LETTERS TO AMERICA

LETTERS TO AMERICA

COURAGEOUS VOICES FROM THE PAST

TOM BLAIR

Foreword by Tom Brokaw

Skyhorse Publishing

Dedication

To the fourth generation Chesapeake waterman, with a face of leather and hands of calluses and scars, who rises an hour before the sun to the absolute promise of a grueling day and only a slim hope of a fair catch; to the young teacher who, while lovingly clutching her soldier husband's pillow, drifts to sleep knowing that in morning's light a ponytailed voice will once again ask where Daddy is; to a graying, stoop-shouldered shop owner who hides within the cruel knowledge that if the bank fails to renew his capital loan the family's home will be lost; to the mother of two who stands rigid at the curb in frigid cold in anticipation of an hour-long bus ride to an office building where, for minimum wage, she will scrub clean public toilets for eight hard hours . . . and to all of those other wonderful Americans.

Contents

Foreword

Tom Blair is an American original.

Aren't we all, you might ask.

True; no nation in the long history of mankind has such a unique citizen DNA. With the exception of the Native Americans, we all arrived here from elsewhere. (My paternal Brokaws were Huguenots from Holland, my maternal Conleys, Irish from County Mayo—working class on both sides.)

Tom Blair, the author, was born to an English mother two weeks after his American soldier father was killed during the invasion of Normandy. Two years later a ship glided past the Statue of Liberty with Tom's hopeful mom holding him. Only opportunity stood at the docks to greet them. The same opportunity that greeted those who landed at Jamestown and Plymouth over three hundred years before.

Tom grew up to embody the American Dream, becoming a successful entrepreneur, overseeing public companies, and raising a family that acknowledged their greatest gift—that they were Americans, and that America is the Greatest Country the world has ever seen.

But America only became the Greatest Country after two hundred and fifty years of sacrifices by past generations of Americans.

Sacrifices beyond the comprehension of those of us with running water and a convenience store within a ten-minute drive. In *Letters to America*, the author demonstrates that most challenges individual Americans are facing today shrink in stature when contrasted with those of the generations before us.

The book is at once an imaginative, sobering, and instructive message to contemporary Americans, the inheritors of all the work, invention, values, and personal and financial interests of those who cleared the way for today's generations.

Tom Blair never met his father, but he knows how to honor his service, and all those generations that sacrificed to give us today's America. In turn, we should honor Citizen Blair by absorbing the lessons—the truths—of *Letters to America*.

Tom Brokaw
June 2015

Introduction from the Past

—⊶⊷—

Dear fellow Americans,

Before you ponder the letters that follow, we wish to lay upon you an indisputable truism. Beginning with that most remarkable year of 1776, generation after generation of Americans have struggled and sacrificed to create a most magnificent America. You, today's Americans, do not have the right to squander this glorious gift from past generations.

Permit us to continue.

Some of us have been observing you for a few years; others for more than two centuries. Most often we watch with utmost fascination and unfettered amazement. And, while we are foremost proud of you, and think proudly of ourselves as one of you, of late we have become heavy with worry.

Today your, our, America stands on two legs, a leg of self-reliance and a leg of compassion for those in need. Over the decades America has shifted its weight, first favoring one leg, then the other. Today's America leans heavily on the leg of compassion . . . mending hurts. While compassion, the noble intent of bending to help the fallen, is a mark of a country's greatness, buried within America's boundless compassion are the seeds to sow a future generation that will expectantly look to government to fulfill their needs. In doing such—in expecting the government to caress their very existence—future generations will forfeit the greatest birth-right of Americans: the unbridled right to succeed by exercising their passions, their skills, their hopes . . . to make their mark. And, know well that the path to success for most human endeavors is sacrifice. A sacrifice—training, studying, risking, working, sav-ing—that renders achievement, once attained, one of the greatest of human experiences.

For those first generations of Americans most families ate only what they killed or grew. An empty belly was an uncompromising motivator for clearing fields and planting crops, pausing only to track deer or build a fish dam. Hunger was not an abstract notion for those citizens of early America; it was a lifelong partner. The absolute need to toil for next week's bread, next season's crop, next year's slaughtering, created not so much an American work ethic as a survival ethic.

Do some of you kind citizens still have fire? Yes, certainly, but not the burning-hot fire of those travelers on the *Mayflower,* or of those pioneers walking in the dust next to their covered wagons so as not to tire the oxen. Today's America shelters its citizens from the rigors and cruelties that its early generations suffered. No longer does one fear starvation, typhoid fever, a whipping by the master, or twelve-hour-a-day, six-day-a-week, mind-numbing, backbreaking work in a textile mill or a blazing-hot foundry. Sharp-fanged fears of yesteryear have been displaced by a basket of less dire concerns: shrinking retirement funds, stagnant wages, the threat of higher taxes and bloated bureaucracies, coupled with the questionable ability of elected officials to govern, to lead, to speak in realities, and to make the hard choices.

We have concluded that the most compelling wake up call to Americans is not a letter drafted to you from one well-known and revered individual from a long-past generation; likely you wouldn't know how to tally "eleven score and nineteen years ago our forefathers." Rather, we have compiled a dozen or so letters from the nondescript among us. None of these individuals accomplished anything of which history made note. Their lives were like thousands of others, and as the country grew, millions of others of their same generation. While their lives were ordinary, we hope that as you read these letters you come to realize that what may have been ordinary in the life of a long-dead American may appear most extraordinary as viewed from today. Our hope is that by reading these letters to you from the past you come to better acknowledge and appreciate the legacy that is America; and in doing so you will accept, individually and collectively, the need to make those difficult decisions that will endow future generations of Americans with no less of a great country than was bestowed upon you.

From afar,
Your fellow citizens

Luke

Except for the Native Americans, the immigrant story is the American story. The majority of European immigrants in the first two centuries of migration to what became the United States settled the land stretching from the Atlantic seaboard to the Mississippi River. Next, from the 1830s onward, wagon trains of settlers pushed west from the Mississippi River to the Pacific Coast. These Americans, these pioneers, abandoned their farms and shops in Iowa, Pennsylvania, Illinois, and other states for a hope. The same

hope that pushed their great-grandparents to abandon their lives in England, Ireland, France, Germany, and Italy to risk perilous sea voyages to the New World . . . the promise of a better life.

This second wave of immigrants colonized the lands between the Mississippi and the Pacific, except for the scattered Californian seaports settled by the Spanish two hundred years earlier. During the long journey west from the Mississippi the wagon trains traveled for months along the Oregon Trail and its offshoots—the California Trail, the Bozeman Trail, and the Mormon Trail—to reach their destinations.

The journey west was spectacularly challenging and often fatal. But the promise of the new territories and new rewards swayed many to the challenge; such is Luke's story.

MA DIDN'T WANT TO GO. DIDN'T WANT TO LEAVE HER FRIENDS. Didn't want to leave her father. Didn't want to leave her church. And no way she wanted to leave her vegetable garden.

Pa said we were going. So's we went. West we went. Sold our Iowa farm. Sold the plow horse. Sold the cows and chickens. Gave most all the furniture away. Ma kept her hope chest. Pa didn't put no money in the bank. Pa used some to buy four oxen and a wagon. What was left got hid in the bottom of Ma's hope chest. Money hid to buy land in California.

There was four of us. There was me and an older sister and Ma and Pa. My sister, Mary, was a girl. I mean a real girl. She liked dresses and cookin' and washin'. A lot of girls I knew weren't like real girls. They was like soft boys. Worked and rode like a boy, they did. But not my sister. That's why I think she was right with going west. Where our farm was there wasn't many boys that could turn into men so's my sister could marry 'em. Think she thought maybe there'd be more where we was going.

Headed to Missouri River first. Took us two weeks. Weren't hard weeks. Only two streams that slowed us down. Weren't deep or wide. 'Course one of our pea-brained oxen broke a leg. Got it stuck in some rocks along the second stream. Pa shot him dead, and the army bought the carcass for three dollars. Said the oxen meat could feed Indians. Pa bought another oxen. Mad that it cost twice what the others cost. Learned real fast further west the more the cost.

Next I thought maybe we'd have to shoot Mary. She was lookin' pretty much like a woman by the time Pa sold the farm. At the farm we had the outhouse. Maybe only fifty steps from the back door. On the trail to Missouri there weren't no outhouses. There were plenty of clumps of trees at first. So's everybody was alone when they were squatting. But then the open fields. Mary stopped going off. Always with the wagon. After a few days she didn't look right. Didn't act right. Stopped eating. Ma knew what was wrong. We had two bottles of medicine. Had them as long as I could remember. One was big for big cures. One was small for small cures. They fixed just about anything but a broken arm or a gouged-out eye. Ma gave Mary two spoonfuls from the little bottle. From sunup till sundown Pa had to keep stoppin' the wagon while Mary went runnin' off to the horizon. Pa got so mad he told Ma never again give anyone the little bottle cure.

When we reached the Missouri River wagon trains were being formed up. Some headed to Oregon. Some to California. Gold or cheap farmland is what the people going to California wanted. Maybe twenty wagons already gathered. Gathered in a California wagon train. Pa talked to the men. Most from Iowa and Illinois. Told we needed fifty wagons before we headed west. Pa said it was 'cause the leader of the train was greedy. Said he was collecting twenty-five dollars a wagon to take them west. Pa said couldn't imagine. Couldn't imagine someone getting over a thousand dollars for four months' work.

Camped outside of Council Bluffs waiting for our wagon train to gather. It took more than two weeks before fifty families joined up. Most leather hands. A few cotton hands. Most every wagon had a ma and pa and a basket of children. Took a tally of the boys in the train. Two close to my age. Arch and Matthew. Both fine fellas. Matthew's pa kept him close to their wagon, so's he couldn't explore with Arch and me. Mary tallied the older boys. More than half a dozen her age or older. Happy she was.

Train had its leader. He was a Captain. He wasn't a real Captain. But since he was in charge he was called Captain. His name was Wrighter. But we didn't call him Wrighter. We called him Captain. Made me feel good though. Made me feel good his name was Wrighter and not Wronger.

Once everyone joined up the men had a meeting. Pa wouldn't let me sit in. But I did. Sorta did. Got my whittling knife out and set down leaning against a tree on the downwind side of the meeting. Not too far away to hear. I sat a-whittling on a stick and listening with my ears. Captain started with the most important. Said for sure only he set the rules. And that was the first rule. If someone didn't want to follow the rules that was fine by him. But they needed to leave straight up and go their own way. Captain said he'd been twice to California and twice back to the United States. He knew what to do and what not to do. Said that some trains took the Sabbath off. Told us only days we'd take off was when there was grass and water for the animals. Said we could take extra Sabbaths off when we got to California if we wanted to get right with the Lord. Captain said Indians wouldn't attack. Said they would steal. Each night there would be guards posted. Two men a night. He would pick who was standing guard. Told us cholera, starving, freezing, and going mad in the Salt Desert is what could kill us. God would decide the cholera. If we did what he told us we wouldn't starve, freeze, or go mad.

Captain said there were four parts to our journey. Some big, some small. Some not so hard, and one that could kill you. Said the first part was the longest. Traveling along the Platte River for five hundred miles past Fort Laramie shouldn't be any worry. Second part was going over the Rockies along the Sweetwater River. Shouldn't be no trouble less it snowed heavy last winter. Snow melting making the water rush over its banks. Talked slow the

Captain did about the Salt Desert. Shortest part of the journey. Worst part. Said he'd seen oxen and men go crazy from burning heat. So hot bacon would fry on a skillet without no fire. Last part was following the Truckee River through the Sierra Mountains. Said he knew everyone heard of settlers being snowed in and starving. Not all starved he said. Some ate the ones that did starve. We wouldn't be getting snowed in, no way. If we didn't get to the Sierras before October we would halt till spring.

Some other things about the women. Said no cussing around the wives and daughters. Said that if a fellow needed to squat he had to be behind a tree or far off. Said the men should tell their women to go off to the right side of the train when they had to be alone. Men should walk a ways out to the left.

Then the Captain asked a question. Strange I thought. Asked which men didn't drink. Which men thought whiskey was the devil's nectar. Three hands went up. Asked if any of the three was only with a wife and no one else. One hand stayed up. Captain said he'd give him ten dollars of his fee back if he'd carry the whiskey in his wagon. For sure, the fellow said. Then the Captain made a rumble. Told everyone to take any whiskey they had and give it to this fellow. The fellow grinning that he got ten dollars.

That night Pa told Ma about the meeting. Left out some things. Put something in. Didn't tell Ma or Mary about the freezing and starving. Didn't say anything about the Salt Desert. Did tell Ma the Captain said men should get a good supper 'cause all the hard work and such. Told her about the whiskey. Said he wished he'd said he didn't drink the devil's cider. Wished he'd got the ten dollars.

Before heading across the Missouri River the Captain looked over every wagon. Cut out a dozen sickly oxen. Made some families get rid of belongings. Only thing Captain wanted in the wagons was stores, tools, and clothes. Told families to sell their potbelly stoves and the like for whatever they could get in Council Bluffs. Said no matter how little they got it would be more than when they threw it out in the middle of the Salt Desert. Thrown out 'cause their cracked-tongue oxen couldn't pull another mile. Got right mad when he found whiskey bottles in two wagons. Found them after they'd all been given over.

Everything took from Iowa was piled on our wagon floor. Couldn't see the floor for the axes, plow heads, clothes, blankets, dried beef, sacks of grain, and Ma's hope chest. No place to lay or even sit. Right away we knew our wagon wasn't no good. Other wagons were better. They had two floors. Bottom one held the family's stores and tools. Maybe two feet above the first floor a second floor with a bunch of trapdoors on rope hinges. So's you could always get whatever you was storing below. The good thing was the second floor was clear. A place for a sickly person to ride in the day. A place big enough for a family to lay their bedding at night when the wind was blowing the rain sideways.

When Ma saw a two-floored wagon she asked Pa right quick. Asked why we didn't have two floors. Pa barked and she didn't say nothing more. But Pa knew we didn't have the best wagon. Somewhere he got a piece of board and cut and nailed a cupboard together. Hung it on a side right behind the wagon seat. Ma had a place for her pans and such.

Kanesville is where the Captain led us to cross the Missouri. A couple of crossings there. The Captain took us to the lower ferry at a place called Traders Point. Cost five dollars for a wagon to be pulled across on a flat boat. The cattle and horses went for free. They swam. Pa wanted to try to float our wagon across. Wanted to save five dollars. Captain told him he was a fool to try. Said if he did make it across he wasn't going any further in the Captain's train.

It took us two days of waiting before Pa had to hand over five dollars. Close to a hundred wagons from other trains waiting for their turn to cross on a flat boat. Waiting in front of us. Captain had us camped some miles away where the cattle had plenty of grass. Afternoon of the second day me and Arch hiked a fair way down to the riverbank. Wanted to watch the goings-on. A family's wagon and its oxen would be driven on this flat boat. Maybe three times longer than a wagon it was. Strung across the river was a rope big around as Pa's arm. All the way across it went. Further than you could recognize a man you knew standing on the other side. When this flat boat got loaded men pulled and poled it across the Missouri. 'Course the river was running mighty fast. So in the middle the rope stretched out toward the downstream side. Arch and me watched maybe four go across and back. Slow they went. Took better part of an hour for a flat to get pulled over and back. There was three of them flat boats. So's they could pull and pole three wagons an hour. The sun was starting down so Arch and I headed back. Just then a bunch of commotion. People hollering. The last flat to load up had a wagon and eight oxen. Didn't have just four. About midstream the oxen get spooked and move right to the front of the flat. So heavy they are the front of the flat dips into the water. But that's not what drowned the family. The wheel lock on the wagon wasn't set. So's this wagon goes rolling right into the oxen. All go a-tumbling into the running river. Some heads for a while. Then nothing. Only thing not drowned was the wagon.

Arch and I back to our train as fast as we could run. Panting heavy we tell the Captain what we saw. Bent way over he did, so's he was looking us in the eyes. Said we shouldn't be telling this story till after our train was across the Missouri. 'Course I told Pa that night. He said he wouldn't talk about what happened. In the morning everybody saying how awful it was the family drowning and all.

Took us most of two days to get all the wagons across the Missouri. Got across we did with no hurts or bothers. River wasn't running as strong as when Arch and I saw the poor family go under. Didn't stop Ma from holding her Bible the whole time she was on the flat boat.

Camped one night right on the west side of the Missouri River. Then started off to the Platte River. Captain said six or seven hundred miles we'd travel on its banks. Stories was that the cholera was bad on the south side. Said whole families dying. So's we crossed to the north side and headed west.

First few days just getting it right. What to do and who should do it. All of us learned the most important thing. Always do what the Captain said to do. A couple of men didn't want to. Didn't want to listen to the Captain. Told them straightaway the Captain did. Told them his way or out of the train. Told them that they should write a letter to their families back home before they split off. Said the letter would be the last they'd ever hear from them. No wagon left. No more talk about leaving. 'Cept Mister Akins. That wasn't till past the Sierras.

Maybe a quarter of a mile long we were. A quarter of a mile of oxen pullin' wagons with most of us walkin' beside. Front of the line wasn't the same as the back. Front was better. When things were dry less dust in the front. After a spell of no rain everyone in back turned brown from walkin' and breathin' in brown dust. If it was raining the trail turned to mud. Each wagon pushed the ruts deeper. Wagon axles started draggin'. Back end of the train had to move off the trail. Had to make a new trail. Had to cut trees and fill in gullies to keep up. Another thing, even if there wasn't dust or mud, the back wagons were pulling through the droppings of more than two hundred oxen. Back of the train wasn't no good. That's why the Captain kept changin' us up. Moved us around so's you weren't always in everyone's mess.

Learned a lesson two families did. Every night we'd stake the wagons down. Hard work pounding stakes. Back-aching work in dried rock-hard ground. But gotta do it. Winds come up strong. A sideways wind blows a wagon over. Right over with a crash. Maybe breaks a couple of wheels. For sure a big mess. Real calm it was. Didn't look like no problem so two fellas didn't drive their stakes. Went to sleep. Wind didn't sleep. In the morning there they was. No broken wheels but pots and clothes all over. Men pushed them right side up. Captain said never again.

Captain did something smart. Always setting a goal that wasn't so far off. Not far off like California. That way we'd be showing ourselves the Captain was right. Right in telling us we'd make it to California. After crossing the Missouri told us about the Loup River. Maybe five days off if it didn't rain. Rolling toward the Loup wasn't much trouble. If I'd known what was ahead of us I'd a said the first days were easy. But at the time they weren't easy. Weren't because we all was used to eating and sleeping under a roof. Just like the Captain said on the fifth day there was the Loup. Flowed down from the north it did. Flowed right to the Platte. Crossed at a shallow ford. After the Loup the Captain always had two men guarding the cattle at night. Indians would steal them, that's what Captain said would happen.

More times than not a big fire was built at the end of the camp. 'Course if the grass was dry and there was a wind nobody built a fire. But the big fire was where the men met after supper. Pa let me come sometimes. Told me to keep my mouth still. Only thing I could move was my ears.

Most talk around the big fire was what was right and what was wrong. Captain kept the yellin' down. Always talk of whose oxen were slowin' us down. Arguments about maybe we should've used horses not oxen. Always talk about where we could find water. And always more complainin' about how's some wagons never shot a deer or a bird, or caught a fish. Talk about why we shared our food with 'em. But the Captain always said the same thing. We was all going to end up the same place. If we wanted to make California, we needed to make sure everyone got there.

Campfire talk wasn't all about the train. 'Course that was most of it. Captain saying what to do and not to do. Sometimes the men talked. Talked about California. Men going for the gold talked different. Talked about what they'd do with the gold. Talked about big houses. Bragged big they'd never work again. Not my Pa. Said California just more farming, what he always did. Sold a hundred acres in Iowa and with the same money he'd buy five hundred acres in California. Pa said he could make more money with five hundred acres, no doubt about it. But he wasn't going to buy anything but more acres with the money he made. Wanted to have the biggest farm in California, he did. Funny thing. Learned more about Pa when he wasn't talking to me. Learned more when he talked like I wasn't nowhere by.

At night the women did most of the work. Washing if we were near a stream, but most nights no water. Cooking and making do with whatever we had or killed. Teaching some, but most learning stopped. After a day on the trail and making camp and cooking and washing no time for learning. Picking up firewood, always picking up firewood. Always needed a fire. Later no wood cause there weren't no trees. Filled burlap bags with buffalo chips for the fire. Mother said she never thought she'd cook on animal droppings. Big job was patching. Making the worn out clothes do. After five hundred miles my britches had parts of old shirts and a horse blanket sewed right in. But it didn't bother me none. Bothered my sister, but not me.

Told you we had four oxen pulling. My sister named them. Called one Miss Brite. She was the teacher at Des Moines. She taught all the grades. So's she taught both my sister and me. Didn't like Miss Brite a bit did we. Happy we were when Pa was swinging his ox whip on a hell hot day.

Those first days along the Platte we covered a fair hunk of land. Maybe twenty miles a day. So's I was thinking it would only take maybe two or three months to California. 'Course I hadn't thought about spending days sitting in mud, not moving a chicken step cause the mud squeezed the wheels tight no matter how hard the whipped oxen pulled. Hadn't thought about unloading the wagons so's the straining oxen could pull them up a rocky rise. Hadn't thought about taking time to make boxes, dig holes, burn names on wooden markers and sing "Nearer My God to Thee."

Maybe two weeks after crossing the Missouri we saw our first marker. Stories of cholera weren't made-up stories. My sister and some other girls put purple wildflowers on the pile of stones that covered the grave. Sticking up from the rocks was a wood headstone with burnt-in writing, "Lived by God, Died by Cholera." Looked at the grave for a spell. Then off to fetch firewood. That night a thunderstorm worse than anything I heard before rolled over. 'Course before I wasn't sleeping under a wagon. Then rain. Rain so hard that a river flowed right under our wagon. Soaked everything. Got up into the wagon we did. Nobody slept. Canvas blowing and rain beating. By morning the rain had slowed a bit. But not enough. Captain came by in a slicker, said we weren't going to break camp. We were staying put. Two days we sat. Not a wheel turning. Never got dry. Never cooked anything. Only bread, salted beef, and cold coffee.

After two days of rain a blue sky morning. But a wind that would have like'd to blow you over. 'Course not as strong as further into the prairie. But bad enough. Turned all our wet clothes cold, it did. Cold like I started to shiver. Was noon before all the wagons got dug out of the mud and we headed out. Some wagons slipping, but the Captain he didn't lead us on any sideways slopes. Oxen could pull you up a slope. The wheel lock could hold you back on a downward slope. Get sliding sideways, for sure going to hit something or fall into something.

Didn't make more than a couple of miles. Camped by a clump of sweetgum on the top of a rise. It was dry. Just about every place else soaked to mud after two days of rain. Down maybe a quarter mile away from camp a stream. A stream flowing into the Platte. Me and Arch and a couple other fellows headed down to fetch buckets of water. Had to keep jumping gullies. Two days of rains had washed deep gullies right down to the stream. Wouldn't you know, jumped over one and slipped backward. Thinking right away how dumb I'm going to look covered in mud. Before I climb out I see them. A pair of blue socks sticking out of the side of the gully. Socks with feet and legs in 'em. I give an Indian yell and Arch pulls me up in a rush. Don't know what I'm looking at. Then

I see the marker. Rain waters washed away half of some poor soul's resting place. Another fella gives out a big yell while pointing. Down the gully a baby. Face down in the mud it is. Ran back to the train. Hardly could speak. Captain had me show him what I'd seen. He read the marker. A young girl it was. Captain walked down to where the baby was. Stared for a spell. Told me to jump down and pick it up. Couldn't do it, no way I could. Captain smiled. Only time I ever seen him smile. Told me it was a doll. He was right. Probably buried with the young girl. Next morning men did the burying. Laid the girl and her doll under a pile of stone on the top of the bluff. Afterward Captain gave each a gulp from one of the safe-kept whiskey bottles.

Maybe a day past Fort Kearny when we met up with the three other wagons. 'Course we didn't go through Fort Kearny. It was on the south side of the Platte. Some wanted to, but the Captain said no. Only thing Fort Kearny had that we didn't was cholera. So there we were on the north side with these wagons fording from the south side. Captain rode over and talked to them for a good while. Told the Captain they wanted to join up with a train going to California. Said they had come up from Independence. Spoke to Pa and some of the men, the Captain did. Musta all agreed 'cause that night the three wagons camped with us. Next day broke camp with us. Captain put 'em at the back of the train. Made them learn their place real quick.

Captain had us driving hard along the Platte to reach Ash Hollow. Most days traveled ten to fifteen miles before staking out camp. Couple of times we had to swing north to go around swamplands. Crossed some streams. Slowed us down, but not much. Worst was the mud if it rained. A day of rain was two days of mud. Two days of pushing and shoving stuck wagons.

Ash Hollow wasn't nothing but a bunch of trees on the South of the Platte. Right after Ash Hollow in rides these two Indians. Didn't sneak up. Just rode in sitting tall. Looping behind them a dog. A dog like you'd see at any farm back in Iowa. Quick like the

Captain rides up to them showin'em we're not scared or nothing. Sitting on their horses like they was chairs, the Captain and Indians talk for a spell. Indians all the time pointing this way and that a way. Captain rides over to a wagon and back. Off ride the Indians toward where they came from.

After setting camp the Captain tells us about the Indians. Sioux they were. Said they are most honest. Not trying to steal when you weren't looking. These Indians wanted to trade. Asked for some salt. In trade would show the Captain where the best hunting was. That was their trade. Captain didn't need no hunting grounds. He did want peaceful Indians. So he gave 'em salt.

Captain told us something else. Made a big speech about where we were headed next. Talked about Courthouse and Jailhouse Rocks and Chimney Rock. I knew he was funning us. Said this stone chimney went straight up to the clouds. Maybe half a mile high. Said it grew out of a pile of sand bigger than anything we'd seen. Couldn't imagine such a thing. Captain said maybe three days. Took us four. Lost a day 'cause of two broken wheels. It wasn't the wheels that broke. It was the spokes. One broke spoke you kept going. Had to stop the whole train when two broke. Couldn't not stop. Couldn't leave a family behind. But we did leave a family behind. Left three families behind. Left behind cause of the cholera and the lying.

Told you how the Captain put the three wagons from Independence at the back of the train. But strange thing. When the Captain said they could move forward, so's they weren't sloping in mud, said they wanted to stay in back. Nobody wanted the tail end of the train. Then one night when the sun's pretty much down the Captain sees them digging. Sees some of the men from the three wagons digging fast like. Finds out he does. Finds out they are digging a grave fast cause they don't want the Captain to know someone died of the cholera. At first they said the poor soul got sick fast. The young boy they was burying. But the boy's sobbing mother told the truth of the story. They'd been traveling with a train on the south side of the Platte. They weren't up from Independence. Left their train cause of the sicknesses. People dying of fevers and constipation.

Captain didn't ask any questions after he found out they were liars. Told them they couldn't have their wagons in our train. Could follow but not close. A fella asked how far back they should stay. Captain said further than his rifle could shoot.

For two days we could see them. White dots on the horizon. Then only their dust. Then nothing. But in front of us there they were. Courthouse Rock and Jailhouse Rock were like God made two giant buildings out of solid stone. So big you'd think the ground couldn't hold them. Started to think the Captain wasn't funning us about Chimney Rock. He wasn't. Next day Pa halted our wagon on a rise and we stared across the Platte at Chimney Rock. It didn't touch the clouds. But for sure it was higher than anything I'd seen before. 'Course there was more. Next day we passed Scotts Bluff. Bigger than both Courthouse and Jailhouse together. One fella said the top reminded him of the Capitol in Washington. Think he just wanted us to think he'd been to Washington.

Something funny. Traveling west along the Platte I got smaller. We all got smaller. 'Course that's not right. But if the world around you gets bigger you are sorta smaller. Back home if I stood on the hill behind the cow barn I could just see the red roof of Drury's farmhouse. Hills and trees got in the way of seeing far. Going west when morning camp was broke you'd spy some big stone outcropping on the horizon, thinking maybe you'd get there by noon. When you made camp after a hard day it didn't look no closer. The West was bigger than the East. No doubt about the truth of it.

Captain told us three days to Fort Laramie. Took us five days. Another broken wheel and a broken wagon tongue. And a whole night of rain. A bad rain and worse mud. But we got there. Fort Laramie was on the south side of the Platte. Just east of where the

Laramie River joined the Platte. Indians camped on the north side across from the Fort. Animal hide tents with smoke coming out the top from their cooking fires. Captain said smoke kept the mosquitoes away. All whichaway naked Indian kids a-running and bone-skinny dogs barking. A bunch of Indians were selling or trading all sorts of things. Pa told me he saw a scalp on a pole. Funning me I think. From an almost naked Indian Pa bought a skillet. Ma left hers on a cooking fire a few camps before. Pa right steaming mad that she did. Bought a horse blanket Pa did. Cost less than a blanket for a bed. Pa told me to pretend I was a horse when I wrapped it around me in the freezing Rockies. A flat boat took folks across the Platte to the Fort. Cost twenty-five cents a head over and back. Pa didn't want to go. Didn't want to spend money. But Ma could see houses along one side of the Fort. After five hundred miles of sleeping on the ground Ma wanted to be around folks that lived like we used to. So's we went. A whole dollar of us went.

Just like the Indians, white people at the Fort selling everything you needed and wanted. Mary and I got Pa to buy two cans of sweet lemon water. One for each of us. And I got a handful of hard candy just for me. Mary got herself a bracelet made of three colored strings weaved together in patterns I'd never seen. Pa bought himself a good sized bag of tobacco. So's he told Ma to pick something. A yellow bonnet with flowers she bought. Hers had blown clean away the first week on the Platte. She'd been wearing one of Pa's old hats.

The whole time going back across the Platte on the flat Pa was complaining. Complaining about the money he'd spent. But I don't think he was really that way. Think he was happy to have got us something. Happy we were safe so far. Happy we was closer to California.

After Fort Laramie we kept on the north side of the Platte heading west. Some men put up a fuss that the south side of the Platte was an easier trail. Captain said no. Owners of flat boats wanting five dollars for taking wagons to the south side told lies about an easy trail. Said that in 1850 he'd been with a Mississippi Company when they used the North route. He knew it was passable. Right he was.

Half a day out of the Laramie the Captain swung the train north. Away from the Platte we swung. Captain said we had to go around a canyon the Platte ran through. Not enough room on the edge of the river for wagons. So north we went. Couldn't hardly tell, but when you looked back you knew. The river kept getting further back and lower on the horizon. After a long spell of flat prairie, the hills were a change. 'Course not a good change if you were an oxen. An oxen pulling a wagon up a slope. Ma and Mary never could have believed so many wildflowers. But the oxen weren't smelling no sweet flowers.

Didn't know what the Captain did till after Fort Laramie. Cut a fella out of the wagon train. Gave him his twenty-five dollars back. Told him he and his family weren't going. Weren't going to California in the Captain's train. Ma told me the reason of it. This fella was always spitting mad. Mostly mad at his wife about this or that. One morning she didn't come out. Stayed in the wagon. Her son cooking supper that day. Then the Captain saw the truth of it. She was bruised and pounded. So the Captain waited till Fort Laramie. Told them not on his train.

After a spell hardly a tree some places. So's no wood for the cooking fires. 'Course you knew what we did. Picked up buffalo chips. "Chips" just a woman's way of saying it. Picked up droppings from oxen and cows and all sorts. Only picked up dried hard ones from trains before. Just people droppings we didn't pick up. First only used two fingers. After a spell didn't bother me any. Held a bunch in my arms.

So's anyway Arch and I fun Matthew one day. He's like us. Has to gather chips for his ma. Puts them in a burlap bag he does. Hung on the side of their wagon the bag is. So's his ma has chips for the morning and evening fires. After a day on the trail Arch and

Matthew and me goes out. Goes out like most times to collect chips. But I come back before them. Quick like I get a big handful. A handful of warm ox dropping. Pack it tight I do. Wait for Arch and Matthew. Sure enough Matthew hangs the bag of chips on the side of his wagon. Then he's off. Walk by I do. Walk by just looking around. Make sure no one's a watching. Drop the warm ball in the bag and keep going. Arch and I sit and wait. For sure it was a loud one. Never heard his ma yell so loud. Never heard nobody's ma yell so loud.

Emigrant Hill is where we buried her. She was from the Ingrams wagon. Maybe five years old she was. Had the fever for days. Even before we got to Fort Laramie she had fever chills. Got 'em from the rain and cold winds. Her ma all the time nursing her tender. But then the little girl got the shakes bad. Shakes stopped. She died. Right on top of the hill men dug her grave. Mister Ingrams pulled some boards from the second floor of their wagon. Used them for her box. Pa took a hunk of board and made a marker. Heated up a piece of iron and burnt in her name. We all stood in a big circle. Silent we stood. Captain read from the Bible. A wind blowing hard. Dark sky like it wanted to rain. Her ma and brother crying. Her father just looking at his boots. Didn't move at all.

It was the Ingrams's girl dying that twisted my life. Turned it all whichaway. Let me tell you why.

Four of the wagons in our train had a passenger. Someone not a part of a family. These people paid to ride in the wagon. Paid a fair amount to the family in the wagon. Ingrams had a passenger. Timothy Akins was his name. Spoke strange. Acted strange. And dressed strange to my way of dressing.

After her daughter passed Missus Ingrams said no more. Didn't want to go to California. She didn't want her son dying on the journey. Her husband put up a fuss. But she just kept saying no. Wanted to go back to Fort Laramie. Wanted to live near where her daughter was buried. So Ingrams pulled away from the train.

Headed back. But not their passenger. Not Mister Akins. He was going to California. That's how I got to know him. 'Cause he rode with us. Almost didn't. Pa said no when Mister Ingrams asked would he take Akins. Pa said we already had too much in our wagon. Mister Ingrams was off and back in a spell. Talked to Pa he did. Pa talked to Ma and then Pa told Mary and me. Akins was traveling with us. Ingrams and Pa was trading wagons. Ingrams didn't need two floors. Back in Fort Laramie they'd be done traveling. So Ma got her two floors. Just like a root cellar it was. She had a place in the wagon for all our belongings. No reason to be sleeping on axes and sacks of grain. 'Course Pa got something. Got twenty-five dollars from Ingrams. That was the fare Akins paid Ingrams. Pa was right happy. Happy till the trunk and the truth of the fare.

I'm going to tell you about the trunk and the fare. But first let me tell you about Timothy Akins. An old fellow he was. Maybe over fifty. More round than straight up and down. Skin was whiter than a lady's skin. Hands didn't have no scars, didn't look like they'd done much. Wore pants that matched his jacket. Same cloth they were. Wore shirts that were white. 'Course they turned a yellow by the Salt Desert. Wore glasses. He read a lot. That's why he wore glasses so much. Never did wear boots. Wore shoes. They looked like his hands. Didn't look like they'd done much working. And Akins spoke strange. Each word had a space between. Like each was special and needed room to stretch.

About the trunk. When we traded wagons everything got moved. Our belongings to their wagon. Ingrams belongings hauled to ours. Pa was loading our new wagon and there it was. Biggest trunk you ever saw. Twice as big as Ma's hope chest. Pa went to move it. Went to slide it to the back of the wagon so's Ingrams could take it with them. It didn't move. Like it was nailed down it sat. Pa down and off. Straight to Ingrams he went. Some loud words and he was back. Mister Akins's trunk it was. Heavy like to be filled with rocks. But not rocks, filled solid it was with books that Akins was taking to California.

Now, a digression and pause if I may. Pause as a gray-black caterpillar pauses for its metamorphosis into a resplendent butterfly. No less did Timothy Akins change my life than God's wonder changes the caterpillar's. As I learned from Mister Akins, there are those seismic-like moments that forever change nature and, perhaps, even mankind itself. Often these changes are recorded, labeled, and studied. Christ's birth being such an event as reflected in the Anno Domini dating system . . . B.C. . . . Before Christ. My life's calendar calibrated against B.A., Before Akins and A.A., After Akins. The remainder of my letter to you is written in the style of an Akins disciple. In no way does my stylistic metamorphosis reflect any malice toward, or disappointment in, my family and life before I met Mister Akins. Both were without blemish. Rather, let my writing acknowledge the teachings of my mentor, and my profound respect for him.

With the burying of the young Ingrams girl and the exchanging of wagons, the train resumed its weave among the hills north of the Platte. Mister Akins sat next to Mother on the wagon seat. My sister more often walked. Mary claimed that she enjoyed the exercise. Perhaps, but physical exercise was not her exercise. Her smiling stroll along the edges of our train allowed her to gauge the young men that might, through looks and demeanor, qualify as a potential biological, economic, and emotional partner for life. Having identified a small subset of eligible male candidates, she proceeded to better know them. This done with the shrewd application of seeming disinterest, followed by random conversation and casual-appearing questions crafted to lay bare the unsuspecting males' core beliefs, aspirations, and frailties. Mother would only ask, "Mary, does he have eyes as blue as your father's?"

Mister Akins had been our passenger, genteel Mother referred to him as our guest, for more than a week before Father learned the awful truth. A truth born from a casual comment at one of the nightly campfire gatherings. Father, feeling financially superior to the others squatting near the flaming centerpiece, boasted how he would spend the twenty-five dollar fare collected from Ingrams for transporting Mister Akins. Father confident that twenty-five dollar fare far exceeded any costs for Akins's transport. Then a dagger to Father's heart as a fellow traveler laughingly reported that all the other passengers had paid fifty dollars. Right back to our wagon Father sprang yelling at Mister Akins; wanting to know how much he paid Ingrams. Looking up from his book he answered fifty dollars. A response served with no more emotion than if Father had asked him what time his pocket watch showed. Only pausing to take a breath so he had sufficient air to shout his words, Father demanded Mister Akins pay him the other twenty-five dollars. Mister Akins looked up again, held his silence for a moment and then softly explained that he had paid Mister Ingrams fifty dollars, and he didn't believe seventy-five dollars was a reasonable fare. Spitting mad, Father made straight off to the Captain, who stoked his already coal-hot consternation. The Captain informed him that Ingrams had used half of Akins's fare to pay his charge for leading their wagon to California. Hence, the Captain concluded, Ingrams had paid Father the full balance of Akins's fare. Not surrendering his right to a full fare, Father pleaded that since the Ingrams weren't going to California the Captain should give him their twenty-five dollar fee. As a judge ruling from the bench, the Captain told Father that only Mister Ingrams could ask for his money back. Father did not sleep this night. But the resolution of his frustration was the single occurrence that most shaped my life.

Father never ceased berating Mister Akins; in Father's universe of fairness his need, yes, unquestionable right, to collect fifty dollars for Akins's fare "stood taller" than Akins's desire to pay no more than fifty dollars for transport. In time a truce. A truce forged by the flame of necessity. A necessity for Mister Akins to tender Father a fig leaf of satisfaction while not depleting his meager personal funds. To my horror, Mister Akins offered an additional consideration; he would provide me an introduction to a classical education. To my greater horror, Father accepted. While Akins verbalized for Father and me the topics he would touch upon, our heads nodded acceptance. Nodded with the same comprehension of the scholarly world as possessed by cattle nodding their heads at a watering trough.

After the evening meal of the day of the truce, Mister Akins attempted to survey my brain to better understand in which classical disciplines I excelled and which would require his tutelage. It was a brief and unpleasant survey. Unpleasant for Akins; he mumbled that he should have paid my Father the contested fare rather than attempt to breastfeed my intellect. When asked if I spoke Latin, I responded by stating no one in my family knew any Indian words . . . no matter what tribe. Further inquiries about the *Iliad,* *Hamlet,* prime numbers, Pythagoras' Theorem, the Battle of Waterloo, Copernicus, and Aristotle were met with like nonsensical responses; thus confirming Miss Brite's inability to concurrently teach diverse subjects to ten grades of farmyard kids cloistered in a one-room clapboard Iowa schoolhouse.

We had just broken camp, the train crawling westward, when my formal education began. Seated on his trunk of books, and I across from him in the wagon as we rolled along the Platte, Atkins explained that he needed to build a foundation before he could raise the walls of my education. First he would add depth and breadth to my vocabulary. Silently I sat for a few minutes as if pondering his decree, then I asked what the word vocabulary meant. He set still for a spell. In time he reached into his jacket pocket to retrieve a key, which he used to unlock the great trunk. The first time I had seen it open; over a hundred books intricately stacked and layered. Books with leather covers of blacks, browns, grays, and crimsons. Most with black lettering across their covers, a few with gold. From his compressed library he handed me *Oliver Twist.* With Mister Dickens's novel he provided a John Jacob Parker fountain pen and a few sheets of the whitest paper I had ever seen. He told me that I should read the first chapter and record each word that I did not understand. He admonished me to write small and neatly, since he had less than fifty sheets of paper, and they would have to suffice for the duration of our journey. Upon providing instruction my new schoolmaster moved forward, climbed up, and took his traditional position next to Mother on the wagon seat.

I sinned. I sinned against the gods of knowledge. I desecrated the work of one of their ministers. But I didn't know.

Try as I might, it was impossible for me to record words neatly on a piece of paper while the wagon swayed and jolted along the uneven trail. In time an idea of immense merit and efficiency washed across me. I merely used the fountain pen to underline those words in the first chapter that held no meaning for me. When we paused for the noon meal Mister Akins requested that I show him my work. We were standing on the north side of our wagon seeking shade from the noon sun as I handed him Dickens's tale. He looked down at the open pages. He stood silent, then gazed at me with an expression that was a close cousin, if not a brother, to disgust. Without a word he climbed into the wagon, placed the book in the trunk, lowered the lid slowly, inserted the key, and clicked the lock shut.

After the noon pause Mister Akins did not take his place next to Mother when the train moved on. He walked far to one side of our wagon. Mostly he looked down. For the supper meal he ate by himself, propped against a boulder. My emotions were torn. Clearly, my actions against *Oliver Twist* offended Mister Akins. Unknowingly, or perhaps better stated, unthinkingly, I had desecrated something Mister Akins held dearly. For this I felt remorse. On the other hand, Arch and I would have more time to explore and conspire if my education had been fortuitously truncated by my ignorance. For this I felt hopeful.

The following morning Mister Akins said that he wished to speak with me. Up into our wheeled classroom he climbed. I followed. Seated on his trunk he began his apology. He told me that he should have explained to me the value of great books. He should have conveyed to me that a great book is no less worthy of respect and reverence than a grave site. As a coffin and tomb may hold the body of a great person, within the covers of a book may be the mind of a great person. Neither should suffer the stain or insult of careless, unthinking men. From the pocket of his coat Mister Akins then pulled *Oliver Twist.* Until halting for the noon meal we dissected the underlined words. Each word he inserted in a sentence and asked me to deduce its meaning. For several weeks each morning was dedicated to vocabulary. Each day new words, as well as a review of those previously discussed. But it was not the steady rising of my reservoir of words that struck my intellectual fancy. Rather it was Mister Akins's afternoon forays into the sciences that swayed me to ponder a pursuit of a quarry that had never been considered before . . . an education.

Since the Captain had ruled there was no Sabbath, no Sundays, one day became as another. The events of a twenty-four hour period gave identity to a day, not the name of the day. Thus it was unexpected, of course we knew it was not distant, when the Captain told the men to set up camp early to celebrate the Fourth of July. After the wagons were anchored and the cooking fires set, a brief oration by the Captain. He spoke of God, George Washington, Thomas Jefferson, and Millard Fillmore. More compliments were bestowed on President Fillmore than God. The Compromise of 1850, the Captain claimed, averted the fracture of the United States and was only made possible by the political acumen of President Fillmore. With a frown, Father looked at me and Mister Akins and mumbled that President Fillmore was made possible by President Taylor dying. Stalking and shooting a buck, Father argued, was for certain not the same as finding a deer dead asleep on the trail.

Once the Captain commanded that every man would be poured two cups of whiskey to celebrate the United States, smiles and pleasant times for all. The red-haired man from Boston with the pretty wife blew his horn with enthusiasm, while the Springfield farmer strummed his fiddle. Matthew all the time beating on an Indian drum that his father bought in Fort Laramie. Draped in a blanket of music, perhaps noise with a melody, the women cooked up extras of everything and those without extras borrowed from others. Quickly hot foods and cool cups of whiskey disappeared into smiling faces; then singing and dancing under the moon, embers from the cooking fires rising into the blackness and cold. Below a camp of laughter and no worries. No worries until the sun rose.

Perhaps a day or two after our Fourth of July celebration I first learned of Mister Akins's life. In an attempt to lead him away from his constant volleys of questions that ricocheted off my ignorance, I asked why, why was he going to California. I did this knowing that any question to Mister Akins resulted in an elaborate answer, elaborate and long. The latter being what I was seeking. Adjusting his posture on the great trunk, Mister Akins related that he was born in Edinburgh, Scotland. There he studied, and taught, at the College of Edinburgh, a college where his father had been a professor of Universal History. He was traveling to California neither seeking land nor gold, but to teach at Santa Clara College, formed by two Italian Jesuits, one of whom long before had studied with Mister Akins.

Then Mister Akins spoke of a subject not raised by me. He spoke of the camp's recent Fourth of July celebration. He said that a friend of his father's, another professor at the College of Edinburgh, had written years before that a democracy will only exist until the voters discover that they can vote themselves gifts from the taxes paid. From that moment on, the majority will vote for the candidates who promise the most benefits from the public treasury; hence, every democracy will in time collapse due to their government's loose purse strings.

Following this dire recounting, Mister Akins went to his trunk; after a few moments of searching I was handed a copy of *General History,* written by Alexander Tytler, his father's friend; then I was tasked to read it and provide him an oral synopsis. Never again did I pose a question to Mister Akins for the sake of delay. Nor did I ever inform the Captain that his beloved United States was doomed.

Slowly the train's journey turned southwest. After a day of no challenges, we rejoined the Platte and set camp just above Deer Creek, snaking in from the south. That night, with the men of the train hunkered around the communal fire, gold shone brighter than flames. Hesitantly two men asked that the Captain delay for a day while they explored whether the rumors were true, that gold mines were only a few miles south of where the Platte and Deer Creek merged. Captain spoke; told them he would delay the train so that they could collect the pots of gold at the end of rainbows, but he wasn't stopping at Deer Creek.

Two days past Deer Creek the train ferried across the Platte River to the south side. No waiting to cross, but another five dollars Father grudgingly fished from the bottom of Mother's hope chest. After the crossing more than fifty miles of no trees, only red dirt, rocks, and prickly sagebrush. Our goal, the Captain always set a goal of a few days, was Devil's Gate. But before Devil's Gate we camped by Independence Rock. Unless a train reached this landmark by July 4th, it well might not be through the mountain passes before the great snows. We were a week behind. Arch and I snuck out early the next morning before camp broke and ran a mile to the base of Independence Rock. Bigger than Scotts Bluff the rock was, and just as rumors said, more than a hundred names of settlers were carved in stone. In the warm light of dawn Arch and I scraped our names on its steep rock wall. I stood back, gazed at the etchings, wondering how many settlers had written their names for the last time. If I had known what the Lord had planned, I would have scraped Mrs. Johnson's name onto the stone.

The night after leaving Independence Rock we heard a woman screaming louder than I had ever heard. An Indian attack, I thought. Father ran with his rifle toward the screams, as Mother pushed Mary and me into our wagon. In the darkness we huddled and listened. No more screaming, then Father was back. It was Johnson's wife, in the cold night air she had gone to lay a blanket on her mother and saw her eyes were open. Open not with life, but with death. Before the sun was fully over the horizon the Captain had her grave dug, the train was going to reach Devil's Gate by the time set.

Even Mister Akins said it was a sight to behold, a granite cliff more than three hundred feet high. Almost straight up; impossible for oxen to climb. Of course oxen didn't have hands that could grab and pull, and oxen had more common sense than Arch and I had back then. After camp was set on the far side of the Devil's Gate, Arch and I made it to the top, we were higher off the ground than ever before. Staring toward the east I claimed that I could see Iowa. Arch turned looking east, squinting his eyes, then he saw my smile. There was something I could see. Below and behind a large boulder shielding them from the camped wagons were Levi and Mary. Levi being one of the young men that Mary thought might have matrimonial potential. Standing together, and as I would have said B.A., they were sparking.

Right through the granite cliff ran Sweetwater River. Mister Akins said a million years of the water flowing wore down the granite, making the "Gate" our wagons rolled through. Captain said we would hug the banks of the Sweetwater River for three days before reaching Parting of the Ways, where the trail split between the Northwest, settlers traveling to Oregon, and the Southwest toward California. Devil's Gate earned its name. After leaving its shadow, three days of a vicious wind, a wind of no pause that blew sand into eyes, mouths, ears, cups of water, and every fold of clothing. Each bite of food a gritting of sand between teeth. For three days we built no fires, ate only hard stale bread and dried beef salted with sand. Blinded by the sand, the oxen staggered forward with eyes closed. Each wagon had some poor soul, mouth covered with cloth, grasping the lead harness, pulling and directing the oxen, each wagon pulled by five beasts, four oxen and one man or woman.

Perfect clear sky when we woke the morning of our camp at Parting of the Ways. First cooking fires since leaving Devil's Gate, hot coffee, hot biscuits, and warm smiles. Good spirits after days of blowing hard sand. Mister Akins said that the greatest happiness is not always the beginning of something wonderful, but often the end of something awful. He said this without having visited truly awful, we had yet to reach the Salt Desert.

After Parting of the Ways we hugged the Sweetwater River into the Rockies. More than a dozen times we forded the river, always seeking the easiest trail. Often in deep canyons, their high walls offering welcomed shade and cool air. Walls that also allowed a yelled voice to be echoed and echoed again. Echoes that somehow made us less small in the dark bottom of the folds of nature's great canvases. Sometimes more than one or two miles we strayed from the Sweetwater's flow. But always came back to its banks, banks that had a backdrop of nature's beauty that I never had seen, or would see again. Touching and framing the churning river were wildflowers, willows and birch, behind these hills of green pine with the smell . . . no, not a smell . . . the aroma, of all that is pure and fresh, and looming over these green hills, great mountains of every shade and texture of gray, in every angular shape known, but all shapes together forming majestic peaks capped in last winter's white.

The Captain claimed the Sweetwater Pass was God's gift to California-bound travelers, without it only a man and his mule would see the Pacific. And our travels over its eight thousand foot pass provided yet more opportunities for Mister Akins's lessons; temperature drops three degrees Fahrenheit for each thousand feet of height, and the formula for converting Fahrenheit temperature to Centigrade temperature is to first subtract thirty from the Fahrenheit temperature and divide by two.

It was the first night after the Rockies, with the men hunkered around our campfire, that the Captain announced that we weren't heading south toward Fort Bridger. We were going to follow close to the Hastings Cutoff, taking a path straight to the south side of the Great Salt Lake. After that we would attack the Salt Desert. Two weeks travel to the Salt Lake, and two weeks of my education being applied by Mister Akins in greater and greater bundles of facts, quotes, theories, formulas, and questions; often questions posed in a manner to cause me to ponder the principles and physics of a hypothetical. Such was the case with a rowboat, pond, sledgehammers, and the two-thousand-year-old Archimedes principle. If I was floating in the middle of the pond in a rowboat and in the rowboat were a score of sledgehammers, and if I threw the sledgehammers overboard and they sank to the bottom of the pond, Mister Akins asked would the level of the pond rise, fall, or stay the same. He asked this as we finished our day's schooling before setting up camp for the evening. I considered the question. I considered it long and hard. I asked Father. He in turn questioned why anyone would toss sledgehammers into a pond. In the morning, with a bucket of water, Mister Akins demonstrated the principles of the matter. Something floating in the water, perhaps a piece of board, displaces its weight in an amount of water equal to the same weight. An item that sinks to the bottom displaces its volume of water. Hence, when the sledgehammers were in the floating boat the combined weight of the boat and tools displaced a volume of water equal to their same weight. When the sledgehammers were thrown overboard, because they sank, they only displaced their volume; weight was of no consequence. Ergo, the answer to Mister Akins question: the level of water in the pond would fall, less water displaced. It wasn't the physics of the matter that etched my memory, but rather the explanation point to the scientific concept recounted by Mister Akins. When Archimedes, during his bath two thousand years before, recognized the principles of displacement, he immediately yelled "Eureka"; the same term yelled by an excited James Marshall when gold was discovered at Sutter's Mill in '49. The latter eureka being the impetus for sev-

eral families in our train to sell their farms and risk death in the
hope of finding a yellow rock fortune in California.

Slowly our train evolved from strangers in wagons to a village
on wheels. Friends were made, strengths were recognized, and
frailties accommodated. Families came to accept that the common
good was only possible through a common struggle. Cooking fires
were shared, clothes exchanged, tools lent, and remedies discussed.
The Captain's declaration that we all, or none, would reach California was silently acknowledged by everyday sacrifices on the trail.
Sacrifices made by individuals for the benefit of all. Such was Mister Graham who, Father claimed, was the best carpenter ever to
drive a nail. But hammering was not what served us best. While
others rested after the supper meal, Mister Graham cut and shaped
spokes. A drop into a gully, or a sideways glance off a stone outcropping, whatever cracked or broke a wheel, Mister Graham
could fix a mend. From Minnesota were the Jurgovans, with them
Mister Jurgovan's mother who each night, if the weather was fair,
would search for edibles; berries, mushrooms, and, perhaps, a
honey nest. Anything found she would first eat; not to quench
hunger, but to make certain no poisons would harm others. Her
son was a blacksmith, always willing to shoe horses and repair the
steel-rimmed wagon wheels for those traveling on the Captain's
train. No consideration paid for his labor other than a thank-you.
And any shoe or boot could be made right by Mister Ebbs. Anything of leather, a harness, a strap to a stirrup, boots with worn-
through bottoms, with his three-inch needles, more as nails, and
cowhides kept stretched and drying on the side of his wagon, all
was made right.

While most all the men would hunt and fish given a chance,
one returned with a kill most often. Mister Visnic was said to be
the best shot in the train. Some thought it was his long-barreled
Springfield, others said he possessed hawk eyes. For whatever reason, while others tracked rabbits, Mister Visnic returned with a
limp elk or antelope burdening his horse. And the meat well butch-

ered by Mister Hanson, so agile with his cleaver and knives that Father said he could divide a two-hundred-pound elk into fifty five-pound cuts.

It wasn't only the men with skills shared. In their wagon Mister Civera's wife had more than a dozen large clay jars, each with colored herbs and spices, many never heard of by Mother. These she shared, explaining which should be rubbed on fish, which sprinkled on cooking meats, and which added to boiling turnips or fried potatoes.

And while each sunset of our trek marked the end of another day of exhaustion, there was one reality that served as the salve for our tired bodies. If not each day, certainly each week the train fought its way closer to California . . . California being that great basket of promise that held the individual dreams of those dirty, tired, bruised, and scared, yes scared, souls of our train. Souls who at night lay on the hard ground and gazed at the night sky—a sky so expansive as to render humble and insecure the most confident—and wonder if they had entered into a fair bargain. A bargain where the price they paid in suffering and hardship was known while the reward was not. But it was known, known because the reward was a nebulous right, not a tangible prize. Those settlers reaching California would have earned the right to continue their struggle to realize their dreams. Dreams that were best dreamt while lying under a clear star-sprinkled night sky of no limits or boundaries.

And it was our steady but slowly measured pace toward California that brought Mister Akins to revise my curriculum. At first he hoped to apply a broad whitewash to my chipped and fading education. As our train drew nearer to California he reconsidered. After crossing the Rockies Mister Akins declared that *Macbeth*, *Hamlet*, and *King Lear* were lost forever in one of its great canyons. For the final weeks of our journey he would only stretch my brain around math and sciences. I smiled a premature smile. That afternoon Akins asked that I calculate the circumference of a rear wagon wheel, it being larger than the front wheels. First, two more vocabulary words added: calculate and circumference. I considered the task. In time a solution. I took a piece of well-worn rope from the wagon, and starting at the bottom of the wheel, carefully "walked" it around the full rim of the wheel, marking the rope where it met at the beginning point of its journey. Knowing that my father's boot was close to a foot long, I walked his boot along the length of the rope and confidently announced to Mister Akins the circumference was just over twenty-one feet. He, as usual, had been reading while I toiled. Looking up he stated that I had not done what he had assigned. I had attempted to measure the circumference. He had directed that I calculate the circumference. Why, I asked, was it necessary to calculate? His answer . . . Because Hipparchus didn't have a rope long enough to reach the moon . . . I came to understand later.

Mister Akins finished the page he was reading, noted the page number, carefully set the book down, and proceeded to calculate the circumference. He took the same rope, marked a length between the center of the axle and the outer portion of the rim. He then reached inside his jacket, unbuttoned the flap over the inside pocket, and removed his wallet. He did this as explaining that while he didn't have a twelve-inch long measuring stick, he did carry a five and three-quarter inch measuring stick. Mister Akins withdrew a five-dollar note from his wallet, then precisely toggled it along the length of the rope, counting seven lengths before a fraction remained. He then folded the note, first in half, then against to fourths and finally to eights and sixteenths. After measuring the folds against the last portion of rope, he announced the radius of the wheel was seven and three-sixteenths of a five-dollar note. Mister Akins then sat down, pulled his Parker pen from his coat, and performed various calculations. In time he peered over the top of his glasses and announced the circumference of the wheel was 21.6 feet. Then he handed me his calculation:

7.1875 times 5.75 times 2.0 times 3.14 divided by 12 equals 21.6

I stared at the numbers, in time I understood two of them. But why multiply by 2 and then 3.14? That day I was introduced to pi. Certain constants exist in the universe, Mister Akins explained. One being pi. Take the diameter of a circle, which is twice the radius . . . or twice the length of a spoke of a wagon wheel . . . and multiply it by pi, 3.14, and the precise circumference of the circle is calculated. Didn't believe him at first. Measured one of Mother's pie pans as best I could, perhaps the ultimate test of pi, and, as predicted, the circumference was touching 3.14 times the diameter.

As Mister Akins taught me equations, the combined variables on each side of the equal sign must agree, in time I came to understand the formula and the equal sign between Mother and Mister Akins. He was at all times a gracious gentlemen to my Mother, offering his hand when she stepped from the wagon. While Father and I would remain seated around the cooking fire, Mister Akins would stand when Mother approached. And when he greeted her each new day, he would tip his narrow-rimmed hat as he offered her a pleasant morning. On the other side of the equal sign never a day passed without Mother performing a kindness for Mister Akins. Washing a shirt, sewing on a button, asking if her cooking met with his approval. Once when Mister Akins tore the sleeve of his coat on a nail head, Mother went from wagon to wagon until she found thread of the color of the ripped apparel. Carefully as a surgeon she repaired the tear.

In time, the challenge the Captain had spoken of during his first meeting with the men of our train in Council Bluffs loomed before us: the Salt Desert. Evening gatherings of the men no longer brought worries of savage Indians, no more complaints about the sharing of food. Crossing the Salt Desert drew everyone's disquiet. Stories were told, some true, some not. It was a tale

Mister Jurgovan repeated that caused those men squatting around the evening campfire to contemplate their mortality. Well, not the story alone, but what the Captain added.

Mister Jurgovan claimed that two years before a train halfway across the Salt Desert was stalled for days by a wind worse than anyone could imagine. Stalled, drinking most all of the little water they had. When the storm took its leave the train broke camp, many wagons were without water, the baking sun and salt air making men and oxen mad of mind. One demented soul with a parched tongue and baked reasoning drank coal oil from his wagon's lamp. Rolling in agony as his stomach tried to squeeze out the burning oil, he shot himself in the gut. As this poor soul was twisting in the sand screaming from the wound, another man from the train fired a bullet into his head, ending his misery. After Jurgovan's tale of woe, all were quiet, then someone offered that it was only a story told in darkness; no one would try to drench a parched throat with coal oil, no matter how mad they be. The Captain spoke; a true recounting, and he knew it to be so because he was the one who shot the screaming man; and they didn't take time to bury him, they had to reach water before they all died.

For two days we hugged the south side of the Salt Lake, a journey that should have been a single day, but the Captain claimed that he didn't want to labor the oxen and cattle before the Salt Desert crossing. Rather, I think he wanted to rest the two-legged animals of our train. Before our assault on the Salt Desert he directed that no one eat bacon, and with each family the Captain met, to make certain their water bladders and kegs were full, and that they knew if any wagon broke down there would be no delay for repair or discussion. Each person to another wagon, only water carried from the abandoned wagon. Oxen cut from their harnesses and free to follow, but the train would not stop.

A long night before the desert crossing, no campfire or meeting of the men. Each wagon tended by their owners, each family speaking softly of the morrow's tasks. Prayers whispered; I saw Mother with her Bible, not seen since the crossing of the Missouri. Its holy grace saved for rivers and deserts.

Camp broke before dawn, the Captain hoping to steal five miles before the sun began its attack. Cold coffee and a torn hunk of dark hard bread our morning meal. The night before we had dug till water, impure and brown, was found; the last drinks for our oxen who knew nothing of what lay before. To the west our savior, mountains. In moonlight only gray against a black sky. Before us an ocean of sand. Flat sand of no threat. But with the rising sun the desert floor a hard anvil under our feet as the sun's hammer tried to bend us as a blacksmith might.

The first hour of no challenge. Easier than most mornings. No hills, no gullies, no trees as sentries on our trail. Only hard sand, white, not gray, after the sun shone its full face. Slowly at first, then as a great oven door cracked open, heat as never before. No one riding in wagons, less burden for the oxen. A roasting heat of every sense of body and mind. By mid-morning a desert of perfection. No dips or rises, no vegetation dead or alive, no sign that any man or beast had ever violated the absolute purity of its vast nothingness. Then, as the Captain had told us, beautiful mirages. First a city. White buildings in the far distance, but not too far to see their pillared facades. As snow on our Iowa fields, in time these buildings, these cities, melted from our view.

One step after another, first one hour, then another; my shadow, slowly it moved close to my body, the sun rising to its highest point. To the south no desert, only a shimmering sea. A sea of no water. A grove of trees on the horizon, a grove that became larger, then smaller. With these trees the mind knew cooling shade and clear, cool water would be ours. Then the trees of hope melted and joined the pillared city.

Walking the full length of the train, the Captain with words of encouragement. From the front to the back, then walking twice as fast as us, back to the front. No man nor beast could maintain such a pace. Thirty, maybe forty miles till any relief.

At noon a respite, but only half our normal pause. Everyone slowly sipped a cup of warm water. For each oxen a half-bucket of brown water. Mister Akins, with a piece of white cloth stretched over his black hat, held the bucket for our oxen. When I asked why white cloth, he told me to first touch the tan wagon cover then the black of the wheel rim. A brief discourse on white reflecting and black absorbing, but I had no interest.

After the noon pause a well-marked trail across the white-hot desert. First a plow and something large and wooden. A chest of drawers it could have been. Then on the horizon another mirage, a wagon. But it did not melt away. Canvas blown to tatters, cooking pots and a single boot by its side. No sign of man or beast. More miles, more tools, kegs, barrels, more bleached and sorry wagons with wheels half covered by sand. Then God's work, not man's. Ox bones. Then whole horses and oxen, dried and shrunk, carcasses stretched over bones.

Somewhere in front an ox fell to its knees, then rolled on its side. No pause, the other oxen cut from their harnesses. A shot to the head of the one not released. Men from the wagons in front and behind carried water bladders from the stricken wagon to others. The train moved on.

Sand as hard as rock, looking down, no footsteps to confirm our progress. Slowly at first, just a breeze. A furnace, but a breeze. Then harder the wind blew, all white. Our goal, the mountains, no longer in front of our path. A glance to the right, to the left, no mountains. In the wind not sand, but a vapor of alkaline. Burning eyes and burning throat, choking and gagging on air of salt. At that moment everything I had, or thought I would ever have, thankfully traded for a gulp of cool water. Walking, staggering on, praying the Captain would scream a halt, commanding everyone to take a swallow from a keg, but he marched on, his head bowed, not bowed in defeat, but bowed to study the compass he held, the compass pointing west.

I glanced back, Arch shuffling, his eyes two slits on a caked white oval. Mother's bonnet pulled from her hair to cover her face. Mary, poor Mary, her arms on Father's shoulders, walking behind his lead, with her face buried in his shirt.

A lifetime we walked and choked toward the mountains. Mountains that were only as real as the Captain's compass. Slowly at first, thinking it might be, but was afraid to hope, but it was true, the winds retreated. Slowly too, the air, air filled with the corruption of the desert, settled. Before us mountains. Onward with no rest, then a shout, Mister Graham shouting at his wife to return. Off to one side, away from the wagons she walked, walked while singing. Two men slowly to her, with a struggle tied with rope, tied while she pleaded that her farm and its pond was just over a rise. Laid in her wagon, the train never stopped.

By late afternoon the hard desert became so much less so. Oxen sinking into pools of salt and sand, pools of no water. Our slow pace of the day slowed as each wagon wheel, each hoof, each boot was grabbed by the soft desert floor. The Captain called a halt. A brief halt. A cup of water for us, a wet cloth on the oxen's mouths. To let them know . . . to make them think . . . water was soon to be. Then rolling again. On the horizon a mirage. A small rise with leafless shrubs. No, not a mirage. More rises beyond, foothills in the distance. Foothills guarding the mountains. The ground no longer salty sand, but gravel and red earth. Then, over several rises, green. The top of a tree. A tree with roots. A tree with roots that fed from a spring. A spring from which we gulped bitter water when camp was made after the sun had long set and the morning's moon became once again the night's moon.

After the Salt Desert an air of calm settled over the train. Met with a collective sigh of relief, the Captain ordered that we rest for two days near a spring, the cattle and oxen grazing while the men hunted. As times before, riding tall Mister Visnic returned with the hindquarters of a mule deer. At night, only laughter around the campfire, laughter and talk of California happiness. Tired and happy men pleaded for a cup of whiskey, imploring the Captain to let them celebrate their crossing. While not agreeing, the Captain promised each would enjoy two full cups when we finished our journey along the Truckee River.

A feeling of accomplishment wrapped the train as Arch, Matthew, and I made our daily pilgrimages to collect fuel for cooking. The first day enough dead wood found by the spring for our mothers' cooking fires. By the second day all dried wood was smoke; so off we walked, knowing only a small effort would fill the well-used burlap bags. On the far horizon dark clouds. Mister Akins had explained, count slowly, sixty to the minute, and for each count of seven between the flash of lightning and the roll of thunder, one mile away the lightning. That day the lightning struck miles away. Running and laughing, tossing stones, picking up chips, no worries, no rush. Then a noise, not a noise, an explosion of all the noises I had ever heard, a blinding light, then silence, tingling in my fingers and a buzz in my bones. There I stood not comprehending what had happened. Facing me Arch, his eyes bulged open and his face frozen stiff in a stare past me. I turned, Matthew on the ground, smoke from his hair and feet.

My friend was buried without a box, his body wrapped tight in the Captain's slicker. Matthew's mother said no to the Captain, no readings from the Bible, no singing of hymns. There is no God, that's what she moaned while lying on the mound of fresh turned dirt that covered her only child. Silently I stood watching her grief, feeling poorly about the warm ball of ox droppings.

While Matthew's death hung over the train, a child's death always the heaviest, the collective weight of relief, relief that the train in a few weeks would be in California, tipped the scale. Only fifty miles of barren land, no challenge after the Salt Desert, until the Sierra Mountains. Once over them, our California. More smiles and hope than since we crossed the Missouri. But not the

Captain. He knew the days, the days remaining before early snows could close the narrow walled canyons through the Sierras. Perhaps that was the reason a week before our planned rendezvous with the Truckee's flow the Captain swung off the most well-traveled trail, taking a cutoff reported to shorten our journey by days. In time this cutoff led to a stream and a crossing not as expected. A torrent of water, not a stream. Far off rains, melting snows, for whatever reason, the narrow crossing was impassable. As always the Captain spoke sharply without hesitation. He said no reason to retreat, to retrace our steps. Surveying the area, he said it would be a fine place to graze the animals and in a day or two the flow would lessen.

Camp was made; in the distance, over the churning waters, the Sierra Mountains. That evening Mister Jurgovan's mother made her daily pilgrimage to the Lord's market, returning with two buckets of wildberries. With some long-saved sugar and biscuit flour, Mrs. Civera baked, using a skillet over a pot as an oven, four pies. Sitting in the early sunset, the mountains rising up to meet the setting sun, I slowly savored a slice of wildberry pie. Then I spoke to Father. He and I didn't talk one to another; Father was my father, he told me what to do and I followed his will. Perhaps because the sun had set and rest was before him, perhaps it was because of the wildberry pie he had eaten, for whatever reason Father offered an explanation, not an answer, when I asked why he had said, as he spoke at the campfire weeks before, that profits from his California farm would be used to buy more land and not to build a large house or hire others to do his work. Father looked at me for a moment, then simply stated they didn't make coffins large enough. I remained silent. Then, not as my father, he spoke some more. He said he didn't want to bury all his hard work in the ground with him; if he consumed his wealth on pleasures, the only thing he would have to show for his hard work would be memories, memories that would be buried with him. Father didn't want the fruits of his labors to be buried, he wanted them to survive his children and their children. I glanced at Mister Akins, who had paused his reading to listen to Father's response. He was nodding, nodding not as a cow at the trough.

By the afternoon of the second day of our rest there was no rest for the Captain. Back and forth along the river's edge he marched, as a sentry guarding a fort. But not guarding, wishing the water would cease its rush; wishing that the train could be on its way. And with each pace the Captain took, with each hour the river's water crashed against boulders, the pressure grew within the Captain. We were here because of him. No one else chose our path. A path only as safe and right as the Captain's judgment.

After waiting three days for the stream to retreat, to drop its level and vigor, Akins softly suggested we search upstream and downstream for a more passable location. His suggestion quickly releasing a cascade of condescending comments. The most simplistic being that the water flowing in front of us for the past three days was the same water that flowed upstream and downstream. Mister Akins responded by saying, "precisely." He added that if the river widened significantly at any point, for whatever reason, the velocity of the water would drop because the same volume as in front of us would be moving through a larger space. Slowly the gathered men nodded in feigned approval. Two men on horseback dispatched in each direction, by evening the duo who headed north returned to report a wide bend where the stream was almost two hundred feet across and the greatest depth was barely two feet. A passable ford for our train. But as with many things in life, a positive holding hands with a negative, a challenge standing in front of opportunity, and fear squeezing hope. To reach the benign ford close to a quarter mile of trees would need to be cleared and after that a hundred foot-bluff ascended.

The Captain rode off to confirm the men's finding and was back at the camp by morning, exhausted and confident. Men were told to sharpen their axes and saws. I was granted a sabbatical by Mister Akins and teamed with Arch. After a long day of cutting and chopping, mostly soft pine, we earned our path through the woods. As combat ribbons displayed, handfuls of blisters for all the men. After the defeated trees, nature's second battalion was attacked; an army of boulders and a bluff. A bluff too steep for oxen pulling a wagon. Almost too steep for oxen dragging nothing but themselves.

First a path through the boulders. Oxen unhitched from the wagon and roped to masses of stone. Poles from just felled trees as levers. Archimedes was right again: ". . . give me a lever long enough and a fulcrum on which to place it, and I shall move the world." A day to make a trail just a few feet wider than a wagon. More than a day. We didn't declare victory till after the sun had set, its glow from over the horizon offering the pale light necessary to defeat the last few rock soldiers. Bent over tired the men were. So tired that Father didn't eat supper. Drank half a bladder of water, laid under our tied-down wagon, and slept an exhausted sleep. It was, I think, the same exhaustion that caused my Father to forego a supper—something never done before—that later caused Mister Akins to be left behind; his trunk on the ground with him sitting on it, a brown cloud of dust stirred by the morning winds his only companion.

To ascend the bluff oxen were unhitched from wagons and driven to the top of the rise. Having provided them level ground for certain footing, a dozen of the strongest were harnessed together and from them four braided ropes pulled down to a wagon. Answering whip and shouts, the oxen strained a wagon to the top of the bluff. After a dozen wagons tugged up, the twelve harnessed oxen given clemency and another twelve lashed together.

To make the oxen's struggle less, wagons were unloaded before the great pull. Contents were hoisted on shoulders or drug behind the men, women, and children of our train. Hauled with strained muscles and sweating bodies to the crest of the rise. For a reason not known with certitude, but for a reason later speculated, our wagon faltered in its climb. Just over halfway up the sloping bluff the oxen halted. No whips, no matter how well applied, no swearing, no matter how loud, moved them. Then one of the oxen collapsed to his knees. The Captain shouting that the wagon could pull the oxen over the crest; broken legs, lost wagons, lost hopes. With another yell from the Captain those men at the top of the bluff quick to the rope; that half a section over the crest of the bluff. More than twenty men cursing, whipping, pulling, straining. Then a small movement. Our wagon lurched forward no more than a quarter of a wheel turn. But forward. Then the ox that had surrendered stood. Up from its haunches it stood. Everyone straining, oxen and man. Another lurch, a slow roll, a steady roll, then mercifully over the crest. Men collapsed where they had stood straining. Silence.

By nightfall all was over the bluff. Sweeping below us the curve of the river. A wide river, a shallow river, a river of no anger. Even though a second day of exhaustion, a night of only elusive rest. A storm of little rain, but fierce wind and thunder that lingered. In the darkness we laid under the swaying and creaking wagon with bolts of lightning offering momentary glimpses of the barren land that was our reality. In the morning an easy few miles to the river's edge and a shallow ford. As always, the Captain rode the length of the train confirming all was as it should be before the train crawled forward. Father standing by our wagon as the Captain passed, this morning hunched over on his mare as if his hat was iron. Father looked up and said sorry, sorry for the trunk of books that almost pulled the oxen over the edge of the bluff.

A quick tug on the reins, his mare to a halt, and as if considering some complex formula the Captain sat silent. Then down to Father, asking what trunk of books. As if questioned by the Lord, Father spun and pointed to the trunk. A trunk that had sat undisturbed since the crossing of the Missouri. Quickly the Captain up and in our wagon. A tug on the rope handle of the trunk. Only the slightest movement. Almost yelling, the Captain had Father and me in the wagon. Together the trunk slid to the back, then with a sorry thud in the red dust. With the Captain's anger boiling, Father sputtered his defense, telling the Captain the trunk was in the wagon when he took it in trade from Ingrams. Hearing a commotion, Mister Akins walked to the rear of the wagon, looked down in silence at his trunk as his orderly mind tried to assimilate and reassemble a disorderly scene. In his always measured voice he asked what the problem might be. Almost a scream from the Captain. A scream that Akins's formidable trunk had come close to crippling oxen and killing men. Then a debate, Mister Akins from the podium of logic and facts, the Captain from the podium of exhaustion and anger. But no amount of logic, no matter how compelling, could douse the Captain's anger. And, the Captain was the Captain. Neither Mister Akins nor logic held any title or rank.

With a shout, as he mounted his mare, the Captain ordered that the trunk wasn't burdening our train. Looking down at Father he told him that he could stay with the trunk, or stay with the wagon train. Quickly Father said we were going, it wasn't his fault the trunk had been in his wagon.

In a low voice Akins spoke to the Captain. Just a few sentences he spoke. He said the sole purpose of his journey was to teach in California. To teach in the first college formed in California. And, most important were the great books he was transporting, books of no less value to him than the plows and seed grain to others of our train. Not as a threat, but as a fact, Mister Akins added that if the books remained in the dust, he would stay to provide them companionship. The Captain hesitated for a few seconds, then said fine and was off. Quickly Mother pleading to Father. But the Captain had given an order; for Father there was no choice. I just stood, understanding, but not understanding. Perhaps because of habit, perhaps because of fear, fear of the Captain, the train broke camp as if no one was being abandoned. In the dust of the train and morning winds sat Mister Timothy Akins. Sitting comfortably on his trunk as if he expected a fine carriage to somehow appear and whisk him and his library to California. No more than a quarter mile had we traveled when Mother turned from her wagon seat and climbed to the back of our wagon. Then a thud, her hope chest on the red earth. A yell and the wagon behind to a halt. In time, a brief time, all the wagons behind to a halt. Father to Mother. The Captain to Father. No compromise, Mother was staying with her hope chest unless the Captain agreed that if she abandoned her hope chest, Mister Akins could bring his trunk.

While not complying with any rule of logic, Mother's action created the opportunity for the Captain to retreat with dignity from his calloused and arbitrary ruling. A ruling made in the fog of exhaustion. In time I came to appreciate not only physical exhaustion, but mental fatigue. Those of us in the train had each other to lean upon when doubts grabbed us, and we all had the Captain to lean upon. He had no one. Always he had to speak with confidence, a confidence that he knew, in the hidden recesses of his being, was not always justified. But not to show confidence would be a greater weight on the train than any trunk, no matter how heavy. He never had the luxury to express or vent his true fears, thus they built until his relief valve of emotions burst open.

So it was ruled by the Captain, Mister Akins and his trunk could ride on our wagon if another family would agree to haul Mother's hope chest. A ruling of no rationale. A ruling easy to implement once Father recovered the farm money hidden in the bottom of Mother's hope chest a lifetime ago.

When we cut and chopped our way through the stand of trees days before, there was a toll. A toll collected late. As with many of the men, Mister Johnson was attacking trees with a well-sharpened ax. It was late in the afternoon, perhaps he was tired, but for whatever reason one swing of his ax glanced off his target and cut through boot, skin and bone; lost most of three toes and a bucket of blood before the bleeding was dammed. Mister Ebbs made him a boot special for his short foot and in a brief few days he was walking, walking with a limp and a grimace, but walking. Then he wasn't. For several days we didn't see him. Before supper, after the train halted for the day, Mister Akins visited Mister Johnson in the back of his wagon. Mister Akins then back to our wagon to retrieve a book I had not seen before, *The Modern Practice of Physic*. Sitting under a birch tree he seemed intent on only one or two pages, he wasn't turning page after page as he did when digesting one of his many other books. Later that evening Mister Akins joined by the Captain and together off to Mister Hanson's wagon, then to Mister Johnson's wagon. The next morning Mister Akins returned his book to his library.

Within a few days Mister Johnson was buried near a clump of pine. It wasn't until later that I considered that we buried him near those that slayed him. There being no planks of wood to construct a box, his body was covered with a piece of stained and torn canvas before the shovels did their work.

It was the evening of the burial, while we were seated around the cooking fire eating beans sprinkled with brown sugar that Mister Akins claimed that Mister Johnson didn't need to have died. He said that if his leg had been removed it was likely that he would have lived a full life. No one spoke, no need to halt the shoveling of beans between plate and mouth. Then Mister Akins, as if speaking to himself, said that Mister Johnson's decision made no sense. When told that if he failed to have the infected leg removed he would likely die, he claimed that he would rather be dead than alive with only one leg. Why, I asked, did his choice make no sense? Mister Akins said that Mister Johnson didn't have any experience to support his conclusion, he had neither been dead nor had he been alive with only one leg; hence, it made no sense for him to say which was better. Father looked up from his plate of beans and mumbled that none of us would be heading to California if we had any sense, so we shouldn't be saying anything poorly about Mister Johnson.

The day before we joined the Truckee River we paused at the noon break and made camp, the Captain wanted to rest the oxen a half-day before a steady climb along the rise to the summit. For our supper Mister Visnic returned with an elk and a story of water steaming out of the earth like a teakettle. Off Arch and I ran off to explore. The smell made discovery easy. Hot pools of water, spurts of water every few minutes. We tasted the earth's tea, thought of the Salt Desert. That evening at the dinner fire Mary moved away from me, complaining I smelled like rotting eggs.

More than a week following the Truckee to the crest of the Sierras. Only perhaps twenty miles, but miles of constant fording, moving from one side of the river to another, crossing to the bank that was passable. Halfway up we lost a whole day, a rock slide covered the only route along the river. A full day of straining ropes, straining oxen, and straining men. But the Lord gave us a magnificent gift for our labors, abundant cold, clean water for a drink; melted water from ice and snow above. And while not spoken, we all understood that once over the Sierras, only God could keep us from California.

After Truckee it was three easy days down to Emigrant Gap. Then a day for grazing and resting. I even saw the Captain sitting, leaning against a tree, staring intently at nothing. That night the men had their two full cups of whiskey, smiling faces everywhere. The Captain joined us, said only two more weeks. Easy weeks. Claimed we could skip and sing our way to the Pacific.

At first nothing that unusual, nothing to raise concern as the train rolled toward Sutter's Fort. Mister Akins was not to supper meals. Perhaps a cup of water and the white of a biscuit. In the morning only half a cup of coffee. Then he sat hunched over one evening, not joining when camp was set. The following morning he did not take his place next to Mother on the wagon seat, remaining in the back of the wagon. In time the ailment made itself felt. Only later would it make itself known. At first only a tenderness of the abdomen; the right side just below the belt line. Mister Akins assured Mother this malady had visited him before and, as all good guests, departed in time. But it did not depart; it lingered and grew in hostility. It was after the night that we heard Mister Akins's moans that he spoke to me. On his bedding lay a book seen before, *The Modern Practice of Physic.* Laying next to him several letters; two were handed to me. He asked that when I reached California one be posted, by whatever means assured, to his brother at the College of Edinburgh in Scotland. The second letter he directed me to forward to a Mister John Nobili at Santa Clara College.

Other letters by his side bound together with a piece of twine. These he kept. As daylight was overlaid by the lamp's yellow glow, we spoke of nothing of consequence, mostly recountings of our journey together. Then Mother came into the darkly lit wagon with a moistened cloth for Mister Akins's forehead, and soft works for his soul. I sat for a few moments, then I knew they should be alone. As I turned to leave, Mister Akins called my name, "Master Luke," I turned to see him smiling faintly. In his always soft words he advised me to be alert for Indians speaking Latin. With eyes swelling I climbed slowly down from our classroom. For me that day was no less a descent than when five decades later I walked down the remnants of the marble steps leading from the Parthenon.

My mentor was buried near an oak tree. An oak tree near a stream. A stream that joined the Sacramento River. A river that flowed through California and into the Pacific.

Father and Mister Graham constructed a coffin with unusual care. The last few boards of the second floor of our wagon were pried loose, measured, sawed, and nailed. Five men and a boy lowered Mister Akins into the ground. Five men shoveled dirt onto the coffin while a boy cried. "Nearer My God to Thee" was sung and then, as it always did, the train rolled on.

The night of burial the Captain visited our wagon to deliver three letters Mister Akins had written in his final days. One each for Father, Mother, and me. That evening, while seated on Mister Akins's trunk, in the glow of our oil lamp, I read my letter. Before opening it I knew. The size and shape were familiar, so many hours I held it tight. A John Jacob Parker fountain pen was his gift to me.

But another gift, a gift more lasting. Mister Akins wrote that in his correspondence to Mister John Nobili he was conveying to the college his collection of great books. In consideration he asked that they accept "his able and worthy student." For several sentences he implored me to attend college; he told me that I had an inquisitive mind and natural inclination toward logic and clear thought; and that I should, by whatever profession chosen, weary my mind and not my back. As a postscript to his letter, Mister Akins asked that I select a book from his library to keep as a reminder of our journey of discovery, discovery of new lands and knowledge.

Father's letter included kind words and the remaining twenty-five dollar fare. An additional ten dollars was tendered to Father. For this sum Mister Akins asked that he deliver, at a time convenient, the well-traveled trunk of books to Santa Clara College. This Father did.

Mother never shared the thoughts laid upon her letter from Mister Akins.

From the time of Mister Akins's death until reaching the Pacific no one in our train died. No more sickness, accidents, or misfortune befell us. Mister Akins was the final toll levied for our trespass on America's wilderness. Or, perhaps better stated, the last cost of admission to our new land of opportunity.

Father bought over three hundred acres in a wide fertile valley south of San Francisco. For years he struggled, then he prospered; with every dollar of profit he bought more land. Mother passed a few years after reaching California. But not before she had a vegetable garden more expansive than the one so carefully tended in Iowa so many years before. In Mother's hope chest Mary found Mister Akins's letter. As did Mother, she never disclosed the contents. Mary married Levi, the boy she was sparking with at Devil's Gate. When Father passed they carried on, nurturing and expanding the farm of Father's dreams, as did their children and grandchildren. Father slept well in his coffin knowing that his grandchildren claimed stake to one of the largest farms in California. No less well did Mister Akins sleep. Hesitantly, and fearful, I enrolled in Santa Clara College. I stayed forty years. First as a student, then as a professor. A professor of physical sciences . . . "Class, before we begin the structured curriculum, a hypothetical question if I may. A person floating in a rowboat with a score of sledgehammers . . ."

As one by one the many years layered over me, the focus of my mind's vision slowly drifted from the future to the past. Of my memories only one held the sting of emotions scraped raw so many years before; that journey on a wagon train rolling on wheels of fear, courage, heartbreak, and triumph. How to sum up this epic time for my children's children? The answer was found in a novel sent to me by my oldest son, Timothy. As my other children, Timothy was raised in a home where one book was held in a reverence higher than even the Bible, that book which I selected from Mister Akins's estate. A book desecrated by me as Father's wagon bumped toward our great hope. My children knew the story of Mister Timothy Akins. They knew the story of Dickens's *Oliver Twist* and the Parker Pen. It was with this understanding that my Timothy sent me *A Tale of Two Cities*, written by Dickens long after our arrival in California. I opened it to the first pages almost expecting to see words clumsily underlined in ink. What I did see was perfection; twelve common words, words that individually held neither weight nor stature, but together shaped perfectly the profile of our long-ago journey.

"It was the best of times, it was the worst of times."

Luke

Junie

The early American Colonies required an army of laborers to clear and till the virgin lands. To fill this need European bond servants paid for their passage across the Atlantic and served as indentured labor. But as the Colonies pushed out their boundaries, more laborers were needed. Then in the dark holds of a Dutch sailing ship the beginning of a solution to the labor shortage . . . African slaves.

By the end of the American Revolution slavery had proven unprofitable in the North, and even in the South slavery was becoming less useful to farmers as the prices paid for their most valuable crop, tobacco, dropped to record lows. Then a seismic shift in the South's economy: in 1793 Eli Whitney invented the cotton gin, making it possible for textile mills to use a species of cotton easily grown in the South.

Cotton replaced tobacco as the South's main cash commodity and this new crop quickly became gloriously profitable. Although most Southerners owned no slaves, by the early 1800s slaves comprised over 30 percent of the population of many Southern states. These slaves were clustered around plantations owned by the "Master." A Master who saw his plantation as a business; hence the absolute need for his slaves to marry and bear children . . . future field laborers for the Master. The treatment of slaves ranged from mild and paternalistic to the most cruel and sadistic. Husbands, wives, and children were frequently sold away from one another and punishment by whipping was not considered extreme.

This was Junie's world, a world where she was one of over two and a half million slaves in the United States.

No one in my family had ever been sold. 'Course, that's not right. If you were black and bent over from pulling cotton or washing clothes, some poor soul in your family had got sold after being beaten and starved on a slave ship coming from Africa. A ship jammed tight, as tight as kernels on the cob, with two-legged animals for sale to plantation owners with their polished boots and ironed jackets. But I couldn't, I didn't, hold no meanness toward Marse Edward for something his granddaddy did a bunch of years before I was born.

For me it was my mama's mama who was bound over from Africa. Till I had my grief she never spoke of Africa. Never answered no questions about Africa. Always just looked away. All I knew about slaves being sold was what I heard from the field hands and then what I saw one day when I was walking down a street in Natchez with Miss Pauline. That's when we happened by the big flat rock. A shiny black girl no older than me was standing with hardly any clothes. She was hunched over in shame. Men looking, poking, and shouting out prices and insults. One turned and walked away, complaining that her hips weren't good for breeding. Miss Pauline, bless her soul, tried to be nice. She was sorry I had to see that, she said. But I remember I was actually glad, glad to my soul that it would never happen to me or my family. Or that's what I believed until my grief time. The time I learned about Binta.

I was born on Belle Normandie, half a day's walk above Natchez. Born into the same plantation as my mama before me, except that she was born when Marse Edward's father had the plantation. Marse Edward's father was old Marse Jack. Everybody said he was the most kindly cotton grower in Mississippi. Never beat his slaves for no good purpose. Never sold his slaves, never tore the families apart, never pulled crying children from their mothers or sold the men away from their women.

Marse Edward was his father's pinecone. Not once did I hear him yell an upset yell. Did hear him shout out happy yells when the jugs and harvesting were both through. Guess I should tell you their yes sir and no sir name. It was Claiborne. To their face they were yes sir or no sir Marse Claiborne. When we was in the smoke-house or somewhere they couldn't hear, they was Marse Jack and Marse Edward. Same with Belle Normandie, when it was just us slaves talking it was the Big House.

I was born at Belle Normandie in 1814, near the end of June, so Mama named me June. But most everyone called me Junie. For my husband Sunshine I was June Bug. 'Course that was when we was alone. I'll tell you more about Sunshine in a bit.

Belle Normandie was the most beautiful house a person could imagine. Like a big white square wedding cake with verandas all the way around both floors. The first floor had six wood columns gleaming from corner to corner. I used to count them as a young 'un, running quickly lest anyone would notice me. On the veranda around the second floor, set back like a cake's top layer, were four of those same columns from one corner to the next. Glossy black shutters along every window. Black till Marse Edward married Miss Pauline. She said blue was a happy color, so's they got painted a sky blue. Two tall chimneys jutted high out of the roof like they were trying to grab a cloud. The whole of the house, except the windows, doors, and Miss Pauline's shutters, was brick painted white. Painted every year so it was whiter than Marse Edward's Sunday shirts. All around the lawns were the big trees—sycamore, tulip, holly, and the giant sweetgum out in back. Altogether a green tablecloth that the wedding cake sat on.

Born into that place, I became a house slave. 'Course that's not what the Claibornes called us. They said we were house servants, not house slaves. I think it made them feel better when they told us to empty out their chamber pots.

And let me tell you right away that being a house servant, no matter what dirty work you did, was Gabriel's heaven for any field slave. With gnarled hands and dead-man stares, field slaves quickly folded over from a life of pulling, digging, hauling, and working harder days than any mule. And the Mississippi sun baked their heads till even the strongest fainted dead away. No cool drink brought them back. A cursing overseer with a frayed baton and mean temper—mean 'cause he was a white man sweating in a field of ignorant blacks—brought the lazy, foaming-at-the-mouth slave back from his sleep to do the Marse's work. But no more talk about that.

Miss Louisa was the sugar in Marse Edward's tea. She was why I became a house servant. Well, it was actually her learning and my learning that got me inside work. She was the only child born to Marse Edward and Miss Belle, born the same year as me. There being no other children, I was her playmate. When she and I got to be five or six she started carrying her little reading books she got from Miss Belle. My favorite was the brown one with drawings. In a while I learned its name, *The New England Primer*.

I couldn't keep my eyes away from Miss Louisa's books. When she was napping, or maybe having her midday meal with Miss

Belle, I'd look at her books and turn the pages ever so carefully. Pretty soon I could put the words to the pictures. Still remember them, pictures of cats, dogs, eagles, lions, moons, something for every letter. Pretty soon the words to sentences. Miss Belle would help little Louisa with reading, and I listened like I wasn't listening. Sometimes Miss Louisa wouldn't know a word. I'd want to speak up, but I didn't.

You all can judge this to have been a foolish thing, but sometimes at night I would dream that Miss Louisa and I were sisters. The dream seemed so natural. More than a few times I used lye soap and bristle brush to scrub the back of my hands. I know this is silliness, but I thought somehow the blackness might scrub off. I knew inside I was the same as Miss Louisa. I just wanted to see if I could be just like her. Another reason for me wanting to be her was Miss Belle and Marse Edward. Miss Louisa had parents, I didn't.

What I'm going to tell you sounds real sad. But it wasn't sad. Well, it was sad, but not to me, 'cause I never knew them. My mother and father both died when I was too little to remember. Father, Big Bo they told me he was called, was a field slave. After one fall harvest the field slaves spent the winter clearing the woods down by Branson's Creek, 'cause cotton was starting to be real important. Nobody knew quite how, but one of the chains on a wagon hauling logs to the mill snapped. Big Bo and another slave got pushed dead flat into the Mississippi red clay. Two days later my mama gave birth to my sister. But it wasn't her time to be born. She was born 'cause of the grief that squeezed my mama. They both went to be with Big Bo in heaven. So that's why I was raised by my mama's mama. But you see, I really didn't grieve for anybody I didn't know. But for certain I thought about them. I always thought about them on my birthday. Truth be, I didn't think much. Thought more about whether maybe Miss Louisa would have a tea party for me on my birthday.

Now Grannie Catfish, she was my mama's mama. She wasn't like any other of my people. My grannie, she didn't ever frown or smile. She wasn't vinegar or syrup. That's how she got her name. People said she was like a fish. A fish has a mouth and eyes, but it doesn't ever show how it's feeling, less maybe it's frying on the skillet. So that's how Grannie got named after a fish. 'Course, I never called her Grannie Catfish. She was just Grannie to me.

When I was maybe eleven or twelve Miss Belle died of the wet cough. For most of a year the days at Belle Normandie felt like dark molasses, full of crying, black armbands, slow shuffles, and soft voices, like if we made a noise even more sorrow would fall on us. Slowly things got right again. That's when a teacher started coming for Miss Louisa every week. She lived in Natchez but stayed at the Marse's house two nights a week so she had three days of teaching. Her name was Miss McBride, made me think of a wedding. She spoke strange. Later I learned it was an accent.

Miss McBride acted like I was just the same as Miss Louisa. Sat us both down on chairs with pens and papers for our lessons. Marse Edward said something to her once about teaching us both. She told him that Miss Louisa learned better when she saw how smart she was next to me. 'Course I'm not for certain that's what Miss McBride thought. I'm pretty certain I was just as smart. But it didn't matter what anybody thought 'cause I got to learn everything Miss Louisa got to learn. And some I learned better.

By the time Miss McBride started coming to the Big House, Miss Louisa and I could read and write more than fair. So she started teaching arithmetic. I learned the figures right away. I learned the addition and subtraction. But, got to tell you, even though Miss Louisa could multiply and divide while humming, I could never make the sense of it.

We studied our history. I felt poorly when I learned the British burned down the president's house the year I was born. We read about Washington and Jefferson and Adams. That's when I made up my mind how I'd name my boys if God gave me any. Nothing said about slaves and how we got here. We studied two things I never heard of before, science and geography. Science seemed to be a lot of fancy words about nothing. If a piece of ice from the ice-house melts you got water. If you put the water in a pan over a fire it boils and you got steam. The dumbest field slave knew that. But science made it a solid, a liquid, and a gas, and somehow it was more important.

But what I learned the best—learned the best cause it let me lay in my cot and travel—was geography. Before Miss McBride I didn't know what geography was. Didn't know the difference between continents, countries, islands, cities, seas, lakes, and rivers. We learned. Well, I learned. Once Miss Louisa found Mississippi on a map she figured she knew all the important geography. But I kept looking at the maps and asking questions, like why isn't England a continent if Australia is one? They're either both continents or both islands, I figured. But mostly I looked at Africa. Looked at the rivers, the names of the countries and lands. I imagined where my grannie lived. I shouldn't have, but I did, I snuck the geography book back to my cot with me. It was Daniel Adams's *Geography: Or, A Description of the World*. Memorized everything between the covers. And that's what brought my grief years later.

'Course when I spent time in the Big House with Miss McBride and Miss Louisa, I learned more than just what was in the books. I learned their ways, the white folks' ways. Two forks, not one, a bath every day, clothes washed before any dirt showed, and words covered with sugar so you could pretend they weren't bitter mean. If the lye and bristle brush would have worked, I could have lived real easy in the Big House.

By the time we turned fourteen our education stopped. No more Miss McBride, no more learning. But that was the way it should have been. Miss Louisa was spending more time at her mirror, and I was spending more time helping Grannie. Maybe helping's not the right way to say it. I was doing most of her work 'cause of her sickness. She had a bad pain in her head for a spell, then her left side didn't move right. She dragged her foot when she walked and held one arm against her side. Said she could still work, and she could. Just took two days to do one day's work. That's why I became the full-time house servant for Marse Edward.

Borrowing from Louisa's education, that was the big part of my learning. The other part was Treefrog. He was an old gray-in-the-hair field slave who knew just about every song anybody could think of. And he had himself a cherrywood mandolin, so's he could dress his songs in music. But that wasn't what made him different from all the rest of us. He had lived where none of us had been. Treefrog had been free, though nobody seemed to know the whole truth of it. Word was he ran away from some place in Virginia and lived in Canada a fair time as a free man. The story was that the bounty hunters followed close behind and he got tired of hiding, but he didn't want to give up. Treefrog was smart, real smart, knew that bounty hunters would be looking up north of Virginia for him, so he snuck around Virginia and went south. So far south he started hearing good things about Belle Normandie and old Marse Jack. So's Treefrog got himself a kindhearted master, and Marse Jack got a slave for free.

I told you I learned from Treefrog. It wasn't his songs I learned, or anything like the learning from Miss McBride. Treefrog knew people. He knew how they thought. Told me I needed to think how people thought. I needed to figure out where they was standing before I tried to hold their hands, so to speak. Told me that if I made sure the people got what they wanted, I could get what I wanted. 'Cause most people just want to feel good about themselves. Treefrog told me something else. Told me always to keep my head bowed down. Never show what you know, 'cause there may be a white man with a whip who knows less, but the whip, and using the whip, lets him show you that he knows more.

Now let me tell you about the best thing in my life. It started in the kitchen. The whole time I was growing up, our cook, the cook for the Claibornes, was Aunt Nina. No one knew for sure how she got her name. When I was little I thought maybe she had eight older brothers and sisters. By the time the top half of my

dress was pushing out Aunt Nina was getting wobbly in the feet
and in the head. One night she served Marse Edward and his guests
a roasted turkey that was still wearing a few feathers and had all its
insides. Another time she baked Miss Louisa's party cake with salt
stead of sugar. That was Nina's last not making it right time. Marse
Edward went off to Jackson. A week later he was back with Sunshine. 'Course I didn't know he was back with my husband.

At first we all thought it strange-like that Marse Edward would
buy a man cook. We giggled that maybe he was one of those butterfly men who didn't do the things men do. I heard of them, but
I didn't know what to look for so I could tell. But all the strangeness went away with Sunshine's cooking. He put more sauces,
more sweet and sours, more hots and colds, and more spices and
herbs on a plate than Aunt Nina could even name. He baked, fried,
roasted, boiled, barbequed, and poached up more flavors than a
body could imagine. Didn't almost need to wash the plates when
Marse Edward and Miss Louisa were done 'cause they were close to
licked clean.

Learned why that cook-man's name was Sunshine. Cause he
was like a big round ball of sunshine on a beautiful Sunday. He
made you feel warm, a happy warm. Biggest smile you ever saw.
Big white teeth and opened mouth, even bigger lips turned up
like a saucer. But the smile was just a window. His insides were
always smiling and his happiness spilled out on others around
him, just like brown sugar maple sauce ladled on slices of baked
ham.

It was the first summer after Sunshine came to the Claibornes
that the cakes showed up on my pillow. At first I thought Grannie
took them from the kitchen for me. 'Course that didn't make sense.
She never really gave me anything that was more than was right.
And Grannie thought right came in a real small package. But I
never could imagine that a body other than Grannie would be near
my cot. Then one night, after I turned down Miss Louisa's com-
forter and sheets, I came back to see a slice of lemon cake on my

pillow. A slice sprinkled with sugar, like dewdrops on a leaf. I knew Grannie was still limping in the Big House. Then I knew.

Sunshine and I were married in the fall, partway through September. Marse Edward and Miss Louisa gave us all of Sunday off, but that wasn't the best present they gave us. Marse Edward let Sunshine use some of his lumber so's he could build a room on the back of the kitchen house, a room just for Sunshine and me. Of course it wasn't just for us a year later. Our boy was born the next summer. I had a hard time. Almost bit clean through the new mama hickory branch. Thought for a spell that maybe I was going to join my mama and little sister.

You might think it somehow not right that I named my son after our president. But let me explain. You know, a slave didn't own a thing. We worked in the Marse's fields, cleaned the Marse's house, ate his food, and wore clothes made from the cloth he gave us. We didn't even own our time. Not except Sunday mornings. The rest of our time was filled tight with the Marse's chores, not ours. Other than teaching him to read and write, a name was the only thing I could give my boy. That's why I gave him the best I could think of, I gave him the president's name. Told him that when God gave him children, he should give them the best names he could. And the best education he could.

Marse Edward thought it funny I gave my son a president's name. Said it didn't matter what I named my baby, that just 'cause I named him Andrew he wouldn't be going to Washington to run the country. I lowered my head a little as I always did when speaking to Marse Edward, said for certain he was right. But as he walked toward the library I thought to myself, thought that we weren't ever going to have no president, whether they be white or black, with a name like Sunshine or Treefrog.

The year after Sunshine and I were married there were two more weddings at Belle Normandie. Now these weren't no jumping-the-broom weddings in the dry barn. These were weddings where fifty of the finest carriages in Mississippi, filled with gentlemen and beautiful ladies, arrived in a line that like to never end. First married was Miss Louisa. Just about every week for almost two years a young gentleman called. Not the same gentleman, different gentlemen, some from over a hundred miles away. But it was Mister Scott from Pascagoula who stole her away. His father owned a bank in Jackson, and his mother's father owned land from Mobile to Mississippi. At least that's what folks said. For certain was that his uncle was governor of Mississippi.

Two months after Miss Louisa's wedding, Marse Edward married Miss Pauline in a wedding even grander. Miss Pauline was a young widow lady who had moved to Natchez. She had the most beautiful curly hair one could imagine. And her face was creamy white, with cheeks that always seemed to be a little red. And Marse Edward did the most wonderful thing for me. The day before his wedding he told me he was gifting me to Miss Pauline as her maid. He was buying a new house servant, and I would only care for Miss Pauline. That afternoon Miss Pauline came to me giddy happy. She hugged me, fussed over me, and said I was her best wedding gift.

After Marse Edward and Miss Pauline were married, life for me and Sunshine and our boy just seemed to go from one good day to another. Never thought anyone could be kinder than Marse Edward's first wife, but Miss Pauline was no less sweet and gentle. I think maybe Miss Pauline was so nice to me 'cause Marse Edward was so happy. 'Course gentlemen aren't happy, wouldn't really be seemly, but he kept talking about the land he was buying in Mobile and how the cotton gin was a gift from the Almighty.

Miss Pauline loved the reading. Just about every month a new book would arrive from Atlanta or Richmond. Once one came all the way from Boston. I remembered what Treefrog told me. I didn't let on, but one day Miss Pauline told me to bring her Miss Jane Austen's *Pride and Prejudice,* and I plucked it out of a stack of ten or so books. She asked could I read, and I told her how I used to read Miss Louisa's books while laying on my cot. Bless her sweet soul, Miss Pauline told me I could borrow any book that I wanted.

Her words were sugar on my ears. Not so much for me, but for Andrew. He was at the learning age. And the best was that way over to one side on the top shelf in Marse Edward's library were all the books from when Miss Louisa and I were taught by Miss McBride. Andrew could learn from the same books as me.

Now to tell you about the black cloud in my life. 'Course, every poor soul on God's earth has a black cloud in their life. Treefrog told me it's not the problems in life that can break us, it's how we hold the problem that makes it a loud problem or a whisper problem. My black cloud was Marse Allan, Marse Edward's younger brother. It was hard to believe both drinks were poured from the same pitcher. Marse Edward was like his father, never wanted to hurt no one. Even if you were a slave, he would sometimes say thank you. All Marse Allan knew is what he wanted, and he wanted everything the fastest way he could get it. And he seemed to be happier if whatever he got cost somebody else something. His place, right next to Belle Normandie, was called Les Moines. It was a French word that came from French monks who traveled up the river in the old days. If you said it right, it sounded like coins.

Marse Allan's plantation was even bigger than Belle Normandie, and seemed always to be getting bigger. Les Moines was a cold-looking big house to my way of thinking. Dark brick and four high stone columns rising up from a porch that needed painting. No green lawns, just rows and rows of cotton. But it wasn't the house that was the talk of all of us, it was the way his slaves were treated. His overseer, Stark was his name, had a whip for an arm. And the whip was only part of his meanness. Word was he would sell off any slave that had a woman he fancied.

Whenever Marse Allan visited Belle Normandie we kept our eyes low and straight. He'd walk around looking like he smelled a two-day-old dead skunk and was nasty loud in telling Marse Edward what he was doing wrong. One of the wrongs was Marse Edward didn't keep the cinches tight on his slaves. Said he didn't make money with his slaves. Told Marse Edward that he should buy them cheap, breed them, and rent them to the railroads to lay track. Marse Edward always sorta nodded like he agreed, but he never changed what he did, never changed how he treated his slaves.

The worst thing about Marse Allan's visits wasn't what he told Marse Edward, it was what he saw and tasted. It wasn't long before I heard tell that Marse Allan said for certain that someday Sunshine would be cooking at Les Moines. Marse Allan had to have the best of everything. Even better if he took it from his brother.

Something else about Marse Allan, he didn't have a wife. Word was that he had woman friends that came and went with all sorts of foolishness, but no wife. Sunshine told me that he heard that Marse Allan proposed to Miss Pauline when she was new to Mississippi, but she said no. I thought maybe this was true. Marse Allan wasn't at Miss Pauline's and Marse Edward's wedding. Maybe if he'd had a wife, a wife who made him a father, maybe then he wouldn't have wanted everything other folks had.

But with me and Miss Pauline, life just seemed one nice thing to the next. One day, and I know the year was 1837 on account of what happened next, we even rode on a steam locomotive from Natchez up to Jackson. Back then they had three tracks all started, one going out to Jackson, one up to Port Gibson, then one coming up from New Orleans. It was a short ride, but it was like nothing else I'd ever done. Miss Pauline, she rode a rail train before, when she visited England with her daddy. It was the first time for me, and for sure I could hardly believe Junie was riding in a train. Not as fast as Miss Pauline's coach and four grays, maybe, but fast enough. There we sat, the window open and air rushing through with the smell of burning wood and a whistle screaming that made everyone for miles know we was coming. The best part was sitting so high up and looking out at the people watching us speed by and knowing they wanted to be riding the train. It was the only day in my life when white folks wished they were where I was.

—⚬⚬—

It was right after we rode the train that the world went wrong side up. It was like they took the glass out the windows and we had a cold wind blowing right through the Big House. Marse Edward and Miss Pauline started to talk low so no one could hear. But I could hear. I heard talk about panic, panic this, panic that. I didn't know what the panic was about, 'cause I only saw worry. After a time they gave the panic a name, they called it the Panic of '37. That's 'cause the year was 1837 when things turned bad. Should have called it the Panic of '37, '38, and '39.

I never really understood the problem, why things were so bad. Treefrog said it was 'cause people bought land with money that wasn't theirs, and 'cause it wasn't their money they paid more than they should've. They was using bank's money, not their money. When the big banks up North stopped giving out money there wasn't no grease on the wagon wheels. Things just stopped. Stopped real bad.

What didn't stop was that Marse Edward owed money to the banks. More days than leaves on a honeysuckle bush Marse Edward was all shut up in his library with this man or that, from this or that place. One of those gentlemen was Mister Robinson, I remember 'cause his accent was the same as Miss McBride's. He was s'posed to build a textile mill in Natchez for Marse Edward, but they had such loud words that it didn't matter the library doors were closed tight. Miss Pauline was all smiles as if nothing at all was the matter. But I knew the matter was really bad or she wouldn't be pretending so hard.

Since he was four or five Andrew had been helping Sunshine in the kitchen, peeling, stirring, washing. As bad went to worse than bad that first year of grief, Marse Edward sold his best field slaves, and Andrew was put out to help tend crops. Happy for us he was still living with us in the kitchen at night. Then one night he told me what the field slaves were saying. Said that Marse

Edward was fixing to sell more slaves so he could keep Belle Normandie. I knew this couldn't be true. Weren't that many to sell. But Sunshine said Marse Edward wouldn't sell Belle Normandie so he could keep us slaves, but for certain he would sell slaves and his right arm to keep the Big House.

It was my learning with Miss Louisa that brought the worst grief. That's not quite right, it's not even right at all. It was that I didn't listen to Treefrog, that's what tore my heart with the worst grief a person could have. I forgot Treefrog's warning that I shouldn't tell others what I knew, 'cause they didn't want to know that I knew anything that they didn't. But I spoke up, one word just jumped from my mouth. It was at a dinner that Marse Edward and Miss Pauline had for some important people from Natchez. Marse Allan was there. If only he hadn't've been there, but he was there.

That night, the night of the special dinner, Sunshine stirred up the best smelling and tasting chicken and mushroom soup a body could imagine. Next was a roasted loin of beef marinated with ginger juice. It was sliced thin-thin and laid comfortable next to collard greens with a touch of lemon and new potatoes rubbed with salt and pepper. Lit bright with all thirty candles burning in the chandelier, the dining room was crowded with important men, food smells, and talk. Wearing my special-guests lace apron, I was dashing from person to person serving and pouring. I shouldn't have, but I couldn't help it, I listened to the conversation.

At first I didn't understand a thing. Most about speculation and banks failing. Then some loud talk about politics. But then conversation I knew. Talk about the world, places in the world, and how the clipper ships were speeding bales of cotton between countries. Between puffs on their cigars the important men spoke of port cities, and I could see them on the map that I had studied with Miss McBride and Miss Louisa years before. Places I had just shown Andrew in the geography book in the Marse's library. Then they spoke of some islands off the east coast of Africa that a clipper ship had foundered against. No one seemed to be sure of the name of the islands. Then Marse Allan spoke up and said Maldives. Lord knows why, but in a very low voice, 'cause I knew they weren't the Maldives, I said Seychelles. Lord help me. I turned as quick as I could and fled to the hall with a tray of clanking plates. Behind me one of the men from Natchez called out laughing, "God damned, she's right. Allan, why don't you find out what else the slave can teach you?"

I was so right about the Seychelles, but I was so wrong. It wasn't just me that was punished, my family was punished. And Marse Edward was punished. 'Cause Marse Allan, as if he had a whip in his hand, took his way with us. Took his time before he cracked it. It was almost a year later. By then Marse Edward had sold or traded just about everything he had at Belle Normandie and still he owed money. His brother, not a brother but a cold-hearted man, wouldn't lend him money. Told him he would give him the money for the banks if he sold him what he wanted. He wanted half Belle Normandie's best-growing land and Sunshine. Marse Allan always had to have the best of everything, and everybody knew Sunshine was the best cook in the state.

For a handful of days Marse Edward didn't look at me straight on, never asked me to do anything for him. In time he had to tell me. It was a rainy morning that Marse Edward fetched me into his library and told me that he had sold Sunshine to his brother. Looked as though he was fit to be sick. As he spoke he stared down at the dark red carpet that was worn bare near the door and behind his desk. Told me that if Andrew and I wanted to go with Sunshine, we could. Said that his brother didn't need no house slaves and we would both be put in the fields. He was quiet for a while, then looked me in the eye and said that since Andrew was too young to do a man's work, Marse Allan's overseer would for sure sell him straight away. Told me that if I wanted I could stay at Belle Normandie with Andrew and we could do the cooking. But then he told me something that made my bones shiver. Marse

Edward said he knew for a fact that Marse Allan would never give Sunshine a pass to visit Belle Normandie. Neither would he ever let me visit Les Moines.

So this was my grief time. Ripped apart was my heart. Sunshine was my sunshine. Andrew was both of our sunshines. Which would I choose? Which grief? Sunshine and I talked low so Andrew didn't hear. I cried a lot, low so Sunshine wouldn't hear. Sunshine figured that he could get Marse Allan to let him use Andrew in the kitchen. He was going to tell him that without Andrew's help he couldn't cook up the good meals. 'Course with me working in Marse Allan's fields, there wouldn't be no more education for Andrew. So the three of us staying together and going to Les Moines meant that Andrew wouldn't be getting no more learning. But that wasn't the worst of it. I knew that Marse Allan's meanness would make him sell Andrew to hurt me. He wouldn't let our boy stay with Sunshine and me, no matter what Sunshine told him.

My insides were torn up and twisted like wrung washrags. No sleeping, no eating, no eating that stayed down. I even thought maybe we should run away, make for the North. Better that we be running together than living apart. Treefrog got me thinking right. Told me that running was hard enough for a young buck who could sleep under the brush during the day and in the darkest night walk straight and fast while stealing whatever he could to eat. Said no way a man and a woman with a boy could outrun the hounds and bounty hunters. 'Course he was right. So I asked Treefrog what I should do. He told me something that made no sense. Told me I should talk to Grannie Catfish. Said that she wouldn't tell me what to do, but afterward I would know what to do.

The sun had just set behind the sycamores when I walked down the curved dirt path to Grannie's cabin, a cabin she shared with another grayhair. Grannie was on her rocker, the one Sunshine made her when Andrew came screaming into the world as her great-grandson. The cabin was pretty much dark, only soft light glowing from red and orange embers in the hearth, no lamps lit. In the far corner a mound on a cot. Only Grannie was awake. She was pushing against the packed dirt floor with her good foot, her shadow rocking across the wall.

I sat on her cot and started to speak, started to tell her of my grief. She spoke two words: "I knows." I was quiet. Grannie was quiet for a spell. Then she spoke, told me about Africa. Told me about men with beards and whips and guns. Men who came to her village and took all the young men and women. Told me about being chained together and walking through the jungle. The chain was as long as the line of slaves, every few feet a shackle around a person's ankle. Men with whips kept the line moving. One of them carried an ax. If a slave fell and couldn't be brought right, they didn't take no time to unlock the shackle. One swing of the ax and the slave was left behind.

After days of death they came to a boat in a wide river. Shackled together they were pushed down into its darkness. No water, no food, just a burning heat, screaming, and fear. After three days everyone taken above. Sun blinding after days in the darkness. When able to see, only ocean, no land. Buckets of water thrown on them to wash off the filth. Some young girls unlocked from their shackles and taken away by laughing men. Some women held babies to their breast, one of the men walked among them grabbing the babies and tossing them into the sea. Screams of a hurt worse than a body could stand, mothers struggling to join their babies, ankle and leg bones broken as steel shackles held them back. With broken bones they were no longer a slave of worth. A swing of the ax and they joined their babies.

Then she told me of Binta. He was my mama's brother. Never did I know that my mother had a brother. Binta was at the breast of my grannie and was tossed into the sea with the others. But my grannie did not struggle. Even though death would have been easiest for her, she didn't struggle against the shackles. 'Cause she carried another. My mother was within her. For my mother's sake the grief of losing Binta was carried by Grannie for weeks in the filth and vomit of the ship. A grief carried by Grannie without a word spoken till her words to me. A grief no slave, no person, no living thing should ever hold within.

When Grannie finished talking she closed her eyes, but her rocking didn't stop. So then I knew. I knew I could do no less. I needed to carry the grief of losing my Sunshine by staying at Belle Normandie for Andrew. This I did.

Junie

Patrick

Even though they represented more than 80 percent of Ireland's populace, during the eighteenth century Irish Catholics were prohibited from purchasing or leasing land, from voting, from holding political office, from living in or within five miles of a corporate town, from obtaining an education, from entering a profession, and from doing many other things necessary for a person to succeed and prosper in society.

Then the Potato Famine. A most cruel and desperate period of mass starvation for the Catholics of Ireland. A blight ravaged potato crops

throughout Europe during the 1840s. But its devastation on the poor
peasants of Ireland was the worst; over 50 percent of the population was
reliant on this cheap crop for their income . . . for their survival. More
than one million Irish men, women, and children starved to death dur-
ing the famine. Another million desperate souls fled Ireland seeking a
better life, or better stated, a less cruel life.

In 1843 a Royal Commission formed to investigate the Potato Famine
reported that, "It would be impossible to adequately describe the privations
which the Irish laborer and his family habitually and silently endure. In
many districts their only food is the potato, their only beverage water, their
cabins are seldom protection against the weather, a bed or a blanket is a
rare luxury, and for nearly all a sickly pig and a manure heap constitute
their only property."

It was this world that Patrick struggled to leave behind for the
hopeful stories of the great open-armed America.

D EFEATED WE WERE AT THE BATTLE OF THE BOYNE IN 1690, BUT
we lived. Afterward the Protestants sat on us like a heavy rock,
but we lived. It wasn't the Protestants that got us Irish Catholics in
the end, it was the potato. It snuck up on us, it pretended to be our
friend, a good friend, then it turned on us. It killed a million of us.

Starting with my grandfather's father our tenant fields were
planted with potatoes. An easy crop. Hoe the fields once, let God
water them, pull four of each five potatoes from the ground for
food, the ones left gave you five more back next season. Ugly to
look at, bland to the taste, but all the things the body needed were
there. A half pinch of salt in boiling water with the potatoes,
dropped in a basket to drain, then stools pulled around and food
for the family. One thumbnail left long to peel the skins, no need
for knives or forks. Potato scraps fed to our landlord's pig, the one
we fattened for him. The head and feet were ours to keep at
slaughtering time.

Then the blight, the Great Hunger. I was nine or ten, maybe
eleven. I know I was born within a year or two of 1838. And I

know for certain I was the oldest son. Our potatoes had a black slime on them. Most rotted in the earth. Within a year everyone's potatoes were born a weed. Thought we could make it through the year. We did make it. Everyone but Grandmother made it. None of us ate much. There wasn't much to eat. Grandmother ate nothing. Said she was anxious to see Grandfather again. Father and I dug her grave where she could hear the creek bubbling.

That first year we ate what wasn't ours to eat. The landlord's pig was picked to the bone by mid-summer. Father became a poacher; we woke to see a chicken. Then no chickens. By the winter of the first year of hunger there was hardly a dog to be seen. A brown collie's hindquarter gave us soup for more days than I had fingers.

It was the second year that killed most of us. By then we were nothing more than hollowed-out heads perched on a clump of rags with sticks for arms and legs. All the hares and birds were eaten or scared away. Each day Paul, little Meaghan, and I walked the fields looking for anything to eat. We searched the wintery fields in our bare feet. Long before our worn boots shredded, boiled, and eaten. Once we found a half-rotten crow. That night we thanked God for His gift.

Starvation is ugly. Little Meaghan went first. Her blue eyes fallen to the back of her head, black gums and bleeding holes where teeth had been. After Meaghan, Mother died. It wasn't the hunger that killed her, it was burying Meaghan. Then my younger brother Paul. For a few long days he never moved from his blanket. One morning he didn't blink any more.

Father died at the end of the year. I didn't see him die, I heard about it. By then I was at the Work House. My last meal in our earthen-floored hut was a scrawny rat that father caught, skinned, and boiled. We sucked twig-like bones and gulped down the hot water broth. Hunched over with hunger in night's blackness I found the rodent fur behind our hut and chewed it until there was nothing. Hunger makes all a feast.

In London the British Parliament argued for free trade, they said there was no need to send food to the starving Irish. Export the extra British crops for coins. Rather more coins than more Irish. The English Protestants hated us Catholics, but when other countries heard about starving Irish children the English claimed to care. Michael said that only after she killed a million of us did the cold-hearted Queen pretend feelings. I don't know why she decided, but it saved my life. I was sent to a Work House for the starving poor. Father with his last breath saved his last child. On a cold morning he stood slumped in front of our hobble and pleaded with a stone-faced man in a cart leading a group of walking skeletons. Pleaded for me to go with them.

I feared the Work House. Stories were the British slaughtered Irish women and sold their meat to the French. Irish men were worked till they dropped and their bodies fed to pigs. It took us a three-day trek to the Granard Work House. On the second day each of us given a single hard turnip. Other than water from creeks we didn't see any food or drink. But we saw death and misery. Not a mile passed without some poor soul laid dead flat on the ground or propped against a tree. Some in whispers begging for food. Most were still. Many were black with death, feeding worms and flies. The worst was a long-dead woman, her child sucking on her flat breast.

The Work House was the finest building I had ever seen. Brick walls with glass windows and a wood-burning stove. A stone wall surrounded three buildings, one for men, one for women, and one for children without their mothers. If thirteen or less you were a child. I was a child because I didn't know for sure how old I was.

The first day we were handed stiff, worn clothes and a pair of tattered shoes. I was told to wash in a large wooden tub. Were they cleaning me before I was slaughtered for my meat? I was given a bed in a dark room with twenty or more Irish children. Never before had seen a bed. Before the sun set I was given more food than I could remember. Everyone but me got a bowl of porridge. I got half a bowl. They told me my stomach couldn't hold a whole bowl. After a few days I got what everybody else got. With each bowl of porridge I thought of Meaghan and Paul. With happiness we could have lived on a single bowl. I thought the porridge was the only food we'd get each day. But in the morning we were handed a slice of hard black bread.

Each building had a warden. A short bony woman was the warden at the children's ward. Malley was her name. Never spoke much, and a stained gray dress was what she wore each day. Malley carried a stick. Only once I got smacked. Told by Malley that the men's warden was Protestant mean. A big fellow he was, smelled like nothing I knew. Later Michael told me it was the smell of ale.

From six to six each day we worked. I didn't know what clock time was, my family worked the land in the light. The happy luck was that Work House children didn't do the hard chores. Men did the sweat-hard work, cut and laid stones for roads and walls. Me and the other children ground corn, scrubbed floors, sawed and hauled firewood, and kept the grounds swept clean. For sure Malley would scream and rant if she saw a single leaf sleeping on a path.

It was a shamrock certainty that I was the tallest in the ward of children. And it was a two-shamrock certainty that I was the dumbest. I didn't know any letters or numbers. We got most of Sunday off if we went to a Protestant service. Even on Sunday we couldn't go outside the stone wall that closed in the Work House. When Malley figured out I couldn't read or write I was made to go to a class on Sunday with little children. Never learned my numbers at the Work House, but I did learn my letters and some words.

Late at night, in the blackness of the ward with the wind pounding the shutters, I would think of my family. I wondered if they remembered me in heaven, wondered if they missed me. I thought that I should be in heaven with them. Thought all the goodness must be in heaven because there wasn't any in Ireland.

Was in the children's ward for most of a year when I turned fourteen. One summer morning Malley told me I was fourteen 'cause they needed more men cutting and laying stone. The men's ward looked just like the children's ward but it was different 'cause of the men. Cursing and fighting all the time. A lot of fights with eyes gouged and ears bitten almost clean off. I didn't talk to anyone, kept my eyes down.

Then I met Michael, a fellow who only stopped talking to chew. He was sixteen, so he was for sure older than me. For more than a year he had been in the Work House. Right off he told me that he had a sister in a convent and a brother in America. After his parents had starved Michael was sent to his uncle's farm at Dingle Bay. For a hurting long time they lived off winkles and barnacles and seaweed. When there was no more to eat his uncle laid down and died, so's Michael walked fifty miles to the Work House.

I was from Connaught, Michael Kelley grew up in Munster. But it didn't matter. We was both Work House lads. His sister was in a convent where nuns had taken in starving Irish girls who promised to do God's work. For a bowl of cold gruel my family would have sworn to do the devil's work. Mostly Michael talked about his older brother Brian and his life in America. I listened with big ears. Wonderful stories of America he told. Someday his brother would send money to bring him and his sister Catherine to America. I didn't believe, but I smiled and told him how lucky he was.

Michael was different than the other fellows in the Work House. He had a bounce to his words and his steps. I hadn't seen a grin or heard a laugh in more time than I could remember. Telling his brother's stories of America made him smile. After a while these stories made me smile. Stories that told that in America every man was his own master with farmland for the asking, more fertile land than any Irish fields of rocks. I knew the stories weren't true. But I knew Grandfather's stories of St. Patrick driving snakes from our land and of Jesus's Trinity being a shamrock weren't true. But

Grandfather's stories were happy stories. Happy stories were more than stories when there weren't any happy times.

In the men's ward Sundays were ours, no need to go to school. And we were allowed to leave the Work House every other Sunday. So it happened that one rainy Sunday Michael asked that I go with him to visit Catherine. Her convent was a good ten miles south of the Work House, so we started our trek when it was more dark than light.

Before the sun shone full Michael and I picked four apples when we crossed through an orchard on our journey. 'Course that's not the truth. The orchard was behind a big stone wall. Michael climbed up on my shoulders and quick like over the wall to pick the apples, a present for his sister. Walked fast we did, and sooner than I thought we were at the stone gray convent. Sat ourselves down on a tree stump and waited.

Walking so slowly with her head down, Catherine came out from the convent after their second Mass. She had a friend with her. A pretty friend. Catherine wasn't so pretty, but her friend was special pretty, with a sweet smile. Her name was Rose. Only family could visit the girls at the convent, so I was Rose's brother. Michael and I were both visiting our sisters. We just sat and talked to Catherine and Rose, eating the apples real slow. After some good words and good apples they smiled, stood, and walked back the path they came, they were off to dinner Mass.

Back at the Work House I thought about what Rose said. She told me that she wanted to be a good Catholic, but she didn't want to be a nun. She said their life was mean like harsh. I thought she meant the nuns didn't have an easy life. That's not what she meant. Told me that harsh meant that the nuns only saw the bad in things. They only saw the sins of the people. Nuns were always trying to scrub away sins. They never saw the happiness in life. Rose wanted to see people's happiness.

No one told us the blight was over but we knew when it was. After almost two years at the Work House we began to have stew and not porridge for supper. At first maybe more a soup than stew. No meat to be seen in the stew but a meat taste was there. Then one evening, right in the middle of my bowl, a hunk of meat. Like a pot of gold at the end of a rainbow, a gristled hunk of meat in front of me. I moved it around in the bowl. I cradled it in my wooden spoon, smelled it, put it back in the bowl. I looked at it some more, then put it in my mouth and slowly, very slowly, I chewed.

I would see Rose twice a month, I would see her on my Sunday off. Some Sundays Michael didn't visit his sister. I went to see Rose anyway. My walk to the convent was short 'cause I was anxious. The walk back was short 'cause I was happy. It was on a bone-cold rainy Sunday, we were standing under an oak tree that was the roof to half the convent's cemetery. With quiet words Rose told me she wasn't going to take her vows in a year when she was supposed to. Said she wanted to smile more than the nuns smiled, wanted to smile at her babies. Got me thinking maybe she liked me not as a friend but maybe as a husband. That night at the Work House I asked Michael to have his sister Catherine find out if Rose cared for me.

And, sure enough, after one of our Sunday visits, Michael told me that his sister said that Rose cared for me more than any boy she knew. Then Michael told me maybe there was a man Rose liked even better. Then he smiled a Michael smile.

By the third year at the Work House potatoes were again plenty. If a lad could show they could find work they were allowed to leave. Michael and I didn't have anywhere to go. Other than his sister in the convent and his brother in America we didn't have family. Then would you believe that one bright spring day Michael's uncle brought the money, the money that Brian sent for Michael and his sister to come to America.

The uncle was a seaman, biggest shoulders and more muscles than I could have imagined. Laced inside a brown belt he wore under his shirt was the money for Michael. Bug-eyed, I stared at a pile of paper money he pulled from the belt. Never imagined there could be so much money. I thought I'd see a singing angel on the windowsill before I'd have seen such a stack of for-real money. There it was, enough for two passages to America, forty pounds plus some kind of money I had never heard of. Dollars, they were, American money. Michael's uncle told him to always wear the money belt. Told it didn't matter if he bathed or laid with a woman, he should never take it off. Michael didn't ever do either so it didn't mean much.

That night Michael stole from the Work House to the convent. He wanted to tell Catherine the news. By morning he was back. A strange look he had. A look of sadness and happiness. The sadness was what his sister told him. Catherine didn't want to go to America. She wanted to be a servant of God at the convent. The happiness was from what he told me. Wearing his big Michael smile asked if I wanted to go with him to America. Of course America was to me as heaven in the sky. Something nice to think of but too far away to ever see. I kept thinking it must be a dream that I could go to America. Sometimes I dreamt that I was with my parents and brother and sister, eating and laughing. But I always woke from the dream. They were buried dead, that was real. Maybe America was a special dream that you didn't wake from. Told him that for sure I would go with him.

A date certain was set, we were to sail from Liverpool in the month of April. A week before we started our walk to Dublin I journeyed to the convent to see Rose. Catherine had told her that Michael and I were going to America. She wished me well. She told me how happy she was for me and that she was for certain that I would have a good life.

It surprised me when I asked. We were at the far end of the cemetery behind the convent, standing near a moss-covered statue of Mary Mother of God. While looking to one side and then the other, I asked if she would join me in America. I asked that when I had work and saved enough money, if I sent her money for the passage, would she come to America. She took my hands in hers.

Rose had never done this. I started to shake. She leaned forward and kissed me on the cheek. Never had I been kissed before. Not even mother had kissed me. And with her head still near mine sweet Rose answered a soft yes.

I drifted above the path on my journey back to the Work House. Never again would I be so happy. But that night, in the darkness, I thought of my family. It could not be right that I was so happy and they were long dead. I prayed for them. Then I thought of the kiss.

It was a seven-day trek from the Work House to Dublin. From there we sailed to Liverpool. Belowdecks cattle, with the Irish on deck in freezing rain. Two weeks in Liverpool waiting for the winds and tides. Our ship was the *Hannah*. I had heard it was a coughing ship. Michael and I thought that meant that most of the passengers would be afflicted with a cough. The crew told us we were wrong. It wasn't a coughing ship, it was a coffin ship. The ship owners insured them for more than their value hoping they would sink. They made more money if the ship sank on a crossing than they did from fares. Sure enough, *Hannah's* sails were tattered and patched, looking like gigantic quilts. Deckboards were rotten and the ropes rubbed thin. No better were the crew. Tattered, patched, and drunk. Not always drunk, but always the smell of ale. They knew for certain they were on a coffin ship.

Over a hundred of us, all belowdecks, not more than five feet between decks, everyone touching close together. At first not enough cots or hammocks for everyone, but the crew said to wait. They were right. Two hatches above the only light. When the weather was rough, and most often it was, they were closed. Meager light and air through the cracked and crumbling deckboards. At first there were babies crying. But they were the first to die, so their screaming went with them to the sea. A few days of moaning by their mothers, then quiet. The really old ones died as we came close to America. I spoke to a few, sorry they had left their Irish homeland. Most were on the journey because they were with their grown children and they had no choice. Death gave them a choice.

Even after twenty or more dead, we were still packed close. No one washed. Most everyone was dark with dirt and filth. Waking up there would maybe be an arm or leg across your body with another's foul breath in your face. Then the amusement. Michael had a hand-carved wooden comb that was a gift from his sister for his journey. We took turns and kept score. Whoever had the highest count won a drink, an ale, from the other when we got to Boston. Of course neither of us had the money to buy a drink. And we didn't know for sure whether we'd get to Boston. And I had never had an ale. So not winning one didn't mean anything to me. But we talked about the bet while we combed each other's hair and picked out lice. I am not sure who won. I picked out more than two hundred and Michael didn't even get one hundred. So I won. But I was scratching more than him, so maybe he really won. And I know he really won because Michael never bought me the ale.

Depending on the winds the Captain bragged the journey would be a quick four to six weeks. It was eight weeks before we saw America. 'Course the *Hannah* was stocked only with enough stale and rotting food for six weeks. The hunger the last two weeks didn't matter, it was an old acquaintance to all of us.

I thought it would look different. I knew it would look different. It had to look different because it was America. But it didn't. Boston wharfs just as Liverpool. Most people in worn clothes. Just a few rode in grand carriages, their drivers yelling harsh words to those blocking their journey. And that first day in America the sky was gray. In my mind America always had blue skies with a bright sun and great white clouds.

Michael and I stood on the edge of the wharf until the sun set. For sure Michael thought Brian would know when the ship had arrived to greet us. I knew this couldn't be, but I knew his brother wouldn't send us money to come to America and I was wrong, so I stood with him. Then a most friendly Irishman smiled a hello. I remember his name. It was Patrick Callahan. The same first name as mine. Said that he saw us standing there looking lost and did we want him to find a place to spend the night, a place where the Irish were welcomed. Michael told him no, that we wanted to find Brian, not a place to sleep. Callahan said not to worry 'cause everyone knew that the inn he was taking us to was where Irishmen went when they first set foot in America.

For most of a mile to the south we walked following Mister Callahan. The last part of the journey only lit by some lantern light from the homes along a cobblestone path. Finally stopped at a red-brick building. Inside a smiling man leaning against a counter. A man wider than he was tall. To the left a tavern with laughter and shouting. Mister Callahan introduced us to the smiling fella. Told him to treat us special good because we were his friends. This big fella told us that for five dollars we could have a room for a month. Michael said we only needed a place to sleep for a few days because his brother would soon be taking us to a fine new home. He smiled and told us that he would give us a dollar back for each week we didn't use of the month.

Michael went outside and then came back and handed the man five dollars. Patrick Callahan with a smile wished us much happiness in America and turned to the tavern. I thought how wonderful that everyone smiled.

While telling us how lucky we were to be in his inn, the big grinning fellow showed us to our room, but it wasn't our room. Eight mats were on the floor, five with snoring men. Told that we could take any of the ones left and that the privy was at the end of the path behind the building.

On our second day in America Michael spent a quarter of a dollar to buy a hard loaf of black bread and some dried fish from a one-armed man that somehow could push a cart while tipping his hat to the ladies. We thought it would be enough for most of a week, but when we woke the next day it wasn't under Michael's mat where he put it for safekeeping. None of the men said they knew anything. Just as we were getting ready to gouge and bite somebody a stranger walked in. He was a stranger until he hugged Michael. It was his brother Brian. They both cried for a little while, then Brian started to yell. Told Michael and me how dumb we were to be staying in the place we were. For sure he was right. When we went to leave the owner wouldn't give Michael his dollars back from the five. But we didn't fuss much.

Brian had found us both good jobs. Later I learned that good jobs for dumb Irish lads weren't good jobs for other fellows. Michael's was in a town south of Boston, mine in Boston proper on Sumner Street, just past Hancock. On the first floor was a dry goods store. Its owner, Mister James Mulcahy, lived on the second floor with his wife and his mother and two daughters. The grandmother was bent-over old and the children just waifs. Just like in the Work House I worked six days. I minded the store, carried boxes, delivered goods to ladies and old men. For this I got five cents a day plus supper and a stained gray blanket and a cot in the root cellar. Once I killed the rats and got myself a lantern it was better than anywhere I had slept in my life.

Almost got let go right away. I couldn't make change 'cause I couldn't count. Missus Mulcahy took pity on me and taught me my numbers. She wrote out on a piece of paper from one cent to fifty cents. Next to each cost she wrote what would be the change depending on the money handed me. Mister Mulcahy didn't talk much. Mostly he gave orders and pushed his forehead down to show he was unhappy about something. His wife smiled when she talked. Men customers, I think for sure, bought from the store so they could talk to a pretty lady that smiled. And she was pretty. But not as pretty as my Rose.

It was at the end of my first Saturday with the Mulcahys that I got paid. Paid a quarter dollar and a half dime. First money I ever had for myself. That night I sat on my cot and stared at the coins in the glow of the lantern. I rubbed them together. I held them together. I held them apart. I wiped them clean with my shirt-sleeve. The next day I walked through Boston with one hand in my pants pocket holding the quarter dollar and half dime. I walked in big steps with a smile.

My first summer in America I saved two dollars and twenty-five cents. I didn't spend one penny. I didn't know at first but I didn't spend any money 'cause Missus Mulcahy spent hers. She gave me socks when she saw I didn't have any. When I asked how I could send a letter to Rose she got me the paper and took my letter to the post office. I never bought stamps. I didn't know what a stamp was then. She helped me with other things. I thought I could read. One day she gave me a day-old newspaper and saw that I couldn't make sense of most of it. Most words were long and strange. So, bless her heart, she became my teacher. When she brought down my supper plate she would bring an old *Boston Post* with one article marked. The next day when her husband was on an errand she would ask me which words I didn't understand. At first most, then a few. I learned a lot about America 'cause of Missus Mulcahy's reading lessons.

Most every night before sleep I would lay awake in the dark of Mulcahy's cellar and think of Rose. I would think about us being together. I would think of the kiss. But then I would see in my mind's eye a starving Meaghan and Paul. I asked God for His forgiveness for thinking of Rose and not praying for my family.

But I kept thinking of Rose. So I wrote to her. My first letter Missus Mulcahy wrote what I said. She told me to say some things I didn't want to say. Since she was a lady and so was Rose I told her all right. But I didn't send Rose the paper Missus Mulcahy wrote. I copied the letter and Missus Mulcahy sent my letter.

Bad I felt that I didn't know how to write a letter. At the Work House I learned to write. But I could only write words. I never wrote sentences. Missus Mulcahy taught me. We started with real short sentences. Learning made me feel worm dumb. At first I did most everything wrong. But I kept trying. You know why? 'Cause

I wanted to write Rose in my words and not copy what Missus Mulcahy wrote.

On my day off Sundays I walked the streets of Boston. When I saw a father and mother with children I would imagine Rose and me with children. If the weather wasn't real cold and windy I would go to the wharfs and sit on a crate and watch the ships unload cargo. Some days a ship would arrive with passengers. I'd watch them come down the gangplank. Most walked slowly and looked scared. But a few saw someone they knew and with a big smile and happy words ran to them. I imagined Rose coming down the gangplank and running to me. I imagined it a lot even when I wasn't at the wharf.

Just about every month Michael visited me. He had a job at a factory that made cloth. Told me a lot of young girls worked at the factory. For that he was happy. But he didn't make much in wages. He was saving for a farm, needed seventy-five dollars for a hundred acres. Figured he wasn't saving as fast as the cost of land was going up. The cost of passage to America wasn't going higher, but it didn't matter. It would be five years of saving each and every cent of my wage before I could send Rose the fare.

I didn't have any way to remember Rose but my mind's painting of her. I would look at young girls trying to find someone that looked like Rose. I thought if I could see someone like Rose it would make me happy. One rainy Saturday a young lady came into Mulcahy's shop. I had never seen this woman before. I had seen her face before. She had the same red hair and beautiful smiling face as Rose. When she left I was sad, not happy.

At first I thought America was like Ireland and that Americans were like the Irish. But after time I saw it wasn't so. Not a big difference but a difference. People in America moved faster. Not like running, but like there was a rush to get somewhere important. Or like there was a need to hurry up and finish what they started. And even when they were rushing about they seemed happy. Americans smiled more than Irishmen. And something else about folks in

America was different. In Ireland people talked about what they did. In America they talked about what they would do. After a while I figured out that was why they hurried about smiling. They were rushing to do something they wanted to do.

By the second year with the Mulcahys I was getting a letter every three months or so from Rose. If more than three months passed without a letter I fretted that Rose maybe met someone that she cared for more than me. But the more I fretted the happier I was when Missus Mulcahy came down with my dinner plate and a letter from Rose. I smiled for the next month, probably smiled when I was sleeping. And even those nights when my bones wanted to sleep, after an extra hard day of Mister Mulcahy's pounding, in the darkness of the cellar I would lay awake and think of Rose. And for most certain I would think about the kiss. How she took my hands in hers and squeezed them tight. How she moved close to me so that our bodies touched. How her face touched mine with her warm breath on my cheek. And how sweet Rose kissed me for such a long moment.

It was the second year in America that Michael got a new job in Worcester, a job making piano wire. Being a dumb Irish lad I didn't know pianos had wire. Took the job 'cause it paid more. Made me think that if I could get another job with better pay I could maybe save Rose's passage fare quicker. So after work I walked around looking in shops, hoping to find a shopkeeper needing to hire a fella. I knew my numbers and after two years of schooling by Missus Mulcahy I could read as good as most and I wrote so that my thoughts were pretty much clear. It wasn't just my brain that got bigger, when I first got to Mulcahy's a strong breeze could have pushed me over, couldn't lift most of the boxes stored in the root cellar, had to drag them up the steep steps. After eating more than good for a time I got some meat on my bones so's I could hoist the heaviest box on my shoulder and be off.

Boston for sure didn't have good jobs for the Irish. The Know Nothing Party was running the city. Argued loud that the Irish were hurting real Americans, said we stole jobs and our Pope wanted to take over the country. Most stores had No Irish Need Apply signs. Jobs building railroads and digging canals had two pay rates. One rate for Irish and a higher one for everyone else. I even saw parades with banners that said that real Americans didn't come on a boat, they were born in America. Wondered if the Indians had the same parades.

The letters from Rose got longer. I kept them in an old tea box Missus Mulcahy gave me. Just about every night I read one or two. 'Course I knew the words pretty much by memory. But I would just stare at the writing. I would study the curves of the letters that made the words. Rose's T's, M's, O's, and S's were beautiful. I'd imagine Rose writing the letters, holding the pen in her small, perfect hand. I knew that when she was writing them she was only thinking of me. I'd imagine where she was sitting when she wrote each letter. I saw her at a small table next to her bed. The table was in front of a window. Sundays she wrote with the sunlight shining in. Other times I imagined her writing at night, seated wearing a nightcap and robe. A lantern was on a small writing desk. As her hand moved with the writing the shadows across her bed followed. Someday we would be together. Until then I had the kiss.

Then the letter that made my heart grin. Rose wrote that she had left the convent. She had to either take her final vows or leave. She could leave because the famine was over and the farms were growing potatoes and workers were needed. And there weren't many workers after the Great Hunger. Rose found a job as a laundress at a grand manor house. She wrote that the lady of the house was most kind and she would be content there until she could join me. My heart jumped. Yes, she was still going to join me. That is what her letter said. I read and read her letter till the corners turned up.

A most busy livery by the wharf was run by Mister Clancey. I said hello to him since his name was the same as my mother's family, but he wasn't from Connaught. When I told him about me saving for Rose and what I was paid he told me his brother needed a good fellow. I went to see him at his saloon on Charter Street. Mister Clancey wanted someone to keep the place clean and move in the full kegs and get rid of the empties, offered me sixty cents a week. Thought about it. I didn't want the job. Real mean-looking customers at the Clancey Saloon. But I did want the sixty cents, it was almost twice as much as Mister Mulcahy paid. When I told Mister Mulcahy I was taking a new job he looked pained and then he looked angry. Told me I wasn't grateful. Then he did something real surprising. Told me I could have sixty cents a week if I stayed. I did. Then something even stranger happened. The next night when Missus Mulcahy brought down my dinner plate she gave me five dollars. Told me it was a gift from her and her husband. Told me that I should buy new pants and two shirts. Also said to make certain not to thank her husband.

Wouldn't you know that after a while Mister Mulcahy gave me more chores. He had me paint the outside of the shop and sand and stain the floor. Had me to do this work after my supper meal. Told me for sixty cents a week I needed to work harder or his two children would starve. Said this with his stomach pushed over his belt. After he said the word starve my heart hurt for Meaghan and Paul. Mister Mulcahy didn't know nothing about starving.

It was by reading the newspaper that I learned about presidents. I liked that America had presidents and not queens and kings. I learned that every four years all the men in America got to say who they wanted to be president. I read that both Douglas and Lincoln wanted to be president. In a loud voice Mister Mulcahy said that Douglas should be America's president. Missus Mulcahy said her thoughts didn't matter. No one asked me who I wanted to be president. I didn't care because I didn't know. Lincoln had more men say they wanted him so he got to be president.

It was a fair time after Lincoln was elected president that Michael came to see me with news. Wonderful news that I couldn't believe. We both could be rich. We could get paid to join the Union Army.

The army of President Lincoln. When he told me how much I would be paid to join I knew he was wrong. Told me I would get 350 dollars. In the Work House when Michael told me his brother was sending forty pounds I knew it couldn't be. But it was. So I listened.

Michael said men were paying Irishmen to serve in their place in the Union Army. He already signed up for Mister Brainard, a fellow married to the daughter of a rich man in Hartford. Michael had his 350 dollars. He told me that I could get 350 dollars for serving in the Union Army. For taking someone else's place I would be made a king. I could own a farm with 100 acres and a farmhouse with glass windows and a stone fireplace. A farm for Rose and me to raise children.

When I told Mister Mulcahy he said that I was a fool to join the Union Army. Said that slaves weren't my bother and I shouldn't get my head shot off for something I knew nothing about. But he was wrong. I did know. I knew because of something I read in one of the papers Missus Mulcahy laid on the counter. A British man by the name of Freeman wrote that the best thing for slavery would be to allow every Irishman in America to kill a slave and then hang the Irishman for murder. If the British who starved us thought slaves should be killed, President Lincoln must be right to free them. And I thought it strange a man named Freeman wanted slaves murdered.

A week after I told Michael I would join up he was back with papers for me to sign. First time I ever signed my full name. Special neat I tried to make it. Two weeks later a smiling Michael was back with my money. I couldn't believe it. In my whole life I didn't think I could have so much money. Ten years before I could have bought food for a thousand starving Irishmen. Michael told me where I would be mustered in. First he had to tell me what mustered in meant. I was joining the 12th Infantry in Hartford, a three or four day walk away.

Told Mister Mulcahy that I was leaving on the first day of August, he turned red in the face and shouted at me. Shouted even though I was standing close enough to smell his tobacco breath. Said I would get my head shot off and I was the dumbest of the dumb Irish. Never spoke another word to me. A few days later an Irish boy named Tadd came to work at the shop. He said that Mister Mulcahy told him that I should teach him everything he should know. I did, for certain I told him of the Clancey Saloon. Told him in a year to see about getting a job there. Told him he could maybe get a raise from Mister Mulcahy if he did.

I was twisted tight worried about Rose. She said she would come to America. But Rose never said she would marry me. 'Course, I never asked her. Scared I was to ask. Scared what she might say to a lad with patched britches. When I told Missus Mulcahy about my worry she said it was silliness. Told me to write Rose a letter telling her how much I wanted to marry her and have children. I did. But it took a long time. Kept thinking of what to say. Finally wrote it all down. I told her right off that I wanted to marry her and have children. Told her that I had money for a farm and that if she came to America and changed her mind about marrying me she could have the money and buy a farm for herself.

A few days before I left for the army Missus Mulcahy took me to the Shawmut Bank on State Street to open an account in the name of Rose. I didn't feel real right about somebody holding most all my money, but Missus Mulcahy told me it was safe. I put in 240 dollars. I had sent 100 dollars with Michael's uncle to give to Rose for her passage. Kept ten dollars for me. Missus Mulcahy promised that she would look after Rose when she got to Boston. After supper that night I went to a shop that sold watches and pretty pins for ladies. For two dollars I bought Missus Mulcahy a silver-colored pin with a real jewel that was red. When I gave it to her she told me it was the most special pin she had ever seen. Wore it every day before I left for Worcester to meet Michael. Most certain I wished I could have bought my mother a pin.

My trek to Worcester was only two days because the blue-sky weather was smiling on the Irish. Thought of my walk to the Work

House so long ago. Thought of the starving children along the path. Thought of the baby at her dead mother's breast.

Michael had a fine room with a window in the attic of Mister Washburn's most grand home. He was the owner of the piano wire factory. I stayed with Michael till it was time for us to be mustered in. It was a full day of walking to Hartford, went straight away to a place called Campfield. There were sixty or so of us being mustered in to the 12th Connecticut Infantry. When I asked why Connecticut Michael told me Hartford was not in Massachusetts. All but two of the fellas joining up were Irish.

The first few days it rained and then rained some more. So there we sat in our tents. Sat there talking mostly about what we were going to do with our mustered-in money. By the second week the sun showed its yellow face and two wagons pulled up loaded heavy with uniforms. I was given the best clothes I had ever seen. A heavy dark-blue coat with metal buttons and boots that weren't worn through. First new boots I had ever owned. But I guess President Lincoln owned them.

We had a captain who acted like our warden at the Work House. Told us what to do and yelled at us. But mostly he stayed in his tent. Then a sergeant joined us. The captain told the sergeant what to tell us. The captain never spoke to us again. I liked the sergeant. He cursed us when we were learning to march. But he cursed in a friendly way, not a mean way, like the wardens in the Work House.

It was the second or maybe the third month that was the best. We got Springfield muzzle-loading rifles. I had never held anything so beautiful. It was almost as long as I was tall. The stock was sanded and stained. The barrel was blue-gray and smooth. I smiled when I looked at it standing in the corner of my tent. I never imagined such a magnificent thing would be trusted to me.

Most every day we practiced with the Springfield. I can still remember. Pull out paper cartridge. Grasp between thumb and finger. Rip open with teeth. Pour powder into barrel. Insert ball.

Ram ball down with rod. Place rod in holding tube. Half-cock hammer. Pull off old cap. Put new cap on nipple. Fully cock. Aim and fire.

Shooting someone I could imagine doing. At a far distance it's not a person, it was just a shape. But there was one thing I couldn't do. No way could I. Each Springfield came with a bayonet. It slid over the end of the barrel and stuck out more than a foot. It made the rifle a big pole with a long knife on the end. Taught we were to lunge at rebel soldiers and stick the bayonet in their chest. Told that when we advanced we should stick any wounded rebel we saw laying on the ground. Stick them even if they were wounded real bad. I just didn't think I could kill someone up close with pain in his face.

A couple of days before we were to march off to war Tadd found me at the camp. Tadd was the Irish boy that Mister Mulcahy hired to do my work. Had a letter from Rose with him. Missus Mulcahy wanted to make certain I got it so she sent Tadd without asking Mister Mulcahy. It was the first letter from Rose since I wrote her about being my wife. The letter I wrote telling her that if she came to America she could have my farm money whether she married me or not.

Quick-like I stole off to my tent. I sat alone on my cot. My stomach churned. Fearful like I opened the letter. It was two sheets of white paper. Each sheet was folded two times. I read each word slowly. I started to shake. Then I read the sentence. Thank you, sweet Jesus! Rose said she wanted to marry me. She wrote the farm money didn't matter. Rose said she would marry me no matter what money I had saved. It was the best happy moment of my life. After three years of hoping that Rose loved me I knew she must.

It was a cold and rainy October day when we marched off to war. The head man of the state came to see us off. Governor Buckingham was what they called him. He rode in a coach and we marched behind. We marched down State Street stepping in horse shit from the governor's carriage. We were marching to the boat that would take us to Washington.

The truth was that even if I was marching to war in a cold rain, stepping in mud and horse shit, I was a happy lad. Let me tell you why I was a happy Irish nobody marching to war. I was doing something for Rose and me. And even if Mister Mulcahy was right and I did get my head shot clean off Rose would be in America. Rose would be in America with enough money for a happy life. Enough money to make her and her family happy. So, you see, no matter if I got killed it was a good bargain I struck for Rose.

And another thing, even if I did get my head shot off, I still had the kiss.

Patrick

Abigail

Unlike many wars, the Revolutionary War was not one nation defending itself against a foreign aggressor. Rather, it was Englishman against Englishman. The American Colonies were founded and populated by those that were both citizens of England and subjects of a monarch.

Beginning in 1765 tensions between the British government and the thirteen American Colonies began to boil. A most divisive issue was the Stamp Act and the Tea Act, which levied taxes on Colonial com-

merce. Colonists, who had no meaningful say in their governance, took to their bosom the chant, "No taxation without representation."

June 17th of 1775 marked the first major hostility between Colonists and the British; heavy casualties were inflicted on a British regiment at Breed's Hill (which became known as the Battle of Bunker Hill). But the first victory was not a harbinger for a quick Colonial victory . . . defeat of the British was seven years distant.

While many Colonists, referred to as Patriots, supported the Revolution, many did not; these individuals were considered to be Loyalists, reflecting their continued loyalty to the Crown . . . to the king.

The British Army was well-trained, well-equipped, and paid. The Continental Army fighting for independence was composed of volunteers. The weapons of most soldiers were their hunting rifles, and their pay was most often no more than meager rations.

A decision for a shop owner or farmer to join the Continental Army and fight for independence was of the heaviest consequence. Families were left behind to fend for themselves; wives took on the burdens of the husband. Pay was nonexistent for months, shelter was often that which the individual Patriot constructed, no consideration was paid to the family of a soldier who fell in battle, and the British promised hanging for those traitors who took up arms against the king . . . welcome to Abigail's struggles as the wife of a Patriot.

1776: At night it is always the worst. During the day I am busy— too busy to think and worry. Always moving. But at night, in the dark, lying on the cot, the wind through the trees and the rattling panes of glass become a chanting crowd of my problems. So many chores, so many tasks, too many things to do. With daybreak the problems do not take their leave, rather they sleep peacefully while I toil. They rest so they will be fresh to attack my constitution yet again under the cover of darkness.

The above is from a journal where I recorded my thoughts while Charles was at war. I intended to make an entry most days. I did not. By the end of many days there was no energy, only despair.

My name is Abigail, Abigail Johnson, once married to my dearest Charles. Before my wedding day I lived with my father, mother, and sister. Father was a gentleman farmer. His ways were of hard work and an acknowledgment of God's blessings. Mother taught my sister and me domestics, by the glow of candles Father read to us from his great books. As a child and young girl a content life wrapped my family. When I married such would be my life, so I believed.

Charles and I wed in the spring of 1771. I was seventeen, he twenty-five. We met on a crisp October Sunday after a rigid sermon of redemption by Reverend Tripwell. Charles, the previous summer, had purchased a small portion of land west of town from Mr. Dear. Even though I met Charles as a woman full grown, I had been praying for him for many years. As a young girl I lay in bed knowing that somewhere my husband-to-be was also resting. Each night I prayed to God that he be kept safe until we met. I knew we would, and we did.

Charles was my answered prayer. His easy smile and gentle manner were like a well-sewn shirt covering a strong back. For me life did not begin until I married Charles. Of all my days on this earth, the happiest were with my husband, nurturing our family.

Then the war.

In 1775 both Charles and I believed that there would be no war or, if it should come to pass, after a few skirmishes the nonsense of British fighting British would show its color. But not so. In 1775 British blood spilled on both sides of the battle line. First Lexington and Concord, then Breed's Hill and Bunker Hill. With a thousand men dead, emotion became the pilot of the Colonies' ship. This emotion stirred and heated to a boil in the early months of 1776 with the publication of Mr. Paine's *Common Sense*:

"Every spot of the old world is overrun with oppression. Freedom hath been hunted round the globe. Asia, and Africa, have long expelled her. Europe regards her like a stranger, and England hath given her warning to depart. O! receive the fugitive, and prepare in time an asylum for mankind."

Words can sway. These words swayed my Charles, they did not sway me. To me a small tax was a just tax, and loyal we should be to the king that granted our lands. But Charles was as the Patriots. He felt conflict was necessary, a belief shaped by a fear that to state otherwise would be a sign of his unwillingness to sacrifice. For my dear Charles the hard decision was the right decision. It did not matter that I believed otherwise, Charles was the man of the house, he and his friend John Dotson would fight the Redcoats. Even though I was told it was only for three months it pained me to know Charles would be in harm's way. In the year to come the pain twisted inside me as the husbands of other women claimed they could not serve. Claimed they were needed on their farms and in their shops. My journal of the many days while Charles was gone began on a warm spring day.

April 18, 1776: Today was the day. With Charles and the children to the path that bends along the stone wall and past our home. Charles held me close and whispered words of love and promises that he would safely return.

He kissed Sarah and Baby Charles, then was down the curved path toward town to meet his friend John Dotson. Together they were off to the Continental Army. Baby Charles was at my bosom with Sarah holding my hand as we watched Charles become smaller in his walk of strong strides along the path to a gentle hill. With my free hand I wanted to brush the tears away, but I feared if he turned he would see my gesture of sorrow. Still I stood, my grief spilling to my cheeks. After Charles crossed the crest of the rise, only his hat and musket were seen. Then nothing, the shrill of a bird of prey in the distance marking the moment. Back to our house, Sarah singing a song and dashing after butterflies. I prepared our Sunday supper, moved Sarah to Charles's place next to mine at the oak table, held her hand, and repeated our blessings. With night the children to bed and I alone. The first night since I married that Charles was not by my side. In the darkness of our home the children slept a good sleep. I did not.

"When you depart from me sorrow abides, and happiness takes his leave."

April 20, 1776: Yesterday was a good day. It was a busy day. With Charles gone, a busy day is a good day. With the chores to be done, with Sarah's and Baby Charles's needs, no time to dwell on loneliness. Yesternight was not good. The children asleep, I was alone. I sat at our table with a precious candle burning and began a letter, but there was nothing new to tell. What I wanted to say I may not say. I wanted to say how much he is missed and how empty I feel. But I don't want Charles to think that I complain. Perhaps he would be right. I did not finish the letter. I snuffed out the candle. Today a heavy rain. Only outside to wish Mrs. Brown good morning and thank her for her milk. With the rain Baby Charles's napkins were hung inside to dry. Sarah could use the chamber pot by her second birthday. Another year for Baby Charles before the napkins become a memory. Two good things the rain brought. Tall drinks for the crops and a washing away of privy well smells.

April 22, 1776: Charles gone four days and I have gained a confidence that those tasks needed to be done can be done. Each morning a visit to Mrs. Brown and then tend the crops. Pulling weeds from their roots and brushing bugs from their leaves. In the afternoon Sarah and I do our domestics together. Washing and baking, then many hours carding, spinning, and sewing.

April 24, 1776: I will fill my empty and lonely time, this time between the sunset and my sleep, the time Charles and I spoke in the glow of the hearth's last flames. Each evening after Baby Charles sleeps I will read to Sarah from my cherished books. As my father to me, I will introduce her to peoples of great drama, emotion, and interest. Tomorrow evening she will meet my friend Juliet.

April 25, 1776: Today I wrote my first letter to my dearest Charles. I told him that all is well and that we spoke of him always. Being gone only a week, I had no new occurrences to share. But not to write would be wrong. I made the letter long. I would have rather just written how much I missed him and how much I hurt at night thinking of him away. But I did not.

Letters to Charles are not certain in their arrival. They are given to merchants who journey to and from Boston, a full day's ride. From there they are carried in manners unknown in the direction of the armies. Mr. Green journeys most often to Boston. Before the war he returned with items dear to us, those things from England that made our life less harsh. Unless there is deep snow on the ground in the coldest time of winter, he goes there and back each week. Mr. Thompson back and forth less, delivering lumber. Both men bear letters to and from our armies. They are not paid for this effort. To each I will offer a cup of cider, good tidings, and appreciations.

April 27, 1776: Sarah has new friends. A family of rabbits lives under our house. She has given each a name, but I think other than the mother rabbit, called Mrs. Hop by Sarah, all the other names change owners day by day. The rabbits are buried deep in their home during daylight's sun, but with dusk we see their noses, ears, and then their wanderings. If the weather is fair Sarah places carrot peelings by their home. I think they now expect dinner to be served each night. Sarah hopes that someday soon they will take a carrot from her hand.

April 29, 1776: When Charles departed I told sweet Sarah he would return in three short months. After only a few days she asked if her father would be back this day. Try as I might, and try as she might, her mind's calendar is not a calendar of the moons I know. To teach her a month's distance, and to ease her questions to me, I took a bowl seldom used and in it I placed ninety dried peas. A single green pea being one day. Each morning, with much ceremony, we remove a waiting pea from the bowl. Told Sarah when the bowl was empty, her father would be home.

May 1, 1776: Not everyone is a Patriot or a Loyalist. Some claim neither side and thus risk nothing nor need to sacrifice. Henry Crabtree is such a person. He and his brother have a small farm not near ours. His brother journeys to Boston each week returning with papers from there, New York, and Philadelphia. These he sells. Most every paper purchased is traded among many. Those who are able read aloud to those who cannot. But I think Henry Crabtree a Loyalist, though he says not. Always he tells of what the Patriots are doing wrong and what the British are doing right. Today in Mr. Cranson's shop he spoke a basket of Patriot mistakes. I quickly took my leave, try not to listen to his words because often they ring true. If Henry Crabtree is right, Charles is wrong.

May 5, 1776: Most sorrowful today. This morning to church; Reverend Tripwell's sermon as his others. Then, to my discontent, in the churchyard gathered families, smiling families of husbands and wives and their children, filled with Sabbath happiness. These were Loyalists. Husbands were not fighting a war—a war that many say is unjust. These Loyalists claim that the Patriots by refusing to pay taxes owed the king mock the crown. Perhaps they are right. Why does Charles choose between a small tax and abandoning his family? Charles would say this is not the choice he made, but on this day it was the choice he made.

From church the long walk back to our farm. Once home thought only of pleasant memories. Did not consider the morning's anger. When Sarah and Baby Charles sleep, I will revisit my favorite pages and join Hamlet in conversation.

May 8, 1776: Our nearest neighbor is Mr. Dear, a most kind man. His wife Margaret was not so. Last winter she died of the putrid fever after a long month in bed. Mr. Dear's temperament is more tranquil after Margaret moved from his house to the house of God. The path, and then the road, from his farm to town passes our house. Before Charles left he made a pact with Mr. Dear. If on his journey to and from town he should see a pail hanging from a nail Charles drove into our door, he will stop to learn what I might need. Today Sarah and I set the signal. Late this afternoon Mr. Dear knocked upon our door, concerned about problems I might have. But I had no problem. Sarah and I had baked fresh bread and gave him a carefully wrapped loaf with a smile and a thank-you for thinking of us. But the gesture was not for kindness only. I alone have the burden for the safety of my children. I am recruiting my army to defend their safety.

May 13, 1776: Today Baby Charles turned one year old. He is plump and hearty. Chores rushed to free time to bake a special cake for him. Baked with sugar saved during the past weeks. But only Sarah and I tasted his cake; he is too young. Sarah made her brother a crown out of paper, glued together with flour paste, then placed it on his head and hailed "King Charles." Also this day Baby Charles tasted his first solid food—not cake—thin gruel sweetened with a touch of molasses. While I prepared our little celebration, my sweet girl told Baby Charles stories about the rabbits that live under the house, but no sense her words made to him.

May 15, 1776: This being Wednesday, I went to the church for the spinning bee. Better Wednesday than Sunday. On Sunday I see all the men in the congregation and wonder why, why is Charles not with me?

On my Wednesdays only women and their children come, women whose husbands are away with Charles. Without their husbands this regiment of women labor their farms and shops and do all the things I do. Our travails leave little time for fellowship. Thus Wednesday mornings are dear—stolen moments to speak with other women, to give advice and share our burdens.

When the shadow falls through the east windowpane we know that it is mid-morning. With our spinning done we pause and give the children milk with bread and jam. Shortbreads and other portions from the week's meals are shared among us. From an earthenware jug raspberry tea, brewed in the sun. If one of us has a newspaper Mary Rogers reads to us. Today, no news. This is good. News when read is only of struggles.

May 24, 1776: Last night to bed with a candle and sonnets. Last one read, "The Passionate Pilgrim," XIV. Its final goodnight stanza:

> *Were I with her, the night would post too soon;*
> *But now are minutes added to the hours;*
> *To spite me now, each minute seems a moon;*
> *Yet not for me, shine sun to succour flowers!*
> *Pack night, peep day; good day, of night now borrow:*
> *Short, night, to-night, and length thyself to-morrow.*

When the candle was out and sleep did come, Charles joined me.

May 25, 1776: Tonight Agnes Meadows came to visit after supper. Her husband serves the Continental Army. She brought her two girls, who ran off to play with Sarah. Agnes after pleasantries dropped her head, was silent for a long moment, then told me she is with child. Agnes wept as she told me this. She fears that if she were to die in childbirth her children would be orphans. I told her this was not true. All would help. I tried to comfort Agnes with some coffee I had saved with a passion. She smiled when she saw me grind the beans; coffee is so scarce. Agnes was content when sipping her coffee, as if it were the potion for all that ailed her in body and spirit. "Perhaps I shall have a son this time," she said. "A fine boy like Baby Charles." Her words were a generous price paid to me for so few swallows of coffee and a pinch of sugar.

May 30, 1776: Charles was supposed to dig a new privy well. He did not. He promised that when he returned it would be dug. Our privy well needs to be covered and forgotten. But before I can do this, a new one needs to be dug. This afternoon I set to the task myself, with a spade and shovel. After an hour, stopping to retrieve Baby Charles from his crawls, I had only scratched the earth. God must have used masons to make the fields of our farm. So many stones. Dirt and a tear on my dress rewarded my labors.

June 3, 1776: Today was bright with a June sun. I walked with the children through our fields. Sarah ran ahead, chasing after the butterflies that have made our farm their village. Baby Charles slept in the sling, content with the swaying and the closeness to me. Try as I might not to, always I steal a glance to the horizon, hoping to see my dear Charles appear over the rise. Always the same, sorry that I glanced.

With the setting sun, Mr. Dear knocked upon our door. The good man brought us a basket of apples and a basket of news. But only news of despair, nothing right for the Patriots. After the candle is out and I lay abed, I will offer prayers that Charles be safe and a letter soon arrive.

June 6, 1776: Before this war, my love was equal between Charles and the children. Since he has been gone, all my attention flows to Sarah and Baby Charles. For this I feel guilt. God knows that I ache for Charles, but, as with a wound, this hurt in time has ebbed. When on the most happy day we meet again, I shall feel as bashful as a girl.

June 8, 1776: A good growing season. The corn is nearly as tall as I, and the beans wrap the stalks like dear friends. The squash are blooming. Each day I attack the beetles as if they were Redcoats. They must be beaten in daily battles to have a full harvest for Charles's return.

June 9, 1776: Reverend Tripwell never before spoke in a manner to give his allegiances. Sermons were confirmations of doing God's work and obeying God's will. Before the war no leanings did the Reverend show. But as I lay these words on the pages of my journal this night, I think I know why. He wished to make the collection plate the most full. Collections from both the Loyalists and the Patriots were sought. Today's sermon was not as others. He spoke of our war, and then he spoke of Matthew 22:21 and Job 1:21. From these scriptures the right and wrong of the war should be known. He said that we should pay our king the taxes that were due him; "render therefore unto Caesar the things which are Caesar's." He then said the lands on which we lived were a gift from the king; "the Lord gave and the Lord hath taken away." Before, monies to the collection plate were from the Loyalists and the Patriots. But now the Patriots are at war. Only their wives and children are in the pews. Families of Patriots have no money for the collection plate, only for food. Reverend Tripwell speaks to the minds of those with money. His scriptures speak to the Loyalists.

"The devil can cite scripture for his purpose."

June 13, 1776: In my letter to Charles today I told him that I would number each letter sent to him and asked that he do the same. If a letter is lost in its journey the truth of the matter will be known.

Together Sarah and I made a pie with apples given by Mr. Dear. A pail hung on the door. When he paused on his journey past, together fruit and sugar wedges much enjoyed.

June 14, 1776: Today in Mr. Cranson's shop men talk of the news. Mr. Cranson reports that a Mr. Richard Lee of Virginia proposes that the Continental Congress should declare the Colonies free of the king. Mr. Crabtree always speaks his opinion in a great voice. Said that only a few colonies would so declare. Other men swaying back and forward, not stating what they believe right. I wonder what army does Charles serve? If colonies are not together in mind, how are our soldiers together on the field of battle?

June 17, 1776: Fewer and fewer dried peas in the bowl. Sarah squeals with pleasure, believing her father will be home soon. I fear he may not and disappointment will be hers. Last night while she slept I placed another fortnight's count in the bowl. Better Charles comes home early than late for Sarah.

June 19, 1776: Charles has an agreement with a farmer neighbor, Mr. Stamps, to tend his pigs. For this labor we will be given the meat of one at slaughtering time. These pigs have been a comfort to me with Charles gone. My sweet Sarah names every animal. This is how our cow became Mrs. Brown. Like Sarah, I named each piglet. I named them after the apostles; even the female piglet. Peter and Paul are the largest, and their sister, James, is the runt.

Perhaps when comes slaughtering time, I will take a slice of one of the apostles to Reverend Tripwell. I will take pleasure when he eats one of God's chosen ones.

"Revenge is best served cold."

June 20, 1776: Our fields are full. God blessed us with sun and rain. Sarah sits outside after supper when the still evening air allows the flowers to give off their most pleasant aromas. She asked me to name the flowers for her, and she revels in reciting their names aloud: "Black-Eyed Susan, Johnny Jump-Up, and Sweet William." Sarah makes up stories about these three, each day giving them a new adventure. Today Miss Black-Eyed Susan married Sweet William, and together they have a son named Johnny Jump-Up. Tonight the flowers are put snug to bed in the drawer of our cabinet. Tomorrow they will sit at our table and join Sarah for bread and jam.

Now too is the season of strawberries. Sarah and I have enjoyed them for a week. Each berry is a treasure. I will put up preserves so the strawberries will be more than a memory when winter comes. A strawberry eaten today is less jam for the winter. Strawberries and jam are as life: always today's sacrifice for tomorrow's hope.

June 24, 1776: I saw Mr. Green driving his cart today, returning from Boston. His horse seemed to look at me askance when he passed by. Why did Mr. Green not bring a letter? Is Charles unwell? I pray not. Yet, if he is well and has not written, in some ways it is worse. I tell myself not to think too much. What is, is. So many reasons a letter so longed for may not find its way to me. It is time for me to lay aside my pen, blow out the candle, repeat my prayers, sleep a good sleep, and rise and smile when Sarah's and Baby Charles's smiles greet me in the morning. I will be content. I must be content.

June 28, 1776: Today with the sun beginning its farewell, Mr. Dear pardoned his journey home from town to wish us good evening and bring us a welcomed basket of cornbread. I think this cornbread may be a gift to him from a widow in town—one of several with an eye on Mr. Dear. After some pleasantries he told me that King George has again refused to accept our olive branch and instead declared the Colonies to still be rebellious. If bad news must be delivered, the package should not arrive at dusk when it will be fresh in my mind as the candle is snuffed; all adversaries become bolder with the darkness.

July 1, 1776: Today as others, up before the sun. The chamber pot emptied and cleaned, some small chores accomplished before Sarah's questions and Baby Charles's needs. Bread and jam for Sarah after her face washed and her hair stroked. Then she pretends to feed her doll as I nurse Baby Charles. To the field all three to say good morning to Mrs. Brown. I on the milking stool with Baby Charles in the sling. Sarah picks handfuls of grass and offers Mrs. Brown her breakfast. My hands once soft are no longer. Mrs. Brown looks back and down as to say, "Why so?" By the time the bucket is half full, Mrs. Brown has no more. Then down the path from the meadow to our house. The foul smell from the privy calls out to be filled with earth. Into our home, then to the field for the day's chores. For each chore done, another one standing ready. A dinner for Sarah with answers to questions always asked. The last nursing of Baby Charles, Sarah's prayers said, then they to sleep. Baby Charles's soiled napkin washed and hung by the stove. An entry in my journal and then in the quiet and darkness of the house I can speak uninterrupted with my worries.

July 4, 1776: Yesterday after Baby Charles fussed and finally was asleep for the night, I finished a letter to Charles before bed. I wanted to tell him that he should have dug the privy well before he left. But then I thought better. I thought where he might be sleeping tonight. I brought Sarah to bed with me. Whenever I felt bitter toward Charles, I hold our children. Charles and God gave me the most precious of treasures. I need not worry about what they did not give me.

July 7, 1776: Today to church and more of the Reverend's admonishments. On my way homeward, I was surprised by the great number of people clustered around Mr. Cranson's shop. The news has come that the Colonies have together declared their independence. These words quickly turned my hands cold. This is the condition so many desire. Is this what my family should desire? We have cast our future to the whims of fate and fighting.

July 10, 1776: Sarah asks questions until my mind feels numb. Most answers I know well. Others I do not. Perhaps no one knows. She wants to know where her father is and why he is gone, even though I have told her more times than there are stones in the pasture. "Father is fighting for our liberty," I say. "What is liberty?" Sarah asks. How do I answer? If we have liberty what will be different? Will Mrs. Brown milk herself and will Baby Charles's napkins wash themselves?

July 12, 1776: Today was as a well baked pudding. The air hot, still, and moist. Chores mostly in the house. Before, Charles's comings and goings punctuated the day and gave them shape, like the poles that prop up a tent. His presence made me feel I could hold on to the day's moments as I lived them. Now it seems as if everything floats by, as if I am adrift on a river of no end and no piers.

July 15, 1776: Before he left Charles asked our neighbor, old Mr. Borrows, to help me dig our potatoes. When I saw him in church yesterday I told him the potatoes were ready for birth and would he be the midwife. He grinned, tipped his hat, and said he would be with us today. He did, but if he is a midwife the babies are bruised.

As he began to dig his thoughts took him back years ago to when he was clearing the land. He cursed the potatoes, calling them "damned stones," flung them far from my collection bushel. Begged him to stop, but his temper grew worse. Sarah was frightened. Quickly I ran to the house and back with a cup of cider. He paused, drank with nary a pause. Then bade me a farewell and down the path as if no potatoes waiting.

July 17, 1776: With a small portion of the potatoes just born, Sarah and I made crisps. Cut thin as a piece of cloth, soaked in cold water, then quick fried with pig grease and salt. Thought of Charles; crisps and ale are his favorite. Sadness descended. I shall not fry crisps again 'til he can partake.

July 21, 1776: Much pleasure in this Sunday. Not from Reverend Tripwell's words, but from Mr. Crabtree's errors. After church I joined many others outside Mr. Cranson's shop, where I read of the Declaration of Independence, agreed to by all the colonies except New York. Crabtree no longer remembers his boast that most colonies would not sign.

Also, Baby Charles took his first steps today. For several days he moved as if walking, but held to walls or chairs. Today his little hands released and his first short steps followed freely. I considered writing Charles of his son's new mark, but thought not.

July 22, 1776: Last month I placed more peas in the bowl. But my Sarah is a smart girl and knows her numbers. Today she counted the ten there, pointed to her fingers, and set the mark. If I add more peas Sarah will need to grow more fingers if she is not to know the truth.

July 27, 1776: Each morning in my walk to and from Mrs. Brown, I pass the privy well. The smell is a righteous stink. I become angry at Charles for not digging the new well before he was off. I need to take a different path or have a new privy well dug. I will put down my pen, go to bed, melt a portion of a candle dear, and speak with Othello about my frustrations.

July 29, 1776: The prayed-for letter arrived yesterday from Charles. My face flushed as Mr. Green pulled it from a sack on the back of his cart—a cart burdened only with leaves and stains from vegetables delivered to Boston. All of my being wanted to tear open the seal and read Charles's words. But first I offered Mr. Green a cup of cider and spoke of the warm July weather. Trying to be most pleasant, Mr. Green played with Baby Charles. All the time I was smiling and wishing him to leave so I could read my letter.

After a game of silly questions with Sarah, Mr. Green took to his cart and down the path. With Sarah sitting next to me on the steps to our home, I read Charles's missive. No words of missing me. No words of love. Only words of his needs and his hardships. He asked that I send a shirt and boots. Why, I thought, did not he just ask for a crown of gold and emeralds? Then words that brought a gasp. Charles is not returning as promised. No fresh troops have come to relieve the struggle of those already serving.

Sarah asked why I was sad. I told her that I was missing her father so. She asked that I read her Charles's words. Slowly I read her the letter, but they were not Charles's words, they were my own. I composed a tale telling how her father would be home soon and would play many games with Baby Charles and Lady Sarah, and how he wanted her to know how he smiled when he thought of her most pretty face.

After the children asleep I poured the few peas still in the bowl back into the sack from which they were so carefully taken. When next in Mr. Cranson's shop I will trade this sack for something else. To see a pea will bring anger. Anger at Charles for his broken promise of return. How does he think I can do his work and my work? When he was tending the fields, did he think I was doing nothing?

"Men's vows are women's traitors!"

July 30, 1776: Today I rushed the chores. Then passed hours with Sarah and Baby Charles. Sliced an apple and baked the wedges with sugar. Even little Charles smiled when one touched his tongue. When he was asleep I read to Sarah a story of a brave knight and a beautiful princess. Once she sleeps, I will burn a candle for more than an hour so I may join Romeo and Juliet—this day my recipe for good temperament to join me once again.

August 2, 1776: For some reason today guilt smothered me. I thought of the wonderful Charles that I married, and then I thought of the anger I had felt toward him for leaving the family. He suffers too. No matter how much we suffer, he suffers more. To sway my guilt I thought what best I could do to make a pleasant surprise. If Baby Charles can speak when Charles returns, the word *father* will be spoken.

August 4, 1776: Much talk today at Mr. Cranson's of the two Howes. General William Howe led the Redcoats' bloody charges at Bunker Hill. As his reward he was made commander-in-chief of the British army in America. His brother is Admiral Howe, commanding the British fleet of two hundred ships along our coast and surrounding our cities. One of the men at Cranson's shop asked if George Washington perhaps had a brother who could help him in his fight against the British. Mr. Crabtree quickly claimed yes and that his brother commanded an open boat with one oar.

I will enter Cranson's shop only when less winds blow.

August 8, 1776: The first day in many the sun pushed aside rain clouds. The Jenkins girl rose early from her bed at home to sit with the children while I walked to the far pasture to milk Mrs. Brown. Emmy does not like to be up so early, but her mother likes the butter and cheese I give her in exchange for her time.

I walked with my empty bucket through the grass; bright sunlight rendered the world reborn. As birds welcomed the rising rays, I felt disbelief that not far away, men who worship my God want to slay dear Charles.

When I rounded the hill Mrs. Brown turned and started in my direction, like an old friend coming to greet me. She has put on flesh from feasting on the summer grass. A stool next to her, and a bucket under her. I listened to the sound of the milk as it streamed into the bucket. I prayed Charles had enough to eat. I prayed he would not stray into harm's way. I prayed he returns home soon. I prayed because it was the right thing to do, otherwise would be wrong. But no one hears this prayer, I fear.

August 12, 1776: I have a dire worry. I could not before write the worry, to write the worry was to anoint its being. But the worry lives. It lives in our root cellar. Charles's letter did not speak of the sentence laid upon this family by his choice not to return by winter. We have not enough food for the winter. While good crops were blessed upon us, they are not enough. Charles hunts, and fresh venison is a staple. His labors for others also bartered for necessary foods. I try not to think, but always the root cellar is in my mind. Not enough stores for the winter.

"Women may fall when there's no strength in men."

August 21, 1776: This being Wednesday I was off to the church with Sarah and little Charles. The women spoke together of our problems and hopes while the young girls carded the flax and watched over the youngest children. Old Mary Rogers read from the *Continental Journal*, only a week old—no good news, only struggles. From eight in the morning 'til noon only our fingers and tongues moved. At midday Arnold Rush came to the door, ready to take our thread and weave it at his shop. A dreamlike time ago when we could purchase cloth cheaply, thanks to the ships always arriving from England. But there is no commerce now with Britain, so we must find the time to spin the thread.

Without these Wednesdays I could not be of a calm temperament. Sarah and Baby Charles are always with me for company, but also with me their needs. At church on Wednesdays other women harken to my problems. Kind and hopeful they be. I know they be this way because this is how they wish other women be to them.

"They who thrive well take counsel of their friends."

August 25, 1776: Again today after church Mr. Crabtree spoke for all to hear. In his voice like a cannonade, he pronounced that he knew George Washington would lose the battle of New York. Mr. Crabtree claimed his brother had served with General Washington when he commanded a force against the French at Fort Duquesne. There, Crabtree boasted, Washington quickly surrendered and only by the kindness of the French did he live.

August 26, 1776: With the burning sun of August, Mrs. Brown's plate is empty. The grasses in her pasture are no longer enough. Mr. Dear kindly told me that his two cows have more than enough tall grasses in the large pasture next to Mrs. Brown's. He pulled down two sections of fence so Mrs. Brown could join them for supper. I wonder if Mr. Dear was always so kind. I wonder if he becomes kinder as he draws nearer to visiting the house of God.

August 27, 1776: Today I stopped at Mr. Cranson's shop. I should not have. Much excited talk. I overheard reports that over eight thousand Hessian troops have arrived by convoy to fight the Patriots. We have so few men against the king. Why does he spend his gold to bring these foreigners to the Colonies? Will he have them do something to us that his army of our cousins would not? I am fearful.

"Hell is empty and all the devils are here."

August 28, 1776: If my mother or father lived, what if I were called home to care for my ailing parent and told my husband that I must do my duty as a daughter? What if I promised to return home, but I did not? I imagine that I write to tell Charles that my stay will last longer. He writes back, wondering why someone else, another daughter, does not help with the burden. I leave the household, the farm, and the children in his care. He asks, "What of your duty to me and the children?" This is how Charles's duty seems to me. He has done his part; it is time for him to return to his familiar work. How unfair is his absence to fight for this thing called liberty! This liberty that to our family is as a drifting cloud in the faraway sky.

August 30, 1776: No longer do I read to Sarah from my treasured books. The emotions of the players make no sense to her. This not be her fault. Her emotions still to bloom.

September 2, 1776: This day for some reason, tea was always on my mind. I smelled tea much today, even though there was no tea near. I remembered pleasant times and conversations with tea as the centerpiece. How long since any of us enjoyed a cup of tea? Warm sweet tea in porcelain cups dressed in hand-painted flowers. I wonder where they are now, the men of Boston who as Indians thrust the tea into the sea. In England they drink their tea. Here only the fish drink tea.

"Praising what is lost makes the remembrance dear."

September 3, 1776: Mr. Dear to our house today. Reported one thousand Patriots captured and three hundred killed in the Battle of Long Island.

Can this be true?

September 6, 1776: Charles in the letter arrived yesterday spoke of the island of New York. Two sides of rivers and a bay beneath. He thinks whoever has the most ships will win the battle for New York City. Unless the British fleet sinks in a great storm, they will win the battle, for Patriots have no ships.

Charles is camped in the middle of the island, and the city is to the south. He writes that he traveled there twice and was much impressed. My heart gladdened to read of his visits to Trinity Church, where he offered prayers for God's care of his family and his safe return.

Charles told of a visit by General Washington. Washington tall and confident, but no king-like notions shown. Then Charles wrote of the trenches they dig for defense of the city. Every day more trenches dug. Could not he have dug a new privy well for our home?

September 11, 1776: It is constantly with me. Whether I am washing or carding, or counting the squash yet to be harvested, I am tallying. Tallying the stores we hold against the days of winter and early spring. We do not have enough. Try as I might, there is no answer other than to ask. Charles would never ask for something that was not earned, but this is what I must do. I must go to Mr. Cranson and ask for stores against credit. For me I would have a choice. For my sweet children I have no choice. Tomorrow the journey of my shame and desperation. But I shall not retreat.

"Boldness, be my friend."

September 12, 1776: Once again this morning I took stock of the root cellar, hoping I erred. Hoping perhaps it held enough to last us through the winter. It did not. I knew it did not. We have cornmeal and flour, apples, squash, potatoes, preserves, pickles, and the smallest portion of salt pork. But I must have fifty pounds of beef to help us weather the harsh days of winter.

To town I go with Baby Charles and Sarah. I am ashamed, and my steps become shorter the closer I draw to Mr. Cranson's shop. When there I wish to turn away, but do not. Into the shop I venture, Baby Charles in the sling, Sarah wondering at items on the shelves. Mr. Cranson nods to me, asks my health and smiles. Mrs. Cranson moves closer, but pretending not to listen. Then I ask. I ask for credit.

Mrs. Cranson, Elizabeth, quickly occupies the space between her husband and me. Tells me in a loud voice that he cannot take care of all the women whose husbands have left them behind. I tell her I will pay her as soon as Charles returns. She looks at me as if I am vermin.

She shakes her head and frowns, hands on ample hips, and tells me that she must protect him from himself, she must protect her family from going to ruin over a war they have no part in.

I turn and then a long remembered walk to our farm, my face hot and red. Red from embarrassment. Red from anger.

When my candle is snuffed tonight, peace will not be with me. It will be frightened away by my anger.

September 16, 1776: This afternoon I had just finished darning leggings for Sarah while nursing Baby Charles. Came a knock at our door, though I expected no one. When I opened the door I was frightened. Not frightened by who it was, but what he said. It was Mr. Cranson, whose wife had been so unkind toward my plea for help. His first words were that he would provide me monies if I promised to do something for him. I shivered with dread.

But my dread quickly became a warm happiness. He asked only that I not speak to his wife of the money he was giving me. He said that he knew that so many were struggling, and his wife was right that not all could be helped. But he said he knew Charles and he knew of our family. He gave me a silver coin and a big smile. He tickled Baby Charles and told Sarah how fair she be, and then he strode quickly away.

Guilt became my partner. I had not offered him a chair or a sip of cider. Within the next week I will stop by his store and wish him a most pleasant day, and when his wife not near, offer a smile and a thank-you. While a single silver coin will not buy beef for the winter, it will buy us a score of contented days. I will include him in my nightly prayers. Perhaps Mr. Cranson is one of the answers to my nightly prayers.

September 23, 1776: Yesterday my sister's husband and his friend came down from Newburyport to harvest the flax. Plants needed to be pulled this week, else their fibers will be too tough for spinning. While the men pulled the plants from the ground, Sarah and I walked behind, laying out the plants to dry properly. Baby Charles napped at Agnes Meadows's home. Next year he will toddle along after us in the fields.

Before they began their journey home I made a fine meal and felt well pleased to have them at table with me. Conversation was a mandolin of music with our supper, not a drumbeat of questions from Sarah with my short, tired answers. But conversation at a cost. One week's meat I used for our meal. Now bread and corn will be our fare for many days.

September 25, 1776: Most sorrowful yesterday. Mr. Dear stopped with only woeful tales. The Hessians and Redcoats drove the Patriots from New York City. Then, he said, the Redcoats burned the city. Can this be? Are they not burning the king's city?

No sleep. Only thoughts of Charles. Where is he? If I could, I would have him a prisoner and safe.

October 6, 1776: Even though it is October, this is as a beautiful spring day. After Reverend Tripwell's sermon, parishioners gathered in the churchyard for conversation. Then Mr. Crabtree stole the gathering in a voice as a trumpet. Said that Virginians claim they are most hurt by British tyranny and believe liberty should be for all. Then in a rising voice he claimed they sleep well on their Virginia estates while the poor farmers of Massachusetts, New York, and Pennsylvania suffer the war. In his loudest blare, shouted that Patriots be fools to fight for our Virginia cousins. Perhaps so, I think.

"The empty vessel makes the loudest sound."

October 21, 1776: An accident today that cannot be forgotten. Back from our visit with Mrs. Brown with a bucket of warm milk, more than her usual. The bucket placed on the table with a cloth across the top. Later I asked Sarah to fetch me the bucket. Then a tumble and a clatter, and somehow the bucket fell to the floor, the milk at first a large puddle and then between the floorboards to our root cellar. Sarah cried, and I sat at our table and joined her, head in hands. Why? I think. But then I think some more, and why not? God did not spill the milk. We spilled the milk. And the spilt milk will not be forgotten. A sour smell will stay with us.

"What's done can't be undone."

October 23, 1776: To town today to use a portion of Mr. Cranson's silver coin for a salt lick for Mrs. Brown. I offered pleasantries to Mr. Cranson, and when certain his wife not near, a thank-you. Sarah curtsied with her much practiced dip and bow. A hard piece of molasses from a brown clay jar was his thank-you to her.

From the store we set forth on our journey home. Men of much energy and little thought gathered in the town square, mocking King George and claiming victories from battles not yet fought. Then the chant. Together they shouted the same words as shouted since Baby Charles has been at my breast, "Give me liberty or give me death." Do they think the decision to go to war with our king is that simple? Should not they scream, "Give me liberty while my wife and children starve"? Everything for men is simple. "Let us have another child," the husband says. Then he goes to the fields and plows and plants as always. The woman carries the baby, mutes her screams during birth, nurses and dresses an infant, teaches it the ways of life, and only then the father pridefully embraces his new child. I will not sleep a quiet sleep tonight.

October 24, 1776: Today a letter from Charles. Told of the Battles of Long Island. Told how Patriots retreated, but he remains confident that New York City will be well defended and not lost to the Redcoats. His letter dated September 10th. Four weeks ago the *Boston Paper* reported our loss of New York City. His letters should only report his health. To write me of the battles makes no sense. Papers and Mr. Dear tell the tales in a louder voice.

October 25, 1776: This morning while helping Sarah with her reading I carded wool, moving it from one brush to the next. I will spin the yarn later tonight, after Sarah sleeps. Then a score of days knitting stockings and mittens for the coming winter. Baby Charles has been unwell with a fever. I hope he is only breeding teeth. I have rubbed oil of cloves on his gums. He sleeps now, but I know not for how long.

October 29, 1776: Sarah was ill, but has recovered. Baby Charles has been unwell for many days. I have not been to the pasture for two days. I am sure that Mrs. Brown is groaning with milk, looking for me to relieve her burden.

October 31, 1776: Much of the day I held my lovely baby. He is hot with fever. I try to coax a smile from him, but his eyes are glassy and far away. I lost a sweet girl after Sarah, a baby dead before she was born to this world. I cannot bear such grief again. I try to think of some way I can bargain with God so he will spare my son. But what can I do, else than that which I am doing?

November 1, 1776: I rocked my little Charles all night and covered him in cool cloths. At dawn his skin felt cooler. I put him at my breast, and he took my milk. Now he sleeps. This morning I write this entry so I may tell God how thankful I am that Baby Charles is well.

Thank you, God.

November 3, 1776: Last night I heard movement and squeals from under our house. Not sure what it be, but I knew it was not good. This morning while Sarah was tending little Charles, I looked to our rabbits' house. With a shovel I moved a small gray-brown rabbit to a final resting place, far from Sarah's daily journeys. The red fox that we saw last week had moved the others. At breakfast I told Sarah that I had seen Mrs. Hope and her family hopping over the hill to a new home. When she showed discontent I told her that with the spring they would surely be back.

November 7, 1776: Mrs. Brown has a shelter behind the garden. Soon I will begin to feed her the hay grown this summer and stored for her winter meals. I feed Mr. Stamps's pigs slops from the kitchen, potato and carrot peelings as well as the cornhusks left over from the last harvest. The chickens roost in their shelter, their feathers a fine coat. This is my family, the children and the creatures great and small. I am as Mrs. Noah, only Noah has abandoned the ark.

November 11, 1776: A bad day and a good day. Both true today were Isaiah 45:15, "Ye work in mysterious ways," and *Poor Richard's Almanac,* "God helps those who help themselves." Last night I lay in bed as a roaring storm passed by. For more than an hour thunder and lightning all around, never heard louder. At first, much time between the flash of the bolt and the roar of the thunder. But then they became one over our house. Sarah quickly to my bed. Baby

Charles did not stir. The roar of the wind gained in its volume, soon so loud that I prayed to God that we should be safe. Perhaps by prayers, perhaps not, the storm moved on.

In morning's light I walked around the house. Some things blown over, but nothing that could not be made right. But then the worst. With my bucket I walked through the gate and to the lean-to that sheltered dear Mrs. Brown. Our lovely cow lay on the ground. Not on the ground with her legs folded under her, but on her side with two legs jutting upwards. A burnt circle on the crown of her head with a portion of the skull showing, a lightning bolt ended her life and took away the milk and butter that our family eat and trade. God did not take away our cow, God took away our life.

I slumped on the ground and cried, no, I sobbed. I had been working as hard as I could, doing everything I could. God was doing nothing to help.

In time back to the house and tried to think of my blessings. But it did not matter. This was not right. Then a thought. With Baby Charles in my arms and Sarah weaving behind off to town, straight to Mr. Cranson's store. The barter, with Elizabeth approving with her silence, was quickly done. Mr. Cranson would have Mrs. Brown butchered, giving me a quarter of the meat and keeping the other for himself. He would also give me a credit at the store and have his eldest son dig a new privy well.

I walked back to the house considering the trade. It was not a good trade. I have sold our future. For the next three months we will have food. At the end of that time we will neither have a cow nor food. I have done what is needed to survive until Charles returns.

"To do a great right, do a little wrong."

November 19, 1776: After supper yesterday Agnes Meadows's daughter Sally came in haste, calling out to say that her mother's travail had started. I took the children's blankets with us, since they were likely to sleep at Agnes's house. I have been with Agnes for two of her births and know that her labors are long. Most pleased to see that Sally had fetched two other women as well. Agnes offered each of us some groaning beer and groaning cakes to mark the occasion.

In time we took turns walking beside Agnes as she crossed the loft from end to end. Mrs. Yiend, the midwife, arrived with her birthing stool. For comfort Agnes took toast dipped in wine. We spoke to her of times past and times to come. When the midwife judged that it was time, Agnes took to the birthing stool. Soon a squalling daughter born, quickly washed and swaddled. Agnes wept; the child is hearty, and she herself survived. The afterbirth taken behind the house and buried. In morning's light back to our house, as always Sarah singing and calling out greetings to things with feathers or fur.

I accept God. But events conspire at times to make God's being suspect. Charles at war against his English cousins is such a time. This morning, in the stillness of our home, I thought of Agnes's newborn. So perfect. God gives us the perfect being. We mortals corrupt the purpose of life, and then we question God's being.

November 24, 1776: Sarah's ears are sharper than I thought. At church today Reverend Tripwell spoke again of heaven and hell. His words are most frightful to anyone other than a saint. Sarah sat silent during his vast river of admonishments, her legs swinging on the edge of the pew, her head tilting one way then another as she took stock of the sights within. But listen she did. On our slow walk home this morning she asked if Mrs. Brown was in heaven. After a few moments of only footsteps being heard, I answered with a certain yes. Sarah then off chasing an imaginary. My answer was partially true. Not all of Mrs. Brown grazes peacefully in heaven. Some of her lies smoked, salted, and resting in our root cellar. Tonight I did not prepare beef for our supper.

November 27, 1776: At the Wednesday spinning bee today, I rued my presence there. Kathryn Johnson's husband returned home last week. She in attendance at our gathering this day spoke of her husband's tales. Said she that in New York City many lewd women sold their companionship to Patriot soldiers. This cannot be true, I think. But whether so or not, why would she tell this tale to women without their husbands near?

I wanted to tell Kathryn our gatherings are for each to be helpful, not hurtful. I did not.

"How hard it is for women to keep counsel."

December 2, 1776: Today I saw myself in the mirror at the far end of Mr. Cranson's shop. Vanity is not good, but my tattered and stained dress reproaches me beyond vanity. Toiling in the fields has taken its measure.

Three dresses I have. One from many years ago, only worn for the heaviest chores. Two others that once were fine dresses, one blue and the other black. The blue one bears no tears or stains that cannot be made right. This one folded away to be worn for Charles. The black dress must suffer my daily chores.

December 8, 1776: As every Sunday, to church this day. Reverend Tripwell spoke words heard before. Need for fasting, prayer, and submission to God's will. I listened, but not with interest or feeling. Thought of all that I must do. I wondered at what I have done and what I have left undone. I must bake tomorrow. Did I set out the sponge for the bread? Did I turn the cheese? Did I close the root cellar? Will the wolves be at my store? This day I must worry about tomorrow's tasks to be done, not worry of my path to our heavenly Father.

December 11, 1776: Tacked to the wall in Mr. Cranson's shop be articles from the Boston and Philadelphia newspapers. Most articles tell of the Continental Army and its struggles. Today an essay not from these papers, from Samuel Johnson of England. It says the signers of the Declaration of Independence speak not the truth. Mr. Johnson argued that the claim "that all men are created equal" is made by those who live in grand estates maintained by men who are slaves. He asked which tyranny is worse, the tyranny of a king who only wished a free-willed colonist to pay a small tax or the tyranny of a Virginia gentleman who enslaves men with the burdens of constant work, then pays them in lashes if they not be grateful for a life of strife?

Think as I might, my mind could construct no retort to Mr. Johnson.

December 13, 1776: Sarah still trails after me always, asking one question after another. Try as I might to answer, my mind becomes tired. I love her so. I know that someday she will leave for her Charles. These should be special days, while her eyes are bright and her mind curious of all. But I am weary. No time to myself, always with me the children with their needs and a village of tasks to be done before I sleep, only to awaken to yet another village of tasks.

"Have patience and endure."

December 19, 1776: Today was not as I thought. A cold day with a heavy wind that made the cold much colder. No word from my husband for nigh on two months. I weighed not going to the church for our Wednesday gathering. But my mind is becoming numb and cold. I need to warm my mind, even though my body shivers in the journey to town.

Sarah and I hurried through the morning chores and then wrapped ourselves with two dresses each and our shawls. Baby Charles held by me, tight in my warmest blanket, with one of my bonnets over his face.

To town. Halfway there I thought of returning, the cold was so hurtful. We stayed the path—would be the same distance to our gray house or a church full of women with conversation and warm food.

Finally at the church we entered, to find no one there. Sarah and I sat on a pew with Baby Charles, the cold dripping from our bodies. Then Reverend Tripwell appeared through a side door. I asked where the other women might be. He told me the gathering was on Wednesday, not Thursday. A day late. No conversation, no food, only a long journey to and from.

This has become my life. Always struggle, no reward. Home we trundled. Now Sarah and Baby Charles asleep; I am writing this by candlelight. A candle that I cannot afford to waste. Despair and disappointment be my companions. Let it be that soon I too sleep and this day be gone.

"Time and the hour run through the roughest day."

December 23, 1776: Last night thunderclaps. Sarah quickly to my bed, then soon asleep. In the darkness, with her body still, I lay quietly next to her. Slowly I rested my hand on the small of her back. Her body warm to my hand. Last night, in the darkness with my eyes closed, her warmth was Charles's warmth. I slept the good sleep.

January 1, 1777: Were the winters so cold and dark when Charles was home? It is the beginning of January and we have two more full months of cold and dark. I scurry throughout the day to complete my chores during the hours of daylight. It is dark by late afternoon and candles must be conserved.

January 5, 1777: For so long the days, no touch of affection, no touch of warmth and love. No one tells me that I am fair. No one tells me all the things that a woman should be told.

January 9, 1777: This morning as most mornings. Before Sarah and Baby Charles up, three half logs into the firebox of the stove. I left the firebox door open to allow the heat to spill through our room. Later, while I busied myself brushing Sarah's hair, little Charles toddled on a morning stroll. To the stove he went and grabbed the iron door to stop his walk. A shriek of pain, then great sobs. I rubbed butter on his fingers and then wrapped them in two portions of clean cloth. Blisters will surely rise, then some days of pain.

January 11, 1777: A pounding on the door this morning. Mr. Dear with not bad news. After months of only defeats, the Patriots stole a victory in Jersey. Much excited, Mr. Dear told me to read the article in the *Boston Paper* in Cranson's shop.

With Sarah wondering why, off I betook my family. At the shop a circle of people gathered around the wall, as if the torn and tacked articles would speak. Finally Mr. Cranson read slowly. Read words so long waited for. On the night of December 25th General Washington led troops across the Delaware River. Across the river, Trenton was attacked and this battle won. Then days later to Princeton, another victory.

Three times Mr. Cranson read the words; read slowly, read clearly, read for all. Each word a kernel of hope; taken together, the kernels gained the weight of confidence for me that the certitude of British victory is not a certitude.

January 22, 1777: At last a letter from Charles—but a letter better lost. The warm glow of December's victories are grown cold to the touch. Problems and hardships plague their winter camp of Morristown. Many soldiers without shoes or boots in the harshness of winter. Few occupy cabins built with their own hard labors; most housed in tents. Each day spent searching for provisions and firewood. Only things plentiful served by the devil: smallpox, dysentery, jaundice, diarrhea, scurvy, piles, and putrid fever. More men have died from disease than battle.

"If you have tears, prepare to shed them now."

How can we fail to provision our soldiers fighting in their lands for no pay while the king provides all for his soldiers a wide ocean away? This cannot be right.

January 23, 1777: Today I read my journal. If I could, I would strike some passages. Anger toward Charles are some of the words written. This should not be. If I cannot write the good of my dear Charles, I should not write.

"Sweet, above thought I love thee."

January 24, 1777: The blue dress that I was guarding for Charles's return is no longer worthy of guarding. This morning it was worn while its sister black dress washed and hung to dry. An ember from the hearth, not seen 'til it smoldered, popped into the folds of the prized dress while I nursed Baby Charles. I should be grateful that the flames were doused without harm to me or my sweet Charles. Nothing is fair. All my efforts to protect are for naught.

January 26, 1777: Young and old are sick with the fever; many funerals. Because so many, and because of the cold, often there is no visitation of the body. Family carry the casket to the church. Reverend Tripwell reads from the liturgy and then speaks words of no significance to the bereaved. Then the procession to the burial ground, where the casket is lowered. Last week two died, one from my Wednesday church group, Mrs. Taft, a widow with no family. I placed her in my nightly prayers.

January 28, 1777: Mr. Dear again so kind. He brought me a dress that once had been his wife's. Did this unasked after I told him of the death of my blue dress. Mrs. Dear was not a tall lady. But I think I can make this dress fine with ruffles to add in length. Perhaps I was wrong; Mr. Dear was clearly a man of kindness all his life. Indeed, he has the habit of kindness.

February 2, 1777: A short letter, stained with mud, from Charles. It is a dying time in the camp, he writes, with the soldiers sick with the fever and the flux. He says the only thing he fears is smallpox. I want to write him that I fear only starving and freezing. I will not.

I see the price we pay; I know not what we receive for our consideration.

February 4, 1777: Baby Charles's first words will not include *Father*. He speaks a small basket of words. *Momma* for me. *Hara*, his try at Sarah, and *bow* for our departed cow. But my wish that he greet Charles with *Father* will not be. A baby's words are only those of things seen.

February 5, 1777: Many afternoons spent spinning wool into yarn. Today I began the knittings. For Charles, gloves, three pair of stockings, and a scarf. The gloves first, for they are the most difficult, with many needles for the fingers and thumb. Though tempted to start knitting the simplest item, the scarf, I feared by the time I finished I would be loath of the difficult work.

As I knitted this winter day, helped Sarah with her lessons and nursed Baby Charles. The click-click of the needles and squeak of the chalk on Sarah's slate lulled me. Did I do this same thing yesterday? Am I living the moment again?

February 7, 1777: Sarah has a fine new blue dress. This I made from my dress of the Great Fire, enough unburned to form a full skirt and blouse. Fitted large to her body, sweet Sarah will quickly fill today's folds.

February 8, 1777: Tonight I will snuff out the candle as always. But a difference wells in the darkness that surrounds me once again—the difference being a peace within. Charles's choice made so many months ago I now understand, all owed to Shakespeare's words so many years ago written.

Yesterday as the sun at its highest point, Mr. Green came to my door. A letter from Charles traded for a cup of cider and a thank-you. This time a trade well made. Charles wrote as always of his struggles and fears. But then he spoke of an essay just written by Mr. Thomas Paine in the cold of a Patriot camp. Words of the essay Charles copied for me: "These are the times that try men's souls. The summer soldier and sunshine Patriot will, in this crisis, shrink from the service of his country; but he that stands it now, deserves the love and thanks of man and woman. Tyranny, like hell, is not easily conquered." Charles wrote that for him, the proof of their struggle was the hardship of the struggle. No man would endure the hardships of this winter, he says, if the rightness of their course was not of the greatest import.

From Mr. Shakespeare's *Julius Caesar* I copied these words: "There is a tide in the affairs of men, which taken at the flood, leads to our fortune. Omitted, all the voyage of their life is bound in shallows and in miseries. On such a full sea are we now afloat. And we must take the current when it serves, or lose our ventures." Only these words, and words of my new understanding of our cause and my eternal love, did I write to my darling Charles, my brave Charles.

February 9, 1777: Again after church Mr. Crabtree with his sermon of what fools we Patriots be. Spoke of the Virginians who caused this war that we suffer. I should not have, but I did. I spoke to him in a loud voice that all could hear. I asked him if it was Virginians who dressed as Indians and threw the king's tea into Boston Harbor. I asked why would a just tax paid sail far from us to another land, is this a tax for services or a tribute to a master? Crabtree was silent, looked at me with surprise. Looked at me as if I were an oak tree that had somehow learned to speak. Then as if nothing had been asked, his song of complaints began again. I turned and with Sarah behind and Baby Charles asleep in the sling, toward our farm we walked. A quick glance back told me I was not alone in my walk. I write this in the dim light of a candle, my smile not easily seen, but it is there.

February 12, 1777: Yesterday I baked bread. I wish it could find its way to Charles, but he is so far away. No matter; I placed a slice on his plate, which I always set at the table for him, imagining that he will be home for dinner. On the bread I spread the fine butter churned with Sarah months ago. With the butter, strawberry preserves prepared last summer. Warm bread to my lips, I imagined that it were Charles I kissed. When he returns home he shall have all the soft warm bread he might want.

February 15, 1777: This winter a colder bite than others. Even our bones are cold. Try as I might, even when the fire blazes at its warmest the house is never warm.

February 19, 1777: We spend much time around the hearth, which I worry over and tend lest the fire go out. The children are bundled up with layers, still Sarah complains of the cold. Baby Charles held much throughout the day to keep him warm. He has no words to complain. I am afraid the children will catch a chill.

February 20, 1777: Shakespeare, dear friend, I beg your forgiveness. Always there for me. Always generous with your players' words. Always enlivening with wit and insight. I rue that I have abandoned you, but I am weary, weary of life. No, that is not right. I am not weary of life; but there is no hope in my life. When hope returns I will return to you. Until then I ask your kind patience, dear friend and teacher.

February 22, 1777: I sleep in my clothes for warmth at night, and I still shiver, even though piled with blankets and rugs and a child on each flank. Before bed I hang little Charles's washed napkins near the hearth to dry while we sleep. With the first light of the new day I stoke the fire with fresh logs. I take a few moments of cold solitude, watching the cloud of my breath before the flames, and children awake and my day's tasks begin. In these few precious moments of quiet, my thoughts of Charles, camped in a frozen field. With shelter and warm clothing I suffer the cold. He, with a tent for shelter and meager clothing—can he endure?

Charles, I am so sorry.

February 23, 1777: Each week men return to their homes. They have had enough of it. They come home to tend their land and be as a family. But what of poor Charles? Can he not leave this war to other men?

February 24, 1777: This war is being waged not by our soldiers alone, but by them and their families. When Charles walked over the low rise last April I thought only he was in harm's way. Harm's way now lodges comfortably in my house.

February 26, 1777: If not for the children I would not have moved from my bed, despair as a black blanket of iron. Fingers too stiff to write.

February 27, 1777: It is not the physical labor that taxes me the hardest, but the mental uncertainties and injustices that give me the most discontent. I am filled with anger. Tonight I am not at peace with God or my station.

"Alas, I am woman friendless, hopeless!"

February 28, 1777: Today with a darning needle I pushed yarn into the cracks between our four window frames and the walls of our house. With a blanket and nails covered the door. Anything to hold back the cold pushed through by the always winds.

March 1, 1777: Ann Boleyn imprisoned in the Tower of London, her needs were served to her. She did not cook nor wash for others. No cries of babies, no interrogation by a young girl inquisitor. No snow blown across her bed by winter's cruel wind.

Today happy I would be as the imprisoned wife of Henry VIII waiting in warmth for a quick, painless death.

March 3, 1777: Firewood, once so ample, now not enough. Each day from Mrs. Brown's pasture I drag into our house two rails from the split rail fence that framed her world. With Charles's saw I render them bite-size to feed to our stove.

When Charles returns there will be no animals, no farm, no stores—only his family in rags.

March 6, 1777: For two days I was nigh consumed by the fever and chills. I longed to lay abed and think of pleasant times past, waiting for the sickness to leave. I did not; hearth tended, food cooked, napkins washed, Sarah answered.

March 8, 1777: Baby Charles is not well. He coughs until I feel my heart will burst from sorrow, wanting to take all of his sickness to myself. My answers to Sarah not kind.

March 10, 1777: Our house is so cold, so dark, so without hope or joy. My life has no punctuation.

March 25, 1777: For two weeks no journal recorded. Grief too great. A deep snow the day Baby Charles died, I could not walk the distance to Mr. Dear's farm, nor did anyone pass our home. I wrapped the tiny perfect body of my baby of innocence in a blue blanket given on our wedding day. A tub of metal filled with hard-packed snow. Then placed the blanket holding my loved in a drawer from my oak chest. This drawer placed over the tub, the tub of packed snow. Baby Charles's body kept cold. No corruption. In time water poured from the tub, new snow added. This I did for a day and night. No more cruel task ever done by a mother. Mr. Dear to our house. He saw the pail on the door. Told him of my sorrow, he gone and later back with a horse and cart. Sarah and I rode with no words spoken, rode with our Baby Charles to the church. Two men had dug my sweet baby's grave in the cold ground. By the hard turned earth we stood. Prayers by Reverend Tripwell. A cutting wind, dark thick clouds, no shadows, only a gray gloom. I looked away, but the sound of frozen soil against shovels and that wooden box told the truth. Sarah to the warmth of the church. I on the ground next to the new mound of earth. Day traded places with night, but I stayed. How can I tell Charles? But his grief could be no greater. A lamplight up the path, Mr. Dear led me to the church. Sarah slept on a pew, next to her I sat. A crushing hurt, a hurt that could not be true, God would not allow this hurt. When the sun rose I back to the path and to my Baby Charles. I knelt, spoke to him softly, spoke words of a mother's love.

"Death lies like an untimely frost upon the sweetest flower of all the field."

March 31, 1777: Today Mr. Green took my letter written to Charles, written many days ago, but I could not bring myself to tender it. The letter as a dagger in Charles. I told of Baby Charles's death. But not to tell Charles was also not right. Wrote also how robust Sarah had become as she grew, but the death of his son will be the only words read. What will he think of me? What did I not do to keep his son from harm?

April 24, 1777: It has been a month since I sent Charles the word of the death of our baby. No letter back. Has my message of miseries reached him? Is Charles alive to read my letter? If no letter from Charles arrives within another week, another letter of grief I will send.

April 27, 1777: Today a letter from Charles. Told me of promises made to the soldiers that monies would be paid and furloughs would be granted. Spoke as always of hardships. No words of Baby Charles. He has not received my letter. My cruel letter to him has taken a journey of no destination. Another letter I will write him. No mother should have to tell the story of her baby's death twice.

May 14, 1777: Today a letter from Charles. His words of no comfort to me; Baby Charles's passing was God's will and he is in a better place. Does Charles think there be a better place than asleep against my warm breast? Told me I was fortunate, surrounded by friends, he has no one to comfort him. Does Charles think that anyone except he can offer me comfort? Charles has his cause and his compatriots; I have an empty house and Sarah crying. He has men to speak; I have Sarah to answer. Could I embark on a long march away from this heartache and take up a musket and aim it at the heart of a Redcoat. Could I do something other than sit here alone strangling in my grief. Perhaps strangling in my guilt.

"The private wound is deepest."

May 25, 1777: Charles will be home soon. The Branson boy returned from the fighting last week. He had only left his father's farm last month, departed with a boastful pride as to how he would slay the Redcoats. One starving month, and the king has become the yeast for his bread. Only when I saw him in church, after he had been home almost a week, did he give me a message from Charles.

After Reverend Tripwell's sermon I had just started up the path with Sarah to visit Baby Charles. The Branson son called my name, so I turned and paused. Up to me he strolled; then, as if merely wishing me a good day, he spoke words that made me faint of heart: Charles had asked him to relay to me that he would be home the week before my birthday.

At first I found his message unclear. Was this a boy's lark? But the message spoke of my birthday, a date not known by this boy. Then happiness squeezed me. This was the message for which I had hoped and prayed for a year! I took his hand and thanked him for such wonderful tidings. Then guilt; turned up the path with Sarah to the grave, the resting place of Baby Charles. Sarah and I knelt and prayed. But my thoughts were not of my baby lost, they were of my husband returning.

May 26, 1777: Last night my head swarmed with thoughts of Charles. I want to make the house a welcome home for my dearest husband. I lay upon my bed and filled a large basket with tasks, tasks to make the house as it was when Charles waved his good-bye last May. Then I thought of the Branson boy. For months I had waited for the message most sought, the message of Charles's return. But the Branson son returned home making no effort to speak with me. Had I not gone to church, I would not know Charles's message. But Branson is a boy with no wife, no family. He does not know the import of Charles's words.

With the greeting of the sun Sarah and I were gladly to our chores.

June 2, 1777: Mr. Dear to our house today, bearing two eggs as a gift. But this was not the gift I received most gladly. He told me that William Winters and John Dotson would soon return from their service—Mr. Winters sick with unknown ills and Mr. Dotson on furlough. John Dotson enlisted with Charles so long ago. His homecoming reassures me of the truth of young Branson's message and my hope that Charles too will soon be with me. After Mr. Dear took his leave, my happiness slowly built to a rush to ready the house for Charles. So many things still to do.

June 4, 1777: Today at our Wednesday meeting Mary Dotson did not join us. The most wonderful news I was told. Her husband arrived on furlough last night from the armies. So Charles too will surely be with us soon. With this news I considered quickly returning to our house. I must be there when he returns.

When home again this afternoon quickly I made everything right. Sarah practiced her curtsy for me. King George would find no curtsy finer. When preparing our dinner meal I made the portions large, hoping perhaps that tonight Charles would be home. After Sarah lay abed I rubbed sweet oils on my hands while thinking of Charles. The most beautiful quilt gifted by Charles's mother I placed on our bed, and the fine dress with the ruffles offered by Mr. Dear carefully folded on our dresser. Tomorrow I will wear it and do nothing that could harm the fine material. For dear Charles I will look as I trust his memory has painted me. This journal kept only for my thoughts while Charles gone. I write this entry praying it will be my last for many, many days. Perhaps when Charles returns to me it will not be for days, but for a lifetime.

The above was the last entry in my nightly journal. The morning after there was a knock at my door. When opened, John Dotson was there. For the briefest moment I did not know who he was, even though many evenings he shared a meal with Charles and me. His skin dark as an Indian. His moon face was no longer round; it was as carved from bone. I smiled. He smiled a faint smile back. Into our house I welcomed him and at our table he sat while I poured a cup of cider. Sarah curtsied and wished him well. Gently and slowly he took her hand, kneeled, told her how fair she is, and how proud her father would be. Then he turned to me. Softly, as a whisper, he told me how sorry he was for me. I told him how my heart hurt for Baby Charles. Then a look of pain on Dotson's face. A heavy quiet, he did not speak, he sat so still. Again I spoke of Baby Charles. Then his face showed pain and confusion together. I thought his words of condolence were for Baby Charles. They were not. They were for Charles. He thought I knew. I did not. Charles was dead. Dead from a skirmish a week before. To the floor I fell. Sarah to my side. She cried, I sobbed.

In time our farm was sold. The farm that Charles and I struggled to make a home. Mr. Dear bought it because of his kindness. Only the smallest sum he paid, but more than offered by any other. Sarah and I moved to my sister's house. I never took another husband. With the war there were many widows. Many sorrowful widows. I lived my life with my sister and her family. I earned my way and Sarah's way by daily domestics done well. For many families I washed and cleaned. The war was long, ending with British surrender years after Charles's death. His grave I never saw; I was told he lay together with many others. After the war the Loyalists quickly became Patriots. In time those loyal to the king while Charles fought spoke of their glorious victory over the unjust monarchy.

I lived to see a new holiday born, Independence Day. I also lived to see a new Charles be born. Sarah married. She wed a man who was as Charles, strong of back and strong of character. To the west and back he went in the great journey directed by President Jefferson. With Sarah, three sons they had. The first of these given the name of Charles. Baby Charles, to me.

In time I frail. My days' tasks were only to rock and think upon the past. This I did. Thought much of the war. For me it was a harsh war. Only grief. Nothing good. How it be for you?

Abigail

Warren

On January 1, 1863, President Abraham Lincoln signed the Emancipation Proclamation. This document proclaimed the freedom of all slaves in the states that were in rebellion . . . the Confederacy. Even though slavery had been abolished by proclamation, the exploitation of blacks, and the stifling of their opportunities to succeed were still an accepted part of the culture of much of America as World War II approached.

While race prejudice was seen in all of the forty-eight states, it was most acute, most harsh and most unforgiving in the Southern states . . . those states that were the subject of the Emancipation Proclama-

tion. And racial prejudice existed in the institutions that were part of the very same federal government that seventy-five years before had declared slavery abolished . . . the army and navy.

MY APOLOGIES. THIS LETTER SUFFERS FROM FLAT EMOTIONS. Mother claimed that in the arts there exists nothing worse than a writer of no artistic flair. Her writings were always resplendent with aesthetically apt adjectives and amplifying adverbs; prose mingling with poetry, artfully composed with a liberal application of Webster's finest atypicals. I was as my father, all prose, no poetry; anemic verbs and diminutive subjects on a bleak white paper stage of drab costumes and stark sets.

My name is Warren, the sole child of Katherine and Benjamin. Another son died when Mother was in the family way with me. A photograph of Woodrow in an oval silver frame, attesting to his residence in heaven, rested during the day on the mahogany table in the parlor. At night Woodrow's sepia likeness carried with care to the nightstand in Mother's bedroom. I was never told the date of his birth or death; to have asked would have been cruelly inappropriate—like the opening of another's diary to entries of the most personal. But the months I knew: Mother's verve took its leave in the first portion of April and the week following Independence Day.

Oakland, California, was my childhood home. More tellingly, I was raised in cloistered academia. Mother was a professor of literature and Father a research microbiologist. Both PhDs, and in time both heads of their department. Mother retired as Assistant Dean of Academic Affairs.

Dinner conversation, try as I might, did not visit long on the exploits of Amelia Earhart, Babe Ruth, or Errol Flynn. During my younger years family meals were not unlike lecture classes, the partaking of sustenance a casual secondary purpose. Once in high school, dinners became much like PhD candidate orals. Ask me about Koch's postulates, endosymbiosis, White's *Sketch of the Phi-*

losophy of American Literature, or Emerson as a Transcendentalist. Sunday dinners a respite from academics, rather discussions of the Bible and dissecting of passages; passages that as a teenager I would rearrange for my amusement during late night Mass:

> As if walking through the Valley of the Shadow of Death I take you for my lawfully wedded wife from this day forward, or until as a rich man driving a Packard I pass through the eye of a needle to Knob Hill, where I will sit on the right-hand side of the mayor of San Francisco.

It was a pleasure when a professor or graduate student joined my parents as a dinner guest—I now relegated to the sidelines, subject to no exams. Nor, as a mere spectator to the intellectual handball played on our inlaid dining room table, was I required to return a hard-hit backhand of opinion.

Our china was calibrated to the academic standing of the dinner guest. Graduate students and unpublished professors were served with plates and silverware of every day. For guests possessing a bubbling intellect evidenced by their status as well-studied authors, Mother reverently set the table with her grandmother's Doulton.

At times a guest challenged my parents' ability to remain tranquil while literature and science scraped against their high-gloss religious beliefs. One such event was the visit by the author Zora Hurston, whose works formed a cornerstone to several of Mother's lectures. After prerequisite cordials we were seated for dinner. As always Father led us with a grace, thus triggering Miss Hurston's passionate discourse as to why she was an avid pagan. Dinner conversation was not as Mother hoped.

One of Father's learned guests, Dr. Ruth Moore, brought forth a not dissimilar twisting of the bowels as had Mother's novelist heroine. As Father carved a leg of lamb Dr. Moore spoke authoritatively as to how Darwin had proven that Genesis 1:27 had no more claim on reality than did the Easter Bunny. Another dinner of unexpected modulations.

My family's dining habits are not the essence of my letter to you. Rather, these small anecdotes provide an insight into the home environment where I nested. Knowledge was both foundation and mortar to my family structure. As the firstborn son of a king will be himself a king, Father and Mother spoke as if my destiny was likewise set: I would become a learned professor in an institution of significance. Alternatively, I would somehow utilize a superb education to wedge myself into an even more notable layer of professional achievement. A prediction that found no resolution.

Something else I should tell you. I was blacker than black on a moonless night. The first several paragraphs of this letter led you down one path—many will have assumed I was a well-educated Caucasian—and then I sucker punched you for dramatic effect.

To my parents, being black was a transient state. Not transient for us as individuals, but for our race. Mother and Father promoted a theory that drew from their academic groundings. Evolution, not revolution, was the process that Father believed would bring the blacks to equal status with whites. He argued that any black slave who had told his master that he wished to become a doctor, lawyer, or professor, or even wanted to own a small parcel of land, would have been ridiculed . . . at best. But a slave who learned to read and write, by whatever means, might be, with the right circumstances, given the opportunity to use these skills. "You, boy, I didn't know you could write. Get yourself some paper and go 'round to the barns and total up how many bushels we got. You'll be a big help each harvest."

Father told of the frog in boiling water. Drop a live frog in boiling hot water and it will react instantly, jumping clear of harm. Put a frog in a pot of lukewarm water and then place the pot on the burner, the frog will remain tranquil, not reacting to the gradual, steady increase in water temperature. As the water reaches a boil the frog will remain calm until its demise. Father said that blacks needed to bring the white race to a slow boil. By possessing the right education and skills, each generation of blacks will be offered—versus attempting to take—more mantles of responsibility. My parents believed that in time a black could be a romantic actor, a big league baseball player and—I'm not sure I believed this—even a Cabinet member. Father said that if each generation of blacks worries about being better than the last, rather than worrying about why they are not at the top, some future generation will be at the top.

While Father leaned on his biology teachings to explain life's events, Mother built her arguments on the need to educate. For her, Father's theory of evolution was contingent upon blacks possessing the requisite skills for their upward spiral. Books, in her view, were the matches and knowledge was the fire to bring the white man's prejudices to that slow boil.

During my life, as I now lay it before you, I was a pilot: first for pleasure, then for survival. The imagined glamour of it caught my eye as a youngster. In the newspaper photos and newsreels airplane pilots looked different, a good different. Having just landed from some great adventure, they posed next to their fabric and aluminum beast. Confidently they stood, clad in leather like knight's armor with goggles hanging loose around their necks, poised for the next aerial struggle.

On my seventeenth birthday flying became real, not imagined. From the slow accumulation of three months of fifteen cents a day for delivering the *Oakland Tribune* I paid for an hour of flight in a buttercup yellow Piper Cub. The instructor pilot smiled. Told me to relax. I sat behind him. Over his shoulders I could barely see dials with numbers measuring things of no meaning. My feet forward, straddling his seat, resting on bars that moved. Between my legs a stick growing from the floor. It moved in all directions. To my left a lever topped with a red ball. To the right, no side, no door, open to the air. A large man moved to the front of the aircraft, and the seated pilot and he exchanged words not understood by me. Then the prop was grabbed by the burly man, he swung one leg for momentum, pulled the prop and the engine to life. Slowly rolling over the smell of just mowed grass, to the end of the field, pivoted to face the wind, the lever to my left moved forward by the pilot, the engine complained in a roar. To my right, to the side open, grass blades became not grass blades, but just green. Then, then for the first time, a time that would be repeated thousands of times, but a first time never again, I flew.

Lifted by a force of magic, we rose. Below, our shadow chasing us, its journey of hills, trees, rivers, all the dips and rises of the earth; our journey, smooth and perfect. Slowly higher. Below, fewer details, only broad brushes of the greens and browns. Before us clouds. Each a mountain of cotton balls, golden white, the tops washed by the sun's uninterrupted blast.

Then the pilot, the pilot who had not spoken since the engine spun to life, turned. Speaking at a yell to pierce the engine's growl and the wind's rush, the pilot told me to place my hand on the stick and follow his movements. This I did, holding the stick with one quavering hand. It moved forward, the nose of the plane tilted down. Then the stick came back, but back further than before, the nose moved up and higher we drifted. Level again, the stick to our right, and as directed the right wing bowed and slowly we turned toward the low wing. The stick reversed, our turn reversed. Then to the neutral and the plane level.

The pilot looked back, grinned his biggest. Turned forward and put his hands behind his head, weaving his fingers as if settling in for a rest. I was the pilot. I flew. Next to clouds. Around clouds. Touching clouds. No edges to my road. My road opened before me wherever my eyes gazed. Before, I had only seen "sensual" from afar; that day it embraced me, never to release.

Even though it was expected, it was a jolt when the news burst upon us that late Sunday morning: We were at war. The economic and political stress fissures that conspired to bring the world to battle had been the entrée of many dinner conversations. Father and I accepted that war was inevitable. Mother argued not. Her argument, unlike most of her positions in life, was not based on a cold analysis, but rather on emotional hope—a hope that I would not journey to harm's way.

Twice I had seen the USS *Wasp* in port, once the *Hornet*. Lashed to their flight decks Wildcat fighters and Devastator torpedo bombers. On the docks where these looming aircraft carriers were nestled, aviators—aviators being naval pilot officers—chatted, not condescendingly, but with a confident aloofness, with the crowds of civilian gawkers. Dressed in their "whites" with gold wings, no better looking uniforms ever draped a soldier or sailor. While I told my parents that I wanted to enlist to "see the world," I felt more than a subliminal urge to wear the uniform.

Six months after Pearl Harbor, and two days after my graduation as a liberal arts major, I finished breakfast with Father, read the morning newspaper, then rode the bus down Market Street, past the police station and firehouse, to the navy recruiting office. Upon returning home in time for dinner I informed Father that the Nobel Prize was mine for the asking. Between breakfast and dinner I had discovered the missing link, the link between *Homo heidelbergensis* and *Homo erectus,* the connector in the evolutionary chain between ape and modern man. A chief petty officer was this elusive link.

After filling out two forms of no intellectual challenge, my number was called and I entered a small office with a fortyish, plump petty officer with a Southern drawl and a complexion more like ground beef than skin; skin drawn over a low forehead and accented with a single eyebrow spanning both eyes. He looked at me as if I was a turtle with fur. When asked what good I might do the navy, I responded by saying that I was a pilot and wanted to train as a naval aviator. His expression changed to someone discovering a turtle with fur that could sing. With no hesitancy nor emotion he explained that I could be either a house slave or a field slave. As a house slave I would be trained as a steward and would clean and cook for naval officers; as a field slave I would load navy cargo ships. Before I could respond he volunteered that a house slave was probably better because I was so scrawny. In silence I pushed back my chair from his desk and departed.

While Mother ever-so-softly touched on the safety of a port assignment, it was not for me. Congress had coerced the US Army into operating an exploratory program for black pilots. I squeezed into the back end of the army's pilot training syllabus because I was a licensed civilian pilot. As if to make certain that there would be as many hurdles as possible, the training base for black cadets was in the heart of the South, Tuskegee, Alabama. In late '42 I burned four bland days on a train weaving from the West Coast to Montgomery. You might think that prejudice became more acute as I journeyed to the Southeast; it didn't, it just became less polite and more direct. In a restaurant in Chicago I was turned away because there were no tables available, even though I could see this was not the case. In the South restaurants merely placed a "No Coloreds" sign in the front window. Less time wasted.

My bunkmate at Tuskegee was a fellow from Lawrence, Kansas, Daryl Clark. We hit it off right away. Both of us felt the pressure; we had the opportunity to achieve something most blacks wouldn't believe possible, and something most whites knew was impossible. In a few months we could be officers in the United States Army, flying the most modern aircraft in the world. Like me, Daryl was a college graduate with parents who pushed and coached. Neither of us suffered fools, no doubt because we both believed that we were exceedingly smart. While we were not as smart as we thought, Daryl and I were smart enough to know our vulnerability. It was us. The ego that bestowed enough confidence to think we deserved to become Air Corps pilots was the same ego that could be sandpaper on the face of whites—especially those white officers at Tuskegee predisposed to see blacks wash out. A confident white man could wear his ego as a top hat, proudly displaying it for all to see. A black man needed to wear his as a pair of socks. Daryl and I chose socks.

I had an advantage over most of the cadets in my class at Tuskegee. I found the academics, while not casual, not daunting either. A lifetime of dinners with my parents had my synapses holding hands, efficiently transmitting neurons. Plus, the army was clever at conveying the technical to percolating sacks of testosterone:

True Course	True
+ or – Variation	Virgins
= Magnetic Course	Make
+ or – Deviation	Dull
= Compass Course	Companions

In addition to a head start on academics, two years of side-slipping a Piper Cub gave me a natural feel for flight. While the PT-19 trainer was heavier, the aircraft was not unlike the Cub. The big difference was aerobatics. I had never been upside-down in a plane before. After a couple of flights where I savored my lunch twice, the unnatural became natural. By the time I moved to the advanced trainer, a T-6 with 600 horsepower and retractable gear, I could consistently perform a crisp four-point roll more precisely than any instructor.

At Tuskegee the most daunting challenge was the environment: "Whites Only" and "Colored Only" marked most every facility. A few of my classmates fought the system. In their minds they were army officers, not black army officers. They conducted a few successful skirmishes, but no battles won. I submissively accepted the prejudiced cuts to my dignity as a toll on the road to excel. At times though, my ability to remain passive was tested. *How Green Was My Valley* challenged my resolve. Actually, not the movie, but the movie theater on the base.

As we had done many times, Daryl and I, along with other cadets, headed to the base theater after dinner mess. I was in a foul mood. A senior check pilot had given me a Fair on my instrument work, not the mark of Good or Exceptional that I knew I had earned; for over an hour I had held the assigned altitude within a hundred feet and the heading within three degrees. As in all theaters in the South, the base theater separated whites and blacks; the seats to the left for whites, the ones on the right for blacks. But this night there was another segment of society seated in the white section: two rows taken by German POWs who worked in the fields around Tuskegee during the day.

There they sat in their prisoner of war uniforms, German officers and enlisted men with sworn allegiance to Hitler. Men who a year earlier had been battling British troops, America's comrades in arms. A *Homo sapiens* masquerading as an officer in the US Army had decided that while it was inappropriate for whites to sit with blacks, white officers would enjoy sharing their popcorn with Nazis.

After stewing in our seats for twenty minutes we got up to leave. One of the white officers called out in the dark, asking if the blacks didn't like the movie. I halted, held my silence for several moments, then spoke to the darkness. I said it wasn't the movie, we just didn't think a US Army officer should be gawking at Maureen O'Hara's tits with Nazis who wanted to kill Americans. We stood across from the theater with our smokes. After a few minutes the white officers strolled from the theater, not glancing our way. The German POWs remained to enjoy American cleavage in solitude.

I prevailed. In March of '43 I earned my Air Corps pilot wings; I was a Tuskegee graduate. All newly minted Air Corps pilots received fifteen days' leave before reporting to advanced training. It took me three days and a half-dozen changes of trains to get to the West Coast. My buddy Daryl traveled as far as Kansas City with me. At one stop an elderly lady pushed a nickel into my hand and instructed me to carry her bag. I did, and I bought a soda with my

wages. A black in a uniform at a train station could only mean por-
ter to most. The navy whites would have looked better, but Mother
and Father made much of the lieutenant bars and pilot wings pinned
to khaki. We passed a pleasant enough visit, but I was anxious to
move on with training—well, move on with flying. Mother and
Father were just anxious. Anxious about my returning safely.

After ninety days of advanced training, those of us who had
avoided shooting down the target tug were off to combat, first to
Camp Shank and then to the transport ship, everyone hoping for
England. Ugly rumors that we would be sent to provide air cover
for the Panama Canal ricocheted through the base. Given the distance from the Axis Powers, Panama offered the same opportunity
to prove ourselves as defending the Grand Canyon.

The crossing was uneventful, uneventful being synonymous
with boring. Fifteen hundred men in a three-hundred-foot-long
gray rusting metal container trading under the euphemism of a
ship. Sleep, think, eat, read, eat, and back to sleep. Reread Stein-
beck's *Grapes of Wrath* and started Sandburg's *Abraham Lincoln*.
Played some poker; not so much for the enjoyment, rather as a
gesture of being one of the guys. Encountered a most thought-
provoking intersection of human experience during my cruise.

Crammed on the ship were elements of the 442nd, an infantry unit comprised of Japanese Americans. One of their second
lieutenants—Miyamoto, I remember his last name, it was the
same as one of Mother's Japanese author friends, Yuriko Miyamoto—saw me reading *Grapes of Wrath*. He asked if he could
borrow it when I was through. I told him for certain and that he
could keep the book. We had a brief shipboard friendship discuss-
ing novels and biographies of the day. Then Miyamoto took the
sting from my experience with the German POWs at the base
theater. He told me of his parents and two sisters, who were living
in a barbed-wire-enclosed compound in the California desert with
ten thousand other Japanese Americans. Living in drafty wooden
barracks with little dignity and no hope, their crime being Japa-

nese descent. Miyamoto asked why not German Americans? Why shouldn't they be in stockades as were Japanese Americans? I told him I could readily explain the differences between Japanese Americans and German Americans once he explained the difference between black Americans and white Americans.

After a couple of days at sea we knew we weren't heading for Panama; and after a week or so it was obvious our course was too southerly for England. In time compass and stars revealed our destiny, the Mediterranean, which could only mean Italy. In the third week we sailed into Taranto, a half-moon harbor dotted with islands, islands of rusting steel—capsized ships. In town, scenes from Miss Mitchell's Atlanta in *Gone with the Wind*. Rubble and more rubble. But it was the human rubble that was the worst, women with sunken eyes, clothed in rags, babies at their bosoms, pleading for garbage.

We had a few days to organize, then a convoy to Montecorvino, a twenty-hour endurance test in trucks with AWOL springs. Nothing as expected. No barracks, just tents in the dust. A sergeant told us to thank God for the dust; after the smallest shower, mud would suck at our boots like flypaper to a fly.

No P-51s either. Rumor had it we'd be equipped with sleek North American fighters, the best the Air Corps had to offer. We were given weary P-39s, hand-me-downs from white squadrons that had been equipped with newer aircraft. The same sergeant who told us to thank God for the dust told us we should thank God for the P-39s. Said the guys before us had been flying P-40s that were more scrap than aircraft. When I saw a couple of the retired P-40s I realized he could have left the "s" off the "scrap."

In the air the P-39 was neither nimble nor light on the controls. Its mid-mounted Allison engine struggled at altitude. Many times we were clawing for altitude, while a formation of Kraut JU-88s disappeared over the horizon. Other than the black squadrons, only the training squadrons and the Russians were given P-39s. America sent our allies what we didn't want.

Daryl and I bunked in a two-man tent, introducing famished Italian mosquitoes to American food. The first morning at our new base, after a hearty breakfast of lukewarm coffee and stale bread, the squadron was formed up to meet Lt. Colonel Davis. He was one of us; Davis had fought the Pentagon to keep black squadrons from being disbanded or deployed to areas of no consequence. Most important he had been in combat; he was a fighter pilot. The first thing he told us was that we weren't fighter pilots, we were merely pilots who flew fighters. Told us that our number one priority for the first two operational flights would be to not get shot down. After two flights our priority would be either to shoot something down or blow something up on the ground. Davis always kept things simple.

Most important, the colonel told us the only way not to be killed was to keep moving when in a combat area. Never fly straight and level for more than fifteen seconds. Never keep looking forward for more than ten seconds. He said that every fighter pilot of longevity had a stiff neck, and that if we didn't keep peering over our shoulders to see what Kraut was at our six o'clock, his adjutant would be drafting a letter of condolences to our parents.

I had imagined combat for months, mostly while lying in the darkness of the barracks. I wondered whether I would panic. Wondered whether the sound and the fury would spook me. After a year of pondering combat, it was about to bolt from the soft abstract to hard reality.

Reality made its appearance on my first operational flight. It was supposed to be just a milk run, a flight led by one of the seasoned squadron pilots, Roland—a fellow I would never forget. But not because of that day's flight. Roland explained that he would be leading a flight of five. He briefed us on frequencies and headings between waypoints. Told us our goal was to get a feel for the topography and landmarks that we could use when our planes were shot up and we only had our wits to get us home. It was the back leg of our tour when Roland called out, "Bogies at twelve o'clock high."

At first I thought he must be kidding. There couldn't really be German aircraft in the air. Krauts were nothing more than an evil force in an unfinished novel. I wasn't ready. I was physically ready, but my brain wasn't ready. I glanced upward, and there they were, six black dots, each with a single white thread trailing behind.

The radio crackled as Roland instructed us to keep our heading, but if they peeled down we should turn in to them. I figured there was no way they could see us. I could barely see them as black dots against a clear blue sky; they couldn't see the same dots against a background of grays and browns. At first I didn't think they peeled. But the black dots stopped moving; then they started to become larger; then they grew wings.

Roland called "Now!" and while I was wondering if I had heard him, his aircraft whipped upward in a tight turn. Onto full power and up with him. Stopping his turn when the Krauts were centered in our windscreens, straight we went. Then, on the front of the Kraut wings, flickers of light—but the lights didn't stay on their wings, they grew larger and flashed over our aircraft.

Roland's aircraft opened fire. Tracers in a line toward the Krauts. I pushed the firing button, nothing, hadn't released the safety. Quickly off, I pressed again. My P-39 shuddered; then in a blur the Krauts passed over. I banked to the right and looked back but couldn't catch a view. Scanned forward and Roland was gone. No one was around. Pulled up and over, rolled the wings level, pushed into a shallow dive, looking. Nothing.

Then to the right a P-39 with a Kraut Me-109 tight behind. With a jerk the P-39 banked and pulled; the Me-109 stayed glued. Another P-39 rose up from below with a deflection shot that was far wide, but the Kraut broke off. Then fear. I had been watching while straight and level. I made a quick bank to the left and a pull to the buffet, pushed down on my seat, and strained to twist my head back for a clear view. Nothing. Then a quick turn in the opposite direction and a scan below, only landscape, no friend or foe. A half hour later I was landing at our base. Straight and level, it would have been a fifteen-minute journey. Even when safely on the ground, taxiing to the ramp, I glanced back to make certain no harm was in my shadow.

As the engine coughed its last, a sergeant up on my wing reached across and threw the safety back on the guns. I was lucky I hadn't killed somebody while taxiing. I unstrapped and got my feet on the ground, looking as if I had gone for a swim. Next to me Daryl's plane was already parked. With a roar, three aircraft overhead peeling off to the downwind: Roland with two rookies in tow.

Excited ground crew called me to the tailplane of my P-39. I gaped at a burnt trough along the side of the vertical stabilizer; a Kraut cannon shell had creased me during the head-on attack. Three feet lower and it would have deceased me.

Once on the ground Roland herded his animated chicks into the operations tent for a debrief. Started off with the basics, said that if everybody gets back it's a good mission. Everybody got back. It was Roland who made the wide deflection shot that got the Me-109 off Daryl's backside. He chewed on Daryl for a while. Told him that he was in a turn, but not a tight turn. Told him that he'd had enough altitude that he should have pulled the nose down and run away from the Me-109 . . . that their ailerons get stiff at the higher speeds. He went through all the basics again: Never try to outclimb a Me-109, and don't try and out turn them at higher altitudes. Asked me why I was late in firing. Before I answered he speculated I hadn't moved the guns off of safety. Then he grinned and said we hadn't done that badly and we should think things through and figure out for ourselves what we did right and wrong.

I couldn't sleep. Felt good about most things. First combat after over a year of contemplation. Two things I checked off. I wasn't a coward. For the past year my mantra against fear had been a line of Stephen Crane's, "Death thrust between the shoulder blades more dreadful than death about to smite between the eyes." I never thought I'd break and run, but I'm not sure that anybody who breaks and runs thought they would. Of course, I had no choice; I was in a flight with others, I did what I was told. A true test of my resolve would be when I was alone in flight, with no one to see me retreat from a fight. The second thing: I pushed the button. I fired the four machine guns and cannon without the slightest hesitation. No consideration of killing a human.

The surprise was the time. Not so much the time, but the pace. One or two minutes at most from the Krauts peeling off to attack to losing sight of everyone. For over a year I had imagined aerial combat as a series of chess moves—a pull, a turn, a dive, a reversal. But there was no choreographed flight; rather, lighting jabs of shells with no finesse, only noise, vibration, and confusion. Reaction, not action, defined my first combat.

Two days later another sightseeing flight with Roland in the lead; this time no Germans joined our group. Then came real missions, missions to destroy inanimate and animate. These first sorties included some momentary skirmishes, but no real gladiator struggles-till-death in coliseums of clouds. Then on a bright spring afternoon my first brief-but-deadly dogfight.

We were escorting a squadron of B-24s that were after the railyards in Palo. On the way to the target we wove back and forth over the lumbering formation, otherwise our speed would have left them behind. Once near the target the fighters broke off and orbited south of Palo—no point in dancing with the Kraut flak. After their string of bombs were laid, the B-24s arced a painfully slow 180 degrees to retrace their path.

Just as we all rejoined came a flash of tracers, and three Kraut Me-109s swept through our flight. Two pulled up and one broke to the left, toward the back of the bomber formation. I yanked and pulled, turning my P-39 on its wing tip in a tightening curve, trying to claw behind the lone Me-109. As my target drew near the bomber formation, other Me-109s darted through the gaggle of B-24s, one of the bombers already trailing dark smoke while firing its .50-calibers at the streaking Krauts.

My prey was five hundred yards in front, his tight arcing turn too acute to lead him into a stream of my shells. As I drew closer he lessened his turn to line up on the trailing B-24. I relaxed my pull as the Me-109 drifted into my sight. Off with the safety and a push on the firing button; tracers showed the stream of shells toward the Kraut. My aim was wide, too wide, but close enough to let the Kraut know death was stalking him. A quick roll to the inverted, a pull, and the Me-109 was in a dive. I followed.

Down almost vertically, the airspeed quickly rose past 300, then toward 400. The flow of air not a rush, but a complaint. From 300 yards another stream of lead from my guns and cannon. A slight waggle of the Me-109's wings, but no fire, no smoke, no sign of damage.

Slowly the distance between pursuer and pursued became less as we hurtled down. At 200 yards I was again poised to fire, my eyes focused past the Me-109, Mother Earth closing at a rate never seen before. With all my might I pulled the stick back. Centrifugal force exercised its prerogative; my vision grayed as blood flowed from my head. Enough tunnel vision remained to show I was about to die.

Then, as first light on a newborn's eyes, the earth in front of my windscreen slowly lowered, replaced by bright sky, replaced by life. Once zooming upward I relaxed back pressure and stole a glance over my shoulder. In a barren field rose a cone of smoke from a circle of flame—a funeral celebration for the Me-109. I felt no sorrow; rather I cursed the bastard German. While my second burst didn't disable his aircraft, it must have killed the Kraut. I'd been so determined to shoot the Me-109 out of the air that I succumbed to target fixation, and this Kraut pilot almost killed me after I had killed him.

Daryl, more by chance than by merit, was my wingman. It would have been no less fair if I had been his. As wingman Daryl's job was simple, but exceedingly difficult. While I twisted in high-g maneuvers to latch on to the tail of an Me-109 or FW-190, Daryl flew behind me and to my side. His role, with two consequences if not done properly—either I would be dead or we would both be dead—was to protect my tail. With my eyes fixed on a Kraut, a Kraut pulling and twisting to save his life, I would not have an instant to check my six o'clock to see what black-crossed agent of death might be twisting behind to rip me with streams of lead. Daryl's job was to keep a watch behind. If a Kraut fighter closed in, Daryl would call break, and both of us would yank and bank, saving ourselves but forcing me to abandon pursuit. Thus Daryl had to watch behind us while simultaneously following my twists, which retraced the most violent maneuvers of my prey.

More than one wingman had chewed off his lead's tail with his ten-foot prop; with the tail gone, a short journey to death. But just as a miscue by Daryl could extinguish my life, I had the same power over him. If he called break but I continued to pursue and not break, Daryl was the first in line for the pursuing Kraut's killing fire.

On average the temperature in the cockpit of the P-39 was a pleasant 70 degrees—problem being that that was the average of 120 and 20 degrees. For each 1,000 feet of altitude, the temperature dropped three degrees. If we took off in comfortable 60 degrees, by the time we reached combat altitude, 20,000 feet, it was frigid—ice crystals clogging the oxygen mask, fingers stiff with pain. Much like Arctic explorers, we dressed in fur-lined leathers with heavy boots and double-thick gloves. Wearing this garb we were shoehorned into the cockpits of our sunbaked P-39s, hothouses once the canopies closed. By liftoff the clothes closest to us were soaked with perspiration—sweat that became stiff and brittle as we climbed to freezing altitudes.

Some days we strafed. Shot up anything that moved, a train, a truck, a car—if nothing better, a tired horse and cart. Flying low on these missions gave every Kraut with a rifle the chance to bring us down. Other days we bombed—rolled over from 10,000 feet in a 60- to 75-degree dive, released our bombs and pulled up while

Krauts perfected skeet shooting with antiaircraft guns. Some days, but not often, we intercepted German bombers, mostly JU-88s. Coming in from behind, I tried mightily to kill the rear gunner before he could put a shell through my windscreen.

Often we flew escort missions, weaving over boxes of B-17s or B-24s. Four hours at 25,000 feet in mind-numbing cold, coaxing the mixture back and the RPMs down to conserve fuel, lest a high-energy dogfight suck down the fuel necessary for a safe return. But always we faced the prospect, the potential, for air-to-air combat, the birthright of every fighter pilot. One man against another, both astride aluminum chariots bolted to a throbbing engine with the power of 1,000 horses to carry the machine guns and cannon for the kill.

If the weather was shit Daryl and I would get a reprieve, no flying. Whatever it took, we would beg or steal a ride to Salerno. While four or five from my squadron might bunk in a single room, a hotel room with a bath was coveted, no matter how many of us shared. As the number of rings of the giant redwoods standing north of Oakland confirmed their great age, so the rings in the tub confirmed how many weary pilots soaked off the grime of Montecorvino. Trying to refresh at base was futile. Every couple of days I would sponge myself down with cold water and a gray soap that smelled like spoiled meat.

Sleeping in our base tents was no better. I'd lie in my cot under the weight of hot, stagnant air churned only by winged entomology surveying me for mineral rights. But the noise, always the noise. Even if they didn't stand a chance in hell of scoring, most nights Krauts would send over a JU-88 to drop a string of bombs. Then came our *ack-ack* shooting into the darkness, threatening no German, but making certain no one slept. Our gunners couldn't have cared less. They rested peacefully during the day as we sweated out yet another mission.

After fifty combat missions pilots were rotated home, perhaps to a training squadron, perhaps to a non-flying post. Most knew precisely their count. Knew how many more times they would be thrust into harm's way. Most never made it to half the count. I tried not to count, but it was involuntary; the brain clicked each mission and totaled.

For whatever reason, mere chance, fate, or perhaps something self-imposed, it was the first and last few missions of the fifty that courted the Grim Reaper. Many fresh-faced pilots never made it past the first half-dozen missions; raw, tender meat obligingly served warm to the Krauts. If a pilot got through the first sorties, he had proved his piloting and survival skills. But then as the last missions were counted down, the missions that were the ticket home, a foreboding arose; a self-fulfilling prophecy permeated the pilot's being. Perhaps it was just the odds; perhaps some sort of survivor's guilt, that it would not be right to return when so many had not. No one knows why. But for whatever reason, the last of the mission count took the highest toll. So it was with Roland.

After a morning sweep over Ravenna, my flight had just shut down on the ramp. No guns fired, no bombs dropped. Nothing to report. Then I saw people walking from the administrative huts to the edge of the operational runway. Roland was circling with two greens; there should have been one more, confirming all three landing gear were down and locked.

Twice Roland flew by on a slow pass. All seemed okay to those on the ground. He could have retracted his landing gear and settled on the runway. No real chance of danger, only a pranged aircraft. But not today; he wasn't going to dent a P-39 on his last sortie, he was going to land with the gear down; likely nothing more than a burnt-out bulb.

As Roland curved from base to final, most of the curious started back to their duties, the landing heralded no drama. Gently Roland's P-39 touched earth on the main gear, and just as the nose rotated down, the right wing dropped to the hard-packed runway as its main gear folded. In an instant the dragging wing arched

Roland's aircraft off the runway. Still no drama—except this day crews were working to add a second taxiway.

A bulldozer and a grader, there they sat. Roland's plane swung to the bulldozer, as if drawn by some great magnet. Then came a noise like thunder, a cloud of dust, a cloud quickly vanished, chased by the rising flames. A dozen or more of us sprinted across the runway.

At twenty yards the air was a furnace. Rippling in the heat, the view of the P-39's nose crumpled against the steel dinosaur earth mover. The Allison engine, the 2,000-pound steel mass behind the cockpit, torn from its mounts and into the cockpit. Our fire truck, merely a jeep with extinguishers, roared past me. Two firemen drew near the blaze, then within a half minute raced back, their clothes smoking, one with molten aluminum burning through his shoes while he rolled in agony.

Then the scream. A scream as never heard before. A scream over the crack of explosions and the pops of ammunition cooking off. In the inferno an arm waving from the cockpit. There we stood, as the flames shot to the sky and the smoke burnt our eyes; there we stood as helpless as if the burning scene were a movie that we wished to have a different plot.

In time the fuel was burned; all that could burn was burned. Only the steel skeleton of the P-39 remained, the engine, a drive shaft, the landing struts. But there was more: a stench of burnt rubber and flesh. I drew closer as the heat retreated. I strained to see Roland, to morbidly confirm that he was there, not sitting in the mess tent laughing at us. Metal parachute buckles marked the mass—a mass of black, a black shell cracked by intestines, and organs boiling and exploding through the charred shell.

I collapsed on my knees and heaved violently.

Roland's death occasioned no pause. Weeks more of flight ops followed. But there was a toll; a toll paid most every day. The empty bed—a bed where another of my squadron mates had slept the night before.

It wasn't the death of a human that took its toll, it was the death of a person, a young man who had laughed with me at dinner messes, who spoke of his mother, his sister, his dreams. Each of these deaths chipped away part of my hope, my humanity, and worst, my sanity.

Not so much from a sharp turn taken following thought, but more as a steady drift away, Daryl and I distanced ourselves from our fellow pilots—easily done because of the relentless attrition. By not making friends with replacement pilots, soon there were few in the squadron we considered comrades. We knew their names, and in time we knew how well they could fly and perform their missions, but we took care not to learn their favorite drink, nor their skills at singing a ditty or dancing a jig. We kept them wrapped in the opaque skin of a human, not permitting the personality of someone intriguingly unique to shine through.

But it was not only the death of others that warped my emotions, it was the prospect of my death, a prospect shackled to my psyche that in time I came to know was a prophecy. After a three-hour sweep north of Milan and back I was on a wide circuit to land, two others from the flight were down, I on an extended downwind with Daryl in trail. My P-39 shook as never before, an explosion and jolt as if rammed by an anvil, the engine spun its last. Smoke and heat in the cockpit, but enough vision to see my prop stop, no longer pulling, but dragging in the airstream. Quickly pushed the nose down to keep up speed. Too low to parachute, too low to glide to an open field, only an expanse of trees in front of me. Tightened my shoulder harness and dropped my external tank. No more than a few brief seconds before I mushed into treetops. But the reciprocal of my bad luck engine played its hand. Trees were not stately hardwoods, rather thin brittle pines that folded compliantly as my wing exchanged air for vegetation to offset gravity. Only in the final instant did the prop plow into hard earth, rotating my aircraft into a somersault. Hanging upside-down from my shoulder harness the sudden silence was only of brief import, the rising flames from the engine behind the cockpit with fifty gallons of avgas in the fuselage tank better marked the moment. Straps released, I fell to the cockpit roof, kicked out a side window, and after a quick sprint slumped under a pine to witness the cremation. Exploding unspent ammunition hastened my scramble to a more distant venue.

Before Italy my mental health was rock solid: traditional passions and flawless logic. But with the grating of battle—the swings between that of pursuer and pursued, the transient and fractured fellowship with squadron mates—my feelings became conflicted. At one apex of my emotional pendulum I wanted to punch anyone who uttered a word of perceived criticism; at the opposite apex I couldn't speak for the fear of sobbing for a reason unknown. Twice I lashed out at Daryl for an imagined slight.

A few days after my second eruption, in the calm of our tent as dusk beckoned night, Daryl broke the virginity of his prized bottle of Barolo Fratelli Minuto. He then offended the pedigreed grape by forcing its intimacy with our army-issued metal cups. After a few words of commentary on the complexity and balance of the sloshing liquid, Daryl told me I wasn't myself. He thought that perhaps I had stolen a concussion when I flipped the P-39 in the woods, told me I needed to see the Doc.

Looking away from Daryl I sat my cup down and left, my thoughts tangled. Waiting until late, I only returned when I was certain that Daryl was asleep. A few days later I lost it, blew my temper at a sergeant who had been sweating all night to get my tired aircraft ready. I chewed him out in front of his men, chewed him out for not having my parachute lying on the wing when I walked to the aircraft. The next morning my name wasn't chalked on the squadron flight board; I was told that I was on sick call, I needed to see the Doc. Dewey, the colonel's adjutant, had seen my histrionics at the flight line and ordered my stand-down.

The Doc checked me over, exploring most orifices. After depositing himself on what appeared to be a Louis XVI chair, likely liberated from a nearby villa, he began the questions: Did I sleep, did I worry, did I have mood swings? I answered; I lied.

To make himself comfortable, perhaps to entice me to candor, the Doc propped his feet up on his desk and lit a pipe as a flight of P-39s tore over, the tent flaps rippling in their wake. Asked me if I would rather have one week's leave or stay on flying status. I told him flying. The Doc took a puff, put his pipe down and looked at me silently for a few moments, then a smile. Told me I needed a week off to untorque my brain; said that if I'd told him I wanted a week furlough he would have known I was okay, but anyone not wanting a furlough needed a furlough.

In a corner of the Doc's tent, on shelves made from a K-ration crate, lined up like miniature soldiers, stood a regiment of jars and bottles. From one of the larger jars the Doc carefully counted out fourteen greenish-blue pills. As if somehow I had won a grand prize, he explained that he was sending me to Naples for a week's R&R. Told me that each night before hitting the rack I should take two pills and wash them down with a stiff drink. He promised me that if I did I would sleep like the dead. I wanted to scream in his face; wanted to scream that I couldn't sleep because of death, the fear of death.

As I stuffed my duffel bag for Naples Daryl provided a monologue send-off. Said he couldn't wait to have our tent to himself, couldn't wait to be the lead, let someone be his wingman, let them try to follow a corkscrewing ace wannabe. While giving me more than a firm handshake, Daryl challenged me, told me that if I didn't have at least two social diseases when I returned I wasn't a real fighter pilot.

For the first few days of my medical-directed furlough I wished to be back at Montecorvino. By the end of the week I didn't want to return. I found myself a room in what had been a first-class apartment, two blocks from the south side of the ruins of Santa Chiara. Only had to share a toilet with three other rooms—all three occupied by British officers who understood the protocols of flushing, a procedure not fully practiced by our Italian hosts. I bought a Kodak from a staff sergeant in dire need of a poker stake; figured I would patch together a photographic record of sights for Father and Mother. We couldn't send photographs home, but I could take them with me when I returned.

Naples' public and royal buildings not pummeled by our Bomber Command had been well picked over by retreating Germans. Wall hooks gave testimony to spots where paintings had hung. Pedestals, supporting nothing, marked the previous residences of marble and bronze sculptures. But still it was there, the grandeur of the city of Bernini, Caravaggio, and Rosa. One evening I savored *La Bohème*. Mimi and Rodolfo so enraptured the audience that little note was made of the battle scars of Teatro di San Carlo. Another warm evening I sat in an outdoor café on the edge of Piazza del Plebiscito and listened to a choir practice, voices flowing through the collapsed church front, while I sipped a bottle of anonymous red to a slow death; this done as young couples strolled by in light clothes and lighter conversation. My problem wasn't sleeping, it was waking.

Much of Naples' ravaged population was desperate for shelter and food. For those with homes not destroyed, food was available, for a price—a high price. In front of many finer residences stood makeshift shops, homeowners selling their valuables for monies to buy food on the black market. This is how I came to acquire my peace offering to Daryl. From a lady looking fifty, but more likely forty, wearing a flowing peach chiffon dress, a remnant of a time and a dignity long gone, I was pleased to overpay for two long-stem crystal wine glasses. As I handed her the consideration she looked away; this day she was selling something more dear than her crystal.

One stain on my Naples sabbatical. On the last day of my therapeutic holiday I was strolling along the curve of Naples Bay, Mt. Vesuvius with its fluffy white bonnet as a backdrop, pondering the weighty problem of the day: which café should host me for lunch, and if I ordered fish would a Fiano di Avellino best complement the aquatic? Then the attempted arrest. Two MPs, Military Police, one a corporal and one a sergeant, stopped me with a harsh call. I was being arrested for impersonating an officer. They assumed that in the army there were no black officers; ergo, I was an impersonator.

For the first time as an adult I used spoken anger not to vent, but to sway. In a deep voice, deeper than usual and certainly louder, I told, I threatened, the MPs that they had fifteen seconds to come to attention and salute me and when they did I would return their salute, to be followed by them quickly spinning 180 degrees and leaving. Otherwise, I barked, they would be the ones behind bars.

Both stood silent. Quick glances passed between them. Hesitantly the corporal clicked his heels together; then, as if dragged by the weight of the corporal's action, the sergeant drew to attention and saluted. I returned his salute sharply. They turned and were soon gone, no doubt doubting what they had just done.

Someone new, a new face, was poised on Daryl's cot when I returned; prone, leaning on one elbow, reading a copy of *Life* magazine with Mary Martin on the cover. When I asked for Daryl, he said he didn't know Daryl, he was just told to bunk in this tent.

Daryl was dead. No details, only that he and his wingman had been seen diving on an FW-190; then all three into a cloud bank. Later two columns of smoke rose from a forest. Most thought Daryl's wingman had tangled with him as they cut blindly through the haze of white. Of no importance how, no importance to me. But the outcome: I paid the price. The price for not diversifying my emotional risk. For months Daryl and I had isolated ourselves; our lives were not entwined with others, lest they be killed and we feel remorse. But with Daryl's death I had no human handhold to steady my sanity. I had lost my only anchor. I was adrift, adrift with anger, an anger that squeezed out all passion save hate.

But hate only defined half of me; the other half was ambivalence. I didn't care. I didn't care about me or anyone other than Krauts. Them I wanted to kill, and I did. I abandoned self-preservation. I twisted and pulled my P-39 beyond what should have been its limits, whatever was necessary for the kill. My wingmen couldn't follow, they couldn't protect my six o'clock, and I didn't care, I was pursuing, pursuing to kill. I felt no concern other than how to best kill a Kraut. Then came the train.

As we had done a score of times before, my squadron escorted a large force of B-17s halfway to their target, in time relieved by a gaggle of P-51s; they had the range to go all the way with the bombers. Heading back to base on the lookout for targets of opportunity, anything moving; I diverted twenty degrees to the south to follow train tracks glinting in the sun; rails that weren't rust-covered, they were well traveled. Just past a small village, heading south toward the front, I spotted a train with no windows in the cars, just flat sides, likely a supply train.

Before I would have flown away, dropped to treetop level, and circled back for my attack. By staying low there wouldn't be time for Kraut gunners to track me. But this day I peeled straight toward them. A half-mile out, the side of the front car dropped and two antiaircraft guns opened fire. Glowing balls of tracers arced over my aircraft. I pushed in the left rudder to track the front car, opened up with the guns, then stabilized to let the train pull itself through my line of fire.

Just before passing low over the last few cars an eruption of force, a car blew up, flame, smoke, and debris higher than my aircraft. In an instant in and out of the fireball . . . but long enough to be battered by rocketing debris. Once at altitude a quick scan of the engine instruments; all the pointers were caressing the appropriate numbers. No damage apparent.

Back at base I taxied to my revetment. With the ground crew on the wing after shutdown, I unbuckled and headed to the operations tent for a debrief. A curt call from my crew chief, I turned. Likely he wanted to show me some damage, some ripped aluminum from shells and flying bits of train and cargo. Often my ground crew pointed out damage so I could feel guilty that by risking death I had damaged their aircraft, an aircraft they would work on long into the night to make right. But not this day. This day they were standing at the leading edge of the starboard wing staring.

It was there, just outside of the gun ports, folded back around the curve of the airfoil, perhaps six or eight inches long, half as wide. It looked like a piece of tan rubber, plastered and sealed against the leading edge by the force of 300-mile-an-hour flow of air. But this wasn't some ordinary scrap of rubber. This rubber had hair growing from it, its edges a dark, caked red. This was of God's making, human skin. A corporal wanted to peel it away, eradicate any testimony to our purpose, killing people. For me, I felt no such concern; I saw a trophy, a trophy to be displayed. I ordered it not to be touched. For more than a full week the skin stayed, slowly dark brown, then black. As I taxied in from each mission the ground crews would steal a glance, hoping it was gone, pleased it was not.

It was the skin, or stories about the skin, that brought about my transfer. Colonel Davis's adjutant, Dewey, called me in to meet with him and the Doc. After a brief exchange of artificials, the Doc asked why the skin, why did I keep it plastered to the edge of my wing. I told him that airmen wear medals reflecting the death and destruction they had wreaked upon the Germans; why not let my P-39 wear its medal? A long silence. Then the adjutant asked if I had a Kraut head in my duffel bag. I frowned, puzzled. He asked if I had seen Spencer Tracy in *Northwest Passage*; I told him I hadn't seen the movie. He said too bad, then more silence.

The Doc and Dewey exchanged glances, and the Doc gave a slight nod. Dewey leaned toward me and spoke softly, told me I was being transferred. It was my call. Did I want to be shipped back to a training squadron, or did I want to take a temporary assignment with the Eighth, the Eighth Air Force, in England? When I didn't reply, he told me to make a choice, or he would. The Eighth was all white; black squadrons were stationed in Italy. I asked by what circumstances a black Air Corps officer would be stationed in England. Dewey said he was being assigned to Doolittle's staff, a non-flying job, and said I could transfer with him. I did.

While not the Mark Hopkins, the American air base at Chester, a hundred miles or so south of London, was quite, as the British would say, posh. Not an extravagant posh, but unquestionably posh as contrasted with the layered dirt at Montecorvino. Not the least notable: hot water, all one could want.

But it wasn't the hot water, or the heated barracks and warm food that were the best, it was the train station. Just over a mile from the base was a farming village with a station whose tracks pointed toward, then intersected, magnificent London. Within two hours of returning the salute of the sentry at the base gatehouse, I was humbly hunched in the back pew of Saint Paul's, giving thanks. After the soul, the body; a pint and some friendly cheeses at the Savoy, interrupted only by Big Ben calling the hour.

Once replenished, I meandered the streets, halting my journey for each whim of curiosity, exploring great public buildings. On one hike through history, strolling through the National Portrait Gallery, a most pleasant surprise. I rounded a corner and froze in the stare from Father's Intellectual God. Gazing down at me from two dark eyes moored in a pond of light skin, white-bearded, and draped in a brown-black coat over rounded shoulders, with his opposable thumb grasping a well-worn fedora, was Charles Robert Darwin wearing an expression of forlorn sorrow—perhaps sorrow that he'd been the one who told the tale. Told us that we were not biblical mystics, but rather comical monkeys.

Italy had been for me the hard crust of Europe: caked earth, bleak browns, stale food, and a defeated people. England was refreshingly green and bright with hope, hope of a population smiling and confident in themselves. Dewey and the Doc had saved me from Dante's Inferno. After Daryl's death my ambivalence toward risk was no less than my own death wish. Without the forced transfer from Italy I would have become a gnarled thorny bush in the middle ring of the Seventh Circle.

General James Doolittle had been Commander of the Fifteenth Air Force in Italy. When he was assigned the Eighth Air Force in England, he was put in charge of the most powerful group of aircraft ever assembled under a single command. The fact that Doolittle brought Dewey to the Eighth in England, where there were less than a dozen black officers, testified to Dewey's strengths.

I was Dewey's adjutant. Although we were both pilots, Dewey's assignments from Doolittle, and mine as his aide, were administrative, collecting ready reports and assessing capabilities of the P-38, P-47, and P-51 fighter squadrons. No one in England was saddled with my old mount, the P-39. At first I enjoyed the desk job. After a year in Italy of solemnly greeting each new day as my last, I savored stability and predictability. But then doubts arose; somehow it didn't feel right. Somehow I wasn't doing my job. A few times I gently probed moving back to flying status. Always a quick response: Absolutely not, no black pilots in the Eighth Air Force. And then remembrances of the navy petty officer . . . house slave or field slave?

In early June of '44, Eisenhower executed the bloody invasion of Fortress Europe. By August, American and British armies were pushing through France and Belgium toward Germany. The Eighth already had forward fighter bases in France. Our group remained in England; most of us expected the European war to be over in a few months.

It was late August when General Doolittle, making a round of all the Air Groups, joined several of the officers at our base. Doolittle was famous for his aviation exploits, both as a civilian and a military pilot. These were not the hallmarks my parents would have noted, however; rather, they would have admired his outstanding education, an education not easily attained nor casually chosen. From MIT he'd earned a master's, then a PhD, both in aeronautical engineering, a daunting science. While most daredevil pilots of the 1920s were hard-drinking exhibitionists, Doolittle had been a doctoral candidate calculating wind velocity gradients. But it was neither Doolittle's education nor his flying skills that swayed me the most; it was his height.

After a formal briefing many of us followed General Doolittle to the Officer's Club for some instructional conversation. Junior officers learned early on that they should limit their interaction with senior officers to responding "good point" and laughing heartily at any humor, no matter how flat. After more than an hour at the bar, the general moved to a table with me, Dewey, and three or four other officers clustered behind us. In time the conversation drifted from operations to stories. Several called out questions about Doolittle's Tokyo Raid, coaxing B-25s off the *Hornet*'s deck, the same carrier I had seen in Oakland while a student. After the first bottle of scotch evaporated, another appeared. More conversation ensued—nothing critical, just random subjects.

Then someone asked Doolittle whether it was true that he had been both a champion bantamweight and middleweight boxer. He responded, with a smile of pride, in the affirmative. Then came the question and answer that sparked my transfer. A young captain asked the general, "Why boxing? Why a brain-pounding sport?" Doolittle's quick answer was a single word: Prejudice. My head involuntarily cocked toward him. He said that at five-foot-four he was shorter than most men. Doolittle went on to claim that tall men had an advantage in their everyday life; for reasons that had no basis in logical thinking, short men were not considered the equal to males of well-developed stature. Boxing, and winning at boxing, and then attaining a PhD, Doolittle said, had been his way of proving to others that a short man was the equal of any tall man.

It may have been the scotch oozing through my cerebrum, or it may have been twenty years of frustration, but whatever the trigger, I spoke up in not a whisper. I told the general that he had framed precisely a valid point. He smiled, a junior officer was acknowledging the logic of his statement. But I did not return the smile and offer a toast. Rather I added that I was five-ten and I would gladly trade him a half foot of my height for his white skin.

Silence. After several long moments a major in our group asked the general when he thought the war in the Pacific would be over. Doolittle didn't respond. Rotating his posture toward me, he asked if I wasn't satisfied that the Air Corps had made me a lieutenant and trained me as a pilot. I responded with a quick yes, but added that I'd only been allowed to fly weary P-39s in Italy. And even though I had proved myself by destroying three Me-109s and a 190 with America's second-rate fighter, and even though I was parented by two PhDs, being black was the overriding consideration of my piloting capabilities. And then—I shouldn't have, but I did—I added that I had seen numbers of short white pilots flying combat aircraft in England.

Doolittle turned to Dewey and asked if I was right; was it actually not possible for an experienced black combat pilot to fill a piloting slot in the Eighth? After a long pause while he likely considered a transfer to the submarine service, Dewey said I was correct; it was not possible.

Two days later I received a transfer to a P-47 fighter squadron. Learning of my rotation, Dewey successfully lobbied for the same. We were transferred to a squadron led by a young captain—a noticeably short young captain—whom Doolittle had mentored. Most squadron pilots greeted us with passive indifference. Real feelings were tempered by the knowledge that we were there by order of the Commanding Officer of the Eighth Air Force.

Only at a distance had I seen P-47s. When a sergeant gave me a walk-around of my new mount, I was in awe. I'd had a similar feeling as a young boy when I first stood next to a steam locomotive. The P-47 was big, not graceful but functional. To overcome drag and gravity, a 2,200-horsepower air-cooled engine swung a twelve-foot prop. The P-38, P-39, P-40, and P-51 all had liquid-cooled engines, coolant flowing around the cylinders, then down from the engine through a maze of pipes and tubes to a radiator. One small leak in the coolant system, from a blown seal or a Kraut's lucky shot, and the pilot had an overheating engine, a fire, and a crash. The P-47's air-cooled engine was simple. As long as it was moving through the air, the engine was cool. A cannon shell from a Kraut FW-190 or Me-109 could blow a cylinder off a P-47 and the engine would likely keep on pulling.

Another thing about the P-47, it was strong. Republic Aviation didn't save any money on aluminum when they built these chariots. An empty P-47 weighed as much as the P-39 loaded. Because it was robust with a powerful engine, it could haul a couple thousand pounds of bombs or extra fuel under the wings. Plus, long-range fuel tanks gave P-47 pilots the range to shepherd B-17s and B-24s during their deep penetration raids into Germany.

Most important for a fighter pilot, no less than eight .50-caliber machines were embedded in the wing. And the "pilot's office" had a view. Our squadron was equipped with the latest model of the P-47, manufactured with a bubble canopy that offered a 360-degree field of vision. Mounted on top of the bubble, a mirror—much like an auto's rear-view mirror—that allowed a pilot to see at a glance if a Kraut was in trail. With a sinister smile, the sergeant providing my walk-around claimed that any Kraut close enough for me to see in the mirror was the last Kraut I would ever see.

On the weakness side, at a low altitude the P-47 was a truck, in fact it was nicknamed "the Jug" after Juggernaut. It wasn't sprightly in its response to control inputs. If you got the plane into a spin much below 5,000 feet, you needed to bail out or have your will witnessed.

Dewey and I quickly learned that most of the squadron's missions were escort, shepherding B-17s and B-24s to Germany and back. By the fall of '44 the Luftwaffe was emasculated. While they were short of fuel and aircraft, their lack of experienced combat pilots was the most deflating. Five years of a two-front war had ravaged their ranks. America and Russia, and England, using the Canadian Territories, could train pilots at bases far from harm's way. The Nazis had no safe incubators to hatch pilots. On many of our escort missions no enemy fighters were seen; if they did make an appearance, often it was a quick hit and run; newly trained— barely trained—Kraut pilots had no stomach for a dogfight till death.

On a given day more than a thousand Allied fighters and bombers streamed across the English Channel, flying missions over France and Germany. These aircraft nested at close to a hundred airfields scattered throughout England and Ireland. When the weather turned nasty over England during a mission, it was often catch-as-catch-can when trying to get back on the ground after a several-hour mission. If my fuel was low, I would drop the gear and flaps and plop myself in the first air base that wasn't weathered in.

I enjoyed these detours. It was always a sour pleasure to see the jaws drop and the eyes bulge. I would taxi along the flight line with ground crew using hand signals to shepherd me to a tie-down ramp. As I shut down the engine some corporal or sergeant would be up on the wing to help with my gear. Off came my goggles, helmet, and oxygen mask; on went their shock. Most had never seen a black pilot. Most didn't even know there were black pilots. For many I was a curiosity, pointed out as I strolled to the operations offices from the flight line. For a few, I was a focus of scorn. "How could a black man do what we do? It's not possible."

Weather-caused displacements gave me the opportunity to become a tourist . . . to explore the nooks and crannies of England. After one four-hour mission to Munich I came back across the channel to see nothing but solid overcast. Most of the bases were socked in. The frequencies were saturated with controllers struggling to put seven pounds of sugar in a five-pound bag. I headed north toward Kimbolton, an airfield that somehow always seemed to be clear. After a few minutes, a tearing break appeared in the cloud layer, and directly below a field with forktailed P-38s parked along the perimeter. A bird in the hand. I pulled back the power, made a long sweeping turn to clear the area, then landed on a wide grass field.

After my normal shutdown and disrobing routine, I headed to the airfield's administrative building where I joined pilots milling around from half the squadrons in the UK. Turns out I was in Duxford. This had been an RAF base in the early part of the war. In time American P-38 and P-51 squadrons exercised squatter's rights. I spent most of two days in Duxford waiting for a stalled cold front to move through. It was a magnificent pause for me. Duxford was only a few miles from the most magnificent cauldron of academia: Cambridge.

For a full day I visited the colleges of Cambridge University, savoring every moment. I made a point of introducing myself to some professors at Christ's College, the college that had educated my father's God, Charles Darwin; his grandson had just retired as Master of the College. When they learned that my father was a biologist with a keen interest in Darwin, they introduced me to a young professor, Giles, who in turn took me to an anteroom off the staircase between the library floors. There Giles, my soon to be friend, handed me a leather case and told me to take whatever time I needed.

For hours I held and perused, with the care of a nurse cradling a newborn, letters from Darwin. Letters sent from the HMS *Beagle* during its five-year exploration of the South Pacific. Letters that hinted of Darwin's first tentative conclusions drawn from observations of the tortoise and finch populations of the Galapagos Islands—conclusions that led to his anti-Christ Theory of Organic Evolution: survival of the fittest.

So engrossed was I with Darwin's handwritten papers that shadows became long with no notice taken. My trance was broken by the young professor asking if all was right. Then Giles, in a tone more like an order than a suggestion, a harbinger of our relationship, recommended that we dine together.

The dinner itself was at Christ's College, in a dark room of darker woods, overseen by ponderous portraits of academia's finest. After typical British fare of starches and fatty meat, Giles pulled me through a discussion I'd never before considered. He transported Darwin's theory of the survival of the fittest from species to cultures and nations. For Giles, unlike most in America, it was as much a certitude that Darwin's theory of evolution explained man's existence as Newton's observation about fruit and gravity. He argued that civilizations, and later in the history of our planet, nations, rise and then fall as the fittest nation becomes less fit.

I questioned this notion. I asked, if it is true the fittest species tends to remain the fittest, why would not the fittest nation hold its place in the world ranking? His answer gave me pause. Man, he argued, is a unique species. And it is man, or men, that form a nation. My furrowed brow elicited further explanation. The Spanish, Giles lectured, were prominent in the 1400s and 1500s. They were a global power in the world as then known. As a nation they had succeeded; boats riding low with gold from the New World confirmed their exalted world status. In time the peoples of Spain used their wealth not to expand, but to enjoy life while paying others to do their bidding. They became lazy. Giles concluded by stating that it was England that was striving the hardest in the 1600s and 1700s, and by the 1800s and early 1900s Britannia ruled the waves, not Spain.

To validate his theory Giles asked that I consider the lion, the King of the Jungle, with no other species challenging its dominance. Imagine, he said, what would happen if the lion killed more game than it needed for survival. Imagine as well that African animals had money that they freely exchanged. The lions could sell their excess meat, and then perhaps save the money they received for selling their surplus kill. Some future generation of lions might use this stored wealth to pay leopards to hunt for them, rather than being bothered to stalk gazelles in the blazing African sun. In time these lions would become fat and lazy; not fleet of paw. Leopards, still being lean and cunning, and noting the lions' laziness, might in time tire of hunting for lions and decide to eat the flabby lions . . . or to sell lion meat.

After a few moments of reflection, I asked if Great Britain would decline. "For certain" was Giles's quick answer, adding that Winston Churchill was spot-on when he spoke of the Battle of Britain being their finest hour. It was not only the grandeur of the event that would make it the finest hour, it would also be the subsequent decline of Great Britain as the world's greatest power.

After dinner I took a wandering stroll through the center of Cambridge, past great colleges founded before the *Mayflower* dropped anchor. On one hidden narrow street I discovered the Eagle Pub; a pub requisitioned by American pilots based at Duxford as "theirs." It was like all pubs—churning conversations lubricated with ale and the always-married fish and chips aromas. One difference: on the ceiling was a testimonial to American pilots who had scrawled their names and squadron numbers across the plaster sky. Hundreds of Williamses, Thomases, Charleses, Jameses, and the like, many already dead in France and Germany, baked black in cratered soufflés of burning fuel, aluminum, flesh and bone. While sipping an ale I considered standing on a chair and adding my name, but thought best not to further stretch the polite tension that my presence had caused among the regulars.

By the afternoon of the second day at Duxford the cold front was over France, leaving only blue sky. I sat on the wing of my P-47 soaking in the warmth, watching aircraft trundle over the uneven grass and lift off toward their home bases. Next to my aircraft was a Spitfire. This sleek fighter was the icon of Britain's struggle against the Nazis, its curved elliptical wings making it more art than aircraft.

In time a British pilot officer strolled toward the Spit. We nodded hellos as he began preflighting it, looking for anything not right. When through, he asked if I was based at Duxford. I told him I was a transient and would be soon heading to my base. He stuck out his hand and introduced himself; Reginald was his name. With names like Reginald one knew the British were smarter than the average Billy Bob American.

For a time we spoke of things only of interest to pilots while staring at aircraft floating off Duxford's green expanses. Then I asked him. I asked if the Spit was as great as the British pilots claimed. He paused for several moments, then said it was a magnificent kite . . . British pilots called their aircraft *kites*. He quickly added that beauty was in the eyes of the beholder. Then Reginald asked if I wanted to take his Spit up. Just like that he asked. No questions about how many hours I had, whether I had ever flown a liquid-cooled aircraft, nothing. As if asking did I want a spot of tea, did I want to fly his Spit. My smile preceded my affirmative answer.

I hopped up on the wing of the Spit and slid into its tight cockpit. Reginald strapped me in, then gave me a quick cockpit brief: master, mags, trim, boost pump, fuel selector, fuel cock, primer, engine settings. "Don't get slower than eighty on short final." Nothing much unlike a US fighter. The big difference was the landing gear, or as they say, undercarriage, selector. It was on the right and didn't look like anything I had seen before. The other big difference was the brakes. Every US aircraft had foot brakes, usually on top of the rudder pedals. The Spit had a handbrake on the stick; probably for the same reason they drove on the wrong side of the road.

With a push on the booster coil and starter buttons the Merlin engine cranked to life. A touch of power and the Spit began its narrow-gear waddle across the Duxford grass. After pausing for the engine oil to warm, I made a quick run-up to check the mags and prop. Then into the wind and power pushed on slowly; I wanted to get the feel. The tail jumped off quickly, and while considering when I should ease the Spit up, it took the lead and we were flying . . . it was flying.

I hesitated with the gear retraction—had to switch hands on the stick to move the lever on the right. The Spitfire climbed faster than anything I had flown before; we were soon level at 10,000 feet. I tried a few quick rolls: ailerons light to the touch. The rudder and elevator even lighter. A Cuban Eight, a Split S, then just random dips and turns.

The Spit didn't go where I directed, it went where I thought. It was a butterfly with the speed and ego of a wasp. I didn't want to overstay my welcome, so back to Duxford, in the pattern, gear down, flaps down, held it off the grass for a gentle three-point . . . I tried to make Americans look competent. I pulled onto the ramp next to my P-47. Reginald was quickly up on the wing, unbuckling parachute straps. I was babbling like a schoolboy—best flight since my first in the yellow Cub! Pointing to my weary mount, I asked Reginald if he wanted to fly it to see what it was like. He told me he didn't need to; said that my wide grin after flying the Spit told him how the P-47 flew. God, the Brits could be cleverly cruel.

After an early November morning sweep over Antwerp on the wing of Dewey, we turned west, back over a churning channel of whitecaps. Halfway across, the oil pressure crossed the boundary between green and yellow, then into red. Whenever a dial reported something wrong with an engine, it was easiest to rationalize the dial was failing, not the contrivance with 5,000 parts twirling at 3,000 RPM as the result of 20,000 contained combustions a minute—this contrivance being a Pratt & Whitney R-2800 that kept my 12,000-pound P-47 in the air. But then more dials took their leave, the amp meter to zero and voltage slipping fast. Then the smell of an electrical fire.

I turned south. If the engine quit I didn't want the headlines screaming YANK's PLANE RAMS BUCKINGHAM PALACE. After a few minutes the rising engine temperature told the tale: no oil pressure. Then came the shakes, rods and pistons protesting before their execution. Quickly tightened the parachute straps, spun in down trim, cranked the canopy open, pulled the mixture to cut off, and rolled inverted. With a firm yank on the quick release, I was borne into rushing air with flailing arms and legs.

One thousand and one, one thousand and two, one thousand and three; I'd been instructed to count to ten. After three I pulled the D-ring. A jerk, and swinging under silk. Below me spread a gray cloud cover, a lumpy quilt. A quick pang of fear: what if somehow I had bailed out over water, not the pastures south of London? In the distance a noise rolled up like a clap of thunder; my P-47 slicing into terra firma, not choppy seas.

Down into the gray overcast I drifted. Crossed my legs so that neither a tree branch nor fence railing could threaten my mother's grandchildren. In an instant a green field below; another instant on my back, in mud, my chute retired from its career, spread limp. The breath knocked out of me, more than a minute refilling my lungs with damp British air, unbuckled my parachute harness and took an unsteady stance.

Over a rise two farmers came running, one with a shotgun. I was pleased to be alive; they were disappointed I was not German. Their second choice would have been a British pilot. I occupied the bottom of their dance card, an American; neither foe nor compatriot.

The older of the two shepherded me back to his cottage. His son hastened off to the village to alert the constable of my arrival while his wife performed the British obligatory: tea was poured. Then the tour; my farmer host proudly introduced me to the pigs and cows that staffed his bucolic factory. I smiled and complimented him while savoring the aroma of great piles of aging manure, making note to thank my parents once again for my expansive education. By nightfall I was back at my base, buying drinks for those who returned with their planes.

I had written Father of my time caressing Darwin's original notes. I considered not telling him; somehow I had stolen moments that should have been his. I also wrote of Giles's theory that nations, once achieving greatness, sowed the seeds of their decline when they used their wealth to pay others to do their bidding. As anticipated, within a few short weeks a letter back from Father with challenging questions of doubt. On a squadron stand-down I hopped a train into London and connected with a northbound to Cambridge. During an enjoyable evening with Giles, I posed Father's questions as if they were mine. With compelling logic and well-chosen analogies Giles dismissed each without even the most meager acknowledgment of the merit of the questions.

For last I had saved my own question, and asked what nation would be the next dominant. Giles quickly replied, "The United States." I then asked if we would tumble from a position of dominance once it was attained. Giles looked at me as if I had asked Newton whether the apple would rise or fall in its journey from the tree. "Of course," he replied, "and it will decline faster than England." Before I could ask he put forth the reason: "The speed of commerce has increased over the centuries and will continue to increase. Just as it took a country with a fleet of steamships less time to move commerce than a nation with a fleet of sailing ships, new technologies will provide for a relentless compression of time, thus accelerating a nation's ability to move from have-not to have . . . to displace the dominant." On the train back to my base later that night I pondered Giles's pronouncements. If he was correct, correct about the rise and fall of nations, I despondently concluded that I was fighting to achieve American greatness so that once achieved my future adult grandchildren could watch America's greatness erode while their hired help cut their lawns and washed their clothes.

Never could I weave my thoughts and words in a manner that conveyed to Mother why flying, why snubbing my nose at gravity, was not a choice made after a precise extrapolation from life events, but was, rather, a passion. Another did convey my passion to paper with a modest sprinkle of perfectly cut and polished words. As with many things in life, I found these words not by a quest, but by circumstance of another journey—a journey to retrieve a wayward pilot of our squadron.

Clifford, our flight leader, asked that I take our squadron hack, a T-6 so tired that I expected its wings to droop until they touched the ground, up to Wellingore to retrieve one of our new pilots who had become lost in the English weather. This poor fellow had circled around most of northern England looking for a break in the overcast, then when a chance opened, dropped into the first airfield he saw—as luck would have it, Wellingore, a British fighter base. So relieved was he to find a field that our frazzled pilot forgot to put his landing gear down. In a few seconds his P-47 went from aircraft to tractor. Our squadron pilot climbed out unhurt, probably with a bunch of stunned Brits wondering how the hell they lost the Revolutionary War.

I flew over to pick up our planeless pilot. Once I was on the ground, dark clouds rolled over bearing rains that would have caused Noah to pause. Waiting for the deluge to disperse my pilot squadron mate wanted to hide in his temporary billet, too embarrassed to be strolling about. I felt no such necessity. It was at a nearby pub I saw the poem posted. The pub owner proudly advised that the composition in verse had been written by a British Spitfire pilot based at Wellingore. Verses that I copied, then memorized.

High Flight

Oh! I have slipped the surly bonds of earth,
And danced the skies on laughter-silvered wings.

Sunward I've climbed and joined the tumbling mirth
Of sun-split clouds and done a hundred things

You have not dreamed of—wheeled and soared and swung
High in the sunlit silence.

Hov'ring there, I've chased the shouting wind along
And flung my eager craft through footless halls of air.

Up, up the long delirious, burning blue
I've topped the windswept-heights with easy grace
Where never lark, nor even eagle flew;
And, while with silent, lifting mind I've trod

The high untrespassed sanctity of space,
Put out my hand, and touched the face of God.

Once back at Wellingore I asked a flight officer if the author of "High Flight" was still stationed at the base. Off-handedly he told me that he had been killed in his Spit two years before.

During the Thanksgiving week, a holiday of no significance to the Brits, Giles and I met at the halfway point, London. We had front center seats for Agatha Christie's *And Then There Were None*, then a superb dinner (somehow the better London restaurants weren't constrained by meat and sugar rations). While our discussions were expansive in their range, the roulette wheel of topics frequently stopped on dissecting the human race. During dinner Giles poured out yet another cataclysmic observation. In the course of a rambling conversation about the ebb and flow of civilization he casually mentioned, as if noting there was no salt in the salt shaker, that mankind as we knew it was a short-term phenomenon. He made this statement heralding the demise of the human race while meticulously removing the last microns of fat from his medium-rare lamb chop.

My stare, accompanied by silence, demanded elaboration. Giles based his conclusion on the primacy of instinct over intellect. He noted that man, in spite of an opposable thumb, was in fact an animal. In the earliest chapters of man's evolutionary development, certain primeval traits were imprinted on our psyche, traits that were necessary for survival—the simplest being to flinch with pain; a more complex example the urge to mate, thus procreating to expand the tribe. These traits in their varied forms and importance,

Giles argued, resulted in unique tendencies of mankind. One of these tendencies being war. He said that Hitler's forays into Poland, France, and Russia were, while on a grander scale, no different than one African tribe attacking another to take possession of their hunting grounds. He argued that no matter how eloquently a human might speak, within him smoldered raw animal passions.

Technology, Giles suggested—of course, Giles really never suggested, he stated—would be mankind's downfall. He believed that technology did two things to the detriment of the human race. First, it allowed any one human exercising a primeval emotion to operate on a scale several magnitudes greater than previous generations. Two hundred years ago an arrow shot into the heart; today a two-thousand-pound bomb dropped on a village. Second, technology dehumanized the event of killing.

When he made this last point, my frown telegraphed my non-agreement. I told him that I felt compassion when the shells from my .50-caliber machine guns raked a German fighter and I saw it enter a flaming death spiral. Giles paused for a moment, then asked how many children did the German pilot that I killed have? Did he enjoy music? Or perhaps, was he a student of the ballet? No, he said, I was not an executioner looping a rope around the neck of someone while peering into his eyes; rather, I killed from afar and feigned compassion.

I remained quiet, abstaining from debate. Then, to make his point that blood never stained my hands, he asked whether, if by some circumstance, I was standing near a German pilot about to take off in his Messerschmidt to shoot down an American bomber, would I, if I had the opportunity, walk up to him and stick a bayonet in his heart? Or would I be more comfortable applying my highly developed intellect to sway him from his mission? Not having a retort of compelling reason, I answered by telling Giles that I would pay a leopard to eat the Nazi pilot.

While I relished the free-ranging intellectual safaris with Giles, there was a price. He was Mr. Atlas and I the ninety-pound weakling when we debated evolution and the itinerary of man from cave to castle. At first his overflowing reservoir of knowledge, which he packaged in small parcels to pummel me, caused self-doubts; was I perhaps best suited to be a field slave? Of course I overstate my intimidation. Giles, I consoled myself, had written a 75,000-word doctoral thesis contrasting Levallois tools to Mousterian tools. He had spent nine months in Java with von Koenigswald confirming that Dubois had in fact discovered *Pithecanthropus erectus*—better known as our cousin *Homo erectus*. When the topic was 50,000 years old, had two legs and a sloping forehead, he possessed a titanic advantage. Let Giles slip into a P-47 and try to fly a mission; he couldn't even bargain the engine to life. But I couldn't compete with Giles in a game he didn't play, so aviation was not my ally.

Mother's teaching rescued my self-esteem. Cleverly, but likely not as cleverly as I thought, I jibed and tacked our banter to literature. Giles held his own initially, as I blundered through Bacon and Shakespeare—both likely direct ancestors to Giles. But American literature, which at first he dismissed as an oxymoron, was my salvation. "So, Giles, don't you agree that of the three scaffold scenes in *The Scarlet Letter*, the night setting with Hester, Pearl, and Dimmesdale is most powerful?" My way of suggesting that Giles should stick a copy of *Tom Sawyer* up *Homo habilis*'s anus.

My correspondence to Mother and Father pasteurized life as a fighter pilot. Once back home I could regale them with my exploits. I did in several letters, however, elaborate on Giles's conclusions regarding the human journey. Father at first only responded in a casual manner. In time, though, Father came to see Giles, at best, as an interloper into his son's mind; at worst, perhaps, as a hijacker of his role as my teacher of all things scientific. Father's letters often included well-crafted arguments as to why Giles's hypothesis was flawed.

While Giles might be wrong, it was not a notion that Giles ever visited. I would reformulate Father's arguments as questions, not challenges, to Giles. "I was wondering, could you help me understand why it's not this way . . . ?" I became the rope in my father's intellectual tug-of-war with Giles.

In one expansive letter from Father, with the breadth and depth of a term paper, he set forth a comprehensive explanation as to why Giles was incorrect in his belief that technology would be the downfall of mankind because our ability to kill each other was developing faster than the erosion of mankind's primeval instincts. Father held that humans are basically benevolent. This notion, when overlaid by the premise that each generation was better educated than the previous generation, was the basis for Father's belief that Giles erred. For Father, education furnished handholds in logical thinking that would force any rational person to "do the right thing."

When I posed this notion to Giles as my own thought, he responded with a smile. If cats could smile, they would wear the same smile while playing with a mouse. Giles attacked my argument at the microcosmic and the macrocosmic levels. In the micro he asked why I was an Air Corps pilot risking death. The ability for the Allies to win the war against the Axis Powers, Giles claimed, did not pivot on the fact that I joined the fight. Simply put, he argued that the risk-to-reward analysis made no sense for me as an individual. In the country that I was fighting to defend, many of my fellow countrymen thought I was not a citizen worthy of all of the benefits of the nation. Nevertheless, I was risking my life for this nation, even though my participation in the fight would not be pivotal. Therefore, my superb education did not funnel me to a rational decision, thus proving that education does not correlate to rational thought.

My retort I thought compelling. On December 7th America was attacked; our president and Congress, both elected by individual Americans, chose to go to war. As a country we went to war, and I was a citizen of that country. Accordingly, there was no decision for me to make, rational or irrational.

Giles then crushed me in the macro, lecturing me as to why the various national and global institutions artificially prolong man's latent primeval instincts. The biggest offender, he said, was the state-church that banded peoples together, then administered false hopes as a tranquilizing opium. "Opium?"

Another sip of Claret and his response. Giles argued that the masses toil in squalor while paying tribute to the state-church leaders—"God Save the King" . . . "God Bless the Pope"—because the same leaders assure them that the meek shall inherit the earth. To embolden his position, Giles claimed he would rather have a flat in the theater district of London today than take his chances on inheriting the earth after death.

While Giles's ramblings became confusing at times, the essence was that religion and sometimes governments were artificial mechanisms to unite a group of people, and this mechanism taught certain absolutes: their God was the only God. And certain religions preached that anyone worshipping a God other than theirs should be slain: "Onward, Christian Soldiers."

I didn't agree. I chose what I thought was the most vulnerable component of Giles's position. Artificiality of religion is not a given, I asserted, hence his entire argument was suspect. Giles eyed me with apparent pity and asked what religion I practiced. "Catholicism" was my quick response. He then asked how many religions had I considered before identifying the Vatican as my mecca? "Why not the Mormon Church? Why not Buddhism? Why not pray in a mosque, or perhaps a synagogue?" For Giles, an individual's choice of one of the world's great religions was of no greater moment than a child deciding—whether based on taste or because it was the only flavor served them as a youngster—what would be their favorite flavor of ice cream throughout life. Some people liked vanilla, others embraced chocolate, and a few worshipped strawberry. The problem being that the people who worshipped strawberry, or whatever flavor, were told that they should kill those who worshipped vanilla. To pay homage to vanilla was to be a heathen and to desecrate strawberry. Giles believed that the downfall of mankind would be religious wars—wars of no logic, just fanatical beliefs, being fought with weapons of greater and greater killing power.

Giles's declaration that religions were fraudulent was not a notion I communicated to Father, lest he incur an aneurism while contemplating his son breaking bread with a devil's disciple. While the teachings of the Catholic Church at times stretched my capacity to believe, I never doubted that God existed. For me, God's existence and the artificiality of religion were not two incompatible beliefs. While religion could not exist without the premise of a God, God could exercise His divine powers without the trumpets and trappings of religion. I planned my counter-attack on Giles, in my quiver carefully sharpened stone-tipped arrows of logical thought as to why God.

Alas, I did not have the opportunity to string my bow.

As the European conflict's center of gravity crawled on its belly toward Berlin, life as a pilot in England drifted toward tranquil— not for the bomber crews being shredded by flak, but for fighter pilots escorting them. American P-47 squadrons in the forward bases, in abandoned Luftwaffe airfields in France and Belgium, flew the low-level support missions, each day playing Russian roulette with Nazi gunners. We flew the milk runs, escorting bombers high above the struggle. Often we would return in the precise formation in which we had departed, no marauding Kraut Me-109s or 190s having disturbed the symmetry of our flight. If the bombers hit a well-defended target we would break off in twos or fours to escort the stragglers, lumbering bombers that had lost an engine to flak.

On a November mission to Merseburg I had my humanity hammered again. Sky of God's indigo blue, only wisps of white at 25,000 feet. More than two hundred B-17s and B-24s had been sent to the target, each with their ten-man crew. As always we rejoined after the bombers laid their TNT eggs, half a score of stragglers limping behind the box formations. Nazi flak had done its job.

We picked our dance partners. Dewey and I joined on a B-17 that was slower than other wounded bombers. One prop feathered, with no thrust, little drag; its engine mate on the same wing was freewheeling, spinning in the airflow, with no thrust and immense drag. The B-17 was slowly trading height for airspeed, the airspeed necessary for flight.

Dewey took his place to the right and behind the crippled bomber, I on the left, as if somehow we could steady the big beast as it wallowed toward England. Even with the power back, my aircraft pulled away. Every couple of minutes I would skid, cross the controls, to chip away at my speed.

Before the invasion the bomber crew would have bailed out miles back. Once on the ground they could have expected a day or two of interrogation, then transport to a stalag with ten thousand other American airmen eating turnips while waiting for liberation. But now it was different. The Nazis had the German civilians whipped to a rage as Yanks were poised to cross onto German soil. Parachuting Allied airmen were welcomed by pitchforks and nooses. Our B-17 was struggling to cross into Allied territory, the boundary marked this day by the Eider River, an agonizing hundred miles or so ahead.

More from curiosity than need, I drifted under our adopted bomber. Sunlight shone through ragged holes in both wings, a portion of the port elevator missing, and worst of all, the lower ball turret, a Plexiglas fishbowl protruding from the belly of the B-17 with two .50-caliber guns and a gunner, was no longer transparent and perfect; it was jagged and blood red.

Slowly I slid back to the side of the lumbering war wagon. From the waist gunner positions came a steady dropping of gear, anything to make the craft lighter in its struggle against gravity, anything to reach the Eider: oxygen bottles, ammunition boxes, a radio, machine guns, and two parachutes. Two of the ten crew members must have been dead. Careful to make certain my wake didn't tip the balance, I slid my P-47 close to the side of the B-17. As if passing a friend on the street, I gave a wave to the waist gunner. A quick wave back, then more hurried tossing of equipment, desperate to lighten the load.

Looking forward in the cockpit, the co-pilot grasping the control yoke with both arms. The ailerons were at maximum deflection, straining to hold the dead wing. The pilot was slumped backward, no worries for him. Slowly the B-17 lost altitude. Ever slower we crawled toward the Eider. After the Eider they could bail out or, if too low, the co-pilot could slide the B-17 into a barren flat field.

I gazed downward; under the bright clear sky, one large shadow bracketed by two smaller, their paths following the rises of the green and brown mosaic of pastures and fields, at times near or across miniature villages, each with their single exclamation point church steeple. Watching the progress of the shadows dehumanized the struggle a hundred feet from my wingtip.

After a several-mile wooded stretch, the shadows descended into a long, wide valley, then across a snaking river. On the eastern side small gray cotton balls appeared and then drifted away; smoke from artillery, Germans and Americans hammering each other; it was the Eider.

One of the gunners, the one who had been tossing out excess weight and had waved earlier, peeled back his oxygen mask. The weary bomber had mushed well below 10,000 feet, no need for oxygen. It had also mushed past the Eider; the crew knew they would live. Across the expanse of rushing air the gunner gave me a thumbs-up and a big grin. Probably like a thousand other grins he had flashed during his young life, the one to his dad when he slammed a well-hit ball over the center field fence, or the one for his girl when she told him how handsome he looked in his uniform. From under his flying cap short locks of red hair jerked in the wind. But the grin that was the essence of the young warrior's being this day.

To share the moment I slipped off my glove and gave the smiling gunner a thumbs-up. Then, as if to crushingly refute my gesture, as if to show who possessed all knowledge and power, the dead wing, the wing with the two dragging engines, dipped. But the dip did not stop. Over the B-17 rolled onto its back, the dirty, oil-stained underside of the cowlings an ugly prelude; then with nose bowed toward the earth, three or four tight spiraling turns, impact, explosion, a churning black cloud of smoke. Silence broken by Dewey keying his mic. "God save their souls"; nothing else said, only a curt call to the tower when we circled to land.

Italy had been a constant, a constant fear of death, a constant of men dying. England was whiplashes of sensory and emotional extremes. Deboned Dover sole presented on fine porcelain with a memorable bottle of white, followed by a musical at the St. James Theatre and a nightcap sherry. Two days later a bright, unblemished sky four miles above Nazi Germany with a front row seat to a theater of B-17s engulfed in flames; dark smoke abstracts against an infinite blue curtain, the final call for the dead and dying crews.

It was time. It was time to transfer, to transfer home. The month before I had exchanged thumbs-ups with the young gunner, I had reached my mission quota. I had voluntarily stayed; now I told the squadron commander I was ready for my transfer home. A few days for paperwork, a week to process, then my orders, thirty days' leave in the United States, then a training squadron in Michigan. I wrote to my parents, their Christmas present welcomed news that I would be shipping home by early January.

On Saturday, December 16th, all hell broke loose. The Germans executed a superbly orchestrated attack across the Allied front. Within twenty-four hours Americans were in retreat, unorganized retreat. The weather gods smiled on the Germans; most all of France and Belgium was blanketed by a solid overcast. No American aircraft could bolster our ground troops. With clear skies, our superior air cover would have saved the day. Kraut tanks and artillery would have been pounded impotent by fighters screaming down with 500- and 1,000-pounders. But it wasn't to be. The weather continued to comfort the Nazis through Christmas.

By the tenth day of the German offensive, the winds of fate shifted. Skies cleared, and our foot soldiers had regrouped and were counterattacking. But while the skies were clear over our forward bases in France and Belgium, most airfields were covered with snow and ice. P-47s and other fighters, with their high-torque engines, needed firm planting for their gear when taking off. Fighter squadrons in England were thrown into ground support. Three flights from my squadron were launched with 500-pound bombs, one shackled to each wing.

Dewey and I were assigned to orbit St. Hubert, west of Bastogne. Pilot officers assigned as observers with the forward ground troops could direct ground strikes by using a discrete radio frequency assigned each flight. Once over St. Hubert, Dewey and I orbited for close to an hour, waiting to be called if some Nazi tank or artillery unit needed pounding. Through the clear Plexiglas of my canopy the sun slowly drifted from behind my head, over my shoulder, directly in front, and then disappeared behind, each circular journey marking my aircraft's rotation around our holding point. Below solid white, God's snowy whitewash of man's desecration of His gift. Above, from horizon to horizon, unstained blue. I was suspended in a world of no blemish or sin; a baptismal font of Mother Earth herself. Soon I would be home, home with family, with my life, a new life. Then, from the boredom of long-ago midnight Masses, arose a scripture, a scripture of John: "I tell you the truth, no one can see the Kingdom of God unless he is born again."

I pulled the mic jack from the radio panel, my voice isolated to me and the perfect day. As the sun once again crossed my shoulder to my face I spoke:

> *I believe in the Holy Spirit*
> *the holy Catholic Church,*
> *the communion of saints,*
> *the forgiveness of sins,*
> *the resurrection of the body,*
> *and the life everlasting.*

A crackle of the radio. Our flight of two was directed to a point fifteen miles northeast of Bastogne. German artillery had our infantry under fire in a wooded killing field. Within a few quick minutes Dewey and I were circling the coordinates; no sign below of artillery. Finally Dewey called our target. To the west, in a forest, flashes and puffs of smoke, artillery shells exploding. Just over a mile away, on the edge of an open field, two Kraut artillery pieces, spitting smoke as shells were fired.

Dewey was in the lead, he took the first pass. Overflying the artillery he rolled inverted, then pulled down and around to a steep dive toward the puffing artillery. Suddenly from a quarter mile away globs of light arched toward Dewey: German antiaircraft, but they weren't leading Dewey enough. At 1,000 feet Dewey released and pulled up. Both bombs arched down, both bombs short of their target.

Dewey keyed his mic. "Sorry."

I keyed mine. "You buy the drinks tonight."

I retraced Dewey's overhead, rolled inverted, and pulled through, the artillery directly in front. Neutralized the controls—didn't want any lateral forces skewing the bombs. Down below 1,000 feet, I toggled the release and pulled up, four or five g's pushing down as I rounded from dive to climb. Across my wing, like glowing baseballs, Kraut antiaircraft shells. An explosion and flash. The port wing folded up and over the cockpit, jerked to a twisting roll to the left, centrifugal force holding me in a death grip as my P-47 plummeted. Quickly the windscreen filled with a spinning and rising earth, no sky. I spoke to Mother, words we both knew.

I have slipped the surly bonds of earth.

Put out my hand, and touched the face of God.

Warren

Milly's Sister

Child labor in America began with the earliest colonists who brought the practice from England. The tremendous expansion of American industry during the last half of the nineteenth century created a heightened demand for child labor. By 1900 it was estimated that 25 percent of factory and mill workers were children between the ages of ten and sixteen. These children were sought after as laborers because their size allowed them to move about in small spaces in factories and mines, they

were easy to manage and control, and, most important, children could be paid less than adults.

The conditions under which the children worked can best be measured by certain child labor reforms various states implemented in the 1880s; such reforms stipulated children under ten years of age couldn't work more than ten hours a day in a six-day workweek without their parents' permission . . . this was the reform.

A most cruel by-product of the sixty-hour work week for children was that it rendered the notion of obtaining an education a fantasy.

Because of the demand for child laborers, a bounty was placed on children. Factory owners and managers paid municipal workers consideration for bringing homeless children to them rather than to county or city homes for abandoned children. These children were given a blanket, a meager ration of food, and a machine to tend for ten to twelve hours a day.

The Triangle Shirtwaist Factory fire in 1911 spurned some sympathy for the overworked factory workers. A hundred and twenty women and children died in this fire; many because stairwell doors had been locked by the factory manager to assure that no unauthorized breaks were taken.

M OMMY AND POPPIE BROUGHT ME AND MY SISTER TO AMERica. I brought my doll Milly. She had button eyes. We went on a ship. The ship was big and made of metal. I ran after my sister in the sun. We watched the waves. We looked for big fish. We lived inside. Mommy helped me sew. Poppie helped me read and write. There were no windows. It smelled bad.

The ship came to a big city. We walked far. We walked to a tall building. It had many rooms. Our room was up many steps. There was one privy for everyone. It smelled bad.

Poppie went to work. Mommy went to work. I stayed with my sister. She got hot and wet. For many days she did not talk. She died. Mommy cried.

I talked to Milly. Milly was my new sister. She was never sick. She was never hungry. She was happy. Poppie and Mommy were not happy. Poppie did not come home. Mommy cried. We did not eat.

Mommy was gone one night. I talked to Milly. Milly loved me. Mommy came home. Mommy had food. We ate. Then we had no food. Mommy was gone many nights. Mommy did not come home. I talked to Milly. Milly loved me.

Big men with gold buttons took me. They took me to a new Poppie. He had many children. He was nice to me. He gave me food and a blanket. He let me keep Milly.

My new Poppie took me to a building. A big building. Many machines. I put thread in machines. They never stopped. Many children were with me. We moved fast. Men yelled at us. Milly sat under my machine. I talked to Milly. Milly loved me.

My new Poppie liked me. He gave me a new job. It was at the top of the building. I cut cloth. I cut the cloth for shirts. I cut it on a big table. Milly sat under the table. I talked to Milly. Milly loved me.

One day people yelled. They yelled fire. The doors would not open. Smoke filled the room. I sat under the table with Milly. I talked to Milly. Milly loved me.

They buried Milly with me.

Milly's Sister

Jack

From the founding of the first American Colonies in the early 1600s until the end of the Civil War, slavery was a most brittle national topic. While slavery was considered an abomination by a few of the drafters of the United States Constitution, their feelings were submerged in order to solicit the participation of Southern representatives to the Constitutional Convention of 1787.

By the 1850s the issue of slavery was at the forefront of national debates. Northern states leaned heavily toward the abolishment of slavery . . . for abolitionists it was a moral imperative. For Southern states slavery was an economic reality of the heaviest consequence. The commerce of the South survived and prospered on the backs of slaves. However, the plantation owners' defense of slavery was not just based on economics, but rather a contrived argument that Southern slaves lived a more content life than Northern laborers.

"The difference is that our slaves are hired for life and well compensated; there is no starvation, no begging, no want of employment, while those laborers in the North have to search for employment."

James H. Hammond
US Congressman
US Senator
Governor of South Carolina

In March 1857 no less than the Supreme Court of the United States ruled that slaves were not citizens, but merely owned property.

One year after the election of Abraham Lincoln in 1860, seven Southern states seceded from the Union to form the Confederate States of America. Then came the Civil War. A war that took the lives of over 550,000 Americans. The equivalent loss of life in today's America would be over five million.

This is the story of Jack, the son of a plantation owner, who joins the Confederate Army to defend the life of privilege he knows. After the defeat of the Confederacy, Jack is forced to reassess the South that he cherished.

IN THE FIRST KING CHARLES'S TIME, A WRITER ON GENTILITY asked, "A gentleman shoots, a gentleman hunts, a gentleman rides; for what is a gentleman but his pleasure?" And that was Clayton's Ride before the Northern War, at least for us young gallants: we worked like the devil, sometimes, but we played like the devil, always.

Then came the fall to earth; broken bones, broken fortune, broken family, broken future. No charge across country, just a hobble uphill, and with the ruins of the Ride on my back. How slowly I crawled, how close my face to the dirt; how I cursed when I thought of the glory days of the family estate.

But somewhere, somehow, in all of this I remembered something I learned at Harvard that stayed most deeply with me, which was Aristotle's observation that happiness is the proper employment of one's capacities. There grew within me not a pride in what I was carrying, not a sense of power rooted in rage, but an almost unwilling, certainly unsought-for, and above all astonished sense that all this toil to support a rabble of old, weary freed black men— as they seemed on bad days, until I remembered that Rebecca had loved them, which made it that bit easier—that all this sweat and frustration and disappointment were the fullest discharge of my capacities in all my life, more so even than when I was with my Confederate regiment; and, while only a philosopher could call this happiness, it had the fitness and rightness of winning the most agonizing and therefore most magnificent footrace.

Paul talks of having fought the good fight; I still think I did that, for four terrible years in Virginia. And he speaks of having kept the faith, which I did for thirty even more difficult years amidst the ruins of my youth. In the end, I only learned satisfaction—funny, that that was the word used by duelists—amidst the loss of all I had thought would satisfy me.

My earliest memory is of running headlong toward a great flaming shrubbery of brilliant flowers—rhododendrons, they must have been, they may still sprawl over what used to be the gardens at Clayton's Ride, now run to wilderness and woodiness. But when I was little, we had slaves to clip and graft them and bring out half a dozen swelling blooms on every stem—scarlet and cream and smoky blue and, as I recalled it, vivid lemon-yellow. But when I told my father this last, one evening when we were reminiscing over a fine brandy, he pulled up and asked me about that in strangely painful detail. And when I had finished telling him again about the big waxy lemon-colored flowers, he looked sadder than I had ever seen before. He asked whether this was all I could bring back to mind—just yellow petals? No silk? No warmth?—and then he told me that there are no lemon-colored rhododendrons, that what I remembered was my mother's dress of that color as she stood in the great thicket with her arms outspread to catch me.

To me it was but another patch of color in a world of play and noise; I have no memory at all of her; and it must have been only a few weeks later that my brothers came into this world and owing to a protracted labor and, perhaps, unsteady fingers on the umbilical cord, she was taken from my father. I do remember being lifted up and wept over, mostly against Aunt Hepsibah's huge black bosom. I had no idea why; but even as a child I did feel that there was something empty at the Ride. Father never looked at another woman, so the twins and I were little kings on the land.

Great-great-great Grandfather Jack Clayton had come along the coast to grow tobacco. The better story was that his grandfather had been an agent of the sinister "Tapski," Lord Shaftesbury, whose personal names, Ashley and Cooper, were given to the rivers that flow to Charleston "to form," as we used to say in youthful times, "the Atlantic Ocean." The other story, more likely the truth of the matter, was that he was the son of a simple lad from the Cotswolds of England—a simple lad, perhaps, but one of great ambition.

Great-great Grandfather learned about indigo. But Great-Grandfather saw the possibilities in cotton, and he helped make that crop king.

The Ride never lacked for money in those days, and we three boys, a little troop of which I was always captain, never lacked for the things we clamored for: ponies; then really fine horses; London guns (we knew how to shoot before we could read and were a danger only to our prey, never to each other or our guests or our hosts away from home); rods and creels, which we packed with rather a curious assortment of fish; little soldier uniforms—and when Scott and Taylor conquered Mexico, how down-in-the-mouth, how chagrined we felt not to be old enough for a real bloody war! Well, one learns.

As we grew up, we did the rounds of our neighbors' properties—and not just all the stuff and nonsense you hear about now, about balls and crinolines and duels. We heard Mr. Ruffin, who may have fired the first shot of the war that taught us what war was about, and who certainly shot himself when that war was over, speak brilliantly about reviving exhausted soil and developing a higher agriculture. We heard Mr. Calhoun speaking about the rights of the South in the voice of our archangel. We met Mr. Petigru, the strongest Union man in the state, but a great gentleman and a character of iron courage.

But, yes, there was a lot of dancing and riding point to point, and, frankly, playing at horseshoes. And I admit, I learned most of my technique from a fellow I could never beat: One-legged Mose, whom we kept on partly because it was our overseer's fault that the tree fell on him and partly because he was the best horseshoes tutor between Florida and Maryland, scandalize half the county though it did. If Chief Justice John Marshall, when he wasn't settling the Constitution of the United States, could judge horseshoe throws on his hands and knees with a straw between his teeth, why not us?

Of course, we were little gentlemen, so cotton money bought us tutors. We had no kind memories of them, but I like to think, even on the other side of the light, that they have worse memories of us. Mr. McTaggart, who taught us proper English and proper English manners, may recall a certain encounter with a billy goat in a locked icehouse. Getting him in there entailed more of a demanding education than anything he managed to teach us directly, because he was not stupid and was much on his guard.

But, of course, tutors are meant to prepare one for college. . . .

———— ❧❧❧ ————

I had always taken it for granted that I would attend the University of Virginia. The country around Charlottesville was splendid for hunting and the undergraduate body perhaps the most consistently constituted band of gentlemen of any learned body in the then Republic. Moreover, the university was founded by Mr. Jefferson—as he had ordered engraved on his tombstone—and the professors were much respected.

I had just told Hosey that he would be my body servant—and he was elated, for he had cut all the swathe he could between Graydon's Roost and the Chattahoochee—when my father laid it down that I would go to Harvard.

"But I'll spend four years among bluenosed Yankees!" I fumed.

"Then you will fully appreciate for the first time the red noses of my friends that you're always making shameful fun of, once you come back."

"They're malignant abolitionist fanatics!"

"Then you will get some truly overdue practice in standing up for our most cherished institutions."

So I went up by ship from Charleston—roads were still terrible, and the railroad was no closer to home than Columbia, even though we had a locomotive before the Yankees did; a foul stormy voyage, and we nearly foundered off Montauk. Still, we got there; and Mr. Peabody, who had fought alongside Father under Scott in Mexico—though both thought it an unwise war, endangering the Union with quarrels over who was to use the land—had his carriage waiting for me at the dock.

I dined and slept at his house on State Street, Hosey being put up, amidst a good deal of to-do, with the servants. Mr. Peabody himself was, I could see, more than a little taken aback, not to say distressed, at having a slave in the house—I suppose we had taken Hosey's status for granted and not mentioned it in our letters. In any event, Hosey was going back once I was settled in, for here he would surely be carried off by abolitionists and told he was free. That was another grievance about having to come to Harvard.

Next day Mr. Peabody took me to Cambridge in his carriage, and once I had found where I was to stay, I left Hosey to deal with my luggage while Mr. Peabody introduced me to President Walker, whom he had known since they bailed Noah's Ark together or something of that sort. Reverend Walker was courtesy itself, if a little aloof; I can only say that I am glad that I didn't find out for a long time that when the college had taken a black undergraduate a couple of years before and the other students threatened to leave, he had only said that if they did, he would see to it that the college's entire resources were dedicated to educating the boy. When first I heard of this (and, as I say, it took a while; all these high-minded people were too embarrassed to admit how it had showed them up) I was furious; then I was amused; and then I'll be damned if I didn't take my hat off to that grim old man. When those people stick to their principles, they're hard to beat. When they do.

So I got back from the president's house, wished Mr. Peabody heartfelt thanks, and hurried up a twisty Bay State staircase—one of the first things I missed were the broad, straight stairways Great-Grandfather put in when he rebuilt Clayton's Ride in the first cotton boom times—and came around the corner on as strange an apparition as I had ever seen.

Hosey had, no blame to him, got the big japanned trunk that we inherited from Uncle Bullough jammed in an awkward corner on those damnable twisty stairs. Give him a little time and his strong back—and he wasn't stupid, in a practical, fixing way—and he'd have heaved it up and around all right. But instead, whether helping him or hindering I was not able to tell, was someone, clearly a gentleman, in an enviable broadcloth coat, taking the weight, plus a lot of the five generations of dirt off the staircase wall, as Hosey heaved. Well, one can work with one's own fellow when the sulky has got a wheel into the ditch, but working with someone else's fellow, when you don't even know the owner? And that was how I met Oliver Sargent.

Oliver had more of a go-to-blazes look about him than most of those cod-chomping psalm singers had, a look as if he might really like a fight, and though back home that would have really got my tail feathers up, it's best not to start something on the other man's ground before you know your way around; so instead of asking what in damnation he was doing with my body servant, I simply introduced myself. He stood free of the portmanteau—whereupon Hosey got it up three whole stairs without breaking a sweat—passed his hand over his handkerchief, and shook hands, bidding me welcome and asking, probably going by my accent, whether I rode.

That ice broken, I soon learned the best stables to hire hacks and hunters anywhere in Cambridge, answered a delicate inquiry as to whether I enjoyed cards, and found myself asked with unforced cordiality—though Oliver had never fully taken his eyes off Hosey—to a wine next evening. I explained that I had to be in Boston next day, putting Hosey on the *Palmetto State* for home; whereupon Oliver's brow entirely cleared, for, as he later admitted, he intended to take advantage of our chat over sherry to explain that it would truly never do for a bondsman to be fetching and carrying under the sacred damp Massachusetts sun.

We set forth at once. Oliver walked me around Harvard Yard, showed me the library, the chapel, a very small and flea-bitten-looking band of Indians camping on the college grounds, and argued, shrewdly and amicably, about the proper length of stirrup for going over rough country; and when all was said and done, he said, with the air of one conferring a truly god-like favor, that I must come over to Beacon Hill that Saturday evening and meet his family. It irked me a little that he seemed to make such a suggestion like a command to dine and sleep at Windsor, but these people had a certain provincial pride of ancestry quite startling to those of the South, who received their land patents from good King Charles and came here of their own free will, and not because their affectedly pious ideas made old England too hot to hold 'em. Well, riches are next best to pedigrees, and heaven knows the Sargents had enough of both to enable them to look kings in the eye—"Their merchants are princes," says Isaiah.

But I am getting ahead of myself. That Saturday, Oliver drove us into Boston behind a very respectable pair of grays, and we went up into a grand enough house, though I for one cannot even now see how anyone of means can live only a walk apart from his neighbor. Even in those days, we could only see the smoke from Old Man Clement's house on the far side of Honeysuckle Hill, and if you went behind the stables at sunset, you might catch a flash from the Lowndes's windows, deep behind their great trees at Mischianza. Our finer Southern homes were, shall I say, clothed in fields and woodlands of a loose fit.

So I found myself being presented to an elegant-looking lady with the whitest hair I ever saw; very firm manners she had, so that, even if she readily volunteered opinions about political economy and the French emperor and a topic you can very readily guess at, she was still obviously a woman of fine breeding; and an old gentleman who was eating walnuts and seemed to have bitten on a real bad one, until it proved that this was his perpetual expression; but however sour his mouth, his eye was very straight and shrewd. There were a couple of lanky younger brothers, not much for speaking, and when they did not very interesting, but no vice to 'em, as Father used to say about his favorite tracking dogs; and three girls; or rather, two girls and Rebecca.

She had a name out of Walter Scott, and a touch of romance to match it. She wasn't tall like the boys—or like her sister Lucinda, whom you could have hammered into the shore at the mouth of Boston Harbor and hung a flag on—nor was she sober and given to good works like the other sister, Kerenhappuch—who was, Oliver later explained to me, shocked that I did not know one of Job's daughters, and who, I must say, looked as if she had suffered enough. The first thing I knew about Rebecca, just as she came into the drawing room, a tad late for having caught her crinoline on the banisters, was her laugh, and that has never left me.

Rebecca and my Harvard mate Oliver were certainly the two bright lights of that evening, not I, although I must say that, not having much to say in this new milieu, I accordingly learned a good deal. Thus, when Mrs. Sargent dispraised the European Powers for their treatment of China, it was greatly and instructively amusing to hear one of the younger boys burst out that "to hear this from Mother was a bit rich, considering that Great-grandfather. . ."—at which there was a clearing of the throats that I swear was the most startling noise I ever heard until the artillery at Gettysburg. Well, that, all unintended, gave so obvious a clue, despite or because of the awful silence that fell amidst Rebecca's attempts to restart conversation, that it was child's play to corner one of the sisters later— you may guess which one. And lo and behold, yes, the family fortune did indeed largely begin with whole schoonersful of opium shipped into Canton. Now *there* was an arrow in my quiver to deal with friend Oliver when he got too high and mighty.

I've no time fully to record those hurrying university years, except to note two matters that now seem, in retrospect, freighted with significance. I rode very rarely unaccompanied by the Sargents, and they showed me their textile mills, from which derived the main part of their mighty fortune. Very imposing and formidable they stood and stand, making anything in the South pale by comparison, and I have to admit they had housed the mill girls very well, with decent dormitories and their own adequate pantry.

But anything good will encounter competition, and times were growing harder and harder at the company—for the mill girls, anyway, though somehow the Sargents seemed no poorer. My friend Miss Sargent—I might, as you may guess, say more than that—was much distressed, and harried her brother with every patch on some worker girl's clothes, every fallen-in cheek and exhausted stoop. It was during one of their exchanges I learned they had the wherewithal to ship unmentionables under their flag because earlier they had traded stranger cargoes yet. I was never able to prove that we Claytons bought from Sargent ships at the

Long Wharf, but I swear that they descend from the Boston ship-master in the chantey:

> *O Captain Ball was a Yankee slaver,*
> *Blow, boys, blow.*
> *He traded in niggers and loved his Savior,*
> *Blow, my bully boys, blow.*

To be fair, Oliver looked quite pained and told me how much they gave to missionaries in Africa and freed slaves in Liberia.

Perhaps that gave me another lever against Master Oliver, though I didn't use it lest I be forbidden the house on Beacon Street, for my feelings, and hers, were not to be denied, and everyone knew how it would come out. Though her mother and her father alike were hor-rified, I give them their New England due that they let her make her choice—as I don't think my father would have done, had any sister of mine fallen in love with an abolitionist.

In 1857, the year Mr. Buchanan became president and we in the South felt that the world was ours—a Northern president utterly bent to our views with Lancashire mills buying every bale we could grow—cotton was king indeed. But then some big insur-ance company failed in Cincinnati and ruin spread eastward.

The Sargents rode out the storm—nothing could sink those iron folk—but half their workers didn't. There were pitiful sights along the road to Lowell. I made myself pretty vocal with what would be said if we treated our people in hard times the way the holy Sargents did theirs. Several of us, not the Sargents, went out there with our pockets full of silver several times a month; but Oliver said they were free to contract where they wished, endowed with liberty, and the sooner they understood the laws of political economics the better for all concerned. He boasted that his father treated his workers as independent adults with a respect that no one who "bartered in lash-cut flesh" could understand, let alone be a sincere Christian.

I resented this, as you might expect, spoke a few choice words, and shoved him hard, whereupon he used the muscles that had assisted my trunk upstairs to pitch me downstairs. We had it out, more or less, and got back to being friends again—or better, man to man, if not North to South; for I think we both could see that one day we must have it out army to army, if not pistol to pistol, just as Mr. Calhoun feared. And I admit I was fearful that *someone* would find out that I had called her brother an uncharitable hypocrite and punched him, and he was, if anything, more afraid that she would find out that he had sent me rolling into the Yard; so I went around in bandages from my "riding accident."

I had expected the years in Cambridge to each have more than twelve months, but of course they swept us along as they always do unless one is in pain, danger, or suspense, of which conditions I was soon to have considerable experience. And then, in spite of a couple of scrapes, at races and in episodes with Yankee ranters whom even Oliver wouldn't stand up for as gentlemen, I more or less got through. Once home, I somehow found myself creating important reasons to return to Boston. Father entirely approved; he was very afraid of looming trouble and wanted to be as well-informed as possible. While home I hunted with my brothers and chatted over wine at Clayton's Ride and at all the neighbors' plantations, heartily glad to be back among plainspoken gentlefolk, red-nosed or not, who laid down truths and spoke to the point.

Grim old Senator Hammond stayed with us during one particular visit by Oliver. He and Oliver at first found mutual intellectual enjoyment; then the senator delivered a magnificent, soaring soliloquy while we enjoyed after-dinner ports. I later learned he had given it in Congress, the first pure and open defense of slavery ever delivered there, that slavery was no evil, rather Providence's greatest blessing upon the South, enabling it to raise the highest-toned, purest, best-organized society to have existed on Earth, an aristocracy of talent, virtue, generosity, and courage, nurtured by republican openness to rule its natural inferiors with justice and humanity. I could see Sargent's hands clenching and unclenching in his lap, and if the senator had not been his father's age, he might have taken advantage of our special ways of honorably asserting our beliefs. But he swallowed, and the topic passed off in an explosion of laughter about the long-armed apelike Lincoln, who was just beginning to be heard about in the South.

On the kitchen porch the following morning, overlooking the western fields of soon-to-be-picked fluffy white coins, Oliver asked how I could tolerate Hammond's thoughts; thoughts that crushed human dignities for no greater crime than excess pigment. I took a few moments to distill my response to fact, not conjecture. I pointed to cabins, the roofs barely visible over a rise. A dozen or more small ones with rooflines as level and true as the ocean's horizon, and then two larger cabins, over twice the size of the others, both with roofs decidedly swaybacked. With Oliver looking as if he wanted to challenge me to a duel, I explained that two of our slave families had asked if they could move to larger cabins if they built them on their own time—larger than the ones that were provided by my father's father. Permission granted. When the first was built, to make less their effort, no foundation of river rock was laid. The cabin was built on earth, earth that settled and moved with spring rains and winter freezes. Two years after the first one was built, another was built just as before, even though they had seen that building on earth was only good for a year at most. Blacks were not the same as us, I concluded.

Oliver shook his head. "They humbly request a larger hovel, and you require them to labor when already exhausted from serving you all day, as if granting them a king's favor. Then you wonder why they take little pride in a house they do not own?" He turned and walked quickly away.

I put Oliver on the boat a few days later; he looked me in the eye, thanked me with obvious sincerity for all our hospitality, then said, "I still cannot believe that a man of your. . ." pulled himself up—he clearly still considered himself our guest—muttered, "Oh well, see you in the autumn," and clumped on board.

Yes, we did see one another that autumn, the last autumn of our youth, of so many others' lives, of so many fast, hard choices. For this was the autumn of 1860, and the Democratic Party, true party of the white man and national compromise, tore itself apart at Charleston, and Mister Lincoln, we Southerners lamented, came gibbering out of the trees into the White House.

I paid my last "business" visit to Boston, and got married, in pretty close order, and by springtime was drilling my baby-faced militiamen to scatter the cowardly Yankees. Of course, I was baby-faced too, but we all grew up fast enough, all except the ones who died.

But I don't think I was ever in a worse battle with Yankees than when I proposed to Rebecca. Oliver himself kept quiet, I thought then because he felt embarrassed and responsible, but Rebecca later made me see that he was entirely on our side, only knowing that if he came out for us it would be the last straw for the old man, and Rebecca would be shut in her room until I had sailed. In the end old Sargent conceded, although in a rage—"But not a penny in dowry or settlement to underwrite your iniquities!"

"Sir," I replied gravely, "I would not contemplate money wrung from one of those pitiful girls who died in the alleys two winters ago." I'm glad I didn't say "we," that might have cooked the goose, but I knew that Rebecca was as firm as I. Of course, she was certain she could turn me from my way of seeing things. . . .

So we were married in Old North Church, with every lady in Boston showing her breeding by her face of horror; went to the cheapest, grimmest reception I have ever attended; and took ship. It was on the dock that Oliver spoke to me alone. "Bad times," he said, then flushed and added, "For the country, not for you."

"For our countries," I said with some emphasis—for South Carolina had been first to secede, though it was then the only state to have done so. "Grave difficulty now, but soon lasting peace."

And, trying to put a laughing face on it, "The mills will have to make so many uniforms their bobbins will break—that is, if your Mr. Lincoln isn't the poltroon he pretty clearly seems to be." True words—there were to be a great many Yankee uniforms.

We looked hard at each other and saw the impasse meant war indeed. We were both young and healthy, and born to be leaders, and absolutely persuaded of our respective causes. And we were to each other as good a friend as either was ever likely to meet. This would, indeed, be a brothers' war. It was as if we heard the screaming and smelled the blood we would soak up for the next four years.

We—a very different "we"—got back to Clayton's Ride, and everyone for thirty miles around fêted us and put us up and held cotillions for us. I wanted to write Sargent to tell him how welcomed Rebecca was by my South. How it made no matter that she was a Boston Yankee. How the South, my friends, saw the person, not the wrapper. To let him know any local society of the South held more of gentlemen and ladies than could be found among his blue-nosed, eyes to the sky, wealth-worshipping friends and relatives. But I didn't. I didn't because Rebecca told me that I should not. And asked me, with a knowing smile, was I most pleased that she was in the South or that I was not in the North? I smiled and replied with a warm kiss. Later, in silence, I considered her question.

When Rebecca wasn't softening Clayton's Ride—in twenty years of men only it was, perhaps, threadbare and blandly utilitarian to her soft blue eyes—she was flitting about those cabins, the cave-like cabins, and coming back with lists of improvements: mats to cover the dirt floors, clothes for their children. Father paid for all of them, because he loved her too and was set on her being happy. She begged the biggest rogues in the plantation off punishment and—this was the talk of three counties—well, let me explain. . . .

Old Colonel Heth at Cowpens Hall was truly a brave man, but never so much as at horserace meetings, for he liked to bet deep, though he could barely tell one end of a thoroughbred from another, and Father, with a shrewd eye, gladly covered him—not to hurt him, but because he loved to be proved a good judge of horseflesh; and, I admit it, we had eighty-something slaves all told, and Father longed to see a hundred at work. The Colonel fancied Buena Vista, a spavined brute if ever I saw one, and Father's muscle-rippled Windermere swept him away. Of course the Colonel couldn't cover his stake, not in coin, but coin was not what Father wanted.

We were all ready to take delivery of the new hands, when Rebecca rode over with me when I was settling the last details and heard the wailing. Good Lord—it wasn't that we were actually splitting up families, but I suppose we were separating sisters and uncles and whatever, and it was all very messy; but what took everyone aback was that Rebecca put Father and old Heth together, and instead of the hands she got old Heth to lease a third of his land and labor to Father for a dollar a year—very profitably, I must say, don't talk figures with a New Englander. She had a way with her, Rebecca.

Then the war . . . and not the war games my brothers and I had played. As children soldiers only half as tall as a man, when one was shot, there was no report of powder and lead, but a yelled "Pow!" and a compliant and silent fall to the ground, all so neat and tidy. Tired of our skirmishes a curt yell to a house servant—lemon water would be quite pleasant. But no make-believe battles for our South. Near the end of the Petersburg siege, a young fellow, maybe fifteen or so, walked past me from the front, his alabaster skin covered with bloody grays. No weapons, but his arms were full: he cradled his intestines as if carrying a bushel of wash. Later the same day, a captain I slightly knew, from Mayesville I recall, was leaning against a stone wall during a pause in the shelling, this officer singing in a soft voice of bluebirds and little girls. When I drew near I could see flies dining; from the top over one ear to his crown, no skull, just brain.

Not much else to say about war, just that it resembled growing old at full gallop—the endless deaths of friends, the continuous likelihood of one's own demise, the chipping away of powers one took for granted until the ordeal struck. Never again did I outrun children to the crest of Luttrell's Hill—the ball lodged next to my shin at Gaines Mill would have seen to that, even without the shell splinter at Suffolk. That burst didn't take my head off, as I thought it might, but it did shatter my leg.

It was after Sharpsburg—or Antietam, as the war's victors commended it to history—with sparse rations, that I ate, gagged, my first horsemeat, repugnant to taste, repugnant to mind. Two years later, with my skin stretched taut over bone, the smallest slice of stallion or mare was most craved for. My father a fine judge of horses, his filthy and spent son a connoisseur of their meat. My South, my dear South.

In time I was told the tale, while my regiment was detached with Longstreet to Suffolk, of how my brothers took part in the glorious victory at Chancellorsville. Derided early in the war as the Pound Cake Regiment, owing to their initial posting in Charleston Harbor, that designation was already long obsolete by the time the South Carolina First Regiment Rifles filled the railroad cut at Second Manassas. My brothers rushed the Yankee line at Chancellorsville, beckoning their men on, and breached the human wall; and though they gave a good account of themselves indeed when they got there, Joseph Hooker's men fought like demons, the ones who held, because they knew so many of their comrades had been routed, and it was their lot to try to save the bluecoat army from complete disaster. So that was the last hill that Joe and Harry would ever climb, and there they lie, brave boys, there their bodies lie. A small comfort, but a comfort no less, that the great Roman centurion Stonewall Jackson marched with them from Chancellorsville to heaven's gate. No comfort at all to find the Yankees swarming back over that same hallowed ground, over their graves, a year later in the Battle of the Wilderness.

It was like that from the first: courage, yes, and glory and victories, but only with bloody losses, losses, losses. Father put all our loose money into Confederate States bonds—"an investment in victory"; the paper kept Black Sally and her new baby warm, the bonds and our bales of shinplaster dollars, for an hour or so on a bad winter's night in '64. The baby died anyway. Then the blockade choked off our trade with Europe, and cotton rotted in the warehouses.

Father broke his neck on an unmaintained road—riding to sit in the Congress at Richmond. Perhaps, I thought at the time, God's blessing; no need for him to see Northern maggots feasting on the carcass. I inherited the plantation; same as inheriting an ingot of lead when swimming from a shipwreck. I'd heard people opine that such were the responsibilities of our class, that the gentry were more the slaves of their slaves than the other way around: mock-self-pity over the Madeira in good times, stark horrid truth in times when holding slaves could only be maintained by seemingly endless war.

Although that great fraud of national humanity, Lincoln, had proclaimed all slaves in our territory to be free, Hosey was by me throughout the war, though never, of course, bearing arms. He had opportunities to slink away in many a bloody retreat or madhouse confusion. And when those Wisconsin boys turned that battery on us at Suffolk, he could have bolted off or shammed dead till the Yankees came; but he got me over his shoulder like a portmanteau on a Harvard staircase, though I was screaming and cursing him, it hurt so. My poor old horse lay dead where I'd been lying—marking the spot until, moments later, it erupted into fragments by a shell. I often wondered if it wasn't my damned bad luck that Hosey didn't run away and leave me to a clean death beside my mount. But he didn't. He worried for me. This I couldn't bring myself to reconcile; I was a master and he a slave. Then I came to understand, my life was not spared for me. My life spared as a present to

Rebecca; for her Hosey, and all his troop of blacks, wished only good, as she wished them.

So we were losing—the war, and our money, and our hopes, and our brothers, and then Rebecca.

She'd been sacrificing, far more than I knew. Brick, the house servant, said that she had fooled him; she ordered good meals and then sneaked them in baskets to old Mrs. Johnson, who really was frail, and to neighbors who had been no worse wounded than I. Brick was a good house manager; he managed for himself; he didn't lose an ounce over the whole war. Food, not Rebecca, was his mistress.

As for the pains of war, and the pains that racked my body, and the far worse pain I would know at seeing my Rebecca fade to a ghost haunting the house she had come so to love, there began another pain gnawing, mounting inside my soul. Our system, our society was not bringing victory. A British officer I had met—Colonel Fremantle of Her Majesty's Brigade of Guards, by heavens, stiff as a ramrod though he never knew it, pleasant enough gentleman when we forgot who he was—who was watching the war from up a tree he climbed at Gettysburg, told me that the English Aristocracy was for us to a man and they loathed the Yankees, but couldn't bring themselves to fight for a slave power, which they found unchristian. In time I climbed the same tree, with the same view, so to speak, as had the good Colonel Fremantle. But before I did, more Southern blood poured on fields of hope, blood necessary to bring our crop of assumed destiny to full growth, only to be cut down by Yankee sickles.

But my mind did not surrender. Neither did my mind's South.

And born from this South the most magnificent human creature ever to lead an army, General Robert E. Lee. Yet we were losing. We were losing to this man, Lincoln, who hated every moment of conflict, every man he sent to his death, every enemy he left to rot in a hospital, every sleeping sentry he had to refuse to pardon and leave to be shot. He had none of General Lee's great-noble-man, high-chivalric love of putting matter to the ultimate test. He saw deeper than the generals he had to discard. He hated it all; he only did for the greatness beyond, greatness that he would never see, could never see. Lincoln was doing better in his misery and ungainliness than Davis and Lee in their shining genius. Perhaps he did so because he hated it, and felt compelled to look deeper. But he was not just a worthy enemy in the end; he was a man not just fit, but right, to be defeated by.

Even the sharp pain of wounds did not draw me from the unthinkable; was the South's cause not a noble cause? Lying awake on the edge of delirium, in what we called a hospital, in fact a barn, with my leg now threatened with amputation, my mind kept returning to the same thing—perhaps because just the week before we'd been arguing with a captured Union officer that the Constitution gave us the complete right to secede. I pondered how the Founders never dared use the words "slave" or "slavery" in the Constitution. Were they ashamed of it, just as Yankees were of the original roots of their wealth? General Washington had not liked slavery and wrote to friends, following the war, that "Among my first wishes is to see some plan adopted, by which slavery in this Country may be abolished by slow, sure and imperceptible degrees." Mr. Jefferson had said that he trembled for his country when he reflected that God was just. General Lee, a hidden abolitionist, did not conceal that he had no love for slavery, that he was fighting for Virginia, not for the human bondage that the vice president had said was our country's cornerstone. And it was a cornerstone, and more: it was the foundation of the South. A magnificent South.

But there was a war to be fought—if only because so many of us had died to win it. If I were to have any prospect of keeping my leg and returning to fight, to paraphrase Falstaff, I had better exercise discretion in the service of valor. I reckoned my wounds would fare better with Mischianza's old Doc Marion than under the tender mercies of the beleaguered army sawyers. And there was a deeper consideration. Rebecca's letters, her hand, had grown so shaky that it was unnerving. I had a word with my divisional adjutant, who requisitioned a wagon too flimsy to be missed, and Hosey hitched our poor horses and hauled me south, as cargo, moaning on my back. For two hard weeks Hosey cared for me as Aunt Hepsibah had done two decades before. By Raleigh, I could manage to sit. By the time we attained the Ride, I could stand, if not much more than that. I thought myself tired, tired to the bone—but that was before I went up to Rebecca.

War teaches many fundamentals: one look, and I knew that I was only just in time, and I could see that she knew as well. So at least we didn't have to say it aloud; I just sat on the bed and we talked of what had happened, and who was left, and how brave everyone had been. But I knew well enough what she would have to say, and in the end she came up with it:

"Jack, let them go."

And I had to say I could not. The Ride had its part to play, however poor, in keeping the war going; and where were they to go, especially the old ones, and the brats, who were thin and wheezy? No, it was better that they stay, and so they needed to have a master. Poor Rebecca had no spirit to sway me. A few brief days and nights together, whispered tender words, and it was over.

I will not write of the black time between Rebecca departing and my love's stark burial, other than to say I leaned heavily on Hosey with my grief; no brothers, no father, I had no one to mitigate.

It was the last hours of the war, and the country was starving. By "the country," I don't mean the Yankees' bloated Union, but rather the Confederate States of America, which in four brief but magnificent years raised itself to a cause unsurpassed in the record of human sacrifice. But sacrifice, yes—that was the very point. You saw maids in Richmond with arms like rods protruding out of ragged clothing, and their mistresses weren't much better. Good men were pulling out and going home—not just the weaker brethren, but some of our best—because their babies were dying of influenza on top of hunger and their wives couldn't keep up a pretense that things were all right in the face of the misery of the children.

You felt sick to see the Provost Marshal after fellows like that. I never did actually see one of our beaten-down starving men appear before a court-martial, although there were people who believed that shooting a few would put spirit into the others. There was death before us and death behind us in those darkening months. For we were a dying dragon. Individually, we were still its deadly sharp teeth and claws; but the fire was burning out in our great beast's belly. We could scratch deep but not strike through muscle or bone. Our armoring scales were falling off, leaving us and ours—poor worn-out women, two-year-old mites with the faces of old men—slow-marching toward death while we soldiers at least had the chance of a quick shot to end it all.

In that summer of 1864, agonizing while hearing news of North Anna and Cold Harbor, I received one bleak official assignment. While we couldn't feed ourselves, one commodity we had in abundance was Yankee prisoners—trophies of our first three glorious years, but now just a drain on our pitifully thin supplies. Some we "galvanized"—recruited into our army—and some of those were to prove pretty darn good, others, of course, going over the hill at first opportunity. But most just sat there eating our scanty food, drawing down our declining number to guard them. They piled up in their starving, unsanitary crowded camps—well, they had surrendered, not us, and our children were getting no better than they, and they were dying even faster. You knew this intellectually, but you thought of it as like battlefield deaths, each side taking its chances. Six thousand died in one North Carolina pen. But as God is my witness, we weren't killing them. We couldn't get the food for them, we didn't have the timber to build them shelters. All very grimly logical. But I still didn't know how that passed from facts on paper to cold, slow horror in life.

After we could no longer hold captives securely in Richmond, and regular prisoner exchanges with the Yankees had broken down, we moved an army-sized mass of bluecoats—at least that's what they had been wearing when they were captured—to an insignificant place in Georgia called Andersonville, where there weren't even enough civilians to supplement the guards to working efficiency. And to make things finally worse, since any man of competence and character was needed at the front, they'd put in charge a Swiss soldier of fortune called Wirz, a man I wouldn't have assigned to shovel horse droppings. And as the saying goes, no money, no Swiss.

I was tasked there from the Ride to see if a thousand prisoners could be assembled for a trade, a swap with the North for some of our captured men, so desperate were we for any man or boy to take up arms. I made a week's trek before riding through the gates of Andersonville on my sad spotted nag, to the indifferent courtesies of a demoralized guard, into the silent stench of living death.

Almost silent. A few voices were yelling with a mechanical brutality. Captain Wirz could not feed his prisoners or keep them clean, but he could set up deadlines and punishment schedules. He presided over a host of skeletons, too wasted to support the weight of their shirts, too parched to lift a cupped palm. He was the only man the Union formally put to death when all was over, when, in fairness to the Yankees, many howled that we should all be hanged as traitors. And the ravages I saw in Wirz's Andersonville haunted my dreams to my dying day.

You ask why? Did I give a care for Yankees? Would I have passed up a chance to shell them down "like demolishing a wall," as Mr. Ruskin said to the Woolwich Military College cadets, panting for glory in some future war? No indeed. But there is something deep within us that we ourselves do not know, cannot know, cannot grasp in others, but whose existence presses upon us, if only to tell us that the world is not empty—that life *lives*. Andersonville trampled men into life's deepest nightmare, impossible to awaken from. And it trampled me, because this was the South; but not the South of my mind.

No trades of men with Yankees; we had nothing to barter.

So there I was again in Virginia in the fall of '64 with my regiment—an ever fewer and more tattered regiment, but you should have seen their spirit—hammering at the Army of the Potomac as it pushed us slowly back around Richmond. As always, at Darbytown Road, and at Strawberry Plains, we killed more of them than they of us, but they always had still more, many more in reserve—and they had more munitions, horses, and—ever more important—more food. A regimental commander, which I was by now—because Haskell and Whitrow had been given brigades, and we had left Kaine in a wood at North Anna and Drew in the mud at Yellow Tavern—spent far more time thinking about corn, no matter how dried up in the fields (and, the next year, no matter how green) than about Sheridan's cavalry.

On the afternoon of April 9, 1865—a date seared on my very soul—I was sleeping, if you can call it that, where I stood, leaning against a white oak, where I had slumped, wearing grays more brown from months of mud, blood, and other intimacies of our gruesome war. We were just west of Farmville, where we'd engaged the Yankees in yet another holding action just two days before. Awakened by a soldier with a message. It was over, the war was over. By dusk a written communication from above: General Lee, our savior, surrendered at a place called Appomattox, until that moment nothing more to me than a crossroads on my field map, on our projected route to relative safety in Lynchburg. Just as sudden as a shot to the head, it was over. We were told to take our horses home, use them to plow—at the moment an empty gesture, but spring plantings saved a few good babies. Justice where justice is due.

What of the Ride? Was it as so many others, brick chimneys rising from a mountain of ash; a mountain of ash attesting to the black souls of that army of Northern invaders? I dreaded what I might find, but Hosey and I rode hard, only stopping to keep our horses from dropping. Still it was close to a full week's journey from the tree where I learned the vile truth, to riding into view of Clayton's Ride. Only despair greeted me. No assets, only liabilities, liabilities with deep-set eyes of hunger. Something else, a letter— not a letter, but an envelope, from Mrs. Sargent. Months before I had written Rebecca's parents, choosing each phrase, each word with the utmost care, trying somehow to make sense of it all, of Rebecca's passing. With my letter to them I'd enclosed a letter to Oliver; I asked that they forward it to him or if, perhaps, he might be at home, they pass it to him.

In the envelope I found only the letter I had posted to Oliver, across it written in large letters "deceased," and then a single sentence scrawled in the script of a woman, a plea to God: "Your South has killed our daughter and our son, God damn you and your South." A plea to God not necessary, her wish already fulfilled.

It was a ruined land, but they had dealt fairly lightly with the Ride—they were in a great hurry to push north toward John- ston's army—we had nevertheless been cleaned out of provisions from cellar to attic, and our cotton gins were smashed, and all the footloose people had gone off with the Yankee column; and I must say that I was so exhausted that I was almost relieved that such possible trouble had walked off.

With Hosey at my side, we took stock of what was left. There would be precious little crop come the fall, even if we had someone to sell it to; most of our sheds and barns and stables were wrecked or burned, some out of malice, more from tired, frightened men drinking and smoking and knowing they'd be moving on to risk getting killed tomorrow—I'd seen enough of that on our side. We had some timber, but the choice had to be made between firewood now or some pathetic bit of money to help rebuild.

I went into what we still called the ballroom, and they were waiting for me. Even Hosey drew in his breath behind me.

They were gaunt—gaunt like an army of bitter cadavers come out of the grave, and ragged, more ragged than the poorest pickaninny's doll; and sores and scabs showed through the tatters. They were gazing at me with eyes that I had never seen, and with more than hunger in their eyes. But not, I think, with hatred. Reproach, yes. Impatience, in some eyes. And it almost seemed that they were looking at me from an equal height. Some were even sitting on the great staircase, and not even Brick or Hosey could find it in himself to shoo them away.

I had not expected this meeting, but the facts were the same to whomever I should tell. I told them that, for those who wished to leave, I would give them my heartfelt wishes for good fortune wherever they might choose to go. Frankly, I would have been glad to see as many depart as possible. A cold prospect chilled the chilly room. Famine might yet grip the Ride, I thought. I told them I would set out a table of rations with Brick. Then a moment of strangeness. I thanked them for their diligent labor; startled myself that I had done so. Perhaps from the habit of thanking my soldiers, merely a mistake of habit.

And so I was not just a temporary insolvent, but a ruined man. More particularly, what ten years before would have been the Ride's most substantial assets, the people of any plantation, had been sieved down to grievous liabilities. We had fought to keep them; now the ones who had not put themselves on the road, the least valuable by commercial reckoning—though I must say I loved many of the rascals—were hangers-on of a broken enterprise. To keep going would be deeper ruin yet. But I thought of Rebecca, and I thought of my life. Born into comfort. Born to be a gentleman. But nothing now. Father gone, sweet Rebecca no longer, no children, no brothers; Clayton not a legacy of name, but perhaps a legacy of action to come. Rebecca's deathbed request I did not grant, "Let them go." Now I would struggle my best for them. I would not cast those whom we had made helplessly dependent into a harsh world of independency. To drive them out would be murder.

That first evening at the Ride, Hosey came to me, came out to the far fields where I was watching hard-shelled beetles dine on my meager future, wondering if perhaps they were Northern bugs seeking retribution; of course they were, everyone would soon be clawing for their share of the little meat still embedded in the crevices and shards of our broken Southern bones. Cast down with a weight of some unknown sorrow, Hosey's eyes did not meet mine. No tears, within him a barrier rigid against his bare emotion. Gasping for air, he told me that Reverend Rolt was on my verandah, that I was to see him quick; then with his voice breaking as the last breath of a dying man, Hosey said that the Reverend demanded to tell me of some grand event. For whatever reason, perhaps because of the hurt that was certainly twisting within him, I didn't question what news could be of boiling import. So I walked the half-mile—I hobbled the half-mile—back to the Ride wondering what occurrence would be of consequence to the wasteland of rubble that was now our Southern states.

With a grin and a pace more of a run Rolt closed the last fifty yards when he saw me approach. Lincoln was dead. Shot by a Southern hero, shot to claim the South's rightful revenge. Those were the Godly Reverend Rolt's declarations, not mine.

Yes, Lincoln was misguided, certainly to my mind when I hotly and publicly debated Sargent and his band of Harvard intellects dripping with obnoxious rightness and obstinate hypocrisy. And, yes, I would have sighed a smile of relief if Lincoln had been mortally wounded by one of General Early's eagle-eyed sharpshooters when he came under fire inspecting Union troops at Fort Stevens. But now, mercifully, the long struggle was over; a war of four years and half a million troops killed. Not troops, let us not soften the carnage, over half a million sons with mothers, and husbands with wives; across the Confederate and Union landscape millions of pillows wet with tears of heartbreak.

No, no soldier who had trudged and crawled on battlefields damp with blood, battlefields with a bountiful crop of ripped fragments of God's greatest gift, no soldier who had witnessed such a scene, no soldier who still clung to the belief, the hope, that men who had been dragged through the furnace of hell could still possess a soul, no such soldier could take felicity in any man's death once the truce had been made. I was such a soldier.

The question was not whether the Ride could somehow prosper with the coming years, but whether it would become some sort of morgue within the coming weeks. I put as good a face on it as I could, if only to keep up credit with the tradesmen from whom we had to buy the tools necessary just to start recovery. But that would not be enough, and though the Freedmen's Bureau imposed by the conquering government actually showed some energy and enterprise, higher wisdom had placed its nearest office a very great distance away, and anyway it was stretched to the utmost.

But then there befell a piece of luck of a kind that I could not have thought to imagine, from a direction entirely outside my thinking.

One day, a captain of the occupying army appeared to present himself with a card from the local commander, a remarkable man, I admit it, called Galusha Pennypacker. He had been a major general of volunteers before he was old enough to vote. After a long convalescence from a wound in early '65, he had transferred to the regular army to oppress us. Well, that may be ungracious to a well-meaning man, and if the Ride had a roof on it, it was his doing.

Pennypacker had a reputation for courtesy and as much fair dealing as you would expect from a Quaker, or actually rather more; though the youngest general in America he was a devout birthright Friend. He had commanded the force we had been attacking along Darbytown Road, was writing an account of his division's actions before memory faded, spoke very warmly of my men's courage and resolution, and asked if he might come over to pay his respects "to a distinguished fellow citizen, no longer an enemy." Well, it would have been ungentlemanly to brush off an admittedly brave and able brother officer; and so I wrote that he might come.

He galloped up without an escort, only an orderly, quite the man of breeding paying a private call. We spoke first in the colonnade; but in due course I needed to consult some papers, and despite his protestations, limped inside, him following. No sooner than we were out of the sun, he stopped.

"But your portraits!" he said.

Well, yes—Grandfather, Great-Grandfather, even Great-Great-Grandfather had set great store by the fine points of such things; for me the old faces were just part of the family, impossible not to imagine on the walls, but not a matter for connoisseur-like discussion. He could see that I was somewhat annoyed—going to patronize our beds next, I supposed—and went along to my study to talk about mighty Stonewall. But somehow things came out, talking to him—he was a man of magical sympathy—and so I told him, through my teeth, of our descent to destruction.

Now, if finding that out was difficult, how was it that with perfect tact he put it to me that there were people in the North who would pay excellent money for my faded ancestors' smoke-marked features— "Copleys, were they? The Sullys I surely know, for I can remember Mr. Sully coming up from Charleston to paint us boys when we were small, and he'd done Father and Mother already.

"The merest letter to a friend . . ." said Pennypacker. And he wrote it, and this fellow came down from New York, and what he offered quite took my breath away. Some fetched more than they likely cost to be painted. It was like driving children into the snow, seeing those protecting house-gods of the family being boxed up for sharepushers and worse out of the Manhattan thoroughfares, but needs must. If what I heard was true, that they were passed off as blood ancestors by the Astors and Drews and Vanderbilts, then I sold my own flesh for dirt. But at least the dirt was put for the crops again.

But more to the point, this Yankee from Pennsylvania saw our silver, and it was like Pizarro seeing the Inca treasure—and that's what got us over the hump. We had to eat with horn spoons for five years, but all those crooked war profiteers paid excellently for two hundred years of our plate. And again it was Hosey, it was his warning, his insistence—if a slave can insist—that two years before the Ride's silver was laid in a great oak chest of Grandmother's and buried under the chicken coop . . . lest our silver trays and goblets fill the saddlebags of Union troops.

Everyone has a use in this world, my godmother used to tell me. Pennypacker's enterprising eye saw us through the storms of peace in which so many foundered. We hacked away at the ruined fields, found brokers for our cotton—though not on such good terms as before the war, because the Yankee blockade got people growing cotton in Egypt and India—and did much patching and repairing. We had epidemics, of course, and many died, the young and old, because there was no medicine; at least Rebecca didn't see that. But not one of our people died of want or cold, and, rather to the horror of several neighbors I need not name, I started a school for the blacks.

I can hear my Harvard classmates hooting, but really it didn't take much to teach what children need to know back then: basic figuring, the Bible, signing their names. People like old Zackary Graystone, our long retired rector, were appalled, however hard he had worked for these people as Christian souls: the sons of Ham were to be our bondservants and need not learn such things above their station for that. Had not God seen to it that they were delivered here? I told him that between '61 and '65 I'd seen enough of God's judgment to know that it pointed both ways, like a rifle. So what we saved in the '68 crop was devoted to books and school. In time, all could read and write and perform simple sums.

Three hard years, but each year better . . . less harsh . . . than the last. We, all the growers, got less for cotton; beaten down, we couldn't bluff when setting price. From our meager income, wages were paid; food and ten cents a day. Each year the good workers stole away, those with muscle and wit. Figured they could do bet-

ter, having been told wondrous stories of Washington and Baltimore. I knew they were fanciful stories, but paid little mind. They
had a chance, and with them they at least took some ability to read
and write.

A few months after the first crop that was really up to the
standards of those dreamlike years before the war was brought in
and sold for profit, a profit tall enough to cast a shadow, Hosey
came to me and told me, to my entire bewilderment, that he was
taking his family to settle some new village of blacks on the far sod-
house frontier. He reckoned that he'd done his part in getting the
Ride going again, and he wanted his children to have more of a
future than they could have inside these gates. Reconstruction was
about over and the South was governing itself again, but not even
an old soldier of Lee's—perhaps especially an old soldier of Lee's—
could dislike all that had taken place.

I argued with him, bitterly, but I couldn't shake him, nor could
I any more hold him, and I despised those who would have been
glad to help me keep him. And in the end, it came to a heartrend-
ing whipsaw: during four years of hard-fought struggles to save my
South, new bonds had formed between us, more vital and humanly
natural than the ugly bonds of slavery; and grieved as I was, power-
less and old as I felt, I suppose I knew that this departure was
inevitable if Hosey was indeed to be a truly free man. So I swallowed, tried vainly to stem the welling in my eyes and faltering
words; strange, only once before did my eyes draw tears and my
voice break as I wished another man a farewell: when in '61 I bid a
long good-bye to my brothers standing proudly resplendent in
their fresh Confederate grays of a lifetime ago . . . tears only for
brothers? I wished Hosey well, and to my amazement, he held out
his hand.

"You've lived by your lights, Colonel Clayton," he said—Colonel
Clayton! That's what the governor of South Carolina called me!—
"and may you do so till you die." His eye went over my twisted leg,
and I did feel very old. "I don't hold against you what your father's

father did to make you a gentleman, and I just hope you don't hold what I'm doing for my children against me, and I hope you is here when I come back twenty years from now to look around." No thought that I might be, of course. "God prosper you."

He bought my unlikeliest wagon with his savings—wouldn't take it as a gift—and creaked off next day. Well, black he might be, but there was no yellow in him at Spotsylvania Courthouse, and I wished this strong fellow, this friend, and yes, this brother, as well as he deserved.

When Hosey's family had disappeared into the dust and heat of the road, I stood on what remained of the balcony, where Father had hoped to see me receiving guests as governor. The order of life we had loved was grown over by wild honeysuckle that wrapped the ruins we had yet to clear. The one thing as resplendently ours as before the war was our good name. But our good name, and the very South, the South for which we had fallen into a self-appreciation, all were built on a foundation of slavery. And as cabins built by our slaves so long ago could not stand firm on a foundation of mere soil, first sagging, then falling, the South could not, did not, survive and prosper on a foundation of slavery.

But if I may, I wish to recall through the looking glass of memory—though it be flawed, perhaps flawed too harsh a word; a looking glass that renders clear what was good, and mercifully soft and blurred what was ugly—the magnificent South of my youth. Cotillions, spinning dresses of beautiful belles, colors of spring, riding to the hunt, cards, ports, noble debate, immoral enjoyments, always money, always a sense—a sense of destiny, not a sense of destiny to succeed, because we had succeeded; but a destiny to carry on with a life above others, a self-perpetuating life of God's chosen, those elegant ladies and courtly gentlemen of the South. And . . . and we knew we had the unalterable right to protect this life, no less than the holy grail of that Northern Nation gave us the right to secede, "When in the course of human events it becomes necessary for one people to dissolve the political bands which have connected them with another and to assume among the powers of the earth, the separate and equal station to which the Laws of Nature and of Nature's God entitle them."

By this standard Lincoln and his misbegotten followers were no less egregious than King George and his court. Only in time, as a beaten man, a hopeless man, a widower with no estate, with eyes lowered by the humility of a broken warrior, did I reflect on the eloquent clause following that which my South held so close to its bosom, a statement perhaps more noble: ". . . that all men are created equal, that they are endowed by their Creator with certain unalienable Rights, that among these are Life, Liberty and the pursuit of Happiness."

Time to put an end to these maunderings. For most Americans, from earliest times, theirs was a struggle to build a better life. My heroic struggle was, at first, to preserve a glorious life. Only after I lost all that I cherished did I strive to build a better life, not for me, but for others; those who with calloused hands and broken spirits had been bent to the ground by the weight of my families. Thus I reluctantly conceded by my deeds the righteousness of that sad, ungainly man called Lincoln.

Jack

Emilie

*In the 1500s, Spain and England were in a struggle for both economic
and military dominance in Europe. With the discovery of gold in the
New World, and with the mining and transport of this gold by Spain,
England believed that it was disadvantaged. Queen Elizabeth, and later
King James, encouraged the exploration and settlement of the New
World so that England could receive its share of the newfound wealth.
England's instrument for this national objective was London merchants
who funded colonial development in the New World. One of these was*

the Virginia Company of London. Their first settlement established was Jamestown, in Virginia, in 1603. This colony and its settlers simply vanished within a year.

To sway Englishmen to abandon their homes to repopulate Jamestown, many inducements were tendered; granting of fifty-acre plots to those who paid for their own passage to the New World. Also, descriptions of the New World were seductive in their imaginative tales of gold and pearls easily attained.

In 1606 a second Jamestown colony was established and within two years the colony grew to over two hundred individuals. At first the relationship between the colonists and the native Algonquins was tranquil, with few instances of hostilities. Trade between the colonists and the Indians was more prevalent than skirmishes; however, in 1607 the Indians turned en masse against the colonists. Between deaths from hostilities and starvation, less than a fifth of the colony survived the winter of 1608–1609; referred to in history as the Starving Period. Cannibalism was exercised.

The Jamestown colony was repopulated from 1608 through 1615. A new crop, tobacco, was raised and sold by the colonists and provided economic justification for the cost of continued support of the Virginia colonies. The population of the colonies grew to just under seven hundred individuals by 1620. In the spring of 1622 a united and coordinated attack was launched by the Algonquins against more than twenty villages around the Jamestown settlement. A third of the settlers were massacred. Another hundred died of starvation during the following winter, this being referred to in history as the Second Starving.

Emilie is a young girl whose family leaves a tranquil life in England for the promise of wondrous opportunities in the New World . . . America.

IF I MAY, I PRAY THAT YOU ALLOW ME TO INTRODUCE MYSELF. MY name is Emilie. My father and mother gave me the name of my great-great-grandmother. Met we never, but many stories of her I was told. All recountings of the most lovely lady.

I born March 1607 to a tranquil home in Tewkesbury, half a day from Cheltenham in Gloucestershire. Told I that the day of my birth more of May than March. My father met Mother when he was home from the sea. They married with a joy. With me in our home was Nathan, my brother, born to this world three years after me. After Nathan was born Rebecca. Born without breath. We prayed for her each day knowing that we would someday meet.

If my father was not a man, an oak tree he would be. No one taller than he in Tewkesbury. His eyes and hair were dark, a narrow face with a jutting firm chin and no beard. His hands were large with skin as rough bark. He spoke little. When he did, the words came from deep. He was kind, shown not from words, but by deeds. Love me he did, but he showed no affection. Mother was the warmth of the family fire. Awake when I awoke, awake when nightly prayers were said. Always there to hold me tight and tell me how loved I was. Rosy cheeks, eyes of the sky, hair of straw, and the smile, always. Father wore dark, Mother light.

Tewkesbury brings a smile to my heart when I gaze at memories. Our stone home, with its hearth of warmth and cooking smells, the shortest of walks from the riverside. Most happy of my happiness was my sweet grandmother, Alice. Mother to my mother. My heart could not love anyone greater than Father and Mother, but no greater than my love for Grandmother Alice. No day turned into night without her affection.

Grandfather passed with heavy hearts for all. Not long after Nathan moved to the loft and Grandmother Alice came to share our cottage. Her cot was placed next to mine. Together we said prayers and held hands in our sleep. She became my teacher of life. To spin, to knit, to play the flute, and to tell me stories of parables, truths and temptations. We read the Bible aloud. Much she explained.

I did not know why, but our home became disquiet. Around our table sat many men with loud talk. On other nights my father would not be home until all were asleep. Mother's smile came less. She and Grandmother Alice spoke where I could not hear. Nathan and I wondered why. In the spring of 1621 Nathan and I were told that we would embark on a wonderful journey. Told this around the plank table after a Sunday afternoon meal of mutton and squash. Going to the New World in a grand ship with white sails larger than the clouds that passed over Tewkesbury. When asked what should I take, the response made my bones cold. I would take everything. Leave nothing behind, there would be no return. Grandmother Alice would stay. Uncle David and Aunt Lindy, with cousin Abby, would live in our cottage with sweet Grandmother. Could this be?

"Why leave?" I asked. "We're so happy in Tewkesbury." Father counseled us of a magnificent new land. Acres for all with opportunity for all. His friend, Mister Raymonds of the Gloucestershire Council, told of the New World. Crops, livestock, and fishes more than one could partake. Told we that in London a play recounted the emeralds and pearls that hung from trees as leaves in the land at our journey's end. When asked how far, told a fortnight to London and two months at sea. At the end of the journey in the most lovely place, Jamestown, on the James River of the New World. Told that those before us built delightful cottages where we could live. Those before would greet us and bestow upon us gracious hospitality.

When at sea before Tewkesbury, Father was a ship's carpenter. In Tewkesbury he was a farmer, but not of his land, a gentleman's land Father plowed, planted, and harvested. Before our journey a great trunk was made by Father under Nathan's gaze. Solid oak, cut two inches thick. These cut again, a good stride in length. Trunk made as high as wide. A heavy lid of oak, with a curved bow.

Hinges, two from the blacksmith, a latch of the same black metal. Two loops of rope, the size of a large man's thumb, made strong to both ends as handles. In this oak safe went life's most valuables for the trek.

The time of our journey was set. We were to leave the first week of April. For our journey Father borrowed Mister Clayton's cart and horse. The cart being as wide as I was tall, and twice in length. It was pulled by a horse the color of wet earth. With us to London traveled Jack, the eldest of Clayton sons, no more than fifteen. After we were secure in London, Jack was to return safely with horse and cart.

As April became nearer my heart was heavy. How could we do this? For Nathan, Mother, Father, and me to leave those behind we loved so. Why would Father take me from Grandmother Alice? Never again would we speak, nor hold hands, nor would she tell me truths that I should know. This choice was Father's, not Mother's. I should not, but I did, one day speak to Father and complained and asked why. He said he knew best and that I should not be ungrateful. A most harsh look given, turned and gone. I trembled.

When to Grandmother Alice I recounted my father's bearing, she counseled my understanding. Told me that socks and shoes are each most important. Shoes without socks rub raw the foot. Without shoes socks shredded by the stones and sticks. Told me Father is the shoe, protects me from the sharpest of life's instruments. Mother the sock, soft and warms me. Both I need, and neither one is better than the other. Told me that Father and Mother only wished Nathan and me the happiest of lives. The New World was a grand gift to Nathan and me from Father.

On this journey I was to leave nothing behind. Both dresses taken, one folded in the trunk, the other worn. My coat, no longer fit, given to a cousin. Grandmother's warm wool shawl became mine. New soles for my boots, Grandmother's Bible for my soul. Only pause was Mantha, should I take? Father thought not, Mother said yes. Only three hands high, she didn't take much space. Head of wood, eyes always open, mouth with a smile. Flowing hair of black thread, a dress of white, more yellow now. Given me many years ago by Aunt Samantha. A toddler's toy, Mantha.

Each day became shorter, but longer with unhappiness. The last night before departure, after my prayers with Grandmother Alice, we lay in our cots and spoke, spoke softly, spoke throughout the night. Told me of the wonderful life I would have, told I would see sights never seen by her. London, with buildings taller than trees. This I could not imagine. Told me I would board the most magnificent of ships with most handsome and brave Captain. In the New World I would live in a most fine cottage in happy contentment. There, she said, I would meet a wonderful young man and we would marry. In the new land with acres for all, my husband and I would own our own cottage. With two large rooms, both with windows, and a loft for the children. There would be a fine hearth, and I would make the finest of meals, cakes, and muffins. She thought I would have two sons and two daughters. I told sweet Grandmother Alice the first daughter will be named Alice. She kissed me.

Later, in full darkness of night, Grandmother Alice made me promise when in the new land, if I saw a full moon, I would speak quietly to the moon. She promised that she would gaze upon any full moon and listen for my words. She asked that if a problem beseech me I ask the moon for help and pause, then listen for her answer. Her answer will be a whisper I barely hear. But, answer she would.

As we spoke through the night of many things, the morn began to peek between the shutters. When I could see the eyes of Grandmother Alice as the first pink light shone, there were tears. We held each other. Grandmother prayed that I be safe. Then it was time to dress and the journey begin.

The cart was full. Most dear the carefully made trunk, full of clothes and soft goods. Also in this trunk, copper pots and utensils.

Most treasured, a silver candlestick holder given by my father's mother. Half our family's plates we took, half we left for Aunt Lindy. Food for the journey was stored. A mound of cornbread, dried fish, and three small kegs of cider. Mother and I in the back of the cart. Father and Nathan beside the cart. Jack led the horse. Father wore a great gray coat. With his size, when standing still, he looked like a statue. Nathan in Grandfather's brown wool coat, patches on the elbows with sleeves too long. A well-worn brown coat for Jack, with a cap of matching color.

The road went east. Through range of hills north and south, then roads through poppy fields we traveled. Stopping to rest the horse and drink from a stream. First night was at Hawling. There some token of money for a room with others. Our trunk slept next to Mother's cot. Much noise and many smells. Before sleep, Mother came to me. A kiss, then a package, brown paper around cloth. A present from Grandmother. I folded the paper back. The cloth I knew, the color of a blanket left behind. From this cloth a coat three hands high, for Mantha's long journey. Across the breast, in thread of fine and white, a heart embroidered.

Early up, off again to the east. This day our journey passed through Natgrave and Torkdene. Each day different, each day the same. Father would take the horse by the lead to pardon Jack. At times he would stroll behind the cart. I measured Jack's gait. Black boot after black boot. Right arm swinging with the stride, left hand in his waistcoat pocket. Eyes not wandering. He was a shy lad. Spoke little and asked for nothing. I guessed him just becoming a man. Once, when stopped to rest the mare from the afternoon sun, I offered Jack a cup of cool spring water. Smile and nod, but nothing said.

Mother and I sat backward, facing the trail of dust. On one side of me my mother, the other side a slowly turning wheel, one spoke loose. With each turn the spoke voiced a groan as it shifted in its place. One turn of the wheel, one groan. Like ticking of a clock measuring the passing of time, each groan marked the march of distance from Grandmother Alice and our home and hearth in Tewkesbury.

Jack shared Father's tasks, all chores done before he sleep. He spoke with Father as they walk. Father did not speak with boys. But next I saw Nathan and Jack by a pond bouncing pebbles with sideways throws.

Several days into our journey, a steep portion of path rose before us, like many before. Lightened the load and Father and Jack carried trunks and tools to the rise. Then with the cart less burdened, encouraged the mare with Jack pulling the lead and Father pushing with his bulk. Running next to the cart Nathan tripped. The solid oaken wheel passed over his hand. A scream of pain. With horse and cart at the top, Father ran to his side. Three fingers broken, not agreeing with the rest. With his knife Father cut and whittled seven wooden tongues. Two each as splints for Nathan's fingers, one for Nathan's bite to ease the pain when bones were pulled and straightened. Nathan took my place on the cart, I walked.

All unsettled the next morning when Jack could not find his father's horse. Not stolen, just strayed to a hay field. Jack said a lesson learned; he'd sleep with one end of rope tied to him, the other to the brown mare.

After a long day's journey, arrived at Harfeyld and lodging, a small room of rough-hewn wood walls with a thatched roof of open disrepair. This leaning against a fine stone cottage. A family of four resided within the cottage. Father, a mother and son and daughter. I recall their name was Newman. The same as my Uncle James. The missus of the cottage took care to welcome Mother and me into her chamber to wash and freshen. A beautiful porcelain pitcher and bowl, covered with painted flowers of a garden. A cloth of soft cotton was offered. Mother and I with great contentment removed the dust of the journey. That night a platter of warm mutton and pickled herring was brought to share. No better food had I ever. The following morning our journey began again. My heart ached. Why did this Newman family stay in their cottage of contentment while we were on a weary journey of unknowns?

At first I thought Jack was not special. But my father, not easily pleased, seemed content with his diligence and labors. For many days Jack did not speak to me. But on one fine bright day he walked to a stream to fill the bladders tied to the cart. Then to the tree under which I shaded myself. He told me the stream water was cool and sweet and that I should partake. I thanked him and made conversation regarding nothing of importance. He spoke with kind words. His brown eyes darted from one side to another, but never to mine.

Mother and I much conversation. Tells me that this will be a most wonderful time and not to despair. During an afternoon trek talked about nothing for some time, then Mother spoke of men. Told me that a husband should be of strong build and character. Pleasant manners and handsome face be good, but most important virtue and acknowledgment of God's intent. Ask I what God's intent be. Mother silent for a few groans of the turning wheel. Then her answer. Ten Commandments should be the strong frame for the painting of life. Our life's painting within the frame must stay. But to each the choice of the painting, for her a loving family. Not certain what this meant, but smile I did. Some more groans of the turning wheel and then I asked, did Mother think Jack a strong man? Her answer with no pause, Jack is a fine boy.

More days of dusty roads, then the rain. Dark clouds, wind, and nothing dry. Mother and I huddled. Nathan with a blanket for a hood. Father and Jack walking as if the sun was shining its warmest. The night of the first rains a barn was our shelter. While a dry roof, no fire to warm our clothes. A second day of rain and cold wind. Mother and I shivered. No fire for cooking, just bread that night. Next day cold with a sharp wind, but no rain. Mother was distressed, a cough and chills. Father stopped and did make a grand fire. Warm tea was passed, and clothes were dried. He told us not to be unhappy, only two more days of travel before the great city of London.

On our final night we lodged in Clerkenwell. Never have I seen so many cottages. For some sum of consideration Father bargained us a room at a tavern; Jack shared with the mare. With an open window, the fresh night air chased out the smells of others before. Mother was unrestful. Coughed until day's light. A surprise before we departed in the morning. Jack, how I do not know, became the owner of four large green apples, roasted, with a sweet syrup in the dimples from which stems grew. One each for Mother, Father, Nathan, and me. Father, pretending perhaps, pleaded no interest and told Jack to eat his apple. Looking somewhat hurt, Jack walked to the cart with apple in hand. At nightfall, after bread and dried fish, Jack came to me when I was alone. With knife in hand, he split his apple in two, one half for me, one half for him.

Off to London on a warm spring morning. Quickly our path of two weeks turned to a road. Soon this road became wider and more traveled. Squeezing the road clusters of cottages. Then shops and cottages, many gathered where our traveled road met another. In the afternoon stopped by a rocky creek, one side weeping willows bending to cool their leaves in the waters. Rest the mare, some bread and cider, some chatter, then off again. On the horizon there it was, home of our ship, London Towne. Buildings, not cottages, broke the sky. Cathedrals, not churches, marked their place. At a distance, no detail. All grays in color. But the size, no question. Together they were a mountain.

Another mile, more carts, more horses, some pulling, some ridden. Many people walking, all with a purpose. Our road, once with fields and a few structures became a journey of structures with a few fields. Then nothing green. Noise, so much noise. Then the smells. Turned right on a road of a kind not seen before. Not dirt, all stone, one laid next to the other. Cottages, higher and higher, no space between, one touching the other. People, people everywhere. On the road, on the walks, peering from windows, standing and eating, carrying packages, pushing carts, doing nothing.

When we departed Tewkesbury, I believed we were so fortunate to have a horse and two-wheel cart to ease our journey. Here, so many four-wheel carriages. Some with roofs and doors. Some painted in splendor, ornaments of polished metals with drivers dressed as a king. We turned to Edgewater Street. Father said it would take us to London gates. Our pace slowed to a walk. Better for me to gauge the sights. Came to a stop.

A splendid structure stood to my side of the cart. A church it could be, but no steeple or bell tower. All brick with a roof not thatched, but of a gray flat stone. Around this structure, a home, a fence of iron. Hundreds of metal spears standing at attention protected those within. Then a yell. From the door and down stone steps ran a well-dressed servant man to open the gate. A clatter of metal-rimmed wheels on stone. Past us a most grand carriage was drawn, stopping only a small distance from me. It was white, with patterned lines of gold. Not one driver, but two. One with the reins stayed, the other off and to the carriage door. Slowly opened the door. From the carriage came a gentleman dressed in black, a black with thin gray stripes. A coat with rounded tails, and britches with buttons of gold. Shoes, not boots, that reflected light. A hat, not for warmth, was more over his head than around his head. He was tall and most, most handsome. By the carriage door he stood. His hand extended in. First the gloved hand. A glove with buttons of white globes. Then the skirt. So much cloth. Not a skirt, more a red cloud. Then the bodice, red and tight to the fit. Around the neck hung a constellation of stars. Then the hat, wide, wide brim dipping to the right, with ribbon flowing behind, all red. So much red.

The lady carefully stepped down. Safely on the road she stood, tall and straight, head back, face beautiful, skin of cream, lips of new strawberries. Words briefly spoke to the gentleman, then turned toward the guarded home. Somehow, I know not why, our eyes meet. She paused. In the sagging cart I sat, her gaze on me, mine on her. Then she smiled. A smile of beauty to me and no one else. Her gentleman saw the lady's pleasant stare. Looked at me he did. Perfect he was. Then! Then his head bowed forward, and with the hand not holding the lady's hand he tipped his hat. All and only for me. A moment forever, a moment no longer. They turned, our cart moved on.

Down Edgewater Street we went. So many sights. Through Moor Gate, then many turns right, many left, then straight, there the dock. Not what I thought. I sought a harbor large, with our fine boat anchored as the centerpiece in fresh waters. Rather, animals at a trough. Ship after ship. One next to the other, bows inwards. No white sails. No fresh breeze. Many questions, then our ship found. No better, no worse than others. Up a plank Father went. The ship is named *Essex*. Back came Father, not pleased. Two nights before we board, a week before we depart.

Off we trekked to find a place to sleep. Stop one place, a tavern with much merriment. Father in, Father out. Not for us this night. The sun was saying farewell. Mother distressed with coughing. A turn up a narrow street. First Father to one home, then to another, then we have our place. One room for everyone to sleep for two nights. But not like any I'd seen before. The room upstairs and down a passage dark. Our room not large, but dry and warm. Father, Jack, and Nathan leave. Mother and I washed with a bucket of water. Then Jack and Nathan back with our trunk. Then Father returned, a brief moment with Mother, then we were told. Tonight, we would go to a tavern.

To the street, lit by glow of lanterns through glass windows, not shuttered for the night. Down the street, more people than horses, walking fast. Nathan ran ahead, and then back at Father's bark. Some doors open, glance inside. So much furniture. Some chairs covered in cloth. Walls of color. On the walls many things of beauty hung. Then something never seen, in one passing room, a wall. As trunks set one upon the other, floor to ceiling. But all sides open. Books, all books, each and every one filled. A wall of books.

Down another street to a tavern. Smoke and noise of many voices not in tune. Closer to Mother I stood. Father off, then back with a large woman. Big smile, few teeth. White apron to the dirt floor. To a table she led, one tattered man there, elbows down, head in hands. Moved by her, not with lady's words. One bench on each side of the stained table. Mother and I to one, the men to the other. Food is brought, one plate for all, fingers for forks and spoons. A large fish. No head, no tail, with a mountain of golden hot potatoes. But not round as new potatoes. Rectangles, like small bricks with salt and vinegar. Then two mugs. One of ale, one of cider. Father the ale, a few sips each of the cider for the others. Before we take our leave Father spoke to Jack of a task well done. Then the mug of ale to Jack. A small drink, a big smile.

In the morning I woke to see Father at the trunk. He lifted out the candlestick holder, silver base and stem, wrapped in a cloth carefully before our journey. Mother watched, then turned away. Into his great gray coat pocket it went, then Father left. I rose, Nathan and Jack gone. Today, we were to wash our clothes, tomorrow to our ship with no certainties. I looked at myself in a smoky mirror on the wall. My face, I knew it well. Just a girl. The lady that smiled, the lady in red, so beautiful. Could this be me someday?

By noon Father returned. Jack spoke to Father, then to Mother. To me Jack came, stopped, and talked to his boots. Asked for a brief walk with me this afternoon, before he departed. Yes I said. He stepped back and fast to the door, then down the steps. To Mother I turned, may I go, should I walk with him? Mother smiled. A cloth wetted across my face, then her brush. Told me to stand still and brushed my hair. To the trunk, and then back. Then she stood facing me, parted my hair, easy for two ribbons to hold. Then the hair clip from the trunk. Fine polished metal and shining blue stones, her mother's mother's. Never before in my hair, holding tight.

Down the steps and to the gray paved street, Jack was there, standing as a sapling. Off we walk. His gait too long. My small steps became many. What to say, "How long is your journey home?" Down a winding street, then down another past a church of stone with ringing bells. The Thames below, London's great river wide. Not with trees on its banks, but buildings, all sizes. To the left, from where the stream flowed, a bridge. Not a wooden span, not a stone arch. This was a highway. People, carts, carriages, and shops with wares across the flow. We walked across. At midpoint stopped. For a coin from the pocket of his frayed coat, Jack bought two ciders from a man in a cart with long red hair, no teeth, one arm, one leg. Our cider poured into well-used tin cups. Told they must stay. So there we drank. To the edge we walked, water below. Noise and bustle behind. Shoulder to shoulder we stood, one hand cups, the other on the stone. We talked. Easy words, only the river's flow in our gaze. At first we recounted our journey together, some good, some with humor. Then talked of the future. Jack thought well of the New World. Someday he will go. He said we will be fine. I neither agreed nor stated other. I asked, though, what price we would pay. We were not leaving bad for good. We were leaving contentment for the hope of contentment in a strange land. A bad trade, I thought. Jack assured that on the journey from Tewkesbury he spoke to Father much as they walked. This I knew. Most words to mark time or day's events. But some not. To Jack, Father spoke of a future. Land for his family, as much as could be cleared and fenced. No limits, other than a man's limit. I was silent. Neither spoke for a time. Dark water drifted below. Then I turned, a glance at Jack. This made no sense, I said. In Tewkesbury we had everything. There was nothing I needed, nothing I wanted. Jack turned to me. A pause. Then a smile. Not of humor. But of a knowledge of something known that someone thought unknown. So he asked, everything I wanted? A long silence before he answered his question to me. "A white carriage trimmed in gold and a dress of red would be nice." Only I saw, I thought.

Tin cups back to the one-legged man, us back to Mother, Father, and Nathan. Up to our room, Mother there, Father below. Out the window I look. Jack off, leading the mare. Home to Tewkesbury. He paused for a moment, looked back, his gaze upward. Saw me in the window, halted his stride. A grin, a bow of his head, a slow tip of his brown cap, then off.

With morning light we rose. A pole Father found, longer than he is tall. With two handles of rope our trunk swung below. Nathan to one end and Father to the other. Off we went. Past no more than a few doors and Nathan pleads for a pause. His fingers hurt. Two more streets and several stops, then I was told to join Nathan's burden. Not that heavy, I think. Finally, the dock and the *Essex*, our cottage for the sea.

As Father and Nathan lifted the pole from under which our trunk swung, a shout from above, then quickly down the plank from the *Essex* a man. If not a man, a beast. Tight britches, many patches. No shirt. Arms as legs. Long hair, one eye open, one closed. Not a beard, but not a shave. Something never seen before. On his arms drawings. Some with scripture. He reached down, removed the pole, and hoisted the trunk to a shoulder, up the plank he went. After a moment Father, holding Mother's arm, climbed the mountain plank. Next Nathan and then me. The plank was twenty good strides long, but many small steps for the steep rise. Halfway up I paused. The smells, a blanket of smells wrapped tight. I looked down. No rushing water. Green-black pond of disgust. A dead rat, a cat, and a hundred things not known. More a chamber pot. My climb resumed, off to the New World.

A man appeared. A patch over one eye, but kind face. Welcomed us, a fair journey we will have. Then down to our quarters, one deck below. The stink was worse than of all the barnyard animals in the hottest month of the hottest summer. No person could suffer this smell. Dark, dark as almost night. The only light those slivers that squeezed through a grate on the deck above. Father did not mask his feelings about our shipboard lodging. A Mister Rountree, an officer with rank and command, reported three other families yet to arrive be berthed in space we thought ours for the journey. Father was ashen, then red. He paced, five paces wide, seven in length. How could this space be divided into fourths, stating not even God could arrange such meager space for four families. Rountree answered, God created man and woman, not families. The space would only need to be divided into two. One half for women, one for men.

Two days before we sailed, others boarded. Four blankets nailed to a beam splitting the space in half. One side for women and children, the opposite for men. For the women the privy was a bucket under a stool nailed to the deck to the women's side. Surrounded this by a large piece of well-worn stained canvas from a sail.

In time the winds and ebb tide spoke kindly, departed to southwest. First fortnight was intriguing and entertaining, like a play. The stage was set and the characters introduced. Some to be cameos, others of note and portents, some kindly and some harsh. The stage was the *Essex*. With the winds pushing us forward, the blanket of smells was no longer, ocean air and water as a new snow, perfect, with not a blemish. Our quarters were shared not with with three other families, but with three couples plus two unmarried gentlemen who had each brought a servant. Since servants were male, only the men's portion of the quarters suffered.

Mother, Nathan, and I, shared with three women. Mrs. Sandys was the most pleasant, with words of kindness. She was first to chores, first to help with others' burdens. Her age, I am not certain, somewhat old, near thirty. Brown hair, but short, perhaps cut for the journey. Sparkling brown eyes and the most white teeth, as a porcelain teacup. And perfect they, all straight and true. Mrs. Sandys wore the most beautiful dresses. She told me that someday I would wear grander. Her husband was older than her by many years. This would be his second time in Jamestown, this her first. His task of importance to represent gentlemen in London. Many books brought by him, many books read.

Mrs. Shelton was so thin, bones showed below her cold white skin. She had dark eyes, dark hair, dark clothes, dark foreboding. Words sparse, a look of despair. She spent most days on her cot, without speaking. Her husband to be a Jamestown blacksmith. As her, he rarely spoke. He became a sailor for our journey, helping those on deck with tasks. His freedom from below. Freedom from his wife I think.

Of the skirted few, Mrs. Forchee was the most uncontent. Nothing good, nothing right. Always spoke of times better. Not pleasant to share our days and nights. Chewed food with mouth open, smelled not good, and slept with loud noises. Her husband never seen, hid I think. He was off to the New World to make glass.

Other players of many importance on our floating stage. Captain Jones was our king. Not of an inclination to dally with his subjects, a crew of twenty-five. The king's ministers were his officers, Mister Rountree, and Mister Johnson. I was never certain as to their rank. Captain Jones was forty or so in years. Taller than even Father. A build of a man of work. Dark hair, fair skin, and eyes squinting. On one hand, two fingers missing. As an apprentice his hand rested wrongly on an anchor chain. Little known of the Captain. Only once he spoke to me, moving from tween deck to main deck we passed. A nod, a good day, and he be gone.

Mister Rountree was shorter by a hand than Captain Jones. A deep voice, much as Father's. Blue eyes, not as blue as Mother's. Brown hair, a brown beard with slivers of gray. Always polite, but never kind. To him passengers were cargo, not to be damaged, no other care needed. Mister Rountree I heard speak often, but not to me. To the crew he gave orders, crisp and short.

Mister Johnson, I think the oldest of all, perhaps fifty. Not tall at all. One arm limp, twisted and torn in a storm many voyages ago. Most teeth, no beard, white hair, long to the sides. One eye bright and gray, the other a patch held by a thin strap around his head. Nose with a scar, from the tip to the patch. Walked with a drift, his path not following his gait. Mister Johnson never a smile for the crew, always harsh his words. Uncertainty in a command is as a ship without a rudder, he said. When told this I nodded acknowledgement while wondering what a rudder be. For Nathan and me, he had a quick smile and soft words of explanation and comfort. I wondered why he was so kind.

First days at sea the food was not good. Then became worse. Prepared by the cook in the forecastle, with its brick hearth. Two meals each day. One in early morning, another before the shadows long. In the morning warm oatmeal. If for me and Nathan, a touch of honey and a smile. After a fortnight, oatmeal no longer. Bread our meal. Evening meal at first warm with a taste. Potatoes boiled and salted with dried meats. Most special if a great fish were caught, then a stew for all. When the seas were rough, no fire to warm, only bread and dried meat. Longer the journey, shorter the flavors, tougher the meat.

Barely a day passed without Mister Johnson interrupting his day to speak to Nathan and me. Often we would ask questions about the sea. Always he took time to respond. Many things we understood. Many things did not. One we did not was the setting sun. During our first days at sea the sun would rise on our left, the port, and set on our right, starboard. I told Mister Johnson that the setting sun always shone through a small grate on the right side of the ship and cast the most lovely patterns on our hanging tarps. His response I could not understand. To Nathan and I he explained by the end of our journey the sun would be setting on the left and rising on the right. How could this be? In our cottage in Tewkesbury the sun's first rays always shone through one window and through another as it bade farewell. He tried to explain, but I could not understand. Several days passed and he came to Nathan and me with apple in hand. With the knife he always carried as partner to his belt, carefully he cut back the skin of a portion of the apple. On the other side of the apple he cut yet another portion. Then with the stem pointing upward he carved what looked to be an arrowhead pointing down next to one portion where the skin had been taken. Then next to the other portion where the skin had been peeled away he carefully carved yet another small arrowhead that was pointing upward toward the stem. When holding the apple upward in the blaze of the sun, he slowly rotated the apple, as the earth rotates around. He explained that during the first part of our journey, south toward the bottom of the apple was our journey, as the direction of the arrow. He then slowly turned the apple so the sunlight hit one side and then the other with the dividing between light and sun slowly moving across the arrow, thus day and night. Then he explained that the second part of the journey we would be moving upward on the earth, along the New World, back to the stem of the apple. He then rotated the apple again from light to shadow and showed the light moved from the other side of the arrow than before. After his explanation he paused. There was silence. I spoke but not sincerely. I thanked him and told him that I then understood. Nathan asked if he could eat the apple.

Mother more quiet, less conversation. Still coughing. Sometimes her eyes stayed closed, but no sleep. I tried to make pleasant conversation. Happy recountings. Happy hopes. Asked her one day to recount her wedding. The story I knew, but it made us feel warm to hear it.

One calm day Mister Johnson took Nathan and me to the quarter deck, above the chart house, never allowed there before. High in the back of the ship, looking down on the crew and passengers. We felt important, seeing what others doing, nothing hidden. A challenge for us, he says. Another month for our journey, a test to be given at the end by him to us. If we pass, a prize to both. "What?" I ask, "A test of what knowledge?" Sailing he said, he would teach us to be apprentices, much to learn, weather, seas, navigation, commands. Mister Johnson then gave us a small plank of wood, no longer than four hands, with a drawing of a ship. A sketch from the side, masts, sails and spars, the deck, both above and below. All with names written next to them. In just a few days Nathan and I learned the names, and how to inscribe them. Still I remember, mizzen, main, fore, and sprit be what I called trees. With plank in hand as a map Mister Johnson went through the ship. With permission of Captain Jones, even the Great Cabin seen. Most interesting the steerage where helmsmen pushed and pulled the whipstaff, rudder. A rudder half the size of a barn door. As a shutter swinging on hinges, the rudder port and starboard to nudge the ship's aft in its journey. This helmsman, with broad shoulders as Father's. This sailor I remembered from before, he was the one who quickly up the plank with our trunk.

While the crew were more old than young, there were five apprentice sailors, twelve to fifteen years, I think. All wore the same dark trousers, loose white or cream shirts, perhaps the cream being white shirts long before. Like squirrels in Tewkesbury, moving from branch to branch and tree to tree, they glided among the masts, spars, and rigging in a manner that seemed not possible. These lads were not often pardoned from their task. One corner of the deck was where they would break. All were young and fresh, one was of particular note. By listening carefully to their yelled exchanges among the sails that pushed and pulled our ship, I came to know his name. It was David, the same as my uncle.

Then one day, a pleasant turn. The young apprentices on a rest, one moved toward me, he was David. I smiled. Then he saw and came to me. Asked if this was my first journey on a ship. My yes was met with his claim of his third passage. As he turned to join his fellows, he was surprised when I spoke his name and wished him a good day.

After twenty, but no more than thirty days at sea, the doldrums. Sea smooth, ship without motion. With no breeze, heat and smells returned. But this was not the worst.

When our space belowdecks was divided between men and women, care was given to the women. A large grate open to fresh air was over the portion of space for women and children. Without wind, the belowdecks air was stale and warm. With wind and movement, a rushing and churning noise was loud and constant, but without there was silence, all conversation overheard. With no winds to move the air belowdecks and with no pitching of the ship, the crew moved to the main deck at night to sleep. Many spoke among themselves, and I listened. Most words of family and home. Sometimes food and ale. It was on the third day of our doldrums that words of a single sailor made my heart stop and my head faint. My only thankfulness was both Nathan and Mother asleep and did not hear. The seaman thought all journeying to the New World as fools. Bragged he had made two journeys to Jamestown. The stories he told could not be true. They were of hunger and savages. Most of the first travelers of 1607 no longer lived. For many starvation was a salvation. Told of savages raiding village, carrying out most horrible of deeds. Settlers set upon by axes and clubs, left to die with arms and legs hacked off. Others tied to trees, fingers were cut free one by one, until God gave them mercy in heaven. Of all recountings, one most horrible. A settler man, starving and desperate, set upon his wife and killed her. Butchered her, cooked her, and ate her. When found out, judged rightly and hanged. Because of the desperation of many, the loved ones of newly dead buried in unmarked sites so not retrieved for sustenance. This could not be. We could not be traveling to such a place.

Morning after, Father saw my distress. Asked Mother why, but she did not know. This day I did not eat nor move from my blanket. The following morning my mother beseeched me to tell her my woe. This I could not do to my mother. I told her I would speak to Father. That afternoon we went to the deck above and to a railing far. I told him the words that I heard. He touched me on the shoulders and turned me around so I looked at the sea with him standing at my back. These were not real stories. These were stories sailors told when ale was plenty. I was told all was well, and a wondrous land was where we would be. I knew this was not true, but I smiled.

Mister Johnson's teaching of the ways of the sea gave relief from the sailor's tales. Clouds, clouds. Mister Johnson points, Mister Johnson speaks. Know their shapes, know their voices. Some flat as dough rolled under the pin, others long and round as a bed sheet rolled. Some tall and round, a mountain of pillows. Some not white but gray. Others not gray but black, with flashes of light. One not seen but spoken of. High gray black saucer, from it a cone with the small point touching the ocean. Told best not to see.

Mister Johnson one day took Nathan and me below. Under the tween deck was the cargo hold. Open wide, only the main mast and windlass intrude. Scores of barrels holding peas, meal, and butter. Tools for every task, spades, shovels, axes, and scythes, more than in Tewkesbury. More barrels, pitch and tar. Soft goods, linen, canvas, rugs, blankets. Also, but not understood, rocks. More than in a garden wall. Asked I why stones to Jamestown. Not cargo, he said, they stay with the ship as ballast. Counter the masts high above. Two rocks I would see again.

From the cargo hold up we go two decks then forward. Then up again to the top of the forecastle looking down. The bow of the *Essex*, parting the sea, as shears through cloth. Leading the bow the beachhead and bowspirit. As the beak of a bird, forward from the bow a bridge to nowhere, ending in a point five strides in front of the bow. Out we go, over the waters rushing forward. Nothing but clean wind in front, nothing but green water below and blue sky above. We were birds.

On the main deck David saw me again today, from his rest he approached. A good day he wished me and then he asked my name. I told him. That night I lay below and think of him. The first young man to seek my name.

Mother did not leave the tween deck. No sun, no fresh breeze. Still a cough. Her voice not hers, breathing not easy. I bathed her with warm water from the forecastle, soap from our trunk. Words of strength from her, but I was fearful. Speak to Father, all will be right. Mrs. Sandys also, Mother to be well. They must be true, any other answer God would not allow.

Again David joined me on the deck for a brief conversation. Unlike Jack, this lad looked right at me, not to the side. His eyes were bright. They seemed to smile. His hair was a dark, dark brown.

His build slender but not frail. Muscles from apprentice tasks were there. His height between me and Father, his complexion reddened brown from the wind and sun.

To interest and occupy the day for me, Mister Johnson taught knots, each with names not heard before. Sailor's knot, rolling hitch, bowline loop, sheet bend, and reef knot be some. Asked me if I would learn a few. I did. Not because of interest, but because he was so kind. I recall some. Make a rabbit hole with one end, pull the rabbit up through the hole, he looks around, runs under one end, and down the hole, a noose knot is made. Nathan also challenged by Mister Johnson. With the loan of his fine large knife with its handle of some stone, Nathan taught to whittle. Small blocks of wood to some object of life. At first nothing to show but wood shavings by a stool and Nathan's bandaged finger. But then a pig's head carved. Later I learned it be a dog.

Another day, more conversation with David. No longer just a sentence or two. Small topics. The weather, the food, the other passengers. As he spoke to me his fellow apprentices noticed from a distance. David said he thought my hair very fair. I washed and brushed to make it even more so. But the wind between the sails on the deck above made it not so.

Seas not calm, heavy winds and spray, the ship and all within a coat of salt. Mister Johnson said only a day and night, but no relief. One day as the day before, ship rolling hard, no passengers above. Crew brings food and drink to our cots, only bread and dried meat, but no matter, no one was hungry. Lay in our cots, blanket's sway marks the time. Mother sleeps, Father quiet, Nathan with a knife. Mrs. Sandys most attentive to Mother, Nathan, and me. The ship rolls and curtsies, Mrs. Sandys smiles. When I move from Mother's side she is there, some water, bread broken small, a folded blanket under her head. Her happiness is others' happiness. At night, when others sleep, I think, why some content, others not? Is it because of a decision made, or the cast of God? Both I think. Then the seas became quiet.

When tested by Mister Johnson, Nathan and I know well the ship's map. All places on board known by their names. Clouds also known. And the knots. The lengths of rope making home to a dozen knots of different purpose. Navigation not understood. Too difficult.

Father never noticed my exchanges with the apprentice David. One morning after a few words of nothing important, David asked if I had seen the great shark swimming to the left, that is port, of our ship. I said not. To the rail we walked. Over he leaned, and next to our hull the shark be, he said. Then he told me to lean over to see the great large fish. This I did. His hand went to my waist. I thought to keep me from a fall. No shark was seen. Another few words were spoken and back to his fellows he walked. Grinning were they, something most amusing. I was perplexed. Nothing amusing I saw. Then from the forward deck strode Mister Johnson, a stride with a purpose. Right to the apprentices he flew. To David he spoke. I know not what, but nothing pleasant. For several days the apprentices did not count David as one. Days later, again, he was on deck. But no conversations.

Mother's health worsened. Cough remained. Breaths more often and shorter. Strange noise as breaths taken. Food not often eaten. Eyes sunk, surrounded by dark. I sat by her, holding her hand. Telling her pleasant stories told me by Grandmother. Each she knew, but each she smiled. Father quiet. Mister Johnson not. Always a subject for Nathan and me. Walk here, see that, do this, keeping us busy. His intent good, but, the more he spoke, the more fearful I became.

If the weather fair, I went to the main deck at the highest sun. This was the time apprentices were relieved from their tasks. While seeming busy with something of importance, perhaps to study another knot on a line, I glanced to the apprentices. David faced my way, a smile I offered, he turned away. Then one day an apprentice, I know not his name, walked past me to the railing. Turned and back to his group, but first by me and passed me a paper. I went down to my cot. Paper unfolded. *Kind Emilie. Not to offend, no disrespect intended. David Lane.* I knew his full name.

Mrs. Sandys spent more hours with Mother. Often they spoke in whispers. Father told me not to worry, Mother would be fine. Worry much I did. Only soup eaten. Eyes closed many hours of the day. Each day the same, then another week the same. Mostly calm seas, but a stiff and steady breeze from the southeast.

For two days Mother did not eat. Then she moved to the far end of the women's share of the tween deck. Her cot blocked from view by a blanket tied from above. Father one cold night took my hand, rarely done, and to my mother. A lamp above swayed with the ship. Shadows also swayed. Still she lay. Head slightly raised, Father's great gray coat folded as a pillow to raise her head and shoulders. Ease her labors. In time her eyes open. When her glance crossed mine, a smile. A smile of warmth and love. My hand went to hers, I felt her bones. Close I moved. Face near dear Mother's. A few soft words, love, hope, and promises, always with me. I had no words, only tears. Minutes passed. Then Father with Nathan came. I stood, then knelt. Kissed her on the cheek. Then back to my cot. Later Nathan was there. Little was said that night. He slept. I did not. With morning light I could see Father by Mother. Finally he stood, moved away, she was with Rebecca.

No casket, no flowers, no grave to visit and speak my thoughts. Her body placed in a long stained gray canvas sack for sails to hold. With her as companions two large stones from the ballast below, they I knew. Then the open end sewed closed forever with an iron needle and black cord. In the evening's fading light the ship turned so that the pink sky of the setting sun was aft, where Father, Nathan, and I and others stood. How could this be? Mother to be plunged into churning sea. Some words spoken by the Captain. I could not hear. I did not care. Nothing worse. A few cried. Toss her body into the sea, my mother of warmth, my mother of gentle love, always there for me. Only Father, rigid and distant, to guide and comfort me. This could not be. This night no prayers said. Shame I felt. Mother dying and David's glance I had sought.

Mrs. Sandys talked to me each day. Nothing of importance. Asked if she could brush my hair. She told me of her niece, who lived in Oxford. Her name was Victoria. Very pretty said Mrs. Sandys, but not as fair as me. I knew she wished to bring happiness to my face. But grief was too much. My sweet Grandmother Alice, home in Tewkesbury, her daughter no longer. Her grief I must have. To the deck I go, over the Great Cabin, sat down on the deck with my back to the mizzen mast, faced the railing, then leaned back, not too far, or the sails I see. But if my gaze just right not the sea or ship cross my eye. Only sky and clouds. With this view I took myself home. Thought of past times, happy times, times with Mother in Tewkesbury.

At night the boat was quiet of voices. I lay in my cot. Only light a far-off yellow glow from a lamp above the decks. While no voices, constant waves against the ship. Thump after thump. Each followed by a muted splash. One after another. As the groaning spoke on the cart measured the greater and greater distance from Grandmother and home, each slapping of a wave made known more distance from dear Mother, with no hope.

Mrs. Sandys came to see me, my dresses she wanted to wash, they'd not touched water and soap since Mother and I laundered our last in London. She asked to wash both, the brown one I wear, the gray one in the trunk. Why wash both together? I wondered. To wear while laundry done, Mrs. Sandys provided a fine dress, one of hers. Much care she takes to pin it to fit. Most beautiful dress ever worn. Blue, a skirt with embroidery, white flowers. Sleeves quite full, with cuffs of white not blue. Sad I was when my dresses back from the wash. But trade not all bad. To my brown dress had new buttons of pearl. White against the brown. So kind.

Days and nights passed. Weeks became our cadence. Father did not speak. Or very seldom. Nathan sad, but busy. Busy doing nothing of matter. Soon, voices of the ship became more. Landfall was hoped and prayed near. Then it was there. Martinique. Nothing more beautiful. Large round green hills dipped to the sea. Between the blue sea, with its whitecap punctuations, and the emerald hills, a wide curved beach. Air warm, sun bright, a breeze of sweet smells. Something pleasant after long despair.

At this island we did not pause. Some said savages there were. Sailed on, past other most beautiful risings from the sea, then to Mevis. Here the anchor dropped. Off to shore went a party of crew. Food and water gathered. Fruit of different colors and flavors than known. Some sweet like honey. Two fine pigs brought aboard. Squealing soon turned to the aroma of meats. Warm weather, still seas, full stomachs, smiling faces, all content. I slept a content sleep. Next morning Mister Johnson spoke to Father, then Nathan and I he took down a steep plank to the ship's boat tied by its side. With a crew on the oars, toward the beach, then pulled to a spit of rocks that arched from the island, thus stopping the marching waves. On the tranquil side of the rocks the boat was held by a small iron tied to rope. Mister Johnson then pointed down. The water clear, sights not seen before. Fish, many fish. But not as any in the streams of Tewkesbury. Not gray. Not black. Color after color. All bright. These rainbows drifted and swam over and around rocks. Perhaps not rocks, bee nests of pinks, blues, and yellows.

From his blouse Mister Johnson pulled a crust of black bread. Broken in two, Nathan and I each given a scrap. Nathan tossed his in the sea. Like chickens to corn, the fish, all colors and sizes, churned the waters. Then my turn. They swam below, I above. What power. I the minister, they my flock. Not toss the bread, but held it right below. Circle. Circle again. Then, one in turn, slow to close, then to dart, as taking communion. Soon the bread gone, and back to the ship. But before the ship, another sight. A yell and gesture by an oarsman, to the port a large upside-down wash basin, with feet of fins and head barely seen. A sea tortoise we told. Fast it swam. But not swim fast enough. Later a bountiful stew there be.

That afternoon another amazement. Two small boats approached. Like none seen before, long and thin, the shape of half a green bean. But their cargo was most strange. People dark, dark like leather boots. All hair black. But clothing not much seen. Women, or young girls, only a scarf wrapped around the hips. Nathan much interest shown. The males, the same scarves. Against their dark faces white teeth in a constant smile. That night I lay in my cot and thought, since Mother joined Rebecca, the first day happiness visited. Perhaps this day was the beginning of the New World. It made me feel content.

One more day and night at anchor, then under the white sails. The day sky bright, moods are bright. Sailed north. The sun now rose on the starboard and bade farewell on the port. Ten or more days at sea, then to land. First Cape Henry. This be the lower lip of the mouth of the Chissiapiack Bay. A calm water, but not colors of Mevis. Trees to the water's edge, no beaches, no clear waters, no green mountains wearing a fluffy white wig. Slowly we went, apprentices at the bow taking measure of the depth. Then up the river named for our king. Not a kingly river I thought. From the river the first view, my new home, Jamestown. From a distance, only grays and browns were seen. Slowly closer, eyes straining to see. No white churches probed the sky. No bells rang. What seemed to be a high fence around the village. Made of logs. Fences are to keep animals contained. I wondered would cottages be built in the pasture of the cows and sheep.

Sails were furled. Two boats, each with strong oarsmen approached from an uneven pier at the river's edge. Ropes were made fast and pulled us to the pier. Scores of faces had gathered, our arrival being much hoped for. Later learned not our arrival, but that of our stores. From our ship to the pier, a long, steep plank leaned. Passengers on deck, toward the aft. Captain and Mister Rountree at the ready, in uniforms not seen since London. Up the plank three men, dark and lean. I think dark from the sun. Conversation, all passengers straining to hear. Then the word, we would spend the night on the ship. Not to our new home till tomorrow. That evening food brought aboard. A meat I had never partook and a sea creature most ugly, but pleasant to the taste. In my cot that night another new creature. Not to be eaten, rather they dined on me. The night air still and hot. No breeze. A buzzing by my ear. Quick to be heard, quick to depart. Then the marks. Large welts felt on my skin where they had set their table. To hide, hands pulled under my blanket with scarf over my face, then sleep.

With the morning Father with other men off to Jamestown. Our home to find. While he gone Mister Johnson spoke to Nathan and me. To Nathan he gave the most dear present, his knife. With this a new belt he had fashioned with a leather pocket for the blade. For me, a comb of white. He said it was ivory from the most strange animal that swam like a dolphin, but could walk like a lumbering sow. In the smallest of small letters, on the comb he had etched my name. I knew not what to say. Nathan's hand he shook, to me a gentle kiss above my eyes.

Before the plank descend, Mrs. Sandys speaks to me, and me alone. Together we sit on a cot, away from all. Smiles she does. Tells me all will be well. To Weyanoke she will go, not a far distance from Jamestown, a day's journey west. If I am ever in harm, somehow to her I should go. Then a package handed me. Ribbon of white around brown paper. Opened slowly. Mrs. Sandys's blue dress, worn by me when mine in the wash. Told to stand and hold it against me. She looked and smiled, said that she made it to fit. Her care in pinning the dress was not for one day worn, it was for alterations. We hugged. She was warm and soft. I think of Mother.

Father back to gather us and our trunk of clothes and household goods. A trunk of memories, memories of Tewkesbury. So sad. A young apprentice directed to help us with our burden. I wished it had been David. Down the plank and into Jamestown Village. What I thought a fence to keep animals in was to keep

savages out I was told. No paved streets. All but a few cottages
one level. Thatched roofs, but not straw. Windows, but not glass.
Only shutters. As we passed people turned their gaze to follow us,
as if judging a heifer at a fair. Some smiled. Most did not. And all
looked weary. Then our home, or half a home. We were given one
room of a two-room cottage. This cottage being no longer than
half the size of our home in Tewkesbury. One cot, one table, two
chairs, one broken, and a hearth. A door to the outside, made of
planks not well fitting. No door to the other room, separated by a
wall of clay. One window, closed with shutters on hinges of rope.
The floor of dirt, with one half covered with a rug of canvas, perhaps from a sail. Not pleased I think, my father. But no complaint.

To the center of town we went. A large building, one end open.
Benches, stools, chairs, and tables. There were other passengers
from our journey. Talked we did, some cottages better, others not.
In a pit meat was roasted. Not certain what animal it be. A hard
bread made by Indians, guinea wheat I told. Some drink was had,
a tease of apple but not cider. A young frail girl I met, her name
Martha. One year younger than Nathan. Over two years at Jamestown with mother and father. Her brother buried in the cemetery.
Pleasant was she, a most nice smile. Then her mother I met, her
face more of a man's than a lady's. Briefly we spoke, then asked to
meet my mother. Father answered, I could not.

Back to our cottage in the dark. There Father lit a candle brought
from Tewkesbury. Sat us down and spoke. But not as before. Always
in Tewkesbury he was Father and we were children. Words were
few, and came with no sauces or sweets. During our journey on the
sea almost no words after Mother's passing. But this night he spoke
to us, and only us. In a voice low Father spoke of Tewkesbury and
our pleasant cottage. He recounted memories of happiness. Then
he spoke of the last year. A hard journey. Then of Mother and love
for her. Then he said we were where we were this night, a cottage of
dark and dust. He paused for several moments. Then said that we

could not make this year better than last year, but we could make next year better than this year. And when we did, contentment and happiness would be ours.

That night, Father laid on the canvas, Nathan and I on the cot. Quickly, they both asleep. My father's words I thought. Spoke not to us as children, but as those grown. He gave Nathan and me a message for life. Not words of a command, but words of wisdom so that we would know how to command our lives. With morning quickly up and tidying. I would make well our modest room. By nightfall our cottage half would not be as well as that in Tewkesbury, but it would be more pleasant than the night before, and for this I would feel contentment. Father was right.

Father to a gathering of some type. Only men. Gone for the morning, then returned. Spoke to Nathan and me. A counsel governed Jamestown, no king or mayor. Jobs assigned, with much hard work for all. Nathan to catch fish. I think we may be hungry. I was to tend the cottage, and domestics with other women. Also, women plant and harvest with the men. Father to work as carpenter, new structures to build, old to repair. Nathan and I were sent to a well for water. Nathan with one bucket in each hand. Passed some cottage and for the first time seen, Indians, or savages they be. A man, two women, or two men and a woman, not certain. A mat, two strides by two strides, looked as heavy straw, with colors of shape. Tall was the man standing. Long black hair, but only on one side, the other shaved. Later I told side shaved so hair and bowstring not get caught. Britches worn, called leggings, with this a breechcloth. Women sitting, wearing something as a dress, more of a coat than a dress. Hair black, hair short. All clothes of deerskin, I think. Boots the same, more as slippers of leather than boots. But most strange the savage color. Skin of Indian not brown, but as brown. And the skin had a wet shine, looked as they just bathed, though in the dust they be. The man moved away, somewhere to go. Two others sitting on the mat busy with a task, I think baskets their labor. Nothing to say, nothing understood, on our way.

With water buckets full, back to the cottage. On the way, near the stockade I saw a sight to cause a pause. The *Essex* not nestled against the pier. A small ship it looked, down the river, to England. Sad, but not certain why. Thought of Mother. Somehow, and no sense to it, with the ship no more, Mother no more.

Next to us, in the half cottage not ours, Mrs. Dear and her son, Jonathan. She not a happy person. Her husband having passed many years before from the fever. Jonathan Nathan's size, but much older. When first arrived in Jamestown, while building a structure of some type, a log fell from a height and broke his leg. Broken bone set and healed. Some muscle torn. Walked with two crutches and one leg dragging behind. Some not kind to Jonathan. He was called snake by many for the snakelike trail in the dirt he left when he walked.

I became the woman of our house. Responsibility I took, direction I gave. But my servant only being Nathan so my instruction was cloaked in challenges. "It be impossible to repair that chair with only a knife." Our room began to appear not dreary. Smooth gray stones from the river were laid at the doorway as a path, to catch the dirt from boots and shoes. From a structure long fallen, planks were taken. Against them a measure was made and cuts applied. A wooden floor was ours. From our trunk an old scarf taken, made of the thinnest cloth. While hurtful, it was cut. Cut to cover the window opening. Then shutters were rehung. With one hinging up to make a canopy over the window. Then at night, even with rain, the shutters could be held open to allow for air while the scarf fenced the winged bugs.

Father became busy. Busy became contentment. A Mister Sullivan, of all the Jamestown persons I met, seemed most not dreary. When spoke to Father enthusiasm was there. Together, they saw a future not seen by others. In time, Father learned the history of Jamestown. This he learned from Mister Sullivan. I also learned a history, but mine from Mrs. Dear. Mister Sullivan to our cottage more days than not. No family in the New World. Came five years ago. In London read an article by a well-respected gentleman, Mister Harriot, "A Brief and True Report of Virginia." The report was half correct, it was brief, he said, but not true. When arrived, much discontentment. No gold, no emeralds, no grand villages. Fever, hunger, and despair welcomed him. But he now content. Labored hard, grows a crop that he barters for food and fine things, more than needed.

Some nights when Mister Sullivan visited, I listened while he spoke to Father. This done while I busied myself with tasks. Talk of a new crop, tobacco, the leaves smoked. Some English gentlemen in Jamestown pay much for this crop. Lands around Jamestown rich with soil for a tobacco from Trinidad. Mister Sullivan and Father speak of growing this tobacco for others. A crop for money, but not eaten, a speculation, I thought.

Nathan more a mason than a fisherman he be. Along the river's edge, where the stream curves in, rocks from the river gathered to make a stone fence. But this fence not in a field, and not high. It was across a portion of the river, then it turn upstream. This stone wall, conspiring with the river's edge, made a bucket larger than a barn. Fish, in their journey with the stream, against a wall they swim, with the strong stream the lid of the bucket. From this pen Nathan scoops dashing village dinners.

Mrs. Dear visited me, brought a flax-wheel. Had told her that Grandmother taught me to spin the thread. Two baskets of flax also brought. Before she left, pointed to a candle. Burn these every night? My response of yes brought surprise. Candles too dear. Turns and leaves, in a minute back. An apron full of wooden coins, but not coins, slices of pine knots from the pitch pine. They be as good as candles, and made by God. That night our cottage bright. Pine candles never sparse.

More to me did my father speak, but not as a child. Sometimes after Nathan asleep. At first our conversations on the day's events and the next day's work. Later on, next year's hopes. One night, after food and Nathan off, Father spoke of land called Martin's

Hundred, no more than a day's journey from Jamestown, and a village there, a strange name, Wolstenholme Towne. Named for a man in England who sends money in hope of rich returns. This town, Father said, was a new village with much promise. Here fifty acres was Father's if he tilled the land for tobacco. Mister Sullivan already was growing tobacco for a Mr. Rolfe. Father said he would journey to Martin's Hundred, and there he would build a fine cottage for Nathan and me, and we would join him before winter. I only first spoke encouragement. Then a small question, should tobacco be our crop? Others must buy our crop, then we trade for food. But if we tilled for corn and wheat, others not of import, we eat. Father silent, then said that he had considered this. Tilling for food served us well in Tewkesbury, but tobacco becomes as water to many. Then a story of Sir Walter Raleigh, gentleman serving at the pleasure of Queen Elizabeth. After her death, Sir Raleigh fell from favor with our King James and ordered beheaded. Last act before head depart, to smoke his tobacco pipe. Tobacco, said Father, becomes a passion, not a choice. That be why a gentleman in London lay a shilling on a scale for equal weight tobacco. More paid for passion than food.

While Father gone, Nathan and I often took our dinner meal with Mrs. Dear and Jonathan. Sometimes food was sparse, conversation never. Many stories. None good. She spoke not kindly of Mister Dear. A fine home in a village near London. Told of veins of gold in Virginia, her husband sold their cottage and shop for promised riches. A long sea journey of forty passengers, twenty-eight arrived. No promised gold. Only recounting of the worst miseries. Savages, they hacked, they burnt. Their contentment the slow torture of the English. The Indians' partner was starvation. A stockade fence built to keep the savages out became the prison to keep the English from fields where crops be grown and game be tracked. She told stories of starvation and worse tales that should not be retold.

A fortnight from his leaving, Father returned. Back to the Hundred he would go again after two days. First evening back, after Nathan asleep, we spoke. Recounted stories told by Mrs. Dear. He turned toward the pine knots' glow, then turned back to me. All true he said. But that was then, and now is a better time. At first the Indians greeted the English, but misdeeds and misunderstandings brought distrust. And, Father said, people distrustful will find cause to be offended. Now Indians and English work and live together. Told how he and Mister Sullivan traded with them and he had seen their villages, with happy children and contentment. Told me not to be sad, that Mrs. Dear was not a happy soul and her happiness was to bring unhappiness to others. This, he said, was not right. But we should show her kindness because much suffering she had.

With next day's morn, Father asked that I join him for a journey not far. Not toward the river we walked, as always my course, but toward the dark of the forest. In we went, a small path, across a wide creek, then to the top of a rise. Along this rise, then down to a field. A field with a crop I had not seen before. Then past the field, voices heard. Strange, but not harsh. Some laughter also. First the smoke seen, then the village. A village of Indians. On level ground their cottages. More like huts, each looking as a large loaf of bread, rectangular with a rounded roof. An opening on the narrow end for an entrance, no wooden door, a skin. Openings for windows, but no glass. Smoke raised from most, a fire within. By many huts gardens, not flowers, but of things to eat. At one place no huts, no garden, just a space, a circle. In the center a pit for fire. I thought this where they meet together. More than a hundred Indians were seen this day. All with some clothes, all dark in color. Hair black, no beards, and mostly smiles. Busy all, skinning, cooking, growing, caring.

At the edge of the village, near a tree long without leaves, was a hut different from the others. From its curved roof a pole stood. From this pole a cloth flew, the colors of England. Not a flag, but the colors of our flag, patched somehow together. Father approached, calling for a Mister Greene. A man appeared, an

Englishman. Greetings to Father, they knew each other from labors together at Martin's Hundred. Pleasantries, then in his hut we went. There we met wife and son. This I did not understand. Wife be an Indian, dark skin, black hair, moccasins, deerskin dress and many necklaces of beads, mostly brown. Son an Englishman, perhaps eighteen or so in age. Mister Greene spoke to his wife in a language I did not know. Her words in English, and most kind to us, a drink being offered. After some talk, Father stood and we bade good-bye. Off to Jamestown by the path taken. Who was this man, who was this Indian woman and boy? I asked. The man, Mister Greene, came to Jamestown many years before, I was told. Married an Indian lady only last year, with much contentment he lived. Their son was of neither, an orphan taken in by him long ago.

In my cot that night I considered the day. Mrs. Dear was wrong. No savages these people. As us, homes, children, work, and smiles. A question was brought by the day. I thought and then decided. The next morn, while Nathan drawing water from the well, I asked Father, would he marry an Indian woman? He was silent. I should not have shown an interest. Why offend, why question? Then he smiled. He never smiled. No, he said. My mother was his wife. His wife before, now, and forever.

Father off to Martin's Hundred. I the lady of the home. Clothes no longer fit. Nathan's britches high on his legs. The pearl buttons on my blouse pulling. Nothing in the trunk to replace. Mrs. Dear had no britches for Nathan, all trousers for her son. Told me of Mrs. Wright, with a young daughter, no husband. Her home also her store. Clothes she had. But only for trade. To her home I went, longer trousers for Nathan, also a dress of a woman's size. Not exchanged for coins, something else needed. That night I considered. Nathan's knife a fine trade, but too dear. Also, in the trunk hidden away, the special hair clip. But this was a gift to me from Mother, I think. Then the answer came. Next morn off to Mrs. Wright with Nathan. Make certain trousers fit, they did. Then for me a well-used lady's dress. Body fine, somewhat long. Easily made right. An exchange was struck, in trade one of my worn dresses and Mantha for Mrs. Wright's daughter.

Some more suppers with Mrs. Dear. Her half cottage with table and four chairs, Nathan, Jonathan, Mrs. Dear, and I could sit as one. Stores considered and a meal planned. Easier one meal for four than two for two. And her bake-kettle most grand. Some talk pleasant, other not. I speak of Tewkesbury, family, and happiness. She of unjust happenings. False promises brought families to the New World. She spoke of those who came with soft hands, no skills, much idleness. Gentlemen arrived, tradesmen, hunters and farmers needed. Mistakes made. Village built where *Discovery*, *Godspeed*, and *Susan Constant* dropped anchor, not where it should. Jamestown marshes with disease, fresh water not always, salt to the taste, fields for crops not near.

Father back and forth. Two days home, several gone. Martin's Hundred he says is most content. Not the heat of Jamestown with its still water smells and bugs. One day a pleasant surprise. Mister Greene's son visited our cottage. Indian bread he brought. His name was Charles. Much like Father, few words. We spoke briefly. Interest he showed in Nathan's knife. From under his smock a hatchet he pulled. No iron. A rock of some kind, but not round, sharp on one end. This bound to a wooden shaft with narrow strips of leather. Most fearsome it looked.

Mrs. Dear visits, a bread baked with cloves brought. Talk of pleasant things. Most things well. Her Jonathan a new friend, the blacksmith. A trade he learn, strong arms needed, walking not much. Then the past, her face darkens. When first they here, Indians give food for not much. One mirrow to the Indians, three families eat for a fortnight. Later, when desperation closer, food more dear. One venison leg, five axes of iron. More given, less received, weaker settlers become. Then the truth. Massacred with the iron traded, heads, arms, and legs severed. These Indian savages, but cunning they are, patient they are, Mrs. Dear said.

Two ladies came to visit. A Mrs. Sing and a Mrs. Smyth. Both most kind. Asked me to tea on the morrow. That night, after prayers, I lay on my cot. A day different. Ladies came to see me, but not as a child. Morning light, up, food for Nathan then the wash. Then time for me. Face clean, hair combed, shoes no dust. Then to the trunk, for this day a hair braid. Only once worn, worn for Jack. Then off to a tea.

Mrs. Smyth's cottage most nice. Curtains of blue, tied back with ribbons of blue. A rug, not canvas, but something of color. A gold, I recall. Chairs, a table, and hearth with a mantel on which large seashells perched. A project for Nathan, I thought. Tea was served. At the table a white porcelain teapot, covered in painted flowers. Hot water poured to cups, they being of tin. Between the stream from the pot and the cup, a strainer, filled with fragments of leaves. Tea. No sugar. Into each cup a large drop of honey, then stirred so slowly, with such care, with small silver spoons. Much ceremony. On a wooden plate, cakes, not sweet, more as small breads. Some square, some round. Then conversation. Much conversation. Asked if I knew why we lived in the cottage that we did. I did not. They did. Mrs. Dear was without husband. Wanted to England return, but she was given promises. Told that one half her cottage be given to the first strong man with no wife partner. Then after the passing of the cakes I was asked, did Father believe Mrs. Dear fair? No response.

Both Mrs. Sing and Mrs. Smyth told me their tales. Came to Jamestown with their husbands. Mrs. Sing's husband strong and able. Mrs. Smyth's the first winter succumbed. Now two families, one cottage. Much more conversation. Spoke of fabrics, food, and home. Nothing distressful muttered. Promises made, again would we meet. As I departed, a question by Mrs. Sing. How old I was and when did my mother pass? I responded. Then a question of confusion. Asked if I knew all that a woman must know. A pause, not sure the import of this question, nor its purpose, I smiled and answered yes.

That night, Nathan asleep, I considered the day. Some sugar, some salt. With women I sat, then perhaps a woman I be. But the question. They asked me if I knew what I did not know. What could this mean? But the most unsettling only I would know. In a cottage I sat this day, with a smile on my face, showing contentment. With me ladies. Fine ladies. But not my mother. And with these ladies, as we smiled, tea was poured. Poured from white porcelain, painted with flowers. Porcelain as the pitcher and bowl my dear sweet Mother and I washed our faces so long, long ago in a happy time together.

As the summer passed, the cottage a home. New furniture made, more chairs, a fine cabinet for the plates and pots, work table, and a new cot. Cloth from the last ship from London become new shirts for Father and Nathan. Also I think Mother proud, cloth for curtains and cloth to cover our table. Most grand, on the last ship glass. One pane for our cottage. Father most carefully framed a window, we would have light in winter with no wind. Each day, but Sunday, chores attacked. Friends made, much conversation and laughter lightens our tasks. Mrs. Dear I know, a good woman she be. When Father and Nathan gone, we speak while laundering, gardening, sewing, and cooking. Her life has been hard with disappointments, but a friend to me.

In my cot, before I sleep, much I consider. Is Jamestown grander than Tewkesbury? I think not for certain. No church with bells tolling, no fine cottages with fenced gardens, no roads without mud, no long curving stone walls embracing the fields of crops, no wooden bridge across the river. Much to do before Jamestown be a Tewkesbury. But another difference. A difference as a heavy weight on the scale. In Tewkesbury people content. A fine village. Most days pleasant, most days the same. And then, each year the same. No satisfaction from sacrificing to make better. In Jamestown, everyone toiling to make life better.

Charles visited again. In a clay jar, honey was brought. Told me it best eaten soon. Together we each bread and honey ate. Then talk. No stories from Charles, only events. Came with his family in 1607 as a small boy. Both parents died. He lived with a minister, then the minister passed. Then it was with others, not friends or relatives, just others. I spoke much. Recounted most happy days in Tewkesbury. Family, foods, gardens, and friends. Charles pleasant, but not warm. No comments about my past happiness. Before he depart, I spoke of the first time we meet. I spoke of how kindly and happy the Indians be. He did not quickly respond. Silent he sat, then he spoke. Words only with time I understood. Charles said if an Indian be a dog, never would it bark before it bite.

Nathan back to our cottage with half a hind leg of venison. Roasted in Mrs. Dear's bake-kettle, served with corn and bread, a fine meal. That evening at Mrs. Dear's table we sat, Nathan and me with Mrs. Dear and Jonathan. Venison enjoyed, Nathan sat tall. Good food, good conversation. Then a casual remark by me, sorry that Charles not share dinner with us. Mrs. Dear flinch, then quiet. She spoke, her voice slow. She knows Charles. Years before many starved, he did not. With a group of men he lived. They survived, human flesh their meal. Said Charles was bound for hell. I said nothing. Then told Mrs. Dear that we would soon depart. This was not good, she say. Again, memories of hardships before. Tortures, burnings, starvation, again told. She thought all Englishmen should stay as one, more men to harvest, more strength to show savages. Perhaps she was right. But I thought she did not want us to leave because she did not want to be alone.

Father, while standing outside our cottage in the evening sun, told Nathan and me his decision, soon our journey to Martin's Hundred. A fine cottage there. Only one long day of travel. Some furniture already. My tasks with a smile. Wash the clothes, Nathan's hair cut, all things packed, all chores of contentment. Prepared us to leave when Father beckoned.

Then our last day in Jamestown. Many farewells. Promises to return. Father and Nathan with our trunk, down to the river's edge. Then on to a shallop. Flat bottom, poles for oars. Two crew, neither the captain, much confusion. Down the river, at first no chore. Turn in a narrow stream, trees low, pushing back, then the shallows. Father and Nathan in the water, more pushing than poling. Nathan's boot stolen by the mud. Much searching, then it reunited to its mate. Hours of labors, then to the firm, a path. Back to Jamestown the shallop, up the path Father, Nathan, I, and the trunk. Not a long trek, then voices, then the sight, the village. I was not rightly fearful. Martin's Hundred a place of contentment. A cottage for us. Greater than Jamestown, smaller than Tewkesbury. The people cheerful. Color not gray. Families with children, one not a year of age. More than a score of cottages. No fence of logs to hold some out and some in. One side of the village a stream, fast moving, clear water for all. On two sides fields, well-tended fields. The fourth edge a backdrop to our village stage, the forest. Tall trees, no pine. Standing at the edge, peering between the wide-rising trunks, with no light from above, a chapel it be.

Our first day there, Mister Sullivan came to visit. Some words, then Father and he departed. As they left, passing through the door a lady appeared. Dark-blue dress, an apron wearing many meals. Round face, hair covered with a scarf. My size, sweet smile. Perhaps thirty years of age, Mrs. Clyde her name. With her presents. A large loaf of bread, not Indian. Dried fish and a small block of salt. Some talk. Most happy she to have another family near. Then she asked a question never heard before. How long was I married? A woman I must be.

At Martin's Hundred many Indians. Jamestown only a few. Many speak words of the Englishman. Many villagers knew their words. I watched, I learned. Indians different, Indians just the same. All emotions and chores are ours, but things done not the same. Crops sowed and harvested, but not by men, Indian women and children tend the fields. Hunting, as English, for the men. No muskets, they bows and snares. As fields become less fertile and game less plenty, Indian village moved. Everything to the next site. This be the reason for no stone structures. All Indian cottages vaulted frameworks of saplings, these covered with skins or mats. Fires in their cottage for cooking and warmth, but no chimney. In the summer smoke kept out mosquitoes.

Most all Indian clothing deerskin. Tanned for color and fringed for style. Both men and women jewelry worn, the most beautiful strings of pearls from river mussels. Copper also for jewelry, and rings of copper for money. Often the Indians skin colored with dyes from the plants, mixed with walnut oil and bear's grease. This what made their skin look as wet when first seen in Jamestown. Most favorite color is that of red from pokeberry, often shoulders and head this red.

Marriage they have, some men more than one wife. Love their children, but not the same. Babies each day in cold water washed. Young not fed until chores done and skills practiced. With death, much grieving. Departed covered in ash from a fire. Mourner also made dark with ash. Shallow grave dug, deceased possessions placed within, then the body. Much wailing, much lamenting, then covered with earth. Comfort given the departed's family by others. Religion not ours. As Greeks and Romans, many gods. Some for war, some for crops, others for disease and sickness. Males be their priests with skins more elaborate than others. Like the Church of England, I think.

But most important, parents smile at children, and Indian children laugh and play. We the same. But, Father and others not think them our equal. Do the Indians think we greater than them, I think not. Do they think we be equal, I hope this be. If they think less we be, fearful I be.

The skills and chores of Jamestown the same needed for a content home in Martin's Hundred. Nathan was now a farmer, a farmer of tobacco. When at the dinner meal, he spoke of problems and solutions. Has begun to sing Father's song, tobacco is wondrous and happiness it will bring. His day was no longer a lark with work being cajoled, toiling in the fields was a race to rewards. For me, no different than Jamestown it be. Domestics each day, meals each evening. Pleasant talk with women. Most things understood, some not. Life not hard, life not easy.

Father to leave with Mister Sullivan, to Weyanoke they go with a Mister John Rolfe. After Nathan asleep one evening, Father spoke of Mister Rolfe. A gentleman from London that first to Jamestown in 1609, a most hard journey. With wife and children shipwrecked on Bermuda. From there to Jamestown, his wife and child soon died. Rolfe struggled but did not fail, took a path different from others. Not a hunter or a farmer of food eaten. Rather he grew tobacco, because it was more dear than food in London marts, a greater coin paid for a bushel of tobacco than corn or wheat. If done right, not a plow drawn, others tend the fields, paid a wage of consideration. With monies from tobacco Mister Rolfe and others purchased all foods and fine domestics for their cottages. But then the story turned sad. A beautiful Indian, Pocahontas, daughter of the Chief Powhatan, was most striking, most kind to all that knew her ways. Married in Jamestown to Mister Rolfe, a contented married life, a fine cottage with a son born, Thomas. Then in 1617 they journey to London. There she was greeted by fine ladies and gentlemen. Much attention, much intrigue. All amazed her beauty, her carriage. Then she became sick and died. Some say from London's cold mists. Buried in England she was, Thomas stayed in England with his uncle, Rolfe back to Virginia alone. At night when all chores done, I thought. So many died in Jamestown, the fever's revenge. An Indian princess to London, and she died. People are people, all the same. What difference where their cottage be? New World or Old World. Then I think. Fish are fish. But fish in a stream cannot in an ocean live, and an ocean fish not be in a flowing stream.

Back from his travel, Father content. Mister Sullivan with him and stayed the night. I prepared the meal and table set. With them a bottle of ale brought. Father and he drank, pleasant talk, then loud talk. Tobacco grown by Mister Sullivan and Father sold for a high price, greater than a fair measure. Father's portion conveyed as another drink taken. In the morn, after Mister Sullivan take his leave, Father spoke. A good summer and winter, the spring will be better. Tomorrow, back to Jamestown, there necessities bought. Nathan and I pleased. Father pleased we are pleased. After Nathan left for his day's tasks, Father came to me by the wash. "Know what month this be?" "Yes," I say, "March." "No," he said, "not March, this the month of your birth, you be fifteen soon. In Jamestown something new for you." Then he turned and was gone. Can this be, I thought, Father both my shoes and socks?

To Jamestown we all went. No trunk to burden us on our journey, no need for a shallop. Walked the paths. Some streams crossed, narrow and not deep. No leaves, but weather more of spring than winter. Some buds seen. A walk of contentment. At the end of the journey not an unknown as other journeys taken, people we knew will greet us. Paused in our trek, rested and took some bread and dried meat, with a cup of cider. Two Indians pass. Indians seen every day. But these are different. Most glanced and smiled, these glanced and looked away. Off to Jamestown before the light is no more. Smoke first seen, then familiar sights. In the village we walked, Father tall in his gray coat. To the counsel, then told where to bed, Mrs. Dear's cottage if we wished, she had returned to England. Not much left in her cottage. Two candles from the cottage next door, a bucket from another, we have enough. We visited others and spoke and heard stories, all good. Winter mild, stores of food ample, ships have arrived, Indians trading and helping. After a dinner Nathan and I to rest, Father to the cottage later.

Before light, a commotion. Father up, people yelling. Father ran from the cottage. Nathan and I peered through the window, much movement, much running, no direction. Then Father returned. Events told quickly, a Mister Pace rowed to Jamestown Island with an alarm. A horrible story he carried. An Indian boy living with him, and now a Christian, visited by his brother of the Pamunkey. This brother told him that all English soon would die and he should slay his master, Martin Pace. Much confused, the Christian Indian told his master what he was told to do. With fear for others, Mister Pace sped to Jamestown.

More we learned of the savages' attack. Much thought, much patience before the blows struck. Four years ago the chief of the Indians, Powhatan, joined his ancestors. This chief being the father of Pocahontas, who had married the tobacco grower John Rolfe and died in England. Powhatan's brother became the chief, soon displaced by Opechancanough. We were told that he hated the English, but he was smart. Claiming that heavens would fall before an Englishman he would kill. Opechancanough traded with the English and in all manner was our friend, all this time planning the attack on Jamestown and twenty villages and plantations. Only Mister Pace's quick call of alarm spared Jamestown.

Father and other men to the stockade walls this night. Nathan and I by the cottage window. Nothing to see, little to hear. In the dark of night, with no glow of flames, I pondered. Summer, fall, and winter good. Why not spring and forever? Why would Indians wish us harm? We intend no harm. Then slowly light, then suddenly reports of muskets. With the dawn four boats of Indian warriors, muskets fire from the stockade, retreat to the boats, no more danger. During the day, slowly news from other villages. Massacres. Women, children are killed, but not quickly without pain. Homes burnt, crops burnt, supplies burnt.

We could not leave Jamestown. As before I made the cottage in Jamestown our home. Borrowed this, borrowed that. Nathan became a fisherman again, but Father not a carpenter, a soldier he became. No one out the stockade by themselves at first. Only groups of men, men with muskets. Then to each village a group of men went, to see what fate they have. Some villages no harm, others most dreadful. Farthest up the river, at Henricus, twenty murdered, at Weyanoke, over thirty murdered, but most fearful to hear, our village in Martin's Hundred over seventy souls gone. Friends hacked and burned. When

I first heard of a village where Indians murdered Englishmen, I felt a grief and anger. Then with each new recounting of murders no more grief, just more anger. Anger at savage Indians.

In Jamestown, days become weeks then months. Some new friends made. Old friends made again. Same chores, easier though. No mistakes of not knowing. Nathan no longer Nathan. Taller, new britches, new shirt to fit. His coat no longer to his wrists, traded with other in consideration for tan deerskin jacket. His voice became deeper also, and from his mouth fewer words of merriment and more of life events. Nathan washed his face and brushed his hair each day, never before. Martha the reason. They met first night in Jamestown, her mother asked to speak to my mother. A pleasant girl, but nothing special, plain to the eye. Her best quality for Nathan, I think, she not a boy.

Father gone one day, and Charles a visit makes. Not seen for months, he was the same, but no gift of bread, honey, or berries. Did not know I was in Jamestown. Saw Nathan by the river and asked where I was. Talk of pleasantries, then I ask, is Mister Greene well, my meaning, does he still live? Yes, the answer. I pause, how can this be, all Englishmen were to be killed by the savages, you and he lived among them, how escape? Not escape, Indians were not fearful of me, he said. No sense this made. Explain, I asked. I did not understand his answer, until long consideration.

Indians were people of the land, not savages, Charles said. Some things they grow, some things they hunt. What they grow they eat. Of what they hunt, most that killed eaten, but some not. Only animals killed that not eaten are those that eat what Indian eats or will kill Indians. A wolf not eaten, poor meat, fur not as large as a deer, or thick as a bear. But wolves eat what Indians eat, and they kill Indians. So an Indian would kill a wolf. But I say, why kill an Englishman? He's not a wolf. His answer a shiver gave me. They kill those who take their land and food, and they be Englishmen. He paused, then spoke, spoke of years ago. When first arrived in Jamestown, curiosity by Englishmen and Indians. Some small exchanges. Then weakness shown by Englishmen to Indians. Not able to raise crops, not able to hunt game, sickly with diseases and fevers. Only survived if Indians helpful, at first this done. But Englishmen, while taking help, were Englishmen. Accepted help from Indians not because they had needed skills, but because they wanted servants. Indian saw a weak new animal, Englishman. This animal ate more than it grew or hunted.

Conversation no more. Two cups taken from an oak shelf. Cider passed. I thought. Then I asked, but Indian is a man and Englishman is a man, not an animal. True he say. But does England not battle Spain? Are they soldiers who fight Spain? Or savages? Uncomfortable I was. Charles was not wrong, but he cannot be right. But they attacked at first light, no warning given. Before I finished he answered, no warning to the wolves, lie quietly in wait, no sign of the hunter given, then the kill. A final question I asked this day, why only in this year did they attack, why not years before? Answer short. A lone wolf no danger, a pack to be feared.

Father to Martin's Hundred and returned. Not good. Many homes burned. Only three families in the village, Indians gone. Father said that we should return. His land was there, our future there. Father was my father, but this did not seem right. Always to the next we go, not to stay. But back we went, a long day's journey. Sorry we did, a sad destination. Many cottages no longer, ours no longer. Ashes and a stone hearth only. Clyde's cottage became ours, they fled to another village long ago. Their cottage not small, and with two windows of glass, the promise of much light in winter.

In the village were the Bradleys, known from Jamestown, and two families, not known, Brites and Anders, they from a village destroyed. Three families shared what they had with us, and that night in a new cottage, blankets, candles, and bread we had. Next day I busy with chores to make the cottage our home. Nathan and Father were carpenters. Repairs made, cots built. After a pause for the noon meal one day, Father to our burnt cottage. Knelt in the ashes, hands sifting. Then he moved a pace or two, more sifting, then stood up and back. With him the two metal hinges and latch, the bones of our family's trunk. I prayed not the bones of our family's future.

Too late in the fall to plant crops, but game plenty. Fewer villagers, same number of deer and turkeys as before. Roast meat every night. During the day, I did chores with Mrs. Bradley, Mrs. Brites, and Mrs. Anders. Few words from Mrs. Anders, sullen look. Mrs. Bradley and Mrs. Brites most content. All things God's will, ours only to be true to God and chores to complete. One day at work we talk as always. Most talk of home and families. Conversation meanders to my journey from England. I tell of beautiful blue dress given me by Mrs. Sandys, such a generous gift. Without pausing in her chores Mrs. Anders said that it was too bad she is dead, Indians butchered her last spring. God, please, be it not so. That night, I lay in my cot, not moving. In the darkness I think; Charles was wrong, only a savage kill Mrs. Sandys. Days passed, each day less hurt, but no less hate. Then one night, Nathan asleep, Father comes to me. Quiet for a moment, then to me handed an ivory comb with my name, ashes cleaned away, only hints of flame.

Nathan join the men in hunting, off every day to track. Almost every day they hunt, return with venison or turkey. I was at the wash with Mrs. Bradley, while men hunted deer. A musket shot heard, fresh venison will be roasted this day. Then another report, then another. One shot for deer, perhaps two. More than two, venison was not the prey. All tasks stopped, all ladies to Mrs. Bradley's cottage. Time passes, worry builds. Then a yell, Nathan's voice. Running our way, three others behind at a distance. They be my father and the husbands. Home safe, Mister Anders wounded. Arrow in his arm. Broken off, pushed through, then coat and shirt off. Washed and dressed the wound. This done by Mrs. Bradley while Mrs. Anders moans.

Then the tale, a deer being tracked as always, our men softly walking to not make noise and frighten prey, looking down at trail. To a clearing, into the middle, then a yell. Savages two hundred strides away, in an instant a flight of arrows, one does not pierce the ground. Muskets fired, perhaps one savage felt the musket's bite. Each party turns, then each gone. This night not much talk, stares at the flames in the hearth. Men decided, one not sleep this night.

With the sun's rise, Mister Anders and Mister Brites made a decision known. With their wives they were leaving for Jamestown. No cart, no boat, little they take. Father and Mister Bradley spoke often and quietly this day. Bradleys stay. We stay. I know not why. Mrs. Bradley a pleasant companion for me. Her share of a burden taken always without a harsh word. Domestics we did, as winter closer, fewer chores, no gardens, no crops, no washes in the stream. Wood collected, meals prepared. Father, Nathan, and Mister Bradley stalk venison together, close to our cottages. All was well, then the break.

Mrs. Bradley and I in her cottage, chores of everyday. Noise outside, the cottage door open. Nathan and Mister Bradley leaned against Father, holding him upright, on one leg, the foot not standing is turned, it not true. To the cot, Father in pain, both hands clenched the folds of the great gray coat, knuckles white. Cut his trouser leg, I was faint, bone through skin. Not a small bone. I am told to leave. To my cottage, then a scream, deep and long, then quiet.

That night events told. Last summer two trees felled and laid across a stream. Next to each other to make a bridge, walk across one foot on one, the other on the log's mate. Today the men cross, no concern. But return, in haste, Father's leg slips between the logs and stumbles to the stream, full weight pulling over a leg grabbed tight by the logs. Two broken bones set, skin sewed, would take weeks to mend, always with a limp. But this was not the worst. Not far from the cottages, across the stream, near a field once for tobacco, many savages. To the cottage our men came, their haste the reason for Father's break.

Next day Nathan crafts crutches for Father. Only one step taken, then to the cot. Not be able to walk for days, perhaps weeks, perhaps never. Mister Bradley visits, ask to be alone with Father, this is done. Nathan and I visit with Mrs. Bradley, she told us they would leave in the morn. Savages only a small travel from our cottages, she fearful of an attack. Mister Bradley returns, his eyes not to mine. To Father I go, go alone. Father speaks to me in words slow and soft. Not Father's voice. Nathan and I would be leaving with Bradleys tomorrow. Father to stay, needs time for contemplation. Has food for the winter, no need to leave the cabin, as a bear in a cave, Indians not know he is here. No, I say, together we go. He is on his cot. He looks away. Nothing said. I stood, taller than Father. He turned back and looked up. This was not my father, this was a man, a man in pain. Pain of muscle and bone, pain of heart and soul. He spoke, of mistakes made, of opportunities no more. Dreams only dreams, hopes only hopes, nothing of good for our sacrifices. I am quiet. Nothing to say, it true.

Nathan and I were to leave with Mister and Mrs. Bradley. No cart, only what we carry. First, all food from Bradley's cottage to our cottage for Father. Nathan moves all chopped wood inside. Father boasted in a fortnight fine he would be, and journey to join us. If not, return in the spring and he would be fat from food and no labors. We move to leave. Father extends his hand to Nathan. Never before. Nathan could not move, then went forward. Father's hand shaken. Then to his cot I went. Told me he would be safe and soon we would be together. Touch him I did not. I knew not what to do, but I knew this was not right. Still I stood. Then off, through the cottage door. With the Bradleys, the four we walked. Through the village, past the ashes of our burnt cottage, to the path. Stride after stride, this was not right. More strides, farther from Father. Mister Bradley's boots heavy and firm. Each stride, a pound of the ground. As on the English paths long ago when the groan of the cart's spoke marked the greater and greater distance from Grandmother never to be seen, and as each slapping wave against the hull marked the growing distance from so much that I loved, the thump of his boots measured the distance from Father. This cannot be, I thought. It shall not be. This was my choice.

Stop I did. Much protest. Mrs. Bradley most impassioned, I will not be swayed. To Nathan, a hug, a kiss on the cheek. See you soon, remember me always. Then back, back to the cottage. Opened the door. Father on the cot. To him I go. Kneel by the cot, a kiss on his hand. Father, I love you, nothing he said, looked away.

Father and I alone. No fire or candles at night, no signals for savages we make. Days long. Father mostly still. Meat we have is dried, small portions eaten before the dark. Father finally up, few steps become more. His crutch be his partner. Then outside he goes, not far. Then not his crutch, but with his musket. Why take a musket? Perhaps hunting his walk. The cold came fast. A small fire during the day for some warmth. Eat less we do. As fall slowly into winter, leaves drifting with the wind, hunger squeezing us tight. My thoughts from loved ones to food. Father cooked our meal, only one each day. Most often soup. Bitter, not good. A cold wrapped the cabin. Then a snow. More snow, less soup. My clothes not fit, Father's face not his. In time, no soup. Only weak tea made with melted snow.

One cold morn my father came to me. Wonderful news, he had seen a large fat deer with a yearling. The snow gave their trail. He would be off to track and then much we would eat. He would butcher them on the spot, and make a coat from the fat one's hide. Asked that I not think poorly of him should he spend the night in the forest eating their roasted flesh. When told this, I in my cot, hiding from the cold. He then silent. Took off his long gray coat and laid it over me, a great blanket it be. Knelt by the cot, took my hands in his. On my finger, one next to my thumb, a ring was placed. My mother's wedding ring. "Hold this tight and think of Mother tonight." Forward he leaned. His face near mine, then our foreheads touched. Moments passed. No words. Then he stood, then I alone.

Father gone. In my cot that day, then night. Prayers I said, but not on my knees. Lay still, so dark. No stars, no moon through the glass. Alone, cold and dark. The wind in the trees my companion. Then a thought, only happy memories for me this night. My home in Tewkesbury. Mother by the hearth, smells of warm bread. Nathan by the river, fishing with Father. Grandmother Alice, spinning and sewing, then holding my hand as prayers said. Jack, walking with me, sharing a roasted apple. His smile, his good-bye. Mister Johnson, so much time, so many lessons learned. Beautiful fish, a tortoise gliding through clear warm waters. Pearl buttons and a fine blue dress from Mrs. Sandys, the most beautiful seen. Tea with ladies, so special. Charles, such pain, but so kind to me. And Father tried so hard. Before sleep, another prayer. God I then spoke, I ask forgiveness for wrongs I did, and know that no one has wronged me. Then sleep.

In the morning I woke, but eyes I did not open. I lay in my cot. On my face the warm sun. No cold. Then I felt the hand. A hand so familiar. A hand held softly. Opened my eyes, sweet Grandmother by my side.

Emilie

John

The Great Depression was the largest and deepest depression in American history, spanning the period of 1929 to 1939. Over 25 percent of the population seeking work were unemployed. Banks failed, savings evaporated, property foreclosed, and in city after city soup lines stretched for blocks.

No group was harder hit by the Depression than farmers and farm workers. During the first three years of the Depression, farm income fell by a staggering two-thirds. A bushel of wheat that sold for

$2.94 before the Depression sold for 30 cents in 1932. Of the farmers, the sharecroppers of the South were particularly fragile and quickly felt the pain of the Depression; their very existence was tenuous even before the Depression.

After the Civil War the bulk of the Southern farmland was owned by a relatively few rich men; rich white men. In the 1870s newly freed slaves and poor whites accepted the sharecropper system. The way of life of most sharecroppers was inferior to that of many people in medieval Europe. Housing consisted of primitive log cabins or clapboard one-room houses. Few homes had glass windows or screens. Indoor plumbing was nonexistent; water was provided from open wells or nearby springs and creeks, and bathrooms were outdoor privies located a few yards behind the hovel that was home.

By the time of the Great Depression sharecroppers represented 65 percent of all Alabama farming. By 1940 it was estimated the average sharecropper family income was less than 65 cents a day. From this amount they had to pay the land owner for the meager sundries he had provided during the year.

I KNEW WE WAS POOR. WASN'T TILL THE ARMY THAT I LEARNED there was good poor and bad poor. We was bad poor. Barefoot poor.

Renfroe is where I grew up. It wasn't more than a long walk in good weather from Talladega. Then Talladega was an hour on the train to Birmingham. Never did ride the train there. Never even saw Birmingham till the army.

In Renfroe there was Pa, Ma, me, and Billy. I was named John after my ma's big brother who was killed in the first war. Blown up in a trench is what they told me. I thought the name John would have matched up good with Ma's maiden name of Green. Both ending with "n," sort of poem-like. But our name, Butcher, didn't go so good with John. Billy Butcher sounded good, but not John Butcher. Too bad for me, 'cause that was my name.

Pa always was a farmer. He didn't own land, he worked mon-
eyed people's land. For sure he wasn't paid. Pa just got a shared part
from the sale of cotton, corn, peanuts, and whatever we could coax
out of the baked Alabama soil. Pa worked fifty acres. Most men
worked twenty-five, maybe thirty-five. Pa worked sixteen hours
most every day, with us kids helping, for those fifty acres. If things
went right Pa could make more money with fifty acres.

Problem was that most times things didn't go right, so Pa
worked twice as hard as a sharecropper with twenty-five acres, and
they both made the same—nothing. I asked Pa once, why fifty
acres, since we had to work twice as hard? What he told me was if
we got lucky for three years or so, and it rained, and the bugs
stayed away, his share of crop money would be enough to buy fifteen or twenty acres outright. Hoped maybe he could give Billy
and me our own land, then we'd get all of the crop money.

That fifty acres of mostly red clay wasn't much good for growing things. Difference between rocks and Alabama clay was maybe
you could break a rock. Coming down through the middle of our
fifty acres was Harkins Creek. Okay for a scoop of drinking water,
but nothing much else. For certain nary a fish. Did have some trees
growing along it. Trees knew where water was. Working in the
fields between the sun and the clay you could start to feel like a
twice-turned-over hoecake. We'd stop for dinner, whatever vittles
were in the tin pail that Ma had put together, and if we was nearby
the creek we'd set ourselves down in some shade.

Our house was better than most. Pa built an extra room in the
back for Billy and me, so's Ma and Pa had their room and we had
ours. In the big room was our stove, table, and some chairs that sat
crooked. I was about twelve or so when we got electricity, got it
from President Roosevelt. Then right before I went off, we got a
radio. We had a better than middling crop that year. Anyway, this
painted brown radio sat on the end of our table that was pushed up
against the wall, so at supper there were five at the table. The five

being Pa, Ma, me, Billy, and the radio. Pa said we could eat faster 'cause no one needed to talk. The radio did all the talking but none of the eating. When there was light, Pa would always want to get a couple more hours in the fields after supper.

Other than the extra room, our house wasn't nothing special. Walls of boards, roof of shingles and tar paper. More tar paper than shingles. Roof sagged in the middle, like it was tired. Two windows in front, two in back, sides plain, no windows. Boards weathered, never painted. The floor was packed-down dirt. Not too much stuff inside. Ma and Pa had a bed. Metal frame with one leg missing, so that corner was propped on a block of wood. Ma had a dresser. When it was her grandmom's it was probably white. Drip pots in the corners, used for when it rained. Me and Billy had a straw tick mattress on the floor.

If we weren't in the fields we did most of our living in the big room. Against one wall was the AVONDALE—that was like the heart of everything. Cast-iron, black, on four short legs. Pipe out the top to the roof, smoke's path to the sky. When I was a half-baked-size kid I would sit and stare at this thing that pushed out the cold and gave us heat and warm vittles. Stared at it like I expected it to speak from the grate or maybe waddle over to me on its stubby legs.

Ma tried to pretty up our home. She would get an old calendar from Mr. Drury down at the feed store. Any month that had a real good picture, she'd tear it off and tack it to the wall. Maybe ten pictures we had, more Julys than anything else. Still remember who made the calendar, the *Progressive Farmer*.

For sure I loved Ma, but I didn't really know what her thinking was. She never really talked to Billy or me. I mean, she talked, but it was talk filled with instructions, not of how are you doing or what are you thinking. And she had a look in her eyes, a gaze into the distance. Years later I saw the same stare in France and Germany and come to know what it meant.

'Course, there was one story Ma told that perked her up. Said her mother's great-grandmother had married a rich brother of a plantation owner during the war. Not the war my mother's brother was killed in, but the Civil War. Said he was killed by Union murderers, said they were paid five Yankee dollars for every Southern landowner they killed. Ma thought maybe someday a lost relative would come walking up our path with money for us. Money from our share of the plantation. Pa grunted that anyone walking up our path wearing shoes wasn't no relative.

Pa was good people. As a youngster I thought he was the strongest man in Alabama. Later, I come to know he wasn't the strongest, he just worked harder than everyone else. Never seen anybody work so hard and have so little. 'Course, he wouldn't have said that. Pa worked for the food on our table. All he wanted was a roof and food, and something for Billy and me. If Ma hadn't took sick and got bedrid, he probably would've never bought the radio.

Something else about Pa, the edges to his life were simple. Work hard and don't lie or cheat. I figured he learned this from his pa. Later on I met a lot of no-count people who said the same thing—work hard and be honest—but when times got tough, they lied and cheated. Sorta thought if they lied and nobody knew it, it was just like the truth. That wasn't Pa. One time Billy was getting paid a dime a day to help the Johnsons with their corn crop. Somehow Pa found out that Billy snuck away for a couple hours and rested under a tree. Next morning he got Billy and me up out of bed and dragged us out to Johnson's place. Had us picking corn from sunup to noon. Didn't ask the Johnsons for anything, neither. That was Pa.

My growing-up days in Renfroe weren't bad. Billy and me never got bad beatings. Maybe once or twice a month we'd get smacked upside the head. Not mean smacks, just getting-our-attention smacks. Some weeks we ate a little higher on the hog than others, but we never went hungry. If there wasn't a stew, there was always corn mash or tomato bread sandwiches. Billy and I really liked them—tomatoes smashed up, mixed with sugar, and spread on bread.

Lucky for Billy and me that school was close by. Some kids walked an hour or more. We'd get there in not much over a half-hour. 'Course we didn't have watches, but it seemed for sure less than an hour. Coloreds went to school closer than ours, but ours was better. Never much liked school. It wasn't that it was bad, it just wasn't good. Billy was two years younger, but we was pretty much in the same grade. Everybody was, pretty much. Figures came real easy for me. I knew my tables and could move them around in my head fast. I could read good, but my writing and grammar, not so good. Never could diagram a sentence. I mean, who can say what the subject is? "A red apple is on the big tree." So what's more important, the tree, the apple, or the color red? I never did understand that.

If everybody showed up, there was probably twenty of us in school. During the seasons, wouldn't be many. Kids didn't go during planting or harvesting. I wasn't there a lot 'cause I was in the fields. Miss Lemmon was our teacher. She wasn't married, and I think I know why. Her face looked like she just ate a lemon. Even so, she was always nice to us, not a sourpuss at all.

I forgot to tell you that I was born on December 28, 1923. It wasn't till years later that I figured out this wasn't a good day to be born. You don't get both Christmas presents and birthday presents, they just give you one present and two cards. But as a kid it didn't matter, 'cause we didn't get presents or cards. If things were good, we got a fruit pie or some other special eats with Christmas supper. Wasn't till I was twenty-one that I got the best birthday present and Christmas present a fellow could get. That birthday I woke up alive.

It was right after spring planting time that Ma got bad sick. I'm not sure when she first started to feel poorly, but by the time I was getting hair on my chest she was looking real frail. Pa and Ma never spoke to us about it. One day when I came back from school there was a car out in front of our house. First visitor that drove a car, a black covered-in-dust Ford with wooden spoke wheels, two bench-like seats and a canvas top. I'd never ridden in a car. I'd seen them passing by—not by our house, but on the concrete road we crossed going to school. The dirt road in front of our place was just an old crookedy wagon path that a car could use.

Quiet, I went up the stoop to steal a quick look. In Ma and Pa's bedroom was the doctor, his black satchel open, sitting on the floor. I remembered him because he had come to the school and checked everybody close up, looking for typhus or something. Anyway, after the doctor left things changed. Billy and I got some of Ma's chores. That's when I learned to wash clothes. Billy did most of the cooking. 'Course, we didn't have a lot of clothes or food, so washing and cooking wasn't much of a chore.

It took about a year from when I saw the doctor's car till Ma passed. She died, but she really didn't die. She got bedrid and slept more and more each day till one morning she just didn't wake up. Sort of like a drop of water in the sunlight. You look at it and you see it, but it just keeps getting smaller and smaller and then it's not there no more.

Pa made a box for Ma out of sidings from the old chicken coop. Billy and me dug the grave, took most of a day. Got a piece of oak board and rounded one edge for a marker. Used a red-hot spike to burn in her name and dates. Tried to get the letters and numbers real straight and perfect. That night, first time ever without Ma. Never gone to sleep without her in the same house. Next morning got up sorta hoping.

Other things changed that year. In Renfroe we had two worries, not enough rain and too many bugs. Those were our worries. 'Course we knew everyone had worries, the country was hurting bad. Pa said there was people without jobs and no way to work for a meal. Told us that the good Lord gave us fifty acres to work, and if we just got up and worked a full day, we could go to bed with something in our stomachs.

After a while the radio talked about other worries. Worries that weren't America's problems. Big commotion about Nazis bombing

England. 'Course, I didn't think much about it. Pa said we needed to take care of ourselves and let them take care of themselves. Ourselves being America. One night I heard Lucky Lindy on the radio. He was in Des Moines or some other place where they grow a lot of corn, remember thinking about the corn when I was listening. Anyway, he was telling us it's their war and we gotta take care of ourselves. If both Pa and Lindbergh told me we needed to take care of ourselves and not worry about someplace an ocean away, I knew it had to be right. Three weeks before my eighteenth birthday things changed.

It was a Sunday. Billy and me and Pa came back early that day from cleaning off the fields. Did some chores around the house, then supper. Beans with a ham bone and pot likker for stale biscuits, tried to eat good on Sundays. Billy flipped on the radio and we heard that the Japs had bombed us. 'Course we didn't know where Pearl Harbor was, guessed California. But then they said the Hawaiian Islands. Billy was still in school so's he had a couple books at home. One had a map. Took a while till we found the islands out in the middle of the Pacific Ocean. Next day President Roosevelt declared war on Japan. A few days later we was at war with Germany too. So from then on we didn't have to decide what was the right thing to do, America was just doing it.

Pa and I talked. Well, we didn't exactly talk. Pa just asked, did I want to go in the army or the navy? I didn't know nothing about boats, so I said the army. It didn't take long. Three months later I had a letter in my pocket from the US Army telling me where to go for my enlistment. The letter listed what to bring. Most things I didn't have.

Just like every day, the day I left for the army I got up early. Coffee and a slice of bread, then out to the fields with Pa and Billy. Pa behind the plow horse, me and Billy hunkered over, pulling stubble. I had on my boots, Billy was barefoot. We both pretty much always went barefoot working in the fields. But today I was going straight off to Renfroe to catch the noon bus.

When the sun was close to halfway up I knew it was time, so I said good-bye to Billy. He asked me to leave a few for him to kill. I walked over to Pa, and with a quick tug, he stopped the brown mare. Looking down, kicking some just plowed clogs of earth, I mumbled good-bye. Pa told me to do the right thing. Then he turned, turned back to his god, work. A grunt and the mare was off. I walked toward Renfroe. Stopped and looked back. Pa in a halo of red dust, hunched over, following the mare's ass to nowhere.

Right in front of Drury's Feed and Sundries was the Renfroe bus stop. Two other boys I knew from school, Robert and Emory, were joining up with me. Every other Robert I knew was called Bob or Bobby, but Robert's middle name was Lee, guess he figured the hero of the Confederacy was never called Bobby Lee. Me and Robert each had nothing but the clothes we were wearing. Emory had a suitcase, never seen one close up. Wondered what all could be inside it.

So there we stood in front of Drury's, waiting for a bus, talking like we knew what we was doing. Emory's ma and pa were standing back so's us three boys could sort of lean on each other. Right off Robert said he wanted to drive a tank. None of us had ever even driven a car, so I think Robert figured the army would start him off in a car or truck, then a tank. Close to what musta been an hour late the bus showed up chased by a cloud of dust.

Never been on a bus, so I wasn't sure what to do. A driver with brown chaw juice on his chin and shirt saw my letter and waved me to the back. Maybe ten or fifteen fellas were already on the bus, most with big eyes, like, *Where the hell are we going?* I set myself down next to a window. Robert was right behind and slid in next to me. Glanced outside, Emory's ma was kissing him good-bye while his pa shook his hand. Quick-like he climbed into the bus, down the aisle, looking away from Robert and me.

Right away I liked the bus ride. Well, I liked the view. Up real high so's I was looking down on everyone and everything. I had a feeling I'd never had before, a feeling of being special. I was on a bus, going someplace. I was sitting high, watching the world go by. That was the good part. The bad part was we were all scared. Not scared like we were going to get killed by some German or Jap. It was just that unknown stuff right in America that had our stomachs twisted tight scared. Fifteen minutes out of Renfroe I was further away from home than I'd ever been in my life. Same with most of the guys. Hard to believe, but for most everyone this would be their first night in their life not sleeping at home.

So anyway, there we all sat. More and more guys getting on the bus. Then some big talk. One corn-mash-brained guy said that if we could take the bus clean to Berlin, we'd win the war. He was really saying that he'd rather take his chances in Berlin than with army training.

Every half hour or so the bus would stop and a few guys would climb on with their army letters and their big wide eyes. Watching the new fellas sliding into empty seats made me feel like an army veteran. After Birmingham the bus went on down to Montgomery, made five or six stops picking up fellas on the way. At one stop we jumped out and ran behind a gas station to take a leak. Out front was a soda machine, a few lucky guys had nickels for Cokes. I'd seen Cokes in Drury's cooler but had never tasted one. Didn't this day either. After Montgomery we headed east to Georgia. Sort of expected Georgia would look different than Alabama, like with red grass or something. 'Course it didn't.

When the sun went down things got quiet, real quiet. Close to midnight we were rumbling down a concrete highway with street-lights on both sides. Never seen so many cars, parked all along the sides. Never imagined such a thing. Two or three quick turns and we pulled into a bus station, big painted sign on the wall said COLUMBUS. A few nasty curses from the driver and we piled out and shuffled into the bus station, lit by a row of flickering neon lights. Rows of wooden benches, probably could hold thirty folks. But not this night. Guys that got there before us took up whole benches, laid out asleep. Other fellas were slumped against the walls, snoring away. Some had letters sticking out of their pockets that looked just like the one I had. We milled around and started to talk until one guy looked up from a bench and told us to shut the hell up. Emory and I went back out and set ourselves down on the grass and waited. My first army training for the next three years, being in the dark and waiting.

After a spell two trucks pulled up. Army trucks with white stars and US ARMY stenciled on the doors. I didn't know my ranks then. Now I know each truck was driven by a private—that's one stripe. With them was a sergeant, three or more stripes. The sergeant didn't have to, but he yelled anyway. *Everybody into the trucks!* We weren't moving fast enough, so he hollered some more. Up we went.

Getting in wasn't easy. Didn't know then that if you pulled two pins, the back of the truck hinged down so's you could hop in. So we lifted one guy into each truck and he pulled and others pushed until everybody was in while the two privates stood back with dumbass grins. When the last guy got muscled in, the sergeant and two privates strolled off and there we sat on wooden benches, squashed like tomato mash. Another lesson, "Hurry up and wait." Maybe more than an hour later the sergeant and privates were back, happier than before. Each had a beer in their hand. Some slams of the cab doors, engines gunning, and we were off.

After a few long hours of bouncing in the back the dawn began to squeeze between the canvas flaps. I glanced around. No one had the look of wanting to go to Berlin. And for sure, I wasn't feeling so special no more. With the sun pretty much up I thought of Billy heading to the fields.

We pulled into Fort Benning, building after building with hundreds of guys marching around. Everyone seemed to know what to do and they were doing it real fast. Finally lurched to a stop, and then the hollering really began. Poured out of the trucks and two sergeants got us in a row with a lot of screaming and pushing, ugly mean things being yelled about our brains, our manhood, and our mothers. Fighting words in the schoolyard back home.

Some fellas had their suitcases next to them. One of the sergeants walked over, picked up each case, and gave it a good toss. Emory's case popped open and we stood at attention, watching his clothes blow away. Then we learned four real quick lessons. Right face, left face, forward march, and halt. They became my new heartbeat. Off we marched. At first our march had a cadence yelled by the sergeant: "Yer left, yer left, yer left, right, left." Later in our training the marking of cadence became more entertaining. I found out more about sex while marching in Benning than I'd ever learned around Renfroe.

Off we marched that first day, right to a haircut. Never had a haircut 'less Ma or Pa gave it to me. Never with an electric shaver before, neither. Some guys had a problem with it. It really didn't bother me at all. Then we stripped down and took showers. I looked around. For sure I was worked hard thin, but there were some really scrawny guys there. A lot of ribs sticking out. Out of thirty or forty of us, I'd say just about everybody was skin-tight thin.

Next was a physical. Even had to bend over stark naked and let them look places that I couldn't understand why they'd want to look. But we were all clean then, so I guessed it was okay. Two guys didn't make it. One boy's foot pointed toward the side when he stood up. I don't mean it pointed a little to the side—I mean it was straight out. The other one was blind as a bat. They asked him to read the chart and he said, "What chart?" Thought he was lying at first, then one of the corporals giving the physical looked in his eyes and said, "Yeah, they're foggy."

After the physical we each got a pair of khaki skivvies. Off we go, marching down the road almost naked. Japs and Germans would have laughed till they wet their pants if they had seen us. Marched probably a quarter mile and then lined up in front of this building, then inside for our uniforms. I never seen so many clothes. Any size you needed. I couldn't believe what I got. Six pair of socks, six skivvies, pants, shirts, jackets, shoes, and boots. I stared with my mouth open like to catch flies. I'd never had new shoes or boots. I'd never had much of anything new. And for certain sure never six of anything.

The sergeant wouldn't let us put anything on, except the boots. Then out again and marched down another road, holding our clothes in front of us. Maybe a half-mile or so, past row after row of buildings, each the same, one story high, about twenty feet wide and sixty or so feet long. 'Course later I learned they were called barracks. Each barrack had a door on both ends and windows along the sides. I looked around because I needed to use a privy, but I didn't see one anywhere. Toward the end of the row of barracks the sergeant yelled a mean "Halt!" There we stood holding bundles of clothes like newborn babies.

More screaming from sergeants and corporals and we got divided up into groups of sixteen. Emory was in my group, Robert in another. Quick like we were herded into one of the barracks, cots along each side. Then another corporal yelling at us, pointing each of us to a cot. At the end of the barracks through a door I could see what I guessed was an inside privy. I'd never seen one before, but I figured it was the privy. I could see it, but I was scared to ask to use it.

In came a private who showed us how to make up a cot. Then the corporal pointed to the fellow next to me and said, "You do it now." When he was done the corporal reached down and pulled the sheet and blanket off and had himself a hissy fit. Said a whole string of things that weren't nice about the guy's parents. He had the private make up another cot while we watched, then each of us had to make up our own.

Cots made up to the corporal's liking, we put on fatigues and formed up out front of the barracks. There we stood at attention with the Georgia sun doing its best to bake our brains. Then the sweat started to pour out. My fatigues looked like they'd been dunked in a well. Worried I'd get yelled at. Shouldn't have worried. The sergeant showed up and marched us off to mess. I didn't know what mess was, but I started to smell food. Hadn't eaten in more than a day.

In we went, never could have imagined the mounds of vittles that were piled high. All sorts of food set out in big metal pans that made a row of eats that stretched out twice as long as our house in Renfroe. On the kitchen side of the pans, two fast-moving GIs filled them as quick as they were emptied. On our side of the pans, each of us got a tray that had bowls and plates punched into them. You'd walk along the line and a GI would plop on your tray whatever was in front of you. At the end of the line there was bread. Some guys were taking two or three pieces. I was scared to take more than one.

Couldn't see anybody I knew, so I took the first empty seat. Felt like I was about to burst and for sure didn't want to eat. Thought about asking somebody, but the sergeant told us he would rip the head off of anybody that talked. At one end of the room there was a doorway, and every once in a while somebody would come out pulling up their zipper. I had to do it. I stood up and walked through the door. Thank you, Lord, it was a toilet. First time I'd peed indoors. First time I'd peed a gallon. As fast as I could, back to my spot, ate in a rush. I'm not sure what the meat was, but it was good. Then the sergeant yelling again, dropped our trays in a stack and back outside.

For two—maybe three—hours, we marched. The top of my boots were higher than my socks so my skin started to get rubbed raw. 'Course, I wasn't going to complain. Then back to the barracks. In came a corporal with assignments. Some of us would clean latrines, some on KP, peeling potatoes and washing pans, and others policing the barracks, picking up cigarette butts, leaves, dead bugs, or anything else that might cause the sergeant a hissy fit.

Finally got a break, half the guys fell asleep in their cots. Most were pushing two days without shut-eye. Good training for the next three years. Then more yelling by the sergeant and the sleepers weren't sleeping. Out front, two rows, and marched to the mess for dinner.

It's funny, once you do something, it becomes easy. Maybe *easy* isn't the right word. I knew what would happen when I walked into the mess for dinner. Like a familiar tune. Down the chow line I went, grabbing my food and taking two pieces of bread without thinking twice.

Back to the barracks, an hour of marching, lights out. Told that we had to be up by 0515, I guessed that meant 5:15 a.m. In the dark I laid dog tired and thought. 'Course I couldn't think long 'cause I was tired. Not tired from marching, but tired from worrying. I didn't like not knowing what I should do. But I figured this wasn't a bad day. I'd gotten the best clothes I ever had, I probably ate more in one day than I'd ever eaten before, and nobody smacked me upside my head. 'Course, never heard so much yelling. Figured I could handle it. I just wouldn't let the army get me riled. I would just do what my pa had always told me to do, work hard, do as I'm told, and tell the truth.

I heard something that night for the first time, something I would hear over the next three years in different places. Somewhere in the darkness a couple of grown guys were crying.

Basic training was okay by me. Some GIs had problems. Most guys from the cities hadn't really worked much, or at least they hadn't done sweat-hard work. For me, a two-mile run and an obstacle course was not a big thing. I'm not saying it was easy, but two miles wasn't that much farther than between my house and school, and when Pa had work to be done, Billy and me ran home from school. Same with the obstacle course. Some guys just couldn't pull themselves up over a barrier. It was no problem for the farm boys. We'd cheat and push a guy we liked, but some just couldn't make it.

There was other problems. Some fellas had corn mash for brains. I'll grant you, an M1 has twenty-two parts that need to be taken apart, cleaned, and then reassembled, but twenty-two ain't that many. 'Specially if you got a week to learn how to do it. A couple other guys just didn't get along with the army. I'm not sure they'd've got along with anything. A guy in the barracks next to us, I think he was from Atlanta, was always mouthing off. The sergeant wouldn't whack him. Instead, he'd have the whole barracks doing push-ups. Some GIs took this fellow out behind the barracks one night and beat the snot out of him. It didn't work. I guess some fellas just had their brains put in backward or something. But most were okay.

Benning wasn't all about running obstacle courses and peeling potatoes, I got to do things I never would've thought I'd do. One day after dinner mess the sergeant told me to pick up a jeep at the PX and drive it to headquarters. Real fast I walked down to the PX. Found the jeep and just stared at it for a while, like maybe it would start by itself and drive me back to the barracks. Finally asked some GIs walking by if they knew how to drive a jeep. Got a yeah. Hopped into the jeep with this GI and off with a lurch. For sure I could understand the steering part. The rest I couldn't, his feet pumping up and down on the pedals and between the seats this stick with a knob on it getting pushed and pulled. I didn't want to get in trouble, so I told the sergeant I let another GI drive the jeep. I think the sergeant sort of liked me, but he told me what a dumbass I was. A few days later, maybe an hour before lights out, a corporal showed up with a jeep. Took me out to learn how to drive. The sergeant probably ordered him to do it. The corporal cussed and I sweated. A couple days of practice after chow and I had it down. Couldn't hardly wait to write Billy.

My pa had a squirrel gun that you loaded and fired one shell at a time. It shot a bullet about as big around as a pencil. The army gave us these M1s with bullets as long as a cigarette and as big around as a dime. And an M1 held clips, so you weren't shooting and stopping and shooting, you just kept pulling the trigger. Almost every day for a week we had practice on the range. I was better than middling, scoring over 160, which was a Sharpshooter rating. Some guys couldn't get over 130 to qualify. But I wanted the Expert rating. I needed 180 or better for Expert. The sergeant worked with me some, but he couldn't see nothing wrong. He got one of the training sergeants to come over. This sergeant watched me shoot a group, leaned over and gave me one drop of advice, then left. I shot 190 the next round.

What did he tell me? It was simple. We'd been instructed to hold our breath, then gently pull the trigger to take up slack before firing. The sergeant told me I should exhale a little of the air and then stop the outflow before holding my breath. By keeping my lungs so full when I held my breath, he said my beating heart moved my arm.

Two months into our training at Benning we were given weekend passes to go into Cusseta. First, we had to watch some army movies about fraternization and VD. They weren't all that bad, with the dirty pictures and all. I'm not sure everybody that saw the film knew exactly what the purpose was. I don't mean the guys didn't know where babies come from, they just were dumb on how to even get a girl to talk to them. Anyway, the weekend passes were better than okay cause Cusseta wasn't all that bad. Probably twenty times bigger than Renfroe. You'd walk up and down the sidewalks and see all sorts of places to spend money. I only bought one thing, something I'd never had before. I bought myself a milk shake. A few times we got milk in trade from Big Sam, and once I'd had ice cream in Renfroe, but a milk shake was new. When I told the guys back at the barracks I got some real hee-haws. A milk shake wasn't what most of them were trying to get for the first time.

That same weekend in Cusseta Emory got himself something for the first time. Got himself a beer. Said the first one was ugly bad, the second one okay, and the third one was his new best friend. Told me I needed to try a beer milk shake next time.

Two letters showed up from Billy during basic training. Pa couldn't write but his name, and we didn't have a phone, so's Billy's letters were the only news. Billy was anxious to join up. Some army guy told him when he was seventeen he could enlist if he had Pa's permission. I gotta say, at the time I thought it was an okay idea. I was eating good, had new clothes, and seemed to be generally getting along. And I'd be getting $21 a month in army pay as a private. For sure Pa never made that much money in a month. 'Course at the time I hadn't thought about getting my head blown off. I hadn't thought about it because I hadn't seen any heads get blown off. So I wrote Billy and told him as long as Pa could manage, joining at seventeen was probably just as good as waiting until eighteen. I think maybe Billy was fretting the war might be over by the time he was eighteen.

Toward the end of our time at Benning, Emory and me were picked out to train with a .50-caliber machine gun. I'll tell you what, just the noise would scare the hair off most anybody. This thing shoots a belt of ammunition that's fed into it by one GI while the other guy is aiming and pulling the trigger. Bullets go flying like water from a hose. The day I shot this .50-caliber for the first time I figured we could never lose the war. In France I learned the problem with machine guns. The Germans had 'em too.

Got a happy surprise right before I made private, like the best Christmas present ever. We all got our own government-issued Benrus watch, with a khaki strap and a shiny steel case. Never had a watch before. No one I knew had a watch. Most expensive thing I was ever given. Figured if I got home alive, it would be a fine present for Pa.

After ninety days of training we were ready to graduate. It's not like they made us generals, we were privates. Close to three hundred of us marched on the parade field and stood at attention in front of the training commander. This colonel said a lot of things that made me feel good. We were well trained and well equipped. We'd be going off for more training at other bases. And, most important, we were fighting for a great country. Then he punched us in the gut as hard as he could. Standing tall in front of us, this colonel told us that in two years many of us would be dead. No matter how many of us were dead, he said, even more would be wounded. Sweet Jesus. I knew GIs were going to get killed, I just didn't need to hear it from some colonel who knew what he was talking about. 'Course, I came to learn that being an officer didn't mean you knew beans.

From basic training we were dealt out like cards to different advanced training groups. Some guys became typists, other guys hospital attendants, other guys cooks. Most of us got the job that the army is all about, foot soldiers in the infantry. I didn't get infantry. Never crossed my mind I wouldn't, but I didn't. They made me an engineer. It's funny now, but when I heard *engineer* I thought of a train. That was the only kind of engineer I knew about. But I found out the army has these soldiers who build bridges, blow things up, and generally act like construction guys. Later on I figured out that I was picked 'cause I tested good with figures. Emory must've done okay, 'cause the army made him an engineer too. Robert got sent off to be a foot soldier, winning all the medals.

Engineers were trained at Fort Belvoir, up in Virginia. I had six days to get there and could do whatever I wanted in between. Thought about going home. I should have, but I didn't. I figured I'd go straightaway to Fort Belvoir so's not to be late. Thought for sure that I would have a chance to get back to Alabama another time. Emory was like me, scared of being late. So we headed straight off to Belvoir to get first shot at the good bunks.

At Benning there was a corporal whose job it was to help GIs get from wherever to wherever. This fellow told us to hop a bus to Atlanta and then a train to Richmond, then another bus up to Belvoir. My second bus trip sure was better than the one from Renfroe. I had my uniform, I had my stripe, and I had some confidence. Once in Atlanta Emory and me got a train that went through Charlotte, up to Durham, and then to Richmond.

I'd never been on a train before, and this one was a real eye-opener. 'Course not for the reasons I thought. Every car was jammed, enlisted guys were sitting three to a bench seat that was supposed to hold two. Some officers were squeezed in our car, but they each got their own seat. There were sleeper cars with little rooms, each with two beds. I got a look into one when I was walking back and forth to get my legs moving again. So anyway, this really good-looking broad walks up and down the aisle, then stops by the officers. She says something about an extra bed in her compartment. One of these young officers walks away with her. A half-hour later, he's back. Takes me a while to figure it out, 'cause three or four other officers each left and then came back after a spell. Well, the truth is, I didn't figure it out. Emory told me she was a Victory Girl. For five dollars she helped your average GI feel patriotic about winning the war.

Fort Belvoir was in Virginia, maybe ten miles or so south of Washington, DC. Right away I could see that Belvoir was different from Benning. For one thing, it had more bricks than boards. Benning looked like it had been thrown up real fast, but Belvoir had rows of big brick buildings. Some could have been a courthouse back in Alabama. And at Belvoir nobody yelled at us when we got there, we just got processed in. Emory and I were assigned to the same three-story barracks. Probably half the GIs in our barracks came up from Benning too. Other guys had been in the army for a spell and were getting reassigned from the infantry.

First thing they had us do was read. Not like, "Here's a couple of pages to read." No, they gave us this *Engineer Soldier's Handbook.* This thing had something like two hundred pages of charts, pictures, formulas—I didn't even know what a formula was—and all kinds of instructions. Almost every day we had a test. Started off with some easy stuff. Y'all won't believe this, but they taught us how to cut down a tree. They even had a section on how to tie knots. Learned how to tie a clove hitch, a becket hitch, a rolling hitch, a mooring hitch. I'm thinking what the hell were we gonna do, tie up the Germans and beat them to death with our rifle butts?

After a time things got more interesting. The army taught us how to build bridges. Not bridges with stone and cement. These were like big sections of metal girders that could be unfolded across a river and not buckle with a tank rolling across it. After bridge building we learned about explosives. I could blow up a bunker with a nonelectric cap or an electric cap, just tell me what you needed. Then more learning. Me and Emory and the other GIs could put down a steel plank runway for the biggest aircraft the Air Corps had, or we could put together a pneumatic bridge made of big inner tubes. If the army wanted me to, I could weld a busted wheel on a half-track, sharpen an ax, or change spark plugs in a jeep. Just tell me what you need.

Belvoir was a quick easy bus ride to Washington, DC. A happy-go-lucky GI could go up and back on a day pass. Walking around Washington was like living in a history book—sorta like plopping yourself down on a bench and having Robert E. Lee sitting right next to you. Standing taller than anything I could imagine, smack dab in the middle of this big grassy hill was the Washington Monument. Any backwoods GI could march right up and touch it, look up past the point and see Air Corps planes heading down the Potomac River to Bolling Field. Peer one way and you'd see the Capitol, in the other direction, the White House, home of our president. Some guys said they saw him, but I never did. I saw his wife, though. Mrs. Roosevelt came to Fort Belvoir on Christmas Day and handed out little presents to a lot of the GIs. She wasn't very pretty, but she sure was nice. Here she was, the president's wife, talking real friendly to a bunch of fellas who didn't used to wear shoes.

In Washington I saw something I'd never seen before. I had no idea there even was such a thing. It was a store that sold animals, not horses and cows, but dogs, cats, fish—animals you keep as pets. Any pets we ever had were half-wild cats that came out of the pines and stayed under our stoop until they figured out we didn't have anything to feed 'em. Anyway, I'm looking in the window at this cage, maybe two feet long, a foot wide, and a foot or so high. Inside is an animal with brown fur. If it'd had a long tail and a longer nose, we would have called it a rat back in Renfroe. But it wasn't a rat. This animal was running real fast on a little wheel, like an endless circle. Around the hub of this wheel a cord looped outside to a box sitting on top of the cage. Running real fast made the cord move. It would only move just a little bit every few minutes. But when it did, a kernel of corn plopped out of the box and into the cage. The not-a-rat would stop, get out of the wheel, and nibble away at the corn till it was gone. Then back to the wheel and his run to nowhere.

Why am I telling y'all about this? Thing is, it made me think real hard about Pa and about the land we worked. The fifty acres Pa, Billy, and me worked was like our cage. If we broke our backs and weren't unlucky, we got enough to eat. That was okay 'cause I didn't know there was anything else. But I'd gotten outside the cage when I joined the army. I'd seen people doing okay, people that weren't working as hard as Pa did. I didn't want to go back and run as hard as I could on a wheel for a kernel of corn. No way. 'Course, I didn't feel all that right about my thinking. My thinking if right, maybe said my pa was wrong. Couldn't make myself think Pa could be wrong. He was my pa.

If the sergeant was pissed off about something, we'd only get a half-day pass on Sundays, not a full day. On a half-day pass I'd go to Alexandria. 'Course, I was on my own pretty much, I wasn't drinking yet. Emory couldn't get enough beer. Spent most of his leave in bars, said he would own one someday.

But let me tell you about Alexandria. It was a little like you were in a foreign city. It had a King Street, Duke Street, Princess Street, and a passel of old red-brick buildings that were strange shapes. It had a lotta stuff for GIs like me to waste our money on, but it had some good stuff for soldiers. Churches had lunches and dances, and there was a USO club. Almost every big town had these clubs for servicemen. Food was free, or cheap, and there were always some nice ladies to talk to. Some were young like they could be your girlfriend or sister, some were older, like they could be your ma.

At Belvoir the barracks talk was mostly about three things, home, women, and war. Y'all probably think we talked about how much we missed home. Well, we didn't. I don't mean to tell you we didn't miss home, we just didn't like to talk about it. Usually when we talked about home, it was about all the great things we'd done. Some guys, the more they talked, the greater the things they did.

But when women came up we agreed that if you're gonna get killed, you might as well enjoy life with the time you've got. I mean, what are you saving yourself for? Another question was, should you get serious with some girl? Should you start talking about love and marriage and all that stuff, the danger being that they're just gonna break your heart when you're thousands of miles away, sleeping in mud while some second lieutenant or 4'Fer with money in his pocket is picking her up for a night on the town. I figured that you probably shouldn't get serious with a gal. This was real easy for me, 'cause I didn't know any gals who wanted to get serious. But I did get to know some Victory Girls on sort of a regular basis. This was easier after I made corporal and my pay went up.

There was a lotta talk in the barracks about the war—how we were doing. While I was in Benning, Doolittle bombed the Japs and we all felt pretty good. Then in Midway we sunk three or four of their carriers. Things seemed to be going okay in the Pacific.

Europe was still a smelly barn. The Brits won the Battle of Britain, but the Nazis were kicking the crap out of the Russians. Americans were in Italy, but nothing seemed to be moving real fast, we were bogged down. Word was that the Germans were real good—they had good equipment, and the scary part, they were real tough killers.

'Course, you know that some bigmouthed GIs in our barracks talked hero talk. Reminded me of my first day on the bus heading out of Alabama, when some guys bragged they wanted to go straight away to Berlin and win the war. I thought about it a lot. I was in the army and I needed to do the right thing—whatever the right thing was. When we graduated from Benning the colonel told us that a lot of us would be killed. But if I could do the right thing and live, I figured that was better than doing the right thing and dying. I mean, if you make like a hero and run up a hill and blow up a Nazi machine-gun nest and kill ten of them, and get killed yourself, is that better than sneaking around the hill, shooting some Germans, and living another year while you kill two or three more each month? I didn't know. Still don't. But one of the things we told ourselves was that being in the engineers, we probably wouldn't be the first to get shot at. We would be building things and tearing things down. Told ourselves the infantry guys would be doing the real fighting.

Never been more wrong.

Ten months of training at Belvoir went pretty fast. When we graduated we figured we would be going to Europe. Europe was army and Army Air Corps, the Pacific was navy and marines. A letter from Billy showed up right before I graduated from Belvoir, he joined the navy, said he wanted to see the world. So my kid brother was headed for the Pacific.

In April of '43 our unit got orders to go to England, leaving out of New York. GIs who had been to New York told a lot of big stories. I'd seen *King Kong* at the base theater and was itching to go to the top of the Empire State Building. Then we learned the truth of it, our destination was Camp Shanks, thirty miles or so north of New York. Crammed in a train heading north past the city, we all strained our eyeballs looking out to the east for the skyline. Didn't see nothing.

Pulled into camp around supper time, detrained, and shuffled off, hauling equipment like Alabama mules. By dark we'd pretty much settled into our barracks, the walls were scrawled with a lot of writing from guys who'd been there before us. Guess they wanted to leave their mark in case they got their asses shot off.

Next day we got some good news and some bad news. Good news was that one of the escort ships was running two days late, so the troopships would be delayed in sailing. Because of the delay we would get one-day passes, enough for the thirty-mile dash south to New York. Bad news was the shots. Neither the devil nor Hitler had come up with any sickness they didn't give us a shot for. Our arms hurt like hell, and just about everybody got real bad headaches.

After a long day of being pricked by pricks, our sergeant dealt out eighteen-hour passes. Said anyone late getting back would be headed straight for the firing squad. Camp buses shuttled between Shanks and New York City pretty regular. I sat with Emory and two other guys in the front of the bus, didn't want to miss anything. After a half-hour or so we pulled onto the biggest damn bridge I'd ever seen, the George Washington Bridge. We crossed over the Hudson River and into New York City. Maybe for a mile the bus rode south along the river. To the left, buildings seemed to touch the clouds. Then we turned into a dark valley of windowed cliffs. People, people everywhere. Squeezed together, all rushing like a bunch of Alabama fire ants after you stomped their mound. A lot of good-looking broads too.

Our bus pulled right up in front of a USO club, I think it was on Eighth Avenue. The pimple-faced corporal driver tells us that buses leave every two hours back to the camp, and the last one would be at 2300. We all spilled out, with big grins and bigger eyes. Me, Emory, and two buddies went into the USO, bellied up to the bar, and gulped some dime beers. Emory had me drinking by then. Asked around on how to get to the Empire State Building, GIs stared at us like we had corn mash for brains. Back out, we walked a few blocks and saw an old fella, wearing baggy green pants and a strange cap, standing next to a booth selling newspapers and stuff. We bought ourselves a city map from him. It wasn't all that easy, the baggy pants fella spoke a real strange English. Not sure for certain what he said.

So anyway, Emory took the map and studied it real hard, like it was a chart for buried treasure. He found the Empire State Building marked real clear, figured we had fifteen or so blocks to walk. We were off, with Emory leading. Strange sights, strange smells. More restaurants than I thought were in the whole country, serving foods I'd never heard of. Just walking and talking, not a care, our heads on a swivel. Finally, I asked Emory if he was sure he knew where we were. A real slow and low yes.

"Okay," I said. "Should we be going north or south?"

Emory pulled out the map and looked at it real careful, then in almost a whisper, "North." I told him that unless the sun was setting in the east, we had been marching south. I grabbed the map and we marched back over our footsteps, thinking that if the Germans could see us lost in New York, they would be sleeping real easy.

There it was, the tallest building in the world. Up the elevators, switching between floors, and then the observation deck. I'd never been so high, never seen so much. South was the Statue of Liberty, maybe two or three miles away. Big ships were crawling past. We'd be on one soon. To the west was the Hudson River. North up the river was the George Washington Bridge. It didn't look so big anymore. If you stood close to the railing and leaned just right, you could see all the way down to the street, people like moving dots on the sidewalks. We stood and gawked. The sun was setting past the river in the west. Looking back to the east, toward Europe, it was gray turning to black. I wondered what was waiting for me there . . . wondered if I'd ever be home again.

Back down on the street, Emory said he wanted to eat supper in a Chinese restaurant. Didn't know why, I guess he just thought it would be different. One of the corn mash GIs in our little squad got the Japs and Chinese mixed up, said he wouldn't eat no enemy food. Anyway, we wandered into a back-alley Chinese restaurant with bright-red cloths on the tables, white napkins, each with a red dragon. At a table in the back, two schoolkids were hunched over their homework. A tiny woman, maybe four and a half feet tall, came by with menus. She probably spoke English, but not for us. So we sat there looking real hard at the menus. I saw some words that I knew, like *chicken, beef,* and *egg.* But each of these words was leaning against words I'd never heard of. So we were all squinting like our eyes were going to burn a hole in the menu.

The tiny Chinese woman circled back to us. There we sat, all stupid quiet. Then Emory speaks up, orders egg rolls. I didn't have a dumbass clue, so I ordered egg rolls. So did everybody else. When she left, I looked at Emory and asked him what the hell an egg roll was. Said he didn't have any idea. So's I asked why he'd ordered them. Real easy, he said, they was the cheapest thing on the menu. I knew Emory was no dummy. They were pretty good, kinda like fried chitlins in a greasy crust.

Next morning at Camp Shanks we packed our gear back onto the trucks. After a short jaunt on the trucks, a train to Weehawken, then a ferryboat. Couple of corn-mash-brained GIs thought we were going to sail to England standing on its deck. A half-hour later we were off the ferry, walking a few hundred feet down a dock, past a half-dozen troopships, rusted and looking pretty tired, and then up a steep gangway.

Our ship was the *Williams,* one of a dozen troopships that were crossing the North Atlantic, with three destroyers as escorts. Back in '41 and '42 the U-boats were killing us. More stuff was getting sunk than was getting across. By '43 things were a lot better, but still "drowning in burning oil" dangerous. More than two thousand of us were packed sardine-tight on a ship that probably held five hundred during peacetime. Most cabins had three sets of three-tier bunks. Some had two sets of three-tier bunks with maybe a half-dozen hammocks strung between. About half of us had our own bunk or hammock. Other guys had to share, in shifts. They called this "warm bunking," 'cause when you got into your bunk, it was warm from the last guy.

Life was simple on the boat. We only did a few things, 'course most of them took a long time. Had two meals a day, stood in line pretty much for an hour to get food and then you had ten minutes to eat it. First few days the lines were short 'cause of seasickness. Depending on what time of the day it was, you waited in line for an hour to use the head (the navy's way of saying *latrine*).

Another hunk of our time was burned up with boat drills and fire drills. Everybody was assigned a lifeboat station in case we got torpe-doed. We figured that they gave us a boat number to feel good—there sure couldn't be enough boats for everybody. Most every day physical training on deck in a cold, damp wind, maybe blowing twenty-five miles an hour or more. Or, as they said in the navy, twenty knots or more, four knots being equal to four and two-thirds miles . . . learned the conversion at Belvoir. Most free time was spent talking. Same things as always: home, women, and war.

A few days before we reached England we got another army manual. Us GIs got manuals for everything, how to have sex with-out getting VD, how to blow up a Nazi Tiger tank, or whatever.

Anyway, this manual explained to GIs how they should act in England. Started off by saying that the average Brit had been bombed for the last three years, so we shouldn't come over and tell them how we're gonna win the war for them. It said that Brits were gracious, and if some family invited a GI for a meal, we shouldn't eat everything put on the table, 'cause they might be using a week's ration of butter and meat for their American cousin. A couple other things caused me to grin. One was that we shouldn't say bad things about their coffee, because they could always say our tea was worse. The most important advice came last. For certain a big warning that no American should ever, ever say anything mean nasty about their king or queen. I don't mean this to sound disrespectful, but after a year over there I came to understand that your average Brit didn't see the king as we saw our president. He was their grandfather, Jesus, and Superman, all rolled together. Piss on their king, you were pissing on their grandfather, Jesus, and Superman.

You know who complained about the manual on how to act in England? Emory, saying that any manual on England should tell a GI about pubs, tell a GI the difference between beer and ale, tell him what he should drink and what it should cost.

After a while the *Williams* began to smell like the inside of somebody's old boot, so I tried to spend more time above decks. I started to peer east when I was up there, like I was Christopher Columbus looking for land. 'Course, he was looking west. The day before we docked, it was maybe 60 degrees. But it was not the temperature that made the day, it was the wind—I mean the direction of the wind. Usually you had a pretty fair breeze across the deck. The *Williams* cruised at fifteen knots. This day the wind was coming from aft, at right around fifteen knots. So even though the ship was plowing through Atlantic waters at fifteen knots, the air on deck was about still. I climbed to the top of what they called the forecastle, sat myself down, and leaned back against some kind of radio mast. If I tilted my head back just a little, I'd only see sky and clouds. With the still air and the view, I could've been leaning against a tree along Harkins Creek. Thought about Ma, Pa, Billy. Thought about home. Wondered if I'd be back.

It was close to midnight in a heavy rain when we docked at Liverpool. Right away I knew we was in a real different place. When we sailed from New York the skyline was carved against the night sky with millions of lights. England lived in a blackout. Nary a light to be seen from the harbor, even though daylight showed us we were nestled in a good-size city. A few years of night bombings had taught 'em to draw blackout curtains and drive with lights off.

By midday we were offloading. A line of GIs snaked down several decks in the *Williams*, then onto a steep gangplank to the dock below. Halfway down the gangplank something in the water caught my eye. A dead cat floating in the black oily water. Hello, England. An hour or so to sort things out, then we loaded onto four-by-fours. It was bone cold and damp so the canvas flaps were kept shut as we pulled out of Liverpool. After a few hours we stopped for a latrine break. I looked around. British cars and trucks—later on I learned they don't have trucks, they have lorries—were for sure smaller than ours. Everything seemed smaller over there. I guess if you've got a small country, you need to make things small so's everything fits.

Anyway, we didn't talk to any Brits that first day. At dusk we pulled into an army base that was nothing more than a bunch of barracks on a field with a few GIs in a guardhouse. Inside the barracks cots, but no bedding, and a few cases of K rations . . . our supper. No electricity, no lights. So we built a fire outside of one of the barracks. Stood close around trying to steal some warmth, rocking from foot to foot. I was sorta thinking, I don't like England.

Next day we were off in the four-by-fours after more K rations for breakfast. Drove the whole morning, then we met our first Brits when we stopped for a latrine break. Them I liked right off. Said hello and told us they were glad to see us. For sure they talked a little different, but not as different as the baggy pants guy who sold us the map of New York City. It was raining like buckets, a real cold rain. The captain spoke with somebody and we went into a big hall where we sat on the floor eating cold K rations, griping that we couldn't get a hot meal. Didn't know it then, but the next year I'd be in a foxhole in Belgium with my ass froze to the ground praying for a K ration meal after days of eating nothing but snow.

The rest of the day and into the night we were crunched in the back of the four-by-fours. In the pitch black we pulled into Ashchurch, some old English city where the army had built a base, 'course all English cities are old. The base was called Ashchurch too. By the time we got processed the mess was closed, so we plopped ourselves down in bunks with our stomachs complaining.

I didn't go right to sleep. Thought about a lot of things. In a year and a half I'd gone from walking around in my bare feet pulling out cotton stubs to learning to drive a jeep, touching the Washington Monument, meeting some Victory Girls, going to the top of the Empire State Building, eating egg rolls, drinking beer, sailing across the Atlantic Ocean, and sleeping where Robin Hood lived. I figured that if the war ended tomorrow I was really one lucky guy. Problem was, the war wasn't going to end tomorrow. The last year and a half had been like one big long movie, but I hadn't paid for the ticket yet. Hoped the ticket wasn't gonna cost too much.

It took us a spell at Ashchurch to get sorted out. The sergeants and lieutenants had to figure out who would be doing all the stuff that made the army work—peeling potatoes, cleaning latrines, standing guard, leading calisthenics, and hurrying up to wait. After some "what the hell is going on" confusion, we got broken down into groups and reorganized. I got assigned to the 5th Engineer Special Brigade. Emory went to another brigade. There wasn't one face in the group that I knew from before. Above us was Sergeant Gibbs and Lieutenant Clyde. The sergeant was okay, but not the lieutenant. He was a ninety-day wonder. Being hard up for officers, the army took college guys and within ninety days made them soldiers and officers. Anyway, we didn't see much of the lieutenant. We figured he was just scared of us, or scared of the job or something. He hid in his office, pushing paper around.

We'd only been at Ashchurch a few days when the whole company was formed up and addressed by Colonel Billings, a big guy with a deep voice. This colonel said that we'd be winning a lot of medals because a lot of us were gonna die. 'Course, he didn't start off with this, he started off with the good stuff. We were the best-trained and best-equipped troops, and we had God on our side. He told us the Russians were complaining that they were carrying all the water. For two years they had been slugging it out with the Nazis and had already lost over ten million civilians and soldiers. Billings said that the Russians wanted the Americans and Brits to get their asses into Europe so's the Germans would need to pull troops out of Russia. That wasn't any big surprise.

But then the colonel got to talking about engineers. Our whole company was engineers, so it was about us. This colonel told us that nobody knew when or exactly where, but it was a dead cinch we'd be landing in Europe, and the Germans were going to try and stop us on the beaches. Then the scary, "You're going to die" shit. Billings said the Krauts had already built ten thousand beach obstacles, most with Teller mines attached, with some underwater just to make things interesting. Told us they had probably buried half a million land mines, built bunkers with three-foot-thick walls, and scattered maybe a few hundred pillbox emplacements on the bluffs. It got real quiet.

Billings kept talking. Told us that the engineers would be the first to wade in to blow up all the obstacles. Stone-statue-still we sat. He didn't stop talking. Told us that after blowing up all the beach defenses, us engineers would be fighting next to the infantry, laying bridges, and repairing roads and train tracks to keep the army moving. Finished off by saying that if we weren't scared now, we should be. The price of my movie ticket went up.

Soon we was into training full steam. First month we had a lot of physical training, we had gotten lazy on the boat ride over. The guy in the bunk next to me in Ashchurch became a friend. A good friend. Tom Lane was from Pennsylvania, and he was like most everybody else I met in the army and pretty much like everyone during the Depression. Tom grew up in a family without much money, had tough times. Now he was just trying to figure out how not to mess up and hoping he wouldn't get killed.

It's funny, when people tell you the most about themselves. It's not when you're sitting across the table, looking them in the eye and talking. Mostly it's when you're both doing some job and not thinking so much about what you're saying. Tom and I would be peeling potatoes or standing guard, all the time shooting the breeze. Real quick I figured out that Tom was an honest, up-straight guy. He always did a little more than his fair share of the work. Sorta like how I thought I was.

When things were going right with the army, and the captain, lieutenant, and sergeants weren't having a hissy fit about something, we'd get a leave pretty much every Sunday. A few miles from Ashchurch was Tewkesbury Abbey. This is like the biggest church y'all ever saw. 'Course, they took a few hundred years to build it, so it shoulda been big. If I remember right, parts of it were started before Columbus bumped into America with his boat. Anyway, on a Sunday we'd walk over to the town of Tewkesbury, a real small town, but not Renfroe small. If the weather was nice, Tom and I would borrow or rent a rowboat and drift down the Severn River to Apperley, or row up the Avon River to Twyning Green, both with pubs serving warm ale and strange food. Strange to us, that is. I didn't eat a lot of egg and eel sandwiches in Alabama. But the Brits probably didn't eat all that much squirrel.

I need to tell y'all about pubs. They're sort of like a diner and bar stuck real tight together. Musta been built by guys who were four feet tall. Ceilings of these pubs touched your hair, and a lot of 'em were really old. Back in Alabama if something was old it was like fifty years old. Tom and I gulped ale at a few pubs that were over two hundred years old. Walls leaned one way or the other, like they was standing at ease after centuries at attention. Wires and pipes ran pretty much all around. Guess they didn't have pipes and wires when they built the places.

You and your buddies would go into one of these pubs and it was most always right happy. People were always laughing and the ale was flowing. And while there were a few Brits that you bumped into who didn't like Yanks, just about everybody was real nice. Guess they forgot about 1776. Tom and I had to learn real fast how to speak English in a pub. The Brits used some of our words to mean different things, and they had some words I never heard of in Alabama or Virginia or New York or wherever. One night I'm standing next to this cute British girl in a pub and she was talking friendly with me. Real happy, she tells me she got knocked up the week before. Just about swallowed my teeth. Later I found out that *knocked up* meant a Brit had had too much to drink.

Another time Tom and I tried to order an egg and sausage sandwich and were told we'd have to queue up. I thought maybe Tom and I would have to hold hands or something. Felt okay once I figured out that for a Brit, *queuing up* meant *lining up.*

By the summer of '43 training was getting pretty tough. Me, Tom, and the other engineers spent most of our time blowing things up. The army had bangalores. Think of a bunch of pipe sections. You're laying down on the ground and on one end of a piece of pipe you have this explosive. Push the pipe forward till you reach the end of it, and then you take another section of pipe and insert it into the end of the piece you just pushed forward. Then you push that section forward. You keep doing this till the explosive is pushed out fifty to a hundred feet. Detonate the charge, blowing up a barbed wire obstacle or some Kraut land mines. We got real good at it. Problem was, we got real good at it on ground that wasn't littered with dead bodies and the pipes weren't slipping in our hands from some GI's just-blown-out innards.

About five miles from Ashchurch was Cheltenham, a pretty big town about the size of Alexandria. Smack-dab in the middle was a town square with flower gardens all around. At one end of the square was the Queen's Hotel. It wasn't as big as the hotels in Washington, but just as fancy. Off the lobby there was a bar to the right and a dining room to the left. It was the Queen's Hotel where Tom met Hazel, a waitress in their dining room. Hazel was seventeen then, with black hair, a pretty face, a nice shape, and long legs. She was always smiling, always had something nice to say. She'd just say it in that funny English way.

On one weekend pass Tom and I figured we'd explore London. After a good two hours on the jammed-tight train we pulled into Paddington Station. It was pretty much like the station back in

Washington, really big with a booming, echoing voice announcing train arrivals and departures. Out we went. First thing we did was come real close to getting killed. Started across the street looking the wrong way and a lorry almost smashed us. London sidewalks were crowded with people, all walking fast. More people were wearing uniforms than in New York.

Tom found a USO, and we plopped ourselves down and made friends with some warm beers. Asked around and decided that we should see Big Ben. Off we went, a three-block walk and we were standing in a big square with a statue that looked like George Washington way up on top of a marble post as tall as three or four telephone poles sitting on top of each other. Wondered why the Brits would have George Washington way up there. Hundreds of people milling around the square, thousands of pigeons flying around. Half a mile walk down from the square we came to this really big old church on the right that made me think of Tewkesbury Abbey. Later I found out it was Westminster Abbey.

Right past the church was Big Ben with a clock face that must have been fifty feet across. I wouldn't have wanted to arm-wrestle the fellow who had to wind it each morning. So we were standing there gawking, probably looking real dumb with our mouths open, and this Brit came up. An old guy. 'Course, Tom and I were just twenty then, so *old* may not have been that old. Anyway, he asked if we'd like him to give us a first-class tour of London for a pound, plus he'd throw in a free ale. A pound being worth maybe five dollars. Tom and I figured that worst case we'd be paying a pound for a couple of ales, so we said yes. I was real glad we did.

Following our guide—Cecil was his name—we trudged back up to the statue on top of the pole. Stopped and gaped up at this fella covered in pigeon shit. Cecil told us he was a most special hero. Told us about Nelson and a big boat battle with the French. But Cecil didn't call them French, he called them frogs. Never did ask why he called the French frogs. Then Cecil marched us down Piccadilly, and pointed out the Ritz Hotel. Said it was so posh that guys like us couldn't get past the doorman. Couple blocks past the Ritz we turned left, marched to Buckingham Palace. Maybe ten or twenty times bigger than the White House, home to the king, queen, and their two daughters.

Bad luck, we just missed the changing of the guard. Hiked down to the Thames River and turned upstream past Parliament and Big Ben. We kept going for more than a mile to the Tower of London. Here Cecil told us all about this King James guy and a bunch of queens, and dungeons. Too much to remember. But I do remember he said that prisoners brought to the Tower for execution would be given free mugs of ale as they passed by the pubs. Before we left, Cecil showed us where one wall of the Tower had crumbled after hundreds of years—thanks to a Nazi bomb.

Then back to Paddington Station and we found ourselves a pub. True to his word, Cecil bought Tom and me an ale. Best part of the tour. We talked and drank, and after an hour or so he got us some fish 'n' chips. Fried fish and fried potatoes served on a page of old newspaper. The ink stained the potatoes, potatoes that weren't long like french fries, but shaped like real small bricks. I'm not sure why, but we dipped them in vinegar. So after a couple of ales I asked Cecil, why Limey? Is it an insult to your average Brit if a Yank calls them a Limey? He thinks for a spell, then says no and yes. Turns out the name came from British sailors eating a slice of lime a day so's they wouldn't get scurvy. Now it meant a not-so-smart bloke.

I liked the British. For the most part they were real nice to us Yanks, always saying "Good day" and smiling, always polite, 'cepting some of the Tommies, Tommies being the name of their soldiers. I never had one be mean to me, but they sorta had a look, like they'd be happy to punch me in the face. Can't say I blamed them. Us GIs made more money than an average Tommie, plus we were buying their women drinks at the pub. They never had a shot at our gals.

By the fall of '43 I'm thinking our brigade's looking pretty good—like we know what we're doing. We got ourselves some confidence. And with confidence we were just getting better. Everybody was standing taller. Then one day we had our first exercise with the navy guys. We actually went to sea, did an about-face, and charged the beaches. 'Course the navy brought the boats.

I gotta tell y'all about these navy boats. They were called "Higgins boats," built especially for putting GIs on the beaches. These Higgins boats had flat sides, a flat bow, and a flat aft. Think of a big bathtub, maybe thirty feet long and ten feet wide. A navy guy, the coxswain, would stand in the back with a big wheel and steer. Us GIs would be hunkered down in the bathtub with our equipment, the boat gave us our own little floating bunker. The Higgins would go right up onto the beach. When you pulled a big lever, the front of the boat would drop down to make a ramp. A GI could drive right off with his equipment, like a jeep pulling a howitzer.

Some army equipment got big-eyed attention—made me feel that maybe I could pay for the movie ticket. The army took these Sherman tanks and put this big rolling-pin thing out in front of it. This steel cylinder hung maybe eight feet off the ground, ten feet or so in front of the tank. On this big metal rolling pin were maybe twenty or thirty big hunks of chain, ten or so feet long. As the tank moved forward it would spin the rolling pin and whip the chains out, slapping the ground in front of the tank. When they hit the ground the chains would set off Kraut land mines. Because it was only the chains setting off the charges, the tank wasn't damaged. A few of these tanks could clear the way for an entire battalion.

The other thing was—and you're not going to believe this— they made the Sherman tanks swim. A Sherman tank weighs like 50,000 pounds. It's got armor plating four inches thick. I gotta give it to the guy who came up with how to make it float. They put a canvas skirt around the tank that went upward, not downward, so you had a Sherman tank that was the bottom of a canvas boat.

The tank's engine pulled in the air from a stovepipe-looking thing that went maybe two or three feet above the tank. You had to see this to believe it.

———— ⬡⬡⬡ ————

Sometimes when you have a tough decision to make, you let something else that has nothing to do with it make the decision for you. Sorta like saying I'll have eggs for breakfast if it's not raining in the morning. The good Lord makes the decision whether or not you have eggs. This is how Tom decided whether he should marry Hazel.

Army chaplains warned us that British girls just wanted to marry GIs so they could get to America. I knew Hazel, and I didn't think she would be that way. She was just like the rest of us. She came from a poor family, but they all worked real hard. Tom liked the idea of having a wife close by who loved him, somebody special who would be worrying about him when he was in combat. Tom figured if he bought the farm, it would be in the next couple of years. Hazel would still be young, and all the Tommies would be coming back from overseas looking for a date, so she would be okay. Plus, the army gave us a $10,000 insurance policy. He thought that if he left half to his ma and half to Hazel, they'd both be all right.

I put Pa's name down for my insurance. Smiled when I imagined Pa fainting dead away if some army guy showed up holding $10,000. 'Course, I'd be in the ground dead.

But let me get back to telling you about Tom and Hazel. Tom and I were both pretty broke 'cause we were both sending money home each month. Tom was helping take care of his ma and younger sisters. I was sending Pa money orders by Western Union since he didn't have Billy or me helping in the fields. Neither one of us had a lot of walking-around-Saturday-spending money. And, no GI was going to lend another GI money. Not when the fella that owed you money might not be breathing much longer.

Tom had an older sister in the United States, Dorothy was her name. I met her a couple of years later. She was married to a guy with a real good office job in the Midwest somewhere. Tom wrote his sis and told her that even though he knew all the reasons it was crazy to get married, he really loved Hazel, and could he borrow $100 from her for a wedding? Sure enough, a month later $100 showed up at Western Union. His sister sending $100 made up Tom's mind to ask Hazel.

The wedding was in October at All Saints Church in Cheltenham. Tom asked me to be his best man. I said yes, but I didn't know what a best man did. Never heard of a best man. Hazel's mother, father, a grandmother, two sisters, and a brother were all there, dressed nice. In the States when someone is poor, most times their clothes are tattered and dirty. In England even the poorest folks seemed to dress okay. Clothes might be threadbare, but they were clean and pressed.

Other than Tom and me, there weren't any other Yanks. Hazel's aunt brought a bottle of sweet wine that we shared at the Council housing after the ceremony. When I'd woken up that day, I thought Tom was making a mistake. By lights out that night, I figured he had done the right thing.

And Tom wasn't the only one getting married. I got a letter from Billy. But first I need to tell y'all about the letters we got during the war. They weren't like regular paper letters, they called 'em V-mail. What the government did was take pictures of everybody's letters. So if Billy wrote me a letter with the right army address, somebody in the army opened it up and took a picture of it, then tossed the letter. Now they got this roll of film with maybe a thousand letters on it. They ship a bunch of this film to England, and some private prints each letter as a picture, but big enough so's you could read it. Same with our letters going back to America. For sure a lot of work, but film took less space than paper on the transport ships.

Let me tell y'all something else. The army was always thinking some corn-mash-brained GI would put something secret in a letter home. 'Course, nobody would tell us any real secrets, but some officers got to read everybody's letters to make sure we weren't telling nothing we shouldn't. Bet you these officers got some laughs.

So I get this letter from Billy saying that he'd married some gal. Could have knocked me over with an acorn. Could you believe? He'd met her in San Francisco, got to spend three days with her before he shipped out of Oakland, heading west. Heading toward the Japs. I can't remember her name. You'll know why later.

I told you I didn't know just how poor we were. We were just like everybody else in Renfroe. Even at Fort Benning I was pretty much like everybody else. But up at Fort Belvoir I started to think I really wasn't like everybody else. Most of the GIs had pictures of their families and would show them around to the other guys. But my family, we never had any photographs. We never had a camera, didn't even know anyone with money enough for a camera. When most guys in the barracks talked about their tough life back home, it sounded real good to me.

Same with Tom. I told you he came from a poor family. I knew he musta been poor 'cause he and his ma and sisters got thrown out of their apartment when they couldn't make rent. Tom's family had to walk down the street dragging almost everything they had and ended up living at an aunt's house till all the kids were grown. But other things made me think he lived in a real different place than Renfroe. Tom told me that he played on his high school basketball team. We didn't play basketball. Never even touched a basketball. Never touched a football. We didn't play anything. We worked, did some schooling, worked, slept, worked, and worked some more. In Renfroe we was for sure bad poor, not good poor.

In '44 training got sledgehammer hard. Sunday leaves became half-day leaves every other Sunday. Five-mile marches with packs went to ten miles, then fifteen. Even a few killer twenty milers. More and more training. I probably lit off a thousand pounds of explosives, and this was using ten-pound charges. Show me something, I'd blow it up. 'Course, as engineers, we weren't just blowing things up. We were also going to construct supply dumps, plus keep any supply lines open by building bridges and repairing roads. If we all got mowed down on the beach we wouldn't need to worry about the other stuff. So we trained mostly to blow up beach obstacles and get our asses off the beach.

There was one thing they tried to teach us that we just couldn't get right. Some Air Corps staff sergeant briefed us on aircraft recognition. He had black profiles of all the US and German aircraft on flash cards, probably twenty or more. He wanted us to be able to recognize each type, so's we wouldn't be shooting down the guys on our side, only Krauts. Problem was, the planes all looked much the same to us foot soldiers. Most every plane had a Hershey bar–shaped wing and a propeller in the front. I could only recognize one, a P-47. It had curved wings.

One morning our sergeant told us that Lieutenant Clyde was gone. We didn't miss him. Then Lieutenant Johnson showed up. He'd been in Italy with Patton's guys. Had a scar that was red and ugly, all the way across his forehead and down to an ear. We figured he didn't get it milking cows or playing checkers. Johnson was tough, real hard. Every cross-country trek we made, he made. One day some guy was sorta cheating on push-ups during calisthenics, the lieutenant went over and kicked him so hard that this sorry-assed GI walked bent over for a day or so. After he kicked this fellow, Johnson went down and did five one-armed push-ups, got up, and walked away.

It was early spring of '44 when I saw my first dead soldier—well, two of 'em. Our brigade was trucked down to Slapton Sands for a landing exercise. The army had built up a section of coast just like what we could expect on the other side of the Channel. Everything from underwater obstacles to fake gun emplacements was there. Even had referees to score how well we did. A hundred boats, mostly Higgins, rushed the beach. Five hundred of us charged forward. We made a bunch of dumbass mistakes, but after a couple crappy dry runs, we started to get things right. Seemed kinda like a game, but nobody was shooting at us.

'Bout late afternoon, our exercise was over. Everybody was milling around, waiting for trucks to pick us up, but they didn't show. Even the dumbest GI knew not to stand if you could sit, so we had GIs sitting around, waiting. A bunch of them leaning back against whatever. Two guys were plopped down in front of a tank that was stopped, with no crew. It was a Sherman with the chains that spun out in front. When the tank was stopped the chains hung straight down, sorta like a curtain of anchor chain, each link weighing five pounds. Anyway, the tank commander didn't see the guys resting their feet, squeezes in, hits the starter, the engine catches, and the chains flail out as they spin. Both guys got whacked by the iron chains whipping around. That's not the worst. The tank commander didn't know anything was wrong and drove forward. Both guys were already dead, but one tank track went right over this private. Looked like somebody poured a hundred pounds of strawberry jam on the beach and shoved a uniform in the mess. Soon I'd be seeing a whole lotta beach covered with jam.

———— ∞∞∞ ————

Everybody knew we'd be going across the Channel, we just didn't know when. Thinking was that fifty thousand or so of us would go on the first day, and probably half a million within a month. Most guessed we'd be hitting the beaches around the middle of June. Guys who didn't have corn mash for brains were looking at calendars and trying to figure out what days had the best tides and moon for an invasion. The big brains thought the smaller the moon and the higher the tide, the better the chance we'd be going.

Something else was expected in June, Hazel's baby. Tom told me at Christmastime that Hazel was in the family way. I shouldn't have, but I asked who the father was. 'Course, I was just funning him, but we weren't getting much leave, so old Tom musta been making hay while the sun was shining.

Starting in May no one was let off the base, MPs walking around the whole perimeter. We couldn't figure out whether they were keeping people out or keeping us in. Every piece of equipment we had got loaded up. On June 3rd we were on our way, a convoy almost a quarter-mile long. I thought the roads were going to give way. Every few miles our convoy would snake through a village. Whole families of Brits stood out in front of their cottages, waving and smiling. Some offered a quick cup of tea, they knew where we were going. Couldn't help but think of the story Cecil told us, how a poor bloke in a cart on the way to the Tower would be offered free drinks before he got his head chopped off.

By dark we were on the Channel coast, up from the Dover cliffs. Took us until midnight to get sorted out, then loaded up on an LSI. Think it stood for Landing Ship for the Infantry. The LSI was 150 feet or so long with most of the space open to the air, sorta like a real big Higgins boat. Stole some sleep. Then daybreak, the 4th of June. The weather was warm, the water calm. Sergeant got us formed up, then Lieutenant Johnson briefed us with big maps of the Normandy coast. 'Course, the army couldn't keep things simple. Over maybe two miles of beach they had sections marked off with code names. We were going in on Fox Green at Omaha. The beach next to our target was called Easy Red. I remember thinking I'd rather be going to Easy Red than Fox Green.

Standing on a crate of mortar shells, the lieutenant told us the beaches would be beat to hell and the Germans would be shell-shocked when we poured off the boats. The Air Corps was sending over a thousand planes to bomb the crap out of the beaches and bunkers. Battleships would be shooting twelve-inch shells that weighed two thousand pounds into the beaches. Sounded good to me. Around midnight we would push off, cut across the Channel for four hours, then down the sides of the LSI and into Higgins boats. A quick two-mile run to the beach and we'd be in France.

Remember I told you that the Air Corps tried to teach us to tell the difference between Kraut planes and our planes, but us foot soldiers couldn't figure out the difference? Some general got a smart idea. Lieutenant Johnson told us they'd painted the bottom of the wings of every American and British plane with zebra-like stripes. If we saw a plane with big black-and-white stripes, it was ours. No stripes, shoot the asshole out of the sky.

We spent the afternoon cleaning equipment and chatting. No big talk. Tom and I gabbed a lot about nothing, mostly joking, some serious stuff. We agreed that if either of us got killed and the other lived, the lucky one would visit the other fella's family when they got back. I was thinking I wouldn't want Tom to see my house in Renfroe. Then I thought if he did, I'd be dead, so's I shouldn't worry.

At 2400, midnight, we were off. The first half-hour wasn't so bad, a couple guys got seasick. Then, we were in the open Channel with big *I want to drown you* waves spraying over the sides. LSIs weren't built to cut through the water, they battled it, a constant rocking, forward, backward, left, right. Most everyone was heaving, slippery vomit all over the decks. Not one GI wasn't soaked with salt water. With the wind and wet clothes we were shivering cold. Then the LSI halted, made a big circle, then moved in a straight line. I pulled out a compass, we were heading back to England.

Anchored in a harbor with fifty other LSIs, all around green pastures—English pastures. The invasion had been called off because of the choppy seas. Maybe we'd go tomorrow. No one was allowed off the boat, so we did what we always did, wait. Broke open some K rations and played some cards. There was some sleeping, probably some praying.

Finally, nightfall. We pushed off again at 2300. The waves were taking a rest. Close to four hours later we were there, the coast of

Normandy, waiting for the sun. Then a noise rolled over us and liked to push our ears shut. For half an hour or more the drone of an army of bombers. We couldn't see them through the overcast but for sure they were there. In the distance explosion after explosion, the bombers were doing their job.

At crack of day we could just make out a hint of the Normandy coast. Everything was black or gray, just a few whitecaps. Ordered down the side of the LSI, into the Higgins. No one was joking. We held next to the LSI till all the Higgins boats in our group were filled. Couple guys got tangled up in the boarding ropes, but nothing bad.

As soon as we pushed off from the LSI we had a big problem. Everybody had more gear than the generals had figured on, so our Higgins boat was scary low in the water. The wind picked up and the seas were high again, with waves four feet or more. Heading toward the beach, our boat was plowing through the waves while the green seawater was pouring in over the sides. The bilge pump wasn't working, so we were all bailing like hell with our helmets. Hadn't practiced this at Slapton.

A quick glance over my shoulder, Tom was bailing with a helmet in each hand, wondered where he got the extra one. The coxswain, the guy steering the Higgins boat, was at the stern. His mouth wide open and his eyes not blinking. After ten or fifteen minutes of bailing like hell less water was breaking over the sides, then almost nothing. I caught my breath and glanced around, we all looked like we'd already been in a battle and lost.

Off to our left, fifty yards or so, two of the Sherman tanks with their canvas skirts that made 'em boats, churning toward the shore. All of a sudden four guys came up from one of the tank's turrets and jumped into the sea. Then the tank disappeared, it sunk. A few moments later the other tank made like a submarine. No one got outta that one.

Closer to the beach, it looked gray, not white. The color wasn't important, all that mattered was that the beach was smooth. No bomb craters, no craters from naval guns. Smooth, just like Slapton, except here we had jacks. Y'all know the metal toy jacks that kids play with? Just like those, except these were maybe eight feet or so tall, obstructions with Teller mines sticking up out of the water.

Up from the beach there was a rise to a bluff, over to the right, halfway down the bluff, a structure. Never seen anything like it before. It looked just like some concrete building had been buried in the bluff with only one side showing. No windows—just a long narrow opening from one side to the other. Out from this slit there was a long black shaft. Wondered for a moment what the hell it was. Then I knew.

I stood halfway up in the Higgins and looked back, saw maybe a couple hundred other Higgins, like a swarm of giant black beetles. Then splashes far to our right. Big splashes. Kraut shells from the beach. But just splashes, nothing hitting our boat.

We were maybe three or four hundred yards offshore. Didn't look like Fox Green Sector to me. Another hundred yards, then the spray. A spray of machine-gun bullets, then mortars. Everybody dropped down below the sides. Water sloshing over the front as we rammed the waves. Bullets were hitting the boat. One ricocheted off some equipment above the sides, hits a guy in his stomach. Fell on his side, screaming. Mortar shells all around.

A sudden jolt and we were stopped. We'd hit a sandbar. The front dropped, the sides and bottom of our boat framed the view forward. A frame for a picture of hell. The beach was a hundred yards away. Between us and the beach the water looked like a hailstorm of ripples in Harkins Creek. But it wasn't ice pellets making the ripples. Both platoon leaders froze, then one folded face forward into the water.

Lieutenant Johnson was yelling and pushing. *Everyone off!* We shuffled and stumbled forward. Down the ramp, into the water. Moving forward, I saw guys falling. Then it was my turn. It was only a foot deep. A few steps forward, and then I was in water over my head. *I'm underwater. I'm going to drown.* Dropped my rifle, tore off my gear. Gagging, I came to the surface, gasping, swimming forward. Then sand under my feet. Fifty yards of wading forward. All around bullets slapping the water. Explosions, mortar shells, hitting with great whooshes, then concussions, then blankets of water.

Crawling forward to an obstacle on the beach. Steel girders welded together in an X shape. Laying behind it, bullets hitting the steel above me. I was in combat. I was heaving salt water. I'd lost all my equipment, and I was hiding behind Kraut girders, scared shitless. I looked back. Boats were burning, abandoned equipment everywhere on the beach, guys sprawled in the sand, most of them facedown. One poor soul was kneeling with a Bible in his hand, then he was gone in a red mist. Guys were wading out of the water and not falling, just slowly crumpling. Some GI comes walking forward, not crouched over, like he didn't have a care in the world, then almost cut in two with the buzz of a machine gun.

More guys to the obstacles. Two other GIs next to me, squeezing together behind the girders. Then Lieutenant Johnson was with us, yelling. Our only hope was to get to the bluff. He pushed off, ran a dozen steps, then an explosion, he'd stepped on a mine. There was a thud as his boot hit the obstacle we were cowering behind, then fell in the sand in front of us. Part of his leg still in the boot.

The guy next to me started forward. A sharp clunk and he was down. A hole in his helmet as big as a fist. I looked at the guy lying next to me. He wasn't moving. His eyes weren't blinking, he wasn't breathing. Someone behind me was crying for his mother.

That night I was at an aid station outside Colleville, about a mile up from the beach. We weren't in the town, the Germans still had it. Fighting was going on a few hundred yards away—not with howitzers and tanks and stuff, just small-arms fire. Both sides were tired. Medics got the aid station squeezed tight to a hedgerow. I was lying on my stomach, thinking *I'm alive.* Most of the men in my platoon weren't. Tom didn't make it, the sergeant didn't, the lieutenant didn't.

For that first half-day on the beach I pretty much knew I was dead. Just waiting to die. By noon we had a foothold. Some infantry got through a ravine and circled behind the Kraut bunkers. By afternoon I was earning my pay, blowing up bunkers and pillboxes. Then some bad-luck GI down the beach stepped on a mine. A shrapnel splinter ripped into my ass. Burned like hell, but I kept going, kept doing my job.

By the time the sun was setting my boots were full of blood. Didn't like to, but I went over to a medic. Felt guilty only being shot in the ass, but figured bleeding to death was going to make me as dead as getting my head blown off. Got shuffled around, then to the aid station by the hedgerow. Dropped my pants for the medic. He told me I'd get two Purple Hearts 'cause the piece of metal ripped through one of my ass cheeks, came out, then ripped into the other. He rubbed in sulfur, and then some guy put in stitches and told me to stay on my stomach for the night.

Me and a handful of tired-ass GIs laid ourselves down next to a stone wall for the night. There I laid, almost too tired to breathe. Fell asleep and didn't move until some sergeant kicked me awake in the morning.

———— ✺ ————

The first week after the invasion was confusion, good confusion. Our job was sorting out all the equipment and men that were coming ashore. No question, the generals really had day one of the invasion screwed up. The only reason we didn't get our butts kicked back to England was that a lotta GIs were willing to die. No fancy equipment got us past the bluffs.

But the generals had things planned pretty smart after the first day. Navy came in and sank these big concrete boxes offshore. Linked together, they made a harbor. Then engineers bulldozed a roadway from the beach right to these blocks, so ships could dock and unload. I'd never seen so much equipment—more than I thought the army had.

By the second week we were building ammo dumps a mile or so back from the beach. Know what our big problem was? I'll tell ya. Craters, damn craters from a few thousand bombs the Air Corps had dropped the morning of the invasion. I'd met some Air Corps guys in pubs. They had it as rough as anybody. Climbing into their B-17s and B-24s and flying in 30-degree-below temperatures, sucking oxygen through a mask for six hours while Krauts were shooting the hell out of their planes. But the day before the invasion some Air Corps general figured he wanted to play it safe and not be blamed for sinking one of our ships. So this chickenshit general had the bombers target their drops one or two miles behind the beach. For all the Air Corps did for us on June 6th, they should have just slept in and enjoyed a real nice breakfast. Same with the battleships. I'm not sure where their shells went, but it sure the hell wasn't on the beaches.

By the end of June I could sit on my ass again and things on the Normandy coast were wrapped up. Nothing more for us engineers to do. My unit was real thin, only one out of four guys left, so we all got reassigned to the 326th Engineer Battalion. They were supporting the 28th Division that was pushing through France. Took me two days to find them, and guess who was there? Emory. Hadn't seen him since late '43. I asked him if he had found his suitcase yet. He was looking good. Emory came ashore the afternoon of June 6th. His guys all made it okay at Normandy, except for one young kid. This dumbass GI went into a Kraut bunker looking for souvenirs. Picked up a German helmet, put it on, and came out with his hands up, pretending to be a Kraut. Right off a GI shot him in the face. Guys that came ashore that morning weren't taking no prisoners.

Anyway, Emory was acting sergeant and got me into his platoon. His sergeant had bought the farm when a Kraut sniper nailed him. We just kept doing what we'd been trained for, laying down bridges and blowing things up. Mostly we built bridges, following right behind the 110th Infantry, about a thousand foot soldiers. They were tough. Real tough. I saw them do some things I shouldn't tell you about.

About half the bridges we built were 'cause the Krauts blew 'em up as they pulled back. The other half were 'cause we blew 'em up. The Air Corps was blowing up any bridge they could find on the Kraut side of the front. Wanted to keep supplies from getting to them, and wanted to keep the Krauts from retreating with their equipment.

By the time July 4th rolled around, I was thinking I might just see Renfroe again. Most times we weren't real close to the killing. And life was easier. 'Course, then easier meant less hard. Once every few days we got a hot meal. Not hot like cooked on a stove, but hot like a trash can sitting on a fire with ten gallons of stew being stirred with a broom handle by a GI that hadn't washed since he'd set foot in France. And if we were lucky, we got a shower. They would have a big can, probably the same one they cooked the stew in, lashed way up in a tree. It was filled with water, and a hose with a clamp came out the side. We could give ourselves a real quick cold shower and then put on the same stiff, filthy clothes we had been sleeping in for weeks.

Every so often we'd get a batch of fresh-faced, bug-eyed replacements. They stood out 'cause their uniforms were clean and they had all the right equipment. Emory would fun them, asking if anyone was a college graduate or had any college schooling. If a hand went up he told them he had a real important job for someone really smart. Told the kid he was the senior private in charge of latrines. Should check them each day, and if one was more than half full of shit, he should fill it and real quick dig another. Sounded funny then. Five months later I would have kissed ass to have been able to jump into a latrine full of shit. Anything to get away from the Kraut 88s.

Sure felt bad about the French. Always coming out of their homes, smiling at us GIs and giving us something to eat or drink. 'Course, you know who grabbed the wine—Emory. Anyway, these French couldn't have been nicer. But I couldn't push it out of my mind that Cecil had called them frogs. Couldn't see why he did.

By August word from the top was that we'd be in Berlin by Christmas. The 326th Engineers had its act together, usually a mile or so behind the guys doing the shooting and earning the medals. We still spent most of our time building bridges. Building is probably not what we did. We put bridges together. Most everything we had was prefab. We'd anchor some cables to both sides of the river, attach some pontoons, lay down the inner connecting steel mats, and we had ourselves a bridge. Problem was, some SOB Kraut with a rifle and a scope hunkered down in the bushes on the other side of the river might use us for target practice. Usually our guys had 'em pushed back enough so's we didn't need to worry too much.

By the time October rolled in, us GIs sleeping on the ground knew we weren't going to be in Berlin by Christmas. We figured we weren't even going to be in Germany by Christmas. The generals sleeping in warm beds told us things were real good, they weren't. These Nazis were tough soldiers. When you'd see them, when they were captured or something, they stood tall. And I figured however good they were fighting now, they'd fight even harder the closer we got to the Fatherland.

Something else about the Krauts, they had better equipment. All the colonels and generals that told us we were the best-equipped were flat-ass wrong. Our hand grenades were about the size of a baseball, but real heavy. Couldn't really throw 'em; we had to heave 'em. The Krauts had this wooden stick, maybe ten inches long, coming out of their grenades. This gave 'em leverage. They could throw one of theirs fifty feet farther—a lot when you're trying to kill a pillbox. Even their shovels for digging foxholes were better. And they had boots that kept your feet warm and dry. Our GI boots would soak right through. We were always fighting off trench foot, always changing socks and drying them by wrapping them around our necks.

But it wasn't the little stuff that was killing us, it was the big stuff. Their 88s shot bigger shells farther than anything we had, plus they had more of a wallop. Our Shermans had four inches of armor, their Tigers had six inches. To stop a Tiger some medal-winning GI had to be brave and lucky. Only thing I figured we had that was better was our trucks. The Germans pretty much moved things with horses. I sorta rethought this when a captured Kraut told me that the next time I was starving, I should try to eat a truck.

By the third week of December we were in Belgium. I started to think of Christmas. Saw some trees decorated with ornaments cut from K-ration cans, but we weren't singing Christmas carols or anything. We were pretty much doing what we always did, building bridges and fixing roads and stuff.

Then we got the crap kicked out of us. Our generals were planning their Christmas party while Kraut generals were planning to take back Antwerp. On the morning of December 16th all hell broke loose. Krauts came pouring across the front. They had put a lot of thought into it, took some of their guys that spoke real good English, outfitted them in American uniforms from dead GIs, and gave them captured American jeeps. Lookin' like GIs these Krauts came across our lines and generally screwed things up every which way. Even changed road signs so our reinforcements headed off in the wrong direction—that kind of thing.

I was maybe twenty miles back from the fighting when the Germans poured across the front. Our guys were surrendering and running. I'm not saying fellas were cowards, I'm just saying we were outmuscled real quick. By the second day the Krauts had pushed us back twenty-five miles in some places. At that rate they'd've been in Renfroe by the next Fourth of July.

So our general, a Southern boy named Middleton, threw everything at 'em. Every GI went to the front. Guys who had been baking bread in the messes were handed M1s and pointed toward the roar. Same with me, Emory, and the whole 326th. Some shouting of orders, a bunch of confusion, and we were in the back of four-by-fours bouncing to the front, carrying rifles.

After six hours of freezing our asses in the back of a careening four-by-four, stopping once for fuel and a latrine break, we pulled into Marvie. It was damn cold. Deep snow on the ground and none of us had winter gear. No long underwear, no winter boots, and most of us didn't even have the full winter coat, we just had our field jackets. Maybe a half hour we rocked back and forth on our feet after we climbed out of the four-by-fours. Rocked back and forth trying not to freeze, waiting for orders. Then this captain shows up. I'd seen dead guys that looked better than this fella. Dark circles under his eyes, three-day beard, a piece of blanket wrapped around his head, covering his ears. Looked like he hadn't slept in days. He walked by using an ax handle as a cane. I was thinking, *I'm in shit trouble.*

To the east of Marvie our guys had established a perimeter, maybe a hundred GIs in foxholes. The captain put one of us—a baker, candlestick maker, or whatever—in a foxhole with one of the infantry guys. I was set down in a foxhole with a guy who made the captain look like Mr. Charles Atlas. His name was Hank, and he probably weighed 130 pounds, and that's only if he was carrying thirty pounds of gear. He told me right off that he'd been in his foxhole a day and a half. No food, only a canteen of soup frozen like a brick. Hank had his rifle under his coat to try and keep it from freezing up. We were dug in on the edge of a wood. In front of us a field a fair piece across, maybe three or four hundred yards till the next tree line. Past this tree line was artillery, Kraut 88s, whooshing like some kinda crazy tornados. The 88s sounded different than everything else.

Hank and me started talking. Even though he said he got his name from a famous hitter for the Detroit Tigers, Hank was from New York. Came ashore in the second wave. Got lucky, only two of the guys in his platoon got whacked. But they had a tough time the next week pushing through the hedgerows, said the Germans had pretargeted the open areas, then they'd leave a spotter behind. When our guys got in the open, the 88s would sausage 'em.

About dark the captain with the ax handle came crawling by, making the rounds of the perimeter. Told us to watch for Kraut patrols, said he'd be back before dawn and he'd shoot us himself if he found us asleep. He knew we didn't have any rations, promised the Air Corps would be dropping supplies the next day. Some more talk with Hank, then the sun set, and the damn cold became unbearable cold. Hank had an army-issue winter coat while I had the standard GI jacket. Neither one made much difference. We were both shivering.

Hank had torn a blanket into strips and wrapped them around his head like a turban. Over this he'd pulled his helmet. He unwrapped a few strips, and I used them to make me some earmuffs. It was a long night. Never stopped shivering. We spoke real low so's we could hear any Kraut patrol. Only good thing about the cold was the crust on top of the snow. No matter how slowly a Kraut walked, he'd make a crunchy noise with every step.

From the time the sun set till daylight was probably fifteen hours. Fifteen hours of bone-hurting cold. By first light I couldn't feel my toes, in spite of rocking back and forth on my feet all night. Captain came by and told us supplies would be dropped. Told us Blood & Guts Patton was on his way, we just needed to hold on. For a couple hours there was a lot of shelling to our left, nothing to bother us. But the sky caused a worry. Couldn't figure out how the Air Corps was going to drop us anything. If I couldn't see up, they couldn't see down.

Sure enough, the captain was right, around noon the roar of aircraft above the overcast. Then some chutes drifting down, each with a box of supplies swinging below. Right through the overcast they drifted, right into the woods held by the Krauts.

The rest of the day Hank and I stared across the snow-covered field in front of us. Nothing moving. Maybe an hour of shelling far to the left, toward Bastogne. Before dusk the captain was back. Same story. I was thinking, *I'd just as soon he shoots me, don't know how I'm getting through another night.* Neither Hank nor I had had anything to eat in almost three days. Right after sunset a strong wind. A real strong wind, strong enough to pick up icy pellets from the crust of the snow and sandblast our faces.

Nothing we could do. We stopped guarding the perimeter and tried to survive. Hank and I hunkered down in the bottom of the foxhole. You may have a problem with this, but I'm not sure we'd have made it another night otherwise. We huddled together—not with our backs touching, but by wrapping our arms around each other and breathing on each other's face for warmth. Long night. Thought I was dead a couple times. Wished I was dead most of the time.

Finally, the light of daybreak. Not a soft light through an over-cast—a sharp light. The sky would be blue. They would fly. The C-47s would know where we were. We might live. Best birthday I ever had.

A sergeant came by with two blankets and told us the 4th Armored was only five miles away. He was gone a couple hours and then three or four dozen C-47s all started dropping supplies behind our lines, dropping them in the right place. Started to think I might make it. So must have Hank, began yakking all about New York City. Wanted to show me around, show me a good time. He wasn't real impressed about my trip to the top of the Empire State Building and eating two egg rolls.

All of a sudden Hank stopped talking and pointed to the field. I didn't see anything. He pointed to a certain tree on the far tree line. Told me to look down from that tree to about halfway across the field we'd been staring at for two days. I looked but didn't see a thing. Told me to look for two tiny black dots. I looked, and then I saw 'em. They were dots, not Krauts. He told me no, they were Krauts in their winter camouflage. Said Krauts had these white blankets with a hole in the middle, sorta like our rain ponchos, that they pulled over themselves so only their square heads and helmets were showing. Everything else was white, like the snow.

Hank and I split them up. He said he'd nail the one on the left and I'd take the other. Our foxhole was just inside the tree line, in the dark shadows. The Krauts were in the bright snow, no way their eyes could focus in the shadows. So we waited for them to get closer. Maybe seventy-five or a hundred yards out, we took our shots. A slow deep breath, exhale some air, hold my breath, squeeze a shot, and the Kraut on the right dropped. Hank took a shot and the Kraut on the left turned back. I could see his legs churning the snow under his white camouflage blanket. He was heading back for the tree line. I sighted him, squeezed, he dropped.

By afternoon the guys from Patton's corps were in Bastogne. Hank and I were relieved from our post. Trudged back to Marvie. After three days of nothing, we got hot food from the airdropped supplies. Can't remember what it was, but I remember it was the best meal I ever ate. Then we crawled into sleeping bags in some sorry-looking barn with maybe fifty other guys. Right in the middle of the roof was a shell hole. We kept a fire going all night, with smoke rising through the blasted open roof. In the morning, another hot meal.

Was scared to look, but I did. Unlaced my boots and pulled off my socks, both pairs. Toes on my right foot were a dark purple, no feeling. Showed a medic, told me that if they turned black I should have 'em cut off, or just wait for 'em to fall off.

They kept us engineers at the front till the Krauts were high-tailing it back to Germany. Got the hell scared out of me before I got off the front line. It happened right outside of Wardin. We'd been moving forward, taking back ground the Krauts had overrun. They weren't putting up much of a fight, they'd used up most of their ammo and fuel the first few days when they'd broken through our lines.

So we were going forward through a forest. Then came the *whoosh* of Kraut 88s. The shells weren't hitting the ground, they were hitting the tops of the trees. It didn't matter if we dropped to the ground—shrapnel was coming straight down. And shrapnel was bad, bad stuff. A Kraut bullet would hit you, then come out the other side, making a hole not much bigger than where it went in. Not shrapnel. This stuff was jagged pieces of metal, maybe half a pound. I'd seen guys hit by shrapnel. It made a hole as big as a baseball where it went in, the size of a football where it came out.

No time to claw out a foxhole in the frozen dirt, so I was laying there in the snow, with guys hit and screaming all around me. Branches were falling out of trees. Hot chunks of shrapnel were slamming into the snow, making cloudy white puffs. Then the roar of aircraft, I looked up. Two P-47s overhead. I could always recognize a P-47 with their birdlike wings. They flew past, then the screams of their dive, and then explosions. The shelling stopped. They nailed the 88s. Sorta made up for the Air Corps missing the beaches last June. Sorta.

———— ∞ ————

By February I was back to building bridges. By March the weather was breaking. No more below-zero nights. So y'all know what happened? Two big army supply trucks dropped off gear. Long johns, winter coats, real boots with lining and rubber soles, even some strange headgear, like a big woolen sock you pull over your head with holes for your eyes and mouth. Just in time for spring.

But no matter how bad we engineers had it, for the GIs on the line it was god-awful worse. Guys coming back from the line had the hundred-yard stare, their eyes didn't seem to focus. Sorta like there was no purpose in them looking. Same with their words. No conversation. They'd mumble a short answer or instruction, but showed no emotion, no interest in anything. They'd surrendered, not to the Germans, they'd surrendered hope. They knew they'd be going back to the line, likely to get themselves killed. It made me sorry. Not for them, but sorry for Ma. She'd had the hundred-yard stare. All that time in Renfroe with me, Billy, and Pa, she musta known she had no future, no hope.

By the end of March, Kraut prisoners were beginning to look real different than before. Before the average Kraut soldier stood tall. Now Hitler and his asshole buddies were getting desperate. The Russians, Brits, and our guys were grinding up their army. But instead of surrendering and saving a few million Germans, the paperhanger created the *Volkssturm*. Kraut soldiers weren't between eighteen and forty years old anymore, they went down to twelve and up to sixty. The Kraut army took these kids and old farts and gave them an armband with a swastika and some rusty old rifle or makeshift antitank rocket. They weren't much more of a threat to us than targets on the Fort Benning rifle range.

Some changes the Germans made worked. Krauts had these land mines, sorta like a big pie tin, maybe a foot across and three or four inches thick. Mostly steel with maybe two or so pounds of explosives. Krauts buried them half a foot under the surface. Each land mine had a pressure switch on the top. Some happy-faced GI would come along and step down on a mine. Next thing you knew, body parts were everywhere and his ma would be getting a telegram.

Us engineers could find most all these mines with a nifty mine detector. Held it in front of us as we walked, about a foot off the ground. It would give off a buzz if it went over more than a half pound of steel. Then real careful like, we'd dig up the mine without pushing down the pressure switch. But the Krauts got smart and started making ceramic mines, using just a few ounces of metal for the pressure switch. This made for two big problems. First, our detectors went right over them with no warning buzz, so all of a sudden we was setting off a bunch of land mines. Second problem was the ceramic mines weren't as powerful as the old metal ones. Metal ones would blast you to pieces. You were dead. The new ones didn't always kill you, they just blew off some body parts. More than one unlucky GI had his manhood blown right off. Couldn't think of nothing much worse. Most of us woulda traded two legs and an arm to keep our manhood.

President Roosevelt died on April 12. We found out about it the next day. Everybody I knew liked the president. His voice made you feel good. He sounded strong, but somehow he seemed a little soft, like he cared for the average Joe. But it's not 'cause the president died that I remember the date. It was the same day I got a letter from Big Sam. I'd never gotten a letter from him before. Other than us trading some eggs for milk back in Renfroe, we'd never really spoken much.

Big Sam sent me a letter to tell me that Pa was dead. Couldn't hardly believe what I was reading. Sat in the mud just staring at the words. Big Sam wrote that he didn't see him in the fields for a long time so he went over to the house. Said Pa was lying in bed real peaceful. He buried him next to the marker we had for Ma. Told me when I got back to see him, he had all of Pa's belongings. I didn't think Pa had belongings. All our flags were at half-mast for the president. For me they were at half-mast for Pa.

With Pa being laid out still, for sure he wouldn't be getting my watch. I'd been trying the best I could to keep it safe for him. Thought about it, decided to give it to Billy. Figured the navy probably didn't give sailors watches. Everyone just did what the ship's captain told them, no need to be looking at the time.

Remember I couldn't describe what it was like on the beaches? Saw something else that I couldn't find the words for. It was a pretty nice day, last week in April. Maybe it was the first week of May. Us engineers were following the infantry guys as usual. If they needed something blown up, something spanned, or whatever, we were there.

So anyway, we were getting close to Munich, a pretty big German city where they made a lot of stuff for the war. I was in my four-by-four, following behind the real fighting. We were going to put a bridge across the Amper River. Still remember the name, thought it sounded like something electrical.

Then we came to this place—I want to say it was a prison, but it wasn't. It was what they called a concentration camp. Dachau. Sorta like a big army base with a lot of barrack-like buildings, and around the whole thing, barbed-wire fences. They weren't like what I'd seen before. Maybe fifteen feet up, on the top, wires with insulators between them and posts, just like you'd see on a road after the electric company come through. Y'all have probably seen pictures of concentration camps. The pictures are bad, real bad. But it was worse. Tear your heart out worse. Sometimes I didn't even know what I was looking at. Once I thought I saw a big pile of old clothes. It wasn't.

Me and Emory were just walking through the camp, numb-like, when we heard shots. A few single shots, then a machine gun. Turned toward the gunfire, GIs shooting German soldiers that they'd lined up against a wall. Didn't seem right, didn't seem wrong. Probably killed fifty or more before a captain showed up and halted the shooting. Didn't stop the killing, didn't stop the payback. Our guys broke Kraut kneecaps with rifle butts. Prisoners who had the strength finished them off with shovels and picks.

At the far end of Dachau were fields of dead people. Looked like skeletons with a sheet of skin wrapped tight around their bones. But it wasn't just the starved dead that made you heartbroke. Emory and me went into this building, bigger than most. Inside a mountain, a brown mountain of shoes and boots. The Krauts kept everything. More boots than shoes, most worn and tattered. But like a wildflower pushing through cold earth in the spring, I saw something white in the mountain of brown leather. A small pair of white satin shoes, each with a strap and a little brass buckle. One strap was looped around the other and then buckled, so the two would stay matched, waiting together for the little girl who wore them.

After Dachau, if I saw a dead bloated Kraut with blowflies going in and out of his nose and mouth, I just thought of the white satin shoes. Let 'em burn in hell. But the truth is that the little girl shoes didn't change just how I thought about Krauts. No, the satin shoes turned some of my thinking upside-down. Not right away, almost twenty years later the shoes changed my thinking. Changed my thinking about the man I respected the most, my pa.

It was at the Amper River, a few days after Dachau. We'd just finished putting the last section of bridge across the pontoons, turned to walk back to my four-by-four, then somebody hit me across my back, real hard, with a shovel or something I'm thinking. Fell face forward, into the dirt, wondering what had hit me. Felt warmth in my jacket, then the taste of blood. I was shot. I didn't feel scared but sorta okay. I was going to die or I was going to an aid station. Either way, *I am outta here.*

I was wrong. Laid where I fell, no one by me. Laid still, worried like if I made a move some part of me was going to fall off. Shooting and footsteps, but no one stopped. I was starting to feel real cold, so I pushed up with one arm and rolled over. Earth dark red where I'd been laying. On my back I could move my one arm, so I waved. Quick-like a medic was over me. Then nothing. I'm not sure how long I drifted in and out before I found myself on a litter strapped to the back of a jeep.

———— ∞ ————

That night I woke up in an evac hospital. Turns out it really wasn't that bad. One of the asshole snipers from the Hitler Youth nailed me in the back of my shoulder. Bullet angled off a collarbone, then out the front. Problem was, one of my lungs got nicked. They cut me open and patched me up. Two days later I was on a train to Paris, a day after that on a plane to England. I was strapped to a litter on my first plane ever. Couldn't see out, couldn't move around.

Everybody seemed real happy on the plane. Wasn't sure why. Then I heard, the war was over. The Nazis had surrendered. Good news, but bad luck for me. If the Krauts had thrown in the towel a week earlier, I'd've been sitting somewhere with a hangover, not laying on a litter feeling like a Kraut tank was on my chest. But I got my head screwed back on real quick. One of the guys on a litter next to me didn't make it—just stopped breathing. An army nurse pulled a blanket over his face and moved on. Thought about how many guys hadn't made it since last June. I was lucky, damn lucky.

So guess where we landed? At an airfield right outside the 160th General Hospital. A top-drawer hospital. But the best part was that it was ten miles from Cheltenham.

In a few days I was walking around, well, walking hunched over in pain. A lot of guys weren't walking at all. Some of them weren't ever going to walk again. A couple real good things, though. Food, hot food, and a lot of it. Took me a while to feel okay eating something that wasn't in a can. And the gals, a lot of them. Most all were American, army nurses. Weren't all lookers, but boy, they all had nice smiles and happy voices.

After a week or so I was able to move around without too much pain, so I figured I'd get over to Cheltenham. Wasn't hard to do, the hospital had buses back and forth to a bunch of nearby towns. Hazel and her family didn't have a phone, so I couldn't tell her I was coming. Anyway, the army bus pulled into Cheltenham and it looked just the same. At a real slow pace—I was still wincing a little—I walked through the town square, past the Queen's Hotel, then down Swindon Road and right on Mercey. Still remembered the number, Number 14 Mercey Road, where Tom, Hazel, me, and the other folks had shared a bottle of wine after Tom's wedding.

Out front was Nano, Hazel's ma. When she saw me, her eyes got real big. Then a smile. They hadn't known whether I was alive or dead.

Hazel and little Tommy were inside. Tom had a son. He was born on June 23rd, just two weeks after his pa and I were in the Higgins boat heading to the beach. Almost eleven months old. Cute kid, seemed to smile a lot. I kept looking at him but couldn't see Tom. Didn't stay too long, felt guilty. Shouldn't have, just did.

It was close to the end of my time at the hospital that I got another V-mail from Big Sam. Worst letter I ever got. He wrote that Western Union had delivered him a telegram that was for Pa.

Billy was dead. Killed in the Pacific. Big Sam printed out in real neat letters just the same as what was on the telegram. One sentence: REGRET TO INFORM YOU THAT YOUR SON WILLIAM BUTCHER WAS KILLED IN ACTION.

I'd never seen "William" printed out before. His name was Billy.

I looked down at my Benrus watch. I'd had it on every day for pretty much three years. Thought about it. Only bad luck for whoever I was saving it for. I gave it to a young redheaded British orderly who emptied out bedpans. Never wore a watch again.

The evening I found out about Billy, went to a market right outside the hospital gates. Bought two tomatoes. Then back to the hospital mess. Got some bread and sugar and made tomato bread sandwiches. Sandwiches just like Billy and me shared after a day in the fields. Ate them slowly. Ate them while thinking of Billy. When they were gone, walked a far way behind the hospital and sat under a tree. Waited till dark. Then I cried. First time I cried since I left Renfroe. Cried for Billy. Cried for Pa. Cried for Ma. Just sat there and cried for a good long spell.

***

Big subject with us GIs in the hospital was how soon we'd all get home. The generals got together and came up with this points idea.

Every guy got points based on how many months he'd been in Europe, whether he'd seen combat, that sorta stuff. Enough points, you got to go home. Depending on which way you leaned, I had enough points. But it didn't really matter. The army figured I was damaged and they were sending me home.

Spent more than a week at the hospital waiting for my transportation home, then it was all downhill. After a couple of trains and a bus, I was back in Liverpool, then on a troopship. Coming over everybody'd had wide eyes. No matter what we said, we were scared. Going back everybody had wide grins. Sailing west the ship was jammed just as tight as the *Williams*, but this time nobody cared. No calisthenics, no boat drills, no cleaning equipment. Time, plenty of time to think of my future. Really hadn't thought much about it since I'd left Belvoir. Seemed like a waste. Only thing I knew for sure was that I didn't want to be in a cage, spinning a wheel. A lot of guys said they was going to college, the GI Bill of Rights pretty much paid for it. I figured I wasn't the dullest Joe around, so I might handle college. Just wasn't sure what I wanted to learn.

A few days out from Liverpool I was on deck, leaning against a rail, having a smoke. My brain was coasting, not thinking of anything, then a hearty laugh from one of GIs on the deck below. Sort of a dumbass donkey hee-haw that I'd heard before. You're not going to believe it, but Emory was on the troopship with me. With a thousand other guys jammed in we hadn't crossed paths till that day. It was great to see him. I'd hoped he hadn't gotten his ass shot off after they'd pulled me off the line. He hadn't, but his right hand was bandaged up like a big white football. The day after the Krauts had thrown in the towel Emory was sitting on the back of a truck bed and some steel mats shifted when the truck swerved. Emory lost most of four fingers on his right hand. Told me his new best friend was his left hand.

Emory had some real bad news. He'd heard from his ma that Robert had been killed. Didn't know where, but our Robert Lee wasn't going home. That night Emory found me in my bunk and took me topside with a bottle of Scotch he had hid in his jacket. Sat under a lifeboat and talked about good times with Robert. Got shitfaced drunk we did.

It was right after daybreak on a Saturday summer morning when our ship pulled into the New York docks. I stayed below-decks for a spell. Most every GI had some family waiting for them. Waiting to hug them and hustle them home. Figured it wouldn't hurt as much, my missing Billy, Pa, and Ma, if I didn't see all the smiling happy families. After sneaking off the troopship I hopped a train from New York down to Philadelphia. The cars were jammed tight—happy jammed, not scared jammed, like when I was going the other direction in '43. Sat in a bar in the Philadelphia station sipping beers for lunch, then I caught a train to Harrisburg, then another up to Altoona. Heading into Altoona we went around the Horseshoe Curve. Tom had told me about it, a curve so tight that if a train was long enough, the front cars were going in the opposite direction from the back cars, so you sorta passed yourself going in the other direction.

Before leaving Harrisburg I'd called Tom's sister Dorothy and told her when I'd be coming in. She and her husband were in from the Midwest, visiting her ma, Tom's ma. Dorothy said that she would pick me up at the station in Altoona. 'Course, I recognized her from the pictures that Tom had showed me. There she stood on the train platform, smiling with tears running down her cheeks. Out to a car we walked, Dorothy's husband started the engine before we opened the door. Thought maybe he wanted to get this day behind him.

The drive to Tyrone was maybe ten, fifteen miles, a lot of conversation, nothing bad, stuff that nobody really cared about. Drove right by Tyrone High School, yellow brick, just like Tom had told me. Another block and we turned onto Pennsylvania Avenue, maybe seven or eight blocks long. A bank building, a lot of stores, a restaurant, a movie theater—all just like Tom had described 'em back in Ashchurch.

Dorothy's husband parked his Chevy in front of a small apartment building on Pennsylvania Avenue, right across from the post office. I knew Tom's ma lived on the second floor of the apartment. To the right was Hap's Meat Store. Tom had had a job there after school. Once in the apartment building up a long, dark staircase. I slowed down toward the top. Dorothy stepped in front of me as we went through the door to the apartment to meet her ma, Tom's ma. On the far side of the parlor was Tom's ma, sitting on a sofa, her hands folded together like she wanted to pray.

For more than an hour we spoke. I knew they would ask, but it still just froze me when they did. They asked how Tom had died. I told them quickly. I lied. I told them that his last words were about his family. I lied again.

'Course we had some pleasant talk, mostly about Hazel and how pretty she was. And you should have seen their faces light up when I started talking about little Tommy and how much he looked like his father. Tom was right when he'd married Hazel in Cheltenham in '43. Little Tommy didn't help Tom, but he was doing a lot to help Tom's family.

By late afternoon I was on a train back to Philadelphia, then riding through the night to Atlanta. Three hours in the station in Atlanta sitting on a bench close to where me and Emory had plopped ourselves down in '42. Then I took an early-morning train west to Birmingham. It wasn't wartime crowded, but pretty much every seat was taken.

An older chap sat next to me, *chap* being one of those words I'd picked up in England. He was dressed in his Sunday best, a suit and tie. There he sat, holding a hat in his lap. We didn't speak for fifteen minutes or so, then he asked if I'd been overseas. Gave him a short yes, and then our conversation just broke open. He wanted to know where I'd been and what I'd done and what I'd seen. I told him where I'd been but didn't say anything about the bad stuff.

Glad I didn't. Turned out he had a son, an only son, who was in the army. He was killed in Italy, Monte Cassino. Told me his son was buried in Italy at an army cemetery, but he was hoping to get him back to Alabama.

This fella's name was Combs, Mr. Richard Combs. He was a retired sergeant—not in the army, but in the Birmingham Police Department. He had been up to Atlanta to visit a sickly sister. He kept asking me about army life, I sorta think he pretended that he was chatting with his son.

After a spell Mr. Combs asked me if I thought I'd get sent over to the Pacific, and what I was planning on doing after the war. Told him I didn't know about the Pacific, but was hoping not. Said I didn't know what I wanted to do, just knew what I *didn't* want to do. I didn't want to break my back working somebody else's land. The two of us probably talked a good hour. He kept staring at me. For sure he was wishing I was his son.

When the train was slowing down coming through Irondale to Birmingham, he took out a pen and wrote down his name and phone number on a piece of torn-off newspaper. Told me I should think about being a police officer. Pretty good pay after a few years, and you got respect from folks. I folded this piece of paper and put it in my wallet, more to be polite than from any real interest. Said I was much obliged and might call him.

I found Emory. He had a little apartment near Kelly Ingram Park. Only problem was the heat. His one-bedroom was on the third floor of a three-floor building, so on a 95-degree Birmingham summer day the heat from three floors of living collected on the top floor. We stayed cool as best we could by opening the windows hoping for a breeze. His apartment came with a kitchen and a sofa that I stole as my bed. Emory said I could stay as long as I wanted. Missing the better part of four fingers, the army had discharged him. He figured he could get himself into Birmingham's Howard College on the GI Bill. Told me I should try. I looked at the application and their brochure, halfway expecting to see a section on VD and fraternization.

Checked in with the army and they didn't seem to be in a rush to get me redeployed. 'Course they made me take a physical, and sure enough some army doc didn't like that I couldn't raise my left arm all the way up. Told him unless I was putting my hands up to surrender to the Japs, I didn't think it would matter much. I finally got orders to get my ass out to Fort Ord in California by September 1st. That gave me six weeks of nothing to do. That's when I decided to head down to our old farm.

The bus pulled into Renfroe just about noon, stopped right in front of Drury's Feed Store, the same place where I'd gotten on the bus with Emory and Robert three years before. Took me about an hour to walk to our old house. Nothing much had changed. Out back was Ma's marker. Couldn't hardly read what Billy and I'd burnt in. There was no marker for Pa. Only thing that showed was a long mound of dirt next to Ma's marker, so they were laying together.

When I went to leave the family living in our old house came out to say hello, sharecroppers, three kids and a pa and a ma. Told them I used to live in their house, told them that was Ma and Pa buried behind the chicken coop. The wife said if she found wildflowers she always put a few on Ma's grave. Gave her a thanks. Kept looking at them, I did. Only the pa had shoes. One of the kids wasn't wearing nothing. Couldn't believe how poor they looked. Looked just like we musta.

Walked to Big Sam's place, nothing much had changed. His daughter was married and living at home, had one kid on her knee and maybe another one in the oven. I didn't ask.

Big Sam was complaining about the bugs and the cost of feed. Nothing much good to say about anything. Left for a minute and then came back with a small wood crate, told me Pa's stuff was in it. There was no top to the crate, and Pa's things didn't even come halfway up. Then Big Sam gave me an envelope and said it was real important and not to lose it. The sharecropper family who'd moved into our house found it and figured it belonged to Pa's family, so he'd been holding it for me.

After thanking Big Sam, took a slow walk back to Renfroe. The bus was late, so I drifted into Drury's. First time I'd ever been there with money in my pocket. Drury didn't recognize me. Don't know why, but I just didn't want to talk, so I didn't say anything. Bought a Coke, turned around to leave, looked up and right over near the door, where it always was, the *Progressive Farmer* calendar. The picture was a wagon being pulled at sunset. Month of July. Thought of Ma.

Back in Birmingham that night I looked through the crate. A pair of boots, same boots Pa was wearing the day I left. A gas lamp with cracked glass. Ma's fancy blue hair clip and a picture she'd had of her ma and pa. Some papers squeezed together with a piece of twine, one saying Billy had done good in school, another one showing Pa's share of the crops after the money he owed and a certificate signed by a judge swearing he married Ma and Pa. Not much else. Stuck down in the corner of the crate was a yellow piece of folded paper. A Western Union telegram from the War Department saying Billy was dead. In the envelope the sharecroppers gave Big Sam was a stack of money orders. Pa had every money order I had ever sent him. He'd never used any of them.

I thought back on the poor folks I'd seen in our old house in Renfroe. They was hurting, hurting bad, but they'd given Pa's money orders to Big Sam. They didn't keep them. Didn't try to pretend they were Pa and cash them. Poor like Pa, honest like him.

———————

Since I had a month to waste before reporting out to California, I spent a fair number of nights drinking, a fair number of mornings sleeping. Plus, if you use your imagination, you can figure out what I was doing between the drinking and the sleeping. Sorta catching up. 'Course I felt guilty. Not sure Pa ever slept past sunup in his life. But I figured there was more than a good chance I'd never be back to Alabama. The Japs weren't caving in. When you went to the movies to get some air-conditioned relief, you'd see a Movietone newsreel. Japs had these pilots who would strap on a sword, get in a plane, and fly right into one of our ships. If they were doing that to the navy, they weren't gonna be treating us army guys any better when we were crawling up their beaches.

But that all changed. First or second week of August we bombed the Japs real good. Dropped two A-bombs. Didn't know what hit 'em. Threw in the towel real quick after that. At the time I was sorta thinking we should've dropped some more before we let 'em say uncle.

Two weeks later it was official, the army was kicking me out on September 30th. I had to sign a bunch of papers and agree that they didn't owe me anything after I got my discharge money. And I had to promise I didn't have any of their stuff, like maybe I had a Sherman tank parked out in front of Emory's apartment.

So by September of '45 I was a retired GI and Emory was a freshman in college. Liked to have died when I saw this beanie cap he had to wear. If we'd worn those through France and Germany we coulda killed the Germans by making them laugh themselves to death. I was okay not working, I had my army discharge pay and a couple of hundred dollars in the bank from the money orders Pa had saved. But after a spell I started to think maybe I was getting rich-guy lazy. So's I went to some interviews, most of them for inside jobs, sweeping floors or standing behind a counter. I figured I'd better get something quick, 'cause more and more guys were gonna be hanging up their uniforms and needing a paycheck. Just couldn't see myself working inside. Couldn't see myself picking cotton either.

Being a policeman seemed to make a whole lot of sense. It was a good job with a for-certain paycheck. You got paid whether it rained or didn't rain, whether bugs came or didn't. And I figured that unless all the bad guys quit their jobs, the police would always have theirs. 'Course, some asshole crook might try to shoot me, but I figured the Krauts had done their best and didn't kill me, so I'd probably be all right.

I called Mr. Combs, the old fella I met on the train. Seemed really happy to hear from me, and he took me to lunch with three fellas in police uniforms. Two weeks later I became a Birmingham policeman. Right after that Emory moved out, got himself in a dorm. Think he liked being closer to the parties. I took over his lease, $35 a month, but I was making $125 a month as a new policeman, so it wasn't a problem.

First thing my sergeant did was have me ride around with an officer who was gonna retire in a few months. His name was Brady. Other than not having a beard, he could've been Santa Claus. Our squad car was parked in front of a lotta diners. But it wasn't bad, sorta like going to school. After spending most of the morning looking for stolen property at the pawn shops on Third Avenue, we'd kill a big hunk of time sitting in booths or at lunch counters with coffee and pie. Brady told me what to do and what not to do. Told me how to get ahead and how I could get into trouble. All pretty simple stuff.

Big thing he told me was to always be in charge. Be like a machine in bad situations, said emotion could get a cop killed. You shouldn't pause, shouldn't negotiate, you had to be firm. Brady was a thirty-five-year veteran, but had never made sergeant. He told me that he didn't kiss ass. Said that if I wanted to make sergeant, I had to pass all the right tests and play up to the right people. He figured that I had a good head start, somebody already liked me 'cause I'd gotten hired. Most guys that got hired were relatives of men on the force or a judge or the mayor.

By the end of my first year as a Birmingham policeman I was feeling good about things. I had my own cruiser, I'd made friends with the other guys, and I figured maybe I could make sergeant in ten or fifteen years. No matter what Brady said, I thought working hard and playing things by the book would get me ahead. 'Course, I did spend some time kissing ass.

As a new guy, I got the bad shifts. A lotta four-to-midnights and a lotta midnight-to-eights. It was on the beginning of a night shift when I met Brenda. I'd gotten a call about a robbery at Randy's Diner on Graymont Avenue, hadn't been there since my schooling ended with Brady. Anyway, two fellas had robbed the place right before midnight. Said they had guns in their pockets. There was only a cook and a waitress in the diner and the cook was in the back and didn't even know they'd been robbed. When I got there the waitress was sitting on a counter stool, shaking. Sorta thin, blonde hair, almost blue eyes, and later I figured out she had a real nice smile. Since the cook didn't know anything, she and I had to fill out the crime sheet. She couldn't really remember too much. Guessed they got fifteen to twenty dollars. Whole time we was talking she kept shaking like to make her teeth rattle. Shouldn't've, but I did, when I was getting all sorts of information, I asked for her phone number. She gave it to me, thinking it was something I needed for my report.

After a week or so I called the diner and asked for Brenda. I could tell she was busy so I kept it short. Told her that I just wanted to let her know we were still working the case and there was nothing new. 'Course, truth be told, we'd stopped working the case when we handed in the crime sheet the morning after the diner was robbed.

Driving around in my squad car at night, I'd be thinking about Brenda, trying to get up the nerve to ask her for a date. Thinking to myself, I've run up Kraut beaches, blown things up, shot people and been shot, but I'm scared to ask her out. Finally gave her a call at home early one morning. Someone answered that wasn't her.

Sounded like an older woman, told me Brenda was working the morning shift. So I had all day to wait before calling her in the late afternoon. All day to lose my nerve.

Right before my shift started at 4:00 p.m. I dialed her up. Brenda answered, and would you believe this, she thanked me for calling. I started to float above the chair. Real quick, I asked her to a movie on Sunday night. That was my day off. She said fine and I hung up quick. Had to call her right back to get her address. I still remember the movie, *The Best Years of Our Lives.* I remember 'cause it was about some guys just like me coming home after the war.

It was June of '47 when I asked Brenda to marry me. I had a regular paycheck coming in, my sergeant seemed to be okay with me, and I had my own apartment over on Wylam Street. Brenda didn't answer right off. Finally she said yes. I'm not sure what was more important to her—marrying me, or moving out of her parents' home. Considered getting married right away, but Brenda thought we should have a church wedding, with people all dressed up in their good clothes it made sense to wait till the Alabama sun took a rest, so that people wouldn't be all sweat-wet sitting in the pews. My sergeant scheduled me for three days off in September, so September 15th was the date.

Brenda had three or four platoons of family and friends filling the church. I didn't have any family, and not too many friends. A handful of my buddies from the force came. And I was surprised happy when Richard Combs accepted our invitation. He brought his wife, a real lady. Emory was my best man. By then he'd quit college, he liked everything but the education part. Wangled himself a job distributing beer, bragged that it kept him drinking on a regular basis.

The wedding went pretty smooth. I wore a blue suit that Brenda picked out at Loveman's. Wearing her mother's wedding dress Brenda looked pretty as a peach blossom walking down the aisle.

After the church wedding we had a real fancy reception. Brenda's father spent more than he should've, a real sit-down dinner and free drinks. Only hiccups were on my side. When Emory stood up to give a toast, he was holding the glass out in front of everybody with his claw hand. I'm looking at the wide eyes of the wedding guests, thinking he shoulda used the other hand. And some of my buddies on the force gulped too much of the free liquor. Toward the end they made some pretty loud comments about what was gonna happen on the honeymoon. Brenda pretended not to hear.

Our first year of marriage was a happy time. Brenda and her ma fixed up the apartment. Everything got painted and all of my furniture that I really liked went someplace else to live. Brenda quit her waitressing job and took a job with the Birmingham Library, putting books back on shelves.

Brenda gave up her library job when John Junior was born in December of '48. He had the same problem I did with birthdays and Christmases. I wanted to name him after my pa, but Brenda never warmed up to the name Calvin. Couldn't blame her, but I'm sure if she'd known Pa, she would've liked the name. Anyway, we named him after me, giving him a different middle name so he wouldn't be a junior. We called him Junior anyway. By the time he got to walking, John Junior got boiled down to JJ. Went through his life answering to JJ. Sarah came along in '51. Sarah was Brenda's ma's name. I guess Brenda forgot she didn't like my pa's name, but I never said nothing about her picking her ma's name.

When JJ was born we moved down the street to a two-bedroom apartment. By the time JJ and Sarah were off to school we signed a lease for a three-bedroom. It was $65 a month, but I was making close to $200, so it wasn't a problem. Brenda kept busy with the kids, washing, cooking, and all that stuff. But she always took time to read. I don't mean magazines and things, I mean books. Books on history and books on how to do things.

When the kids were in bed, and if I wasn't on the night shift, sometimes Brenda and me would sit on the sofa and talk quiet like about the future. We imagined some hard-to-get good stuff. Maybe buying a house or maybe taking a real get-on-a-train kind of vacation. And we talked about some easier-to-get good stuff. Maybe buying a TV or an air conditioner. But we talked mostly about real-life important things. I wanted to make sergeant in a few years. Pay would be better and I wouldn't have to work so many night shifts. Brenda hoped to be a librarian, and not just putting books back on the shelves. If she made librarian she'd have people working for her, sort of like she was the lieutenant at the library. But neither me making sergeant or Brenda becoming a librarian were jump-off-the-fence easy. In the police department every time a sergeant retired there was probably close to ten guys elbowing for the job. It wasn't any easier for Brenda. A librarian needed a college degree.

By the middle of the fifties I was starting to think I could maybe make sergeant. Hadn't shot myself in the foot and I always showed up on time. Well, that's not fair to me. I was working hard. I passed all the tests, and they weren't easy. I had to learn a bunch of law and police science. Got a big break when I was assigned to drive for Jimmy Morgan, the Birmingham mayor. If he had official business or just wanted to impress people, I would drive him in his black Oldsmobile Super 88 with one of my guys leading in a cruiser with the sirens and lights going. Gotta say, every time I saw the chrome 88 emblem on the trunk of his Oldsmobile I thought of those Kraut 88s. *Whoosh*.

Anyway, the mayor seemed to like me. We talked quite a few times. His nephew had dragged his ass through Guadalcanal as an army private. The mayor kept complaining that the marines got all the credit for beating the Japs. Once I drove the mayor and our police chief all the way to New Orleans. Spent two nights there. Real happy nights for them after they found a couple young friends.

I sorta figured they'd take care of me after that. Funny thing, in New Orleans we passed the Higgins boatyard. They made the boat that took Tom and me to Omaha Beach back in '44.

In '57, there was good news for me, but bad news for Sergeant Billy Bob Livingston—a heart attack, fell over dead wearing his police uniform. Billy Bob was only in his forties. Good news for me was that he'd just made sergeant a couple years before, so instead of waiting twenty years for the guy to retire for an open slot, there it was. I couldn't hardly believe it when they told me I'd made sergeant. I like to think the mayor put in a good word for me. Other than being alive when the sun was setting on June 6th, 1944, I don't think I've ever been happier. My pay went to $250 a month. Plus, and this was real important, I would only have the night shift one week a month.

I needed to stop working so many night shifts because of JJ. I wasn't spending much time with him. It's not like I needed to, he was a good kid. Both he and Sarah were good kids, and we made sure they always had chores to do. 'Course, living in an apartment, there weren't too many chores to hand out. JJ had been delivering the *Post-Herald* since he was ten. Got fifteen cents a day for doing it. In the summers he cut grass, plus some Saturdays he worked in the back of Morey's Hardware. Morey's son had gotten skunk drunk and ran over some colored kid, and his pa was real grateful when I let him go.

Gotta be fair. I wouldn't've made sergeant without Brenda. The department gave me two books to study, one on criminal law, another on municipal codes. I would've never learned them on my own. Brenda studied each chapter and wrote down an outline, then made up ten or twenty questions for each chapter. Made 'em up with the answers so's I got maybe two hundred questions and answers to study. Each night I'd read 'em over once. After a few weeks they were like the Pledge of Allegiance, I knew 'em by heart. When I took the test most of the questions looked familiar and friendly, just like the ones Brenda made up. I passed the first time.

Most guys never passed. My buddies at the station figured I was smart. Brenda was the smart one.

With my sergeant's pay we could afford a mortgage. For $9,500 you got yourself a brand-new house with three bedrooms, two baths, a carport, and a yard. 'Course, not a yard you could plant corn or peanuts in, but a yard for a vegetable garden. But we decided to hide our acorns and put away fifty dollars a month. Figured in a couple years Brenda could start some college classes. Figured maybe JJ would want to go to college, so we saved some money for him too.

After I made sergeant we did live a little higher on the hog. Bought ourselves an air conditioner at Sears, Roebuck. Me and a buddy slid it into the living-room window. It cooled the living room real good. In each bedroom we put in a window fan that blew the air out, not in. The fans were turned off during the day so the bedrooms were real hot during the daytime, while the living room was cool like a movie theater. At night you just turned on the fans and they blew out, pulling the cold air from the air conditioner through the bedrooms. Worked real good.

Police work wasn't all that hard in Birmingham. It's not like we had a bunch of Al Capones shooting people with tommy guns. Most stuff was pretty simple. Directing traffic downtown, handing out speeding tickets, and a lot of just walking around. It made the shop owners feel good and let the bad guys know we was watching. One or two robberies each week, nothing big like banks. Maybe a TV from somebody's house or money from a shop owner. Each year five or six murders, mostly a colored fella stabbing his sister's boyfriend, that kind of stuff. Nothing like Perry Mason.

Moving through the fifties to the sixties was like watching a bad movie. Russians were putting up satellites, made us look as dumb as Mississippi mules. I'd turn on the TV and there'd be this pencil-shaped rocket down in Florida blowing up with our satellite burnt black like a marshmallow that fell in the fire. When I was growing up we had Hitler. Now Khrushchev was flying into New York on a plane twice as big as anything we got, telling us the Commies are gonna bury us.

Then the election. We got a Catholic president. Me and the other guys at the station were thinking we were gonna have to learn to talk Latin, eat fish on Fridays, and pray to the Pope. But that wasn't the worst of it. I couldn't believe the trouble the coloreds stirred up. We had always treated them good. They had schools and jobs. Anytime they didn't like something, our coloreds could get on a bus and leave. Wasn't like they was slaves and would get whipped if they tried to run. Then this Reverend Shuttlesworth guy started to stir up all the Birmingham coloreds. Coloreds that were real happy till he told 'em they shouldn't be. All of a sudden things that everybody was okay with for a hundred years was a corncob-up-your-ass problem.

By the spring of '63 Birmingham was going crazy, our coloreds standing at lunch counters wanting a seat right next to the white folks, complaining about all sorts of crap. Commissioner Conner ordered paddy wagons and billy clubs. And this is what really got me all-fired mad, a swarm of reporters from the North taking pictures—not taking pictures of anything good, just trying to make us look bad.

When things were really starting to heat up, King showed up. That's Martin Luther King. Martin Luther Coon was what we called him. Everything I heard about him told me he was a troublemaker. Figured he was sorta like a colored Hitler or Khrushchev.

Then the coloreds brought out their kids, a thousand colored kids marching, chanting that they needed better schools and wanted to be treated just like whites. Commissioner Conner called out the fire department and they hosed 'em down with high-pressure hoses that could peel bricks off a building. That's not everything they used. A lotta German shepherds learned to eat dark meat. I'm not saying it made me feel good to see a sharp-toothed dog ripping skin off, but I figured if the coloreds didn't like our town, they shoulda just got the hell out.

By August we had used up most of our overtime budget for the whole year. My guys weren't working day shifts or night shifts, they were working day-*and*-night shifts. Just about the time we were getting things quieted down the KKK showed up and stirred the pot to a boil.

Right in the middle of all this commotion was Brenda's and my fifteenth anniversary. September 15, 1963, was the day. We'd never had a storybook kind of honeymoon. We hardly ever had a vacation. Twice we drove over to Holiday Beach with the kids for a week, laid on the beach, doing nothing. So we planned a get-it-right honeymoon in New York City for our anniversary. Other than one trip to Macon, Brenda had never been out of Alabama. I'd told her about New York, told her she wouldn't believe how big the buildings were, and what it was like to stand on top of the Empire State Building. Everything was planned just right. On Sunday we were taking the train to New York and would be up there for three days, then back. The kids were staying with the Brown family down the street. Johnny Brown was looking to make sergeant someday.

On Saturday night before the Sunday we were jumping on a train for New York we had an anniversary party at the VFW. Rented a room, had barbecue brought in, and even had a guy with an electric guitar playing and singing. It being a VFW, there was plenty to drink. 'Course, the VFW only had beer. Emory brought two bottles of Scotch. Said one was for him and the other for me and my friends. He wasn't kidding. Sarah and JJ were with us, dressed in their Sunday best. Pretended not to see, but JJ was sipping a beer that Emory snuck him. All our close-by neighbors came and a lot of the guys under me showed up. They were doing their bit to become sergeants by kissing ass. I felt real proud that I could have a fancy party and pay for everything with no trouble. I'm not sure Brenda had a good time, but I knew she was real bubbly about New York. Guess she was tired of my stories and wanted to have a few of her own.

Sunday morning I was heading down to the station house to make sure all was well before we caught the train in the afternoon. Then the radio call, an explosion at the Sixteenth Street Baptist Church, right across from Ingram Park. A big explosion.

I was off. Didn't have my uniform on, turned on the siren and the lights. Within ten minutes I was pulling up to the church. Three other squad cars were already there, parked in the middle of the street. One wall of the church had collapsed, bricks and concrete all across the sidewalk and halfway into the street. No fire but a lotta smoke. A hundred colored people rushing around screaming.

A quick nod from my guys and I knew they recognized me without my uniform. I climbed the front steps of the church and walked in. At first I was sorta thinking, *This is what you get when you stir things up.* Toward the back of the church there was a staircase down to the basement. I heard screaming and started down. Through the dust and smoke I could see a dozen or so coloreds, some men, some women, all dressed in their Sunday best, wailing.

I didn't have my uniform on, so the look I got was not the same as usual. It was a look of despair. Over in a far corner a colored man in a dark suit was holding a girl. He was sitting on the floor covered with dust and rubble. This little girl, maybe ten years old, was dressed all in white. Pretty little thing, 'cepting part of her head was missing. You could see her brain. This fellow cradling her real careful looked up, he stared at me. Tears were running down his face. I stared back, but not at him. I wasn't looking at the girl, either. I was staring at her shoes. White satin shoes, a single strap each, with little brass buckles. That's when my thinking started to change.

Brenda and I didn't go to New York. Everybody on the force was working sixteen-hour shifts. Birmingham was the talk of the world. TVs in most every country were showing pictures of the bombed church and the four colored girls who were killed. World leaders rubbed our faces in it. Mao Tse-tung sent the Birmingham coloreds his regrets and told them to persevere. Malcolm X threatened bullet for bullet. Even some of our white folks were saying the coloreds weren't being treated right. 'Course, the KKK threw gas on the fire, and Governor Wallace gave everybody matches.

There were more of them than us. More coloreds than cops. Gotta tell ya, when you got fewer than two hundred policemen holding back five thousand spitting-angry protestors, angry 'cause somebody killed four little girls going to Sunday school, even when you got dogs and fire hoses, you could lose. The whole city could get burned down real quick. But I was thinking about something else. I was thinking about white satin shoes with little brass buckles. It just couldn't be right. The Nazis were evil. Seeing the white satin shoes at Dachau proved it to me. Was something evil in Birmingham? I didn't think so. But if the little girls dying wasn't right, what was wrong?

For days after the bombing everybody on the force was working sharecropper hours, just trying to keep the coloreds and whites apart and things calm. Then a church service for three of the girls was announced, to be held at the Sixth Avenue Baptist Church, near the one that was bombed. Martin Luther King would give the eulogy. Our captain figured King would get everybody riled up and there could be looting and burning for a week. Our mayor and the captain put their heads together and decided we'd arrest him as soon as he said something to incite. 'Course, if we had a bunch of police there, he wouldn't be saying anything. So it was decided I'd go to the church service, but I'd be wearing my civilian clothes so's I'd look like one of the Northerners that was down for the funeral. Soon as King said something to stir up the blacks I'd blow my whistle and my buddies would pour in and arrest him.

More people attended than the church could seat, but most everyone got in. I stood way in the back. Better for my guys to hear the whistle. King spoke for ten minutes, no more. A lotta whites had been talking about bombings and shootings and lynchings. Even Governor Wallace said we needed some first-class funerals to fix things. What did King say? Let me tell you. "We must not lose faith in our white brothers. Somehow we must believe that the most misguided among them can learn to respect the dignity and the worth of all human personality." I can quote it pretty good, 'cause I read it and reread it in the newspaper. Not a Birmingham newspaper, but a New York newspaper Brenda got me at the library. At the time he said it, when I was standing in the back of the church, my brain kind of stopped. It was something I just couldn't understand. It was something I just couldn't believe a colored could say after us whites had killed their little girls.

In the war I knew which side was right and which side wrong. I was on the right side. But it wasn't right just because it was the side I was on. It was the right side because Americans stood for good things. Nazis and Japs did bad things. Dachau with its piles of skin stretched over skeletons showed me why we were fighting. In Birmingham I wasn't sure about what I was doing. My mind churned on it for a spell, then I came to think that maybe the only reason I thought us whites were right was because it was the side I was on. I was a white, so we were right.

And I started to have a lot of confused thinking about Pa. No person I respected more. Most hardworking, honest man that God ever gave breath to. So if Pa said something, it was right. Pa told Billy and me coloreds weren't like us. They weren't smart like us and they didn't work hard like us. You had to be good to them, like you would be good to a mule or a horse. But if you didn't keep a close eye on them they wouldn't work. And you had to keep a bridle or a yoke on 'em, otherwise they wouldn't be doing the right thing. As kids JJ and Sarah thought there was a Santa Claus 'cause their ma and I promised them that there was. If some kid's pa tells 'em something, they're gonna believe it.

It was late one night, I had worked two shifts, when Brenda and I talked serious about the coloreds and all the hubbub. I asked her what she thought. She didn't say much. It was maybe a week or so later that Brenda put the note in my lunch pail. There it was, on a small folded piece of paper in Brenda's handwriting: *Prejudice is the child of ignorance.* Brenda wrote out the name of the fellow who said it, some fellow who had been dead for hundreds of years, some guy named Hazlitt. Brenda wrote something else—that *ignorant* didn't mean *stupid*. It just meant you didn't know. Made me feel better. Pa wasn't stupid. Pa wasn't mean. Pa just didn't know better.

By the middle sixties things had pretty much settled down in Birmingham. They had big problems later in Washington and Detroit and LA. Wouldn't say we were happy about it, but it made us feel a little less poorly about ourselves. By '66 we even got ourselves a colored policeman. JJ went off to college in '67, dropped out a year later. Said nothing he was learning meant anything to him. I looked at his books and couldn't say I disagreed. Anyway, he wanted to join the army. I never talked much about the army, so JJ didn't get the notion from me. Some recruiter was telling him the good stuff. We were at war in Vietnam, and I didn't see anything wrong with him joining up. If the country's at war, that's what young guys should do.

In the spring of 1968 JJ went off to Benning and from there to Vietnam. He visited us twice before he shipped out. Looked real good in his uniform, better than I ever looked. That same year Brenda finished up her night classes and got a job as an assistant librarian. It didn't pay a lot but I was real proud of her. She had three people working for her.

Sarah was smart like her ma. Got herself a scholarship to a school I never heard of before, Berkeley, out in California. Found it on a map, it was in Oakland. That's where my brother Billy met his wife, a wife that didn't ever look us up. It never crossed my mind that Sarah would want to go to college. But she did real good, and by the third year she was a professor's assistant. Not quite certain what that was, but they paid her to stay out there during the summer. Just about every week she'd call all excited and tell Brenda and me about all the excavating she did, looking for fossilized bones and stuff older than dirt.

After a long year JJ was back from Vietnam, with sergeant stripes. I never got close to being a sergeant. Making sergeant is probably what made him re-enlist. In '70 the army sent JJ on his second tour in Vietnam. It was half a year later on a Saturday afternoon when the captain and a minister knocked on our apartment door. Two weeks later we had JJ's funeral at the Woodlawn Methodist Church, the same church that Brenda and I were married in. Other than the Sixteenth Street and the Sixth Avenue Baptist churches, the only church I'd been in since we got married.

Brenda kept working, but there was no happiness. Her eyes were pretty much always red, red like she'd been crying. Later she told me. Told me she would take a shower so she could bawl and scream her hurts without anybody knowing.

I didn't cry. No, I didn't. But my insides were twisted sick with anger. I wanted to punch somebody, I wanted to kick somebody, I wanted to make somebody hurt because of JJ. The guys on the force told me they were sorry and all, but they didn't stop laughing at jokes, didn't stop playing catch with their sons, didn't stop sleeping sound at night.

We lost JJ, but Sarah found a fella. Called us one day and tells us she met some special guy that was in her class. Told us she was going to marry him. Didn't ask us, just told us. And this fella didn't take time to travel east to meet us so's we could look him in the eye before he married our girl. Making it worse, Sarah told us they just wanted a small wedding with a few friends at something called Half Moon Bay. Said there wouldn't be family at the wedding. I never hinted to Brenda, but I think maybe we were an embarrassment to Sarah. Once Sarah told Brenda that the father of the guy she married was the biggest lettuce farmer in California. Not impressed a bit, who needs lettuce? Maybe rabbits. Real farmers grew real food. The kind of food that people who worked hard and sweated wanted to eat.

Brenda and I had saved up a nice bundle for JJ's college. Since JJ didn't use it and Sarah pretty much paid her own way with scholarships and things, we sent Sarah and her husband a check for $5,000 as their wedding present. Told them to use it as a down payment on a house. I wanted her husband to know that Sarah's daddy was doing better than okay.

A few years after Sarah got married Brenda got the cancer. A woman's cancer, a bad one. She didn't go like Ma, didn't go peaceful-like. We had two years of all sorts of medicines and stays at hospitals. The last bedrid weeks were real bad. A lotta tubes, lotta pain, lotta embarrassment. That's when I met Sarah's husband, he came to the funeral with Sarah. We all sat in the church where we'd had JJ's funeral.

Emory passed a few months after Brenda. A year before his doctor told him that his liver was turning rock hard and that he had to stop drinking. I could have guessed what Emory was going to do, sent the doctor a bottle of Scotch and told him to enjoy life. Neither of Emory's ex-wives showed up for his funeral. Just me, some old-fart neighbor of Emory's in a wheelchair, a bartender friend, and the minister gave a damn. I took a bottle of Scotch Emory had given me for Christmas a few years back and after the service we each had a short one. Emory would have liked that.

I retired from the police force the year after Brenda passed. A surefire mistake. It made missing Brenda much worse. Spent the first week at home packing her things in boxes. Spent the next week unpacking them. Just couldn't give her belongings away, no way. So there I sat in our living room. Most evenings when the sun went down didn't get up to turn on the lights. Just sat there in the dark wishing I would have told Brenda things I didn't.

Finally did something to help stop the hurting. I got myself a part-time job at Eastwood Mall. Sarah thought it was a good idea.

Spent the day walking around in a uniform that made me look like a real policeman. Didn't carry a gun. Helped parents find their lost kids and herded teenagers toward the exits. Didn't do anything important. But it kept me busy, kept me not thinking too much.

That first Christmas I was working at the mall Sarah sent me a round-trip ticket to California. After the holiday rush I took a week off and got on a Delta flight in Birmingham that went up to Atlanta, then all the way out to San Francisco. The flight to Atlanta was the first time I'd been on a plane since '45, when I flew from Paris to England. Didn't have to lay in a litter this time. Had a seat next to a window, right over the wing. This really sweet gal with a big smile came by and gave me a Coke and some peanuts. Got off in Atlanta and sat in a terminal that made the train station in Washington look teeny. The flight out to San Francisco was really something. Delta even showed a movie. Didn't think it was fair, I had to give two dollars to get some headphones so I could hear what they were saying.

Sarah and her husband met me at San Francisco Airport. Parked outside was this shiny station wagon with wooden sides. I got pushed in the back with their kids. Drove clean through the middle of downtown San Francisco. Streets ran up and down these steep hills that I couldn't believe a car should be on. Crossed the Golden Gate Bridge and pulled into a little park and stopped for a spell. Had a great view of the bridge and the whole city. Sorta reminded me of '43, looked like the George Washington Bridge going into New York.

Sarah's house was in Santa Rosa, maybe an hour up north from San Francisco. Real nice, with a two-car garage. Other than the station wagon they had a bright-red sports car. I'd seen Corvettes before, just never gotten to ride in one. A few okay days visiting. One Sunday we had a picnic by the Russian River, all around these Paul Bunyan redwood trees like you couldn't believe. Some hollowed out so's you could walk right through 'em, standing up. But mostly things were either too quiet or too noisy during my stay.

Both Sarah and her husband worked and the kids were in some kind of nursery school. I could only watch *General Hospital* and *As the World Turns* a couple of days before my brain started to turn to corn mash. When everybody got home, with the kids yelling and all, it was on the real noisy side. Headache-noisy. It was a nice visit and everything, but I was happy to get back to Birmingham.

Maybe a year or so after visiting Sarah she called real excited. She and her family were moving to Virginia. Sarah got the head job digging for old stuff in a place called Jamestown. Figured I'd see 'em more, them being closer and all. But I didn't. Well, I didn't see her till she came down to put me away with the other oldies.

After a while each month in Birmingham was like the last one. And each year was pretty much the same. After work at the mall I spent more and more time on my easy chair, just napping and thinking. With JJ gone there weren't going to be any more Butchers. And for sure there weren't going to be any more Calvin Butchers, my pa's name. The name I'd wanted to give JJ. Decided to do something about it.

No question, I had more acorns in the bank than I needed. Didn't need any money for Brenda's old age. Didn't have JJ to leave money to. And Sarah and her husband were driving a Corvette, for sure they didn't need no help. So I sorta gave the money to my pa, to Calvin. I took the bus to the Sixteenth Street Baptist Church and spoke to the minister, a colored fellow named Hamlin. At first he was nervous when I told him about me being there the day of the bombing. But by the time I left he was happy. I gave him a check, the biggest check I'd ever written. I'll tell you why I did it. Reverend Hamlin had them put a brass plaque on the side of one of the pews, right in the front. You know what it said? Etched real clear was IN APPRECIATION OF CALVIN BUTCHER. Made up for burying Pa next to Ma with no marker. Maybe helped to make up for some other things both Pa and I needed to get right with.

In early '94 got a call from the governor's office. A fella wanted to see me. Okay, I said, wondering if I forgot to turn in my police revolver or something. This young guy came by, had a nice suit and spoke college smart. In June they was planning an event in Normandy. There was going to be a big show for the fiftieth anniversary. Each state was sending two veterans who had been there when the fighting was tough and they wanted me to represent Alabama. Told me I was picked 'cause I had a Purple Heart. Figured the real reason was that I was one of the few guys alive not wearing diapers. Anyway, this fellow said the State of Alabama would pay for everything. Wanted to ask him if they would give me two dollars for earphones so I could hear the airplane movie. I didn't. And, I didn't give an answer right away, told him I'd think on it.

In a few days he called back. I said no. Told him I was too old to be traveling around the world. That wasn't the honest truth. I'd read the materials and stuff he left on his visit. President Clinton was going to be at Normandy giving a big speech. I liked Clinton. He was an Arkansas boy who came from a poor family, worked hard, and made president. But when JJ was in Vietnam, Bill Clinton was hiding in college and saying bad stuff about our GIs. Didn't think he should be standing tall and proud at Normandy. Shoulda let his generals do the speeches.

It was the winter of 1995 that I gave up my security job at the mall. Well, that's not really the truth of the matter. My boss told me I was too old, told me to quit. So I did. Watched some TV if there was a movie or a baseball game. If it wasn't too hot or too cold, I'd take a walk. Pretty much every morning I'd go down the block to a little coffee shop. Everybody knew everybody, so we talked real friendly, like we were family. Then I stopped going. I was just tired. So I'd sit and think. Thought a lot about a lotta things. Mostly thought about my life. 'Course I did wonder some what I could have done better. Not much, I figured. I'd worked pretty hard, joined the army, raised a family. I might not have always known the right thing, but whatever I thought was right, I tried to do.

One thing I felt real sorry about. More than thirty years Brenda and I were married. Probably not a week went by without me telling her something good about Pa. Always bragging Pa was the best man I ever knew. I shouldn't have been looking backward. Should have been looking next to me. Should have been telling Brenda she was the best most wonderful person ever. But I didn't. Never told her how special lucky I was to have her. Hoped maybe sometime I would get the chance.

After a spell Sarah put me in an old folks home. I was there for the better part of a year. Then back to the Woodlawn Methodist Church for the last time.

John

Mordecai's Uncle

Two hundred and fifty years after a few brave and hopeful English struggled to establish the first colonies in America, colonies that held the promise of religious freedom and the opportunity to work for a better life, Europeans were still fleeing from their homelands for America. And America still, after two hundred and fifty years, held out the beacon of religious freedom and greater rewards for greater work.

Between 1880 and 1920 over two million persecuted Jews fled Russia, and what is now Poland and Ukraine, for America. After a long and difficult journey, the last portion being in damp and dark steerage of a rusting or rotting ship, only opportunity stood at the pier to greet them. But opportunity was the large white canvas on which many painted their life's work, achievements, and legacy. One such painter was Mordecai's Uncle.

I F IT WASN'T THE COSSACKS, IT WAS THE COLD; AND IF NOT THE cold, it was hunger.

One winter night Shlomo ben Jezekiel dropped from his dying horse outside what passed for our tavern and beat on door after door, crying that at Kishinev our people had been slaughtered like rats, baled up like corn for the reapings, and he passed from one hand to the next no one believing, yet all knowing they had to, broken bricks with what looked like gray worms in them—brains, Jewish brains. So we left.

We sold everything (a lot, ha!) and borrowed a little that the Staronometz pressed on us, the only rich folk in the shtetl, guilty at being on such good, well-paid terms with the colonel of Cossacks and the vice-governor.

We wouldn't take all that they offered—we'd never have the chance to repay it—but what we took made all the difference.

It was five weeks to the sea, to harsh Odessa with our children and our nephew Mordecai, breaking our backs when their legs gave out.

Oh, but they had a great spirit, to walk so far through the icy ruts, our shoes filled with blood on those foul roads and every joint a chilblain.

Dos Kleyne Mentshele, the Little Man, I thought of these unforgiving potholes, the little little man in the big indifferent world; I'd have settled in a blits for its being indifferent, but it seemed as hostile as the Cossack major who robbed us outside the city.

Praise be for money sewed up in girls' flowers, torn to look ragged.

And so finally we got there, three children sick, neither of us free from lameness for the rest of our lives.

But none dead, and the ship at the quay!

We worked our way through those horse-drawn carts and proud-driven carriages, their coachmen anxious to frighten the poor who worked for no noble family, cracking their whips from the box; and always the horsemen in the foul Tsar's uniform, smashing off *shtrayml*, sending those fur hats flying like crows with their wretched tin sabres that had done them no good with the Japanese.

(How we laughed when we heard!)

And people shrieked at us, "Where d'you think you're going, Jew?"

We answered clear, under our breath: "We're off to America. America, where *our* shoes and mittens won't have holes. *Die Goldene Medina.* The Golden Land."

And so we arrived at the ship. We knew we weren't going easy. We were going to sail like the old women's children who went to sea in a sieve; but not even that quite prepared us for our particular sieve. Worm-ridden, rat-riddled, vomit-clung, and, we suspected, heavily insured so the owners wouldn't be too grieved if the sea ate us off Iceland, or fire claimed us off the Grand Banks.

We sold our lucky pieces for bread rations. They rotted. But we were off to the Golden Land.

The ship met the big waves, and it staggered, leaving legs and arms broken in every hold.

Icebergs we saw, where a few years later that great liner sank with a thousand of the richest—and the sea piled up like the mountains of Megiddo between us and dry land and no fear and hard earth.

But each face of water was one wet mountaintop nearer the Golden Land.

We lost our steering for hours off some unlit lighthouse. But we made it. God preserved His poor children. We creaked into

New York Harbor—some thought it was Boston—with three feet of water in the hold and our bread blue for so many days.

But though our legs swayed under us when we arrived, we stood firm on the land we never again left—not even a trip on a pleasure barge!

We staggered to Immigrant Aid and got ourselves jobs, I for a hard man that made factory soft shirts. Only calluses for me on my throat, yelling at the little ones. Thread those bobbins! Cut that cloth!

Rebekah scrubbed floors and thought they were joking when she worked out she was getting ten kopeks for work that would have got her one, and a curse, from the squire uphill in the Old Country.

We found schools for the children, so Rebekah and I could go also, alternate nights, to learn this strange country, golden or not.

But then the schools began to take hold, and we found the library. And now there were more books than you could read in a lifetime, most the kind Rebbe Aron always warned against.

But some—wicked smart Gibbon, peace be upon the clever old pagan; kindly Lincoln, who agonized over a bloody war among brothers; proud Jefferson, who loved liberty while he held slaves and "remembered that God was just"—reminded you why you were in a free country. You were still always tired—everyone was. You heard of Mr. Morgan's partners dying of overwork, him shedding no tears, this was America. And you always wanted something to eat, but not the way you did in the Old Country.

Each day you made money—maybe just pennies—but you wanted to spend it, because you could not walk down the street without seeing something you wanted, something new to eat, new to wear. In a shop window, on a wall, on a leaf of the *New York Herald* blowing jerkily downstreet, inducements uppermost; and it made it so hard to chink those few pennies back and put them under the brick (from which we both stole, I'm sorry, sorry when temptation hurt too much, for an apple, or an orange, or God help us, one stick of chocolate. But we put it back, and put the blows and outcries behind us, and went short to make up).

Then that terrible March, that awful factory fire. Doors were locked, little lives lost. No factory, no job, no money.

So we got a cart, just for coffee and sandwiches—but Lord, how people wanted fresher things than their lunch boxes held.

Hotter coffee at break—couldn't call it lunchtime—after five hours already at work. Then I hired a man. Kal Ivanov worked hard, but never lost a smile.

Three years, then we had two carts, and three. First to work, then to dream; next to dream and work even harder.

A shop, yes, and another, and buying the building, but not forgetting to send money five thousand miles to get more of our people on ships—just slightly better ships—before their luck ran out in the darkening Old Country, before the murderous horsemen were given free rein, and the golden doors slammed on this country. Some we got out, some we didn't. God help us.

Come the day we'd been off the boat for twenty-five years—like five when you take stock, like fifty when you remember the work, one day on another—and we thought of working only six days a week.

(*Shabes* we felt embarrassed, driving past Synagogue; fair Sabbath-keepers we were!)

But too golden a sun rose on Wall Street, and we found most of our gold magicked to paper. We were hurt enough in the fall, and laughed bitterly when pushy little Harry Golden went down with his firm and went to prison for mail fraud. (Well, he made it back, that I'll give him.)

But we had our hearts and our heads, and dammit our good name, and back we came. Rebekah went to Florida for her pleurisy. Being a fool she bought a stretch of sand on a place called Palm Beach and has laughed ever since at how furious I was. And then—I nearly was too annoyed to say it—there was my nephew Mordecai.

We brought him over, saw he got a good schooling, couldn't miss how sharp he was, working through Stevens College—but then he passed up a good job! Went for this PhD thing. Oy, we were mortified.

Still and all—rather good, I think—one year he had to go to Stockholm, shake hands with the king. Because he invented something that no one needed. Even got a medal, and half a cart full of money!

Only in America, my America.

Die Goldene Medina.

Mordecai's Uncle

Nananawtunu

Within the first few decades of the seventeenth century, the British had colonies established along the New England coast and the Chesapeake Bay. At first, trade with the European settlers brought Native Americans material advantages: knives, axes, cooking utensils, fish hooks, and a host of other goods. Those Indians who traded with colonists initially had significant advantage over their rivals who did not.

Early colonial–Indian relations were an uneasy mix of initial cooperation and conflict. Conflicts grew into a long series of skirmishes and wars. At first the Indian was most often the victor, then as the population of Europeans grew in the colonies the balance shifted, and the Native Americans were forced to retreat in defeat.

The first of the important Indian uprisings occurred in Virginia in 1622, when over three hundred colonists were killed, including a number of missionaries who had just recently come to Jamestown. The Pequot War followed in 1637, as local tribes tried to prevent settlement of the Connecticut River region. Then with the colonies' population advantage and deadly weapons, began a 250-year long slow decimation, from the Atlantic to the Pacific, of a race and its culture.

Before the sun was up I was down the path, moving from our village to a stream that wrapped past our round-topped wigwams. I paused, I lay in the water, my scent washed away. Then across the shallow flow and back to the path. Up a small ridge spotted with pine, down and through a dark forest of beech, off the path, following beside a slow-running creek that cut through a lone tribe of hemlock. Once across I moved softly through a clearing, the sun now on the horizon. Across the open yellow grasses and into the forest, then to the blind my son and I made days before. Today, fresh tracks in the dew. One set of hooves no more than two fingers across, a yearling. With these tracks another with hoof marks three fingers across, the back hooves farther apart than the front hooves, an older doe. As I moved from the tracks to the blind, rabbits darted far to my right, to their burrows for the day.

I squatted behind the blind with my longbow, made from ash, as long as I am tall. The back flat, the front rounded by a shale scraping rock, then smoothed with a quartz rubbing stone. A bowstring of dressed and twisted sinew from a moose leg. Arrows nested in a quiver of dark bark with a strap of hide for the shoulder. Arrows from a hardwood sapling, almost a stride in length and thick as the small finger. Long ago cut from their mother tree with a blade made from the leg bone of a deer; split down the middle to make two sharp edges, these edges given a cutting bite with a flint notching stone. Shafts then carefully smoothed with a sandstone. A notched quartz arrowhead fashioned. To receive the arrowhead one end of the shaft notched with a large beaver tooth or antler from a young buck. To guide its flight, tail feathers from an eagle, split down the middle, three halves lashed to the shaft with dried gut from a small animal.

This morning, the air was still. No scents drifting. A sweet smell of a nearby honeysuckle. Another sweet smell of flesh decaying.

I knelt, one knee on the earth. In the distance turkeys called. Traps for these birds set far away yesterday. Between the clouds of foliage above, the sky was bright. A fox trotted slowly down the trail, then sensed me and disappeared into the brush. Above, a hawk stalked in drifting circles. Squirrels rushed in the trees, muted squeals and the feathered hunter tearing flesh. The sun slowly higher, in time straight above me. Next to me red ants moved in a line from their mound, disappearing under gray-brown leaves. Another row of ants marched back from the leaves and down their hole with prizes.

I ate red berries. No food that would carry the scent of my village. I thought of days as a young Indian, of days with my father, Mixanno. Many days hunting, learning the ways. I thought of my son Quannopin, how much I must teach him. The sun began its journey downward. A hemlock next to me, beetles of a shining green at its base. Their journey up and under the bark. Around the tree a floor of pinecones, some newly fallen, others gray and cracked. Among them a chestnut, but no chestnut tree near. A squirrel's lost meal, or perhaps from above, pigeon dropped.

A movement of air. Dung from a bear in the breeze. Also the scent of blood. Perhaps the blood of the hawk's kill. When the direction of the wind shifted, my blind no longer a blind to the deer.

Clouds sneaked in, long and flat. No thunder. Past me a snake on a zagging course, leaving curves in the soil, a bulge in its middle, a chipmunk, young heron, or frog. The sun drifted low. Another fox loped by, and then hurried away. A noise of leaves rustling. As the colors of the forest turned from greens and browns to grays and blacks, I stood. Footsteps in the distance, footsteps of my son. Coming to help me carry a slain deer back to our village. But no fresh meat today. Together we walked, told me of his day's task. Well-soaked birch bark carefully lashed to a curved frame of white cedar. Another few days the canoe will be married to the rivers.

Why do I recount this day for you? Because it is an Indian day. A day of seeing nature, smelling nature, touching nature. A day of being nature. Let me explain. Our women wove mats. Every wigwam hosted many mats. They were sat upon, they were slept upon, they were ate upon. A frame of wood as large as the reach of a warrior was used by our squaws to weave these mats. Each mat, thousands of strands from bulrushes, the inner bark of cedar and the roots of evergreens. All intertwined among each other in a careful pattern. Some strands colored with the dyes made from pine root, other dyes from the bark of walnut and flender root mixed with crabapple juice. To the Indian nature is as a mat. The earth, rivers, trees, plants, fish, birds, animals, rain, and the sun, all together intertwined and dependent on each other to create nature. The Indian saw himself as one of the strands of the mat. He is part of nature.

The white man did not see himself of nature. This was the strangest of the white man's many strange ways. Even the greatest of white men, Roger Williams, saw nature as only a servant. The white man walked upon the mat, he scuffed the mat with his boots. For those settlers among us nature was only to serve. As we could not understand their ways, they could not reason our reverence to nature. As an old and wise chief said, "The white man asked the Indian to dig for stones of value. Should we dig under the skin of our mother for her bones? The white man asked the

Indian to cut grass, make hay, and sell it. How could we cut our mother's hair?"

Let me tell you of my life. My name is Nananawtunu, son of Mixanno, one of the three sons of Ousamequin. This Great Chief was known as Massasoit, the honored leader of the Pokanoket people. Our lands were those surrounding Narragansett Bay. You know this land as Rhode Island. Because of his wisdom and spirit, the Indians of the Wampanong sought Massasoit's counsel. Their lands spanned the forests and streams of Rhode Island and the lands of Massachusetts, including what you call Martha's Vineyard and Nantucket. In the year 1620, by your calendar, Massasoit and Canonicus, another great leader, met with the chiefs of the white men who journeyed to our lands on the *Mayflower*. Before this, many council meetings of Massasoit and other sachems from many Indian villages. Much discussion on the white man's fate. Some believed the English as a forest fire, they would destroy land and game. Others saw them as an Indian, gentle love for their children and hard work for shelter and food. Others believed the white men's big canoes with their own clouds and their thunder muskets showed they were wise. After paced and considered discussion, the council decided the English should be welcomed and given knowledge of the land. For years the white man and our nation lived together in peace.

In time Massasoit and the elders learned that other white men came to lands far south from our nation. In our land the white man came to worship their god, not the god of their chiefs in England. Settlers in the south came seeking gold and pearls. Neither were found. To survive they grew the leaf that is smoked. This crop they bartered in England for supplies. For them tobacco was more valuable than food. In time white men in great numbers came to the south to grow the crop. Indian forests were cleared. Game became fewer. More settlers, more Indian lands taken. Battles between settlers and Indians.

I had just turned from a boy to a man when my father took me to Massasoit's wigwam. Grandfather told me of his days with the

English. Spoke to me of his friendship with Roger Williams, a man who saw the Indian as no less than a white settler. Williams wished to write an English translation of Indian words to create a record of the ways of the Indian. Neither I nor my grandfather knew of a book. Only later did I learn a book of Indian language would be printed for those English far away.

Grandfather believed the more the English understood of us, the better our contentment. Told that I would assist Roger Williams. His home was in Providence, there I would make my wigwam. Over the summer and into the fall in Providence I met with Roger Williams most days. It was a labor of discovery and humor, for both of us. He learned the Indian's ways as well as the Indian words. I learned of the white man's ways, as I learned their language. The humor was because Williams did not understand all Indian's words, and I only a few of theirs. He pointed to his mouth and rubbed his stomach. I gave him the phrase for not hungry, *matta niccattuppummin*. Days later, before a meal, I learned he wanted the word for hungry.

As my understanding of the English language grew, Williams asked me to join him with other settlers. Many meals I ate with them, many discussions I heard. The thoughts of the white man were not strange. Most were as of the Indian. But they spoke not as an Indian. An Indian speaks as a slow walk. Few words after thought, not many words with no thought. In council meetings, while an elder spoke all would be silent. Before the next spoke, only silence would be heard. The words spoken were considered before a response. To speak quickly after another was an insult. It meant the others' words were of no importance. White men spoke as a flock of ducks quacking, all louder than another.

I wrote the above as a white man. An Indian would have said only, "Thoughts as boulders, words as feathers."

Let me tell you of Roger Williams. In 1630 Williams and his wife sailed for Massachusetts to join those who had come to our lands to escape the chiefs of the English Church. Settling in Plymouth he was given a congregation to lead. There Williams came in conflict with the Puritans who dominated life. Roger Williams was not as most white men. He believed that man should be free to worship any god. He also had beliefs about the Indians that other English did not. William Bradford instructed Williams to write a paper telling that all the lands around Plymouth Colony were discovered by the English. Our friend Roger Williams asked how could the English claim right of discovery if the Indian was already happily living upon those lands?

Thinking that Williams's beliefs and teaching were hostile, he was banished from his congregation. Later a summons was issued for his arrest. Fearing for his life, Williams fled to the south and became stranded in a blizzard. Befriended by Massasoit he was given shelter in Indian lodges. Canonicus was one of the first to befriend Roger Williams on his arrival in the land known as Rhode Island. Williams founded the village of Providence, lands for this town and the farms around it were bought from Massasoit and Canonicus for a consideration. That consideration being Williams's promise that he and other settlers would live peacefully and not disturb Indian happiness.

Williams saw himself no greater than the Indian. Many times we spoke of things other than our work on the book of translation. His father, James, was not a hunter. Sold wares in a village in England called Smithfield. As a young man Roger Williams went to a school in Cambridge village. His tribe there was Pembroke. Williams told me of their council houses made from stone blocks. Some buildings higher than trees. This I could not imagine. He spoke of a river that went through their village and of the flat-bottom boats that would be poled to the fields outside their village. But he never spoke in a manner that made the Indian village lesser than the Cambridge village.

Even though he was a great man, Roger Williams was a white man. About nature he told me things that only the white man do. In Cambridge village the fields were cleared of trees and many high stone council houses were built, blocking the view of the mountains, rivers, and fields. Inside one of these stone council houses many painted canvases framed in wood and hung on the walls. The most beautiful canvases hung in one special council house. Some of these pictures were of mountains, rivers, and fields. The white men block the view of mountains, rivers, and fields by building the stone council houses, then go into a stone council house to look at a canvas painting of mountains, rivers, and fields.

Most of what I learned from Williams I understood: how the sails moved their canoes with the pushing wind, how to divide life into years, months, days, hours, and minutes, how to load, aim, and fire a musket, and how to eat with metal tools. Some things I could not understand, least of all their religion. Their religion was as ours, many stories, many miracles. One of their ministers spoke to our elders. He told of how their god created the earth and man. Told of how woman was from the rib of a man and god's son was born from a woman untouched. My people listened with interest. After some thought one of our elders spoke. Told the minister of our Spirit, the magic of the winds and our stories of the fish and deer. The minister spoke quickly and harshly. Told us these were falsehoods. After silence, the elder spoke again, "Is it not true that the logical person must either deny all miracles or accept all miracles?" The minister stood and was quickly gone.

I pondered the English claim that there is only one true god. I considered the sunrise that greets us each day. For the Pokanuket of Narragansett Bay the sun rose from the great sea each morning. For those in the Nation of Nipinu in Massachusetts, the sun rose from the cape that jutted around to the ocean. For the Indians of the Mohegan Nation to our west, the sun rose from the hills that surrounded them. All saw the sun from a different birthplace. But for all, the sun gave light, warmth, and life. One nation could not claim their sun was best. All nations had their sun. I thought the same for god. All nations have their god. All gods are true gods, unless their followers claim theirs is the only true god.

In England the fur of the beaver was sought by many. Such a high value was placed on the fur that white man paid the Poka-noket for pelts. Payment in the form of metal knives, hatchets, and, then, muskets. Pokanokets in turn paid other tribes wampum to trap the beavers. Our nation was rewarded for trading between the white man and hunters from other tribes. Many elders argued this was not the way of the Indian. Never before had an Indian traded the labors of others.

In 1643 my work with Roger Williams was at an end. Before he set sail for England, he told me that he had learned much from me. He was the first to ever say such a thing. He promised me he would return to our lands.

Later in the year much grief. My father, Mixanno, was killed. His death was not claimed by any enemy. Settlers argued that the Indians who traded beaver with the Pokanokets were guilty. Many of our tribe thought his death was by English hands, since my father had counseled against trapping beaver for the English. A few of our tribe argued for revenge against the English, Massasoit counseled otherwise. He spoke of years of peace with the English, he spoke of the English he knew who were of good heart, and he spoke that no one knew for certain whose hands had taken Mix-anno's life. Because Massasoit spoke not only as our chief, but also as Mixanno's father, his words were heavy and no one spoke con-trary.

My grandfather's words did not comfort me. My father was gone. In time the words of another wise Indian gave me comfort. He said that death will come always out of season. It is the com-mand of the Spirit, and all nations and people must obey. What is past and what cannot be prevented should not be grieved for. Mis-fortunes do not flourish particularly in our lives, they grow every-where.

With the death of my father I was asked to take his place at council meetings. Before the first Grandfather Massasoit spoke to me. Told me to listen carefully and thoughtfully and to speak nothing. He said I should only learn from others and that I had nothing to teach. If some question about the ways of the white man were to be asked, he would ask me to speak of my time with our friend Williams. I should be as the smoke in the council house, seen but not heard.

I chewed my grandfather's words. His belief that I had nothing to teach cut me. One evening in the soft light of dusk, when all was quiet, I spoke to him. Told him of my last meeting with our friend Roger Williams. Told him Roger Williams said he learned from me. Grandfather silent for not a short time. Then he spoke slowly, "With Williams you are as a rabbit speaking to a fish in the stream. Here you are a rabbit among foxes."

I took a wife, Weetamoe. The eyes of the deer, skin of a new doe, and always a smile. I was not the fleetest of our tribe. My songs were not sung by many. But as a young man I saw her glances. At first no attention to her, only spoke to her father. Then, I spoke. I spoke to her. Nothing of matter, nothing to remember. But it was the beginning. The beginning of my life. Once married, one always thinking of the other. Her pain was mine. Her happiness was mine. Together we slept. Together we taught our son.

For many years I had a contented life. A life of Indian ways. Living and teaching my son. But always there, as storm clouds on the horizon, the white man. Always another forest cleared for their cattle, sheep, and corn. Game was no longer our companion, white man was our companion.

A dark year for the Pokanoket laid on us. My grandfather, the wisest of our chiefs, died in 1660. As with my father's death, there was much lamenting. All the women and maids darkened their faces with soot and other blackings. Indians of esteem buried him as many wept. He was laid in a shallow grave with the mat from his wigwam, his bow, his ax, the clay dish that held his food, and a warm blanket of dark gray fox pelts. All surrounded the grave, many sat, all showed anguish, many moaned softly. Body to rot, his spirit to soar with birds of prey.

After the death of my grandfather, his son, my father's brother, Wamsutta, became the leader of the Pokanokets. He was called by the name of Alexander by the English. Wamsutta saw the good in the English and counseled to compromise when challenged. As the English settlers' numbers grew, conflicts grew. In England the demand for the pelts of our beaver became less. Settlers in our land could no longer live by selling the Indians' trappings. The English stopped taking our beaver and began to take our land for their farms. In response, Wamsutta, Alexander, no longer sought compromise. He learned that a compromise of today was only the new mark from which the English would seek greater demands.

Williams returned as promised. I journeyed to Providence to see my friend. For one day and long into the night we spoke. Many stories. Mostly good. But the bad stories were heavier. I spoke of my father's death. Williams spoke of Massasoit, his friend, dying. I spoke of our lands being taken. Williams looked sad. He had no words to comfort me.

In the morning before I journeyed home, my friend gave me a gift of a book, bound in dark leather. Printed on the cover in a color as the sun, "A Key Into the LANGUAGE OF AMERICA." Inside the cover, Williams wrote to me:

Nananawtunu,

It hath pleased God in wonderful manner that together this work was done. Without our forbearance this work not be complete. May it conduce the happy end intended by us.

His writing brought happiness to me, it was written by Williams in Narrogánset dialect. He used the word "work" for "book," as book is not a word for the Indians.

As settlers took greater portions of our land, they were assured that it was god's will. One of their chiefs of the church, Reverend Mather, wrote to his followers that, "Heathen people live amongst

us and their land the Lord God has given us for rightful possession." Before the Indian only had to argue with the white man that
he should be permitted to keep his land and live in peace. Now the
Indians were told their grievance would be with the white man's
god. Where should we meet this god to plead our rights?

Our elders spoke in response, "Before the white man we owned
nothing, because everything is from the Spirit. Food was free, land
as free as sunshine and rain. Who has changed all this? The white
man. And yet he says he is a believer in god. He does not seem to
inherit any of the traits of his Father, nor follow the example of
Jesus." Another of the elders, called upon for his thoughts, kept a
long silence. Finally he said, "They tell us Jesus was opposed to
material things and to great possessions. And they tell us he was
inclined to peace and was as unpractical as any Indian and set no
price upon his labor of love. These are not the principles upon
which the white man lives in our land. I have come to know that
this Jesus was an Indian."

The more I thought about the white man's god, the more clever
the white man seemed to me. Their ministers preach that their god
is a benevolent god. They tell us that his son Jesus taught forgiveness and kindness. Then the white man states to all that he is godly
and does god's work. When the white man takes all before him, he
tells all that it is god's will. He feels no remorse. He does god's
work.

When news of Alexander's unwillingness to bend to each English breeze reached the Plymouth Colony, the colony that was
blessed to survive by the benevolence of his father Massasoit, the
General Court in Plymouth demanded that he appear before them.
He refused. In 1662 Major Winslow was sent to retrieve Alexander
with the order, "If he refuses to go, he be a dead man." Alexander,
my uncle, was taken under guard to Massachusetts to be questioned by those of high office in the Plymouth Colony. He never
returned. The English claimed he became ill and perished. The
Indians believe he was poisoned.

With the death of Alexander, two of Massasoit's three sons were no longer. Only his youngest son, Metacom, my uncle, survived. He became the leader of the Pokanokets. Known as Philip by the English, Metacom did not benefit from long friendships with some of the earliest settlers. As with Alexander, at first he attempted reconciliation and compromise with the English. But English settlers were as a tide that always rose and never receded. Indian pleadings were not heard over the pounding English waves.

In the summer of 1674 Williams traveled to speak with me as a man. He was fearful. Fearful for the Indian. He came to our lands from Massachusetts because he wanted freedom. A religious freedom and a freedom of thought. In consideration for being given lands to form his colony in Providence the only price asked by Massasoit was that the English exist peacefully with the Pokanokets and other tribes. This he promised, this he meant. But now Williams feared his word was being broken by others, new settlers. Settlers who came to our lands not for tranquility, but for opportunity. Settlers who had no sense of the bond between Indians and English. A history made possible only by the kindness of Massasoit and others.

What Williams told me had been spoken of at our council meetings. At first our concerns were more a curious concern. As one of our wise elders said, "The English, in general, are a noble people. They pride themselves on their civil and religious ways and they think that no other nation is equal to them. They are truly industrious. But their close attention to business is not our way. They forget to think enough about their souls and their god. English fly about in every direction, as a swarm of bees, in search of the treasure that lies so near their hearts."

As time passed, and new settlers clustered in our lands, the words of our elders became as spears. "They are a heartless nation that is certain. The greatest object of their lives seems to be to acquire possessions. They have divided the day into hours, like the moons of the year. They measure everything. Not one of them would let a handful of corn go from his field unless he received value. I am also told that each year their Great Chief compels every man to pay him for the land he lives upon. In war they have leaders that do not fight. The common warriors are driven forward like a herd of deer to face the enemy. Fighting from compulsion and not bravery is not as with the Indian."

Over many more changes of the face of the moon council meetings were held. Elders spoke. All opinions considered. The words of Philip were heaviest. He spoke as the only living son of Massasoit, "When the English first came to our land Massasoit was a great man and the English as little children in the forest. My father restrained the other Indians from wronging the English, and gave them corn and showed them how to plant and harvest. Now there are many English. They have taken the earth as theirs, they believe the Indian is only to be used. Now that they are strong they show us no kindness as Massasoit showed them. We may lose a war with them, but not to go to war is to lose the war." All knew what he meant.

In the spring of 1675, I traveled to Providence to see my good friend Williams, a troubled man. I told him that breeze was now a gathering storm, my people would no longer bow to the English. He did not argue that English injustices were not grave. But he warned that the Indian was a single canoe on a stormy sea of English fury. I told him that our canoe was already overturned.

War came. First in Swansea in June of 1675. By mid-July most of Rhode Island and Massachusetts Bay hosted the struggle between us and the white man. Even in Providence, founded by our friend Williams, houses were burnt and settlers slain. But Williams's life was spared by Chief Canonchet. All Indians knew of Williams's kindness. It was a cruel war. My Indian brothers placed hooks through the jaws of captured settlers, then hung them from trees for a slow death. In Springfield a captured Indian woman was beaten to a bloody death, then fed to the settlers' dogs. Through the summer of 1675 Philip's war parties had more victories than losses. Then the turn. The Englishmen by their herd numbers began to show advantage of strength. As 1675 moved to 1676 there was no hope for Indian victory. Over three thousand Indians were killed. My wife one. I cannot speak of how she died.

Some tribes joined with the English, hoping to curry favor after the war. Others fled to the lands in Canada and New York. The Indian leader who had spared Williams, Canonchet, was captured in Pawtucket. Told he could spare his life in return for ending hostilities, he replied, "He liked it well, he should die before his heart was soft." Quickly executed by the English, his head was carried to Hartford.

The English gave our struggle a name, King Philip's War. It made Philip, my uncle, and his warrior Indians seem as a mighty force. The English wished to claim they defeated a powerful enemy. Another purpose for the name was that the English claimed that the war was by Philip's choice. An Indian would have called our struggle "The War of Despair."

By spring of the year it was over. Philip was killed in March, ending the Indian war. By order of Benjamin Church, a commander of the English, Philip's head was hacked from his body, his arms and legs then severed. His head was placed on a pole in Plymouth. There it was displayed for more than a year so all the Christians of the colony could see their defeated enemy. One of his hands in a bottle of alcohol, a tavern curiosity for many years.

After Philip's death, his brother-in-law, Tispaquim, surrendered to Benjamin Church with the assurance he and his family would be spared. He was beheaded. A similar fate to many who accepted amnesty: beheading or hanging. Some of us who accepted the English truce met a fate worse than death. We were sold as slaves, monies traded for our bodies to pay for the war.

As an old and tired man Roger Williams journeyed to Plymouth to plead against slavery of the Indians. His words were of no weight. Arguing against Williams, the governor of Plymouth, Josiah Winslow, ruled that "Native men, women and children joined in the uprising against the colony and were guilty of many

notorious killings and should be condemned to perpetual slavery."
Josiah Winslow was the son of Edward and Susanna Winslow, two
of the English settlers who arrived on the *Mayflower* and who were
embraced by my grandfather, Massasoit.

To spare me and my son from slavery, Williams offered to pay
three times our worth to the officials of Plymouth. But they remembered his banishment from their colony. We were to be sent away. On
a fall evening Williams came to the stockade that held me. When I
first met Williams I was a boy becoming a man. This day, with ropes
of iron around my legs, I was neither a boy nor a man. We spoke for
a long time, mostly of good memories, of our work on the Language
of America, and of his friend, my grandfather, Massasoit. Then he
spoke of other things. It was with heavy heart that he couldn't keep
his pledge to Massasoit and Canonicus. A pledge that the white man
would live in peace with the Indians. As he departed, he handed a
package and spoke the words, "*matta niccattuppummin*"; words that
caused much humor over thirty years ago. In the package, dried deer
meat for my son and me.

Your history books tell of the *Mayflower*. Nothing is written of
the *Seaflower*. In 1620 the *Mayflower* sailed to our land with English as passengers. In 1676 the *Seaflower* sailed from our land with
Indians as cargo. I and my son were cargo. A long journey, a hard
journey. Before the *Seaflower* touched land many went to meet the
Spirits. My son was one.

My journey ended in a faraway land, a different land, a land of
more water than earth. Here I lived and did my master's tasks. As
the sun began to set on my life I had much time to think. Why the
English were now in our land, while the Indian was in a strange
land as a slave. Was the Indian weak, was the Indian not clever, was
this the intent of nature? All these questions I considered. After
much time I came to understand. The Indian saw the white man as
himself. As a dog might see a wolf. But a wolf is not a dog. A white
man is not an Indian.

What made the white man different, not much. They worked, they slept, they loved their children. But there was a difference. Their want was not a certainty. Their want was greater than whatever they possessed. A farmer with two cornfields wanted three. A settler with one cow wanted another. Their wants were the distance of their vision, not their reach. This caused a stirring, a discontentment, a willingness to sacrifice themselves and others to move closer to their wants. Wants that always outpaced them no matter how mightily they struggled.

Was the Indian's contentment wrong when measured against the settlers' always wanting more? I thought not. The white man's hunger to take more made them as a locust in a field, moving quickly forward and devouring the grasses. I came to believe that the settlers would surely move from our lands to the lands of other Indian nations. They would not relent until all before them was theirs. Their nation would be greater than all the Indian nations together. But the white man may have another war to fight. An enemy stronger than the Indian. The Indians waited, then fought the settlers and were defeated. A new enemy of the white man is waiting. This enemy is nature. The white man takes what he wants from nature, just as he took from the Indian. But nature is stronger than the white man. It will not lose when it attacks.

Taubot mequaun nemêan,
Nananawtunu

Alice's Husband (Tom)

Americans suffered the Great Depression of the 1930s, sacrificed during the 1940s in order to claim victory over Germany and Japan, and entered the 1950s with the confidence that they were citizens of the Greatest Country the world had ever seen. As the calendar pages were turned over during the 1960s, 1970s, and into the 1980s, the majority of Americans strutted with a confidence. For the first time in America's life there was a feeling of being "the chosen one." Ford had launched the

Mustang, NASA had landed men on the moon, and color TVs nested in most homes.

This American confidence was coupled with a middle class that rode a wave of economic expansion. An expansion that resulted in higher and higher disposable family incomes, thus creating a vast pool of millions of new consumers. Consumers who responded to the seductive calls of Madison Avenue, "You deserve the best, drive a Buick home today." Materialism and instant gratification became the twin altars for many American consumers. Stories of Lewis and Clark were replaced by the recounting of Gates's and Jobs's successes. Making money transformed from being a by-product of a company to being the product of many companies.

And, for the first time in American history, the focus of many parents moved from one single well-defined objective to another: "My kids will have it better than me" became "I can own one of those, too."

This is the story of Alice's Husband, and his striving for greater and greater financial rewards at the expense . . . at the risk . . . of what he held most dear.

I N THE CORNER OF OUR LIVING ROOM SAT THE TV, BLACK-AND-white for most of my childhood. Later an RCA color TV arrived for Mother's birthday; she wanted to see, perhaps adore, Dean Martin in color. But back to black-and-white. In the early fifties there were three channels: CBS, NBC, and ABC. For the first few years they only broadcast in the afternoon and at night; no morning TV. A family favorite was *Wild Kingdom* with Marlin Perkins and his sidekick. In early TV most everyone had a sidekick: the Lone Ranger and Tonto, Captain Video and the Ranger, and Sky King and his perky niece Penny.

Perkins's weekly travels on *Wild Kingdom* took him and his companion to exotic lands. Of course I was growing up in Des Moines, so most places qualified as exotic. Episode after episode Perkins, in his obligatory safari jacket with cameras purring, would stalk the most elusive of animals. During one of his quests for the rarest of God's creatures, Perkins was flown to a clearing far from civilization. Once the plane landed on a just-cleared dirt strip, natives moved from the darkness of the forest, slowly circled the aircraft, hesitantly drew near, reached out, touched it, and sprang backward. Having never seen a plane before, it was a winged god to them.

I encountered my first winged god in the calm of an early evening in Teterboro, New Jersey. The plane was one of many, clustered together, having brought their warlords to pay homage to the ministers of Wall Street gospel at Morgan, Goldman, Merrill, and Hutton. These were corporate aircraft, not winged Greyhound buses for the masses. Only the anointed titans of industry ascended their stairs into cabins of plush New Zealand wool carpets, polished cherrywood, and finely stitched Italian leathers. In the security of his royal coach, the prince of commerce sipped a mixed drink in Baccarat while considering a selection of poached salmon, Dover sole, or filet mignon, offered by a stunning young woman whose professional destiny was linked to a single objective: The warlord should be a content warlord.

That evening in Teterboro I was not a warlord, I was a road warrior. Delta, United, American, TWA, Braniff—all had hosted me in their battle-worn DC-9s and 727s, thrusting me to my next meeting of imagined importance. Always with me the unwashed multitudes: businessmen with zombie stares and haggard mothers cradling unweaned babies.

My epiphany that warm evening in Teterboro was the midwife to the birth of a new personal goal. I coveted a winged chariot of luxury. Not a second home in the Hamptons or Telluride; not a Harry Winston ten-carat VS-1 diamond in an asscher cut for Alice; not a fine arts building at my alma mater with my name chiseled in stone above the entrance. No, I lusted for one of these magnificent, opulent time machines to serve me and no one else; poised to rush my body and soul to wherever my whim beckoned. But let's rewind forty or so years.

Back in Des Moines, Iowa, where much family time was consumed sitting around watching *Father Knows Best*, *Ozzie and Harriet*, and half a score of other happy, benign shows homogenized to offend no one. Dad comfortable in his chair, Mom on the sofa next to the far table lamp in case she wanted to browse through *Life* magazine or *Ladies' Home Journal*. As kids my sister Barbara and I would sit Indian-style on the floor to watch TV. As teenagers we assumed a more leisurely posture, lying prone with head propped on an arm. The best way to describe my growing-up days is to tell you that *Father Knows Best* could have been a documentary of our home life in Windsor Heights. Every day but Saturday Dad wore a suit. When he arrived home from work or church, Dad would remove his jacket and dutifully hang it in the hall closet. Only on particularly hot summer days would his tie disappear. Mom, Dorothy, never wore shorts or even a pantsuit. A few times I saw her in a robe, and occasionally a bathing suit during our two weeks at the lake. Otherwise her uniform consisted of a dress or a skirt and blouse.

Dad drove his Chevrolet Bel Air to and from work, arriving back between 5:30 and 5:45. We immediately sat down to a meal that took my mother hours to prepare. Beef, ham, pork chops, lamb chops, anything with a heartbeat we ate. Potatoes, mashed or baked, and a variety of vegetables; most often our revered state vegetable, corn. Two or three times a week Mom would bake rolls, keeping them hot in the oven until the sound of the Bel Air crunching driveway gravel. Dad never discussed business at the dinner table. Most of the conversation, or perhaps interrogation, centered on school. Since my sister was brighter than me, his inquisition focused on yours truly. While I never made the honor roll, my grades weren't embarrassingly mediocre; they were pleasantly mediocre. Dinner was not overly lengthy because Dad needed to nest himself in his maroon leatherette recliner and soak in Douglas Edwards and, later, Uncle Walter—Walter Cronkite. We viewed the world through the window of these two gentlemen. One knew they were telling the truth, "And that's the way it is."

I started off by telling you about *Wild Kingdom*. More precisely, it was *Mutual of Omaha's Wild Kingdom*. Probably another reason I remember the TV series so well is that Mutual of Omaha was Dad's competitor. Actually, a competitor of the company that employed Dad. Headquartered in Des Moines, Dad's firm, Bankers Life, sold insurance products. Later I learned that both of these companies were outliers to the insurance industry mecca and epicenter, Hartford.

My growing-up days were easy, just like Bud's on *Father Knows Best*. I got my bike when I was eight and my BB gun when I was ten. Joined the Cub Scouts, where Mom was a Den Mother. Learned my oaths and motto, "Do your best," and over time Mom, with much ceremony, sewed my tiger, wolf, and bear badges on the pocket of my blue Cub Scout shirt. With the awarding of my Webelos ("We'll Be Loyal Scouts") rank, I moved on to the Boy Scouts.

Boy Scouts was more challenging; one had to earn a variety of merit badges before moving up the organizational chart. Dad had made Eagle, the top rung. I peaked at Second Class. My enthusiasm for mastering the seemingly quaint skills—need to know how to build a fish dam—to earn merit badges waned as Betty's breasts bloomed. Betty being Bud's older sister on *Father Knows Best*. Thankfully, my education as a Boy Scout didn't cease. On a piss-freezing night in December, huddled inside a tent that provided meager shelter next to the Christmas tree lot sponsored by my troop, I was introduced to a new friend for life, cigarettes. The next year at summer camp, more education. An Explorer Scout—this being one up from Boy Scout—in charge of our care and feeding provided knowledge not represented by merit badges. Back in the sixties we didn't have sex education in Des Moines schools. I'm not sure we even had sex back in the sixties in Des Moines. Every kid was probably adopted from out of town. They definitely didn't have sex on TV; Lucy and Desi had separate beds. Maybe little Ricky was adopted too. Anyway, this Explorer Scout had a bunch of wide-eyed guys sitting around a campfire taking mental notes: "Girls do *what*?"

It was right after the Explorer Scout's ad hoc sex education class that I figured that I needed to change my name to have a chance at snagging a date; told my parents I was Tom, not Tommy. Didn't really help, only after my acne was in full retreat was I able to steal my first kiss.

As I was sneaking up on my senior year of high school, Dad started to brief me on college. Brief me, as in he knew exactly what I should do. Off to the University of Iowa, where I would earn a business degree back-loaded with statistics and actuarial science. Immediately upon removing my cap and gown, I would submit a job application to Bankers Life. Dad's belief about education and career reflected self-confirming logic. This had been his professional path, and he was happy.

If a company could be a religion, the Bankers Life headquarters at 711 High Street was a cathedral. Our Moses was Edward Temple, whose deeds were spoken of in reverent tones by employees. On May 1, 1879, a date no less significant than July 4th to many in Des Moines, Temple formed Bankers Life; always more than fair to its policyholders and Republican conservative in its finances.

While other insurance companies floundered and defaulted during the Great Depression, Bankers Life remained pure of purpose and resolute in its obligations. Only later, as I began to forage through the business wilderness, did I learn the differences between a mutual company, as was Bankers Life, and a for-profit stock company. The essence of a mutual company was to serve its policyholders. Profits were only generated to be added to reserves, thus allowing the company to provide more protection at a modest cost to the Ozzies and Harriets of the world. Every decision at Bankers Life pivoted on what was best for the policyholder versus how to maximize profits. Likewise with the employees: All were treated with benevolence. The competent were given raises, the incompetent were given slightly smaller raises and a watch when they retired.

My father was an actuary. "Stimulating job" being the antonym to "actuary." Trends, loss rates, standard deviations, outliers, a sea of numbers washed across his desk. Dad's bible was the writings of Pascal and Halley. Like a scientist examining slides under a microscope, Dad studied and extrapolated death rates, accident rates, trends of diseases and illnesses, and shifts in demographics. If the average family size went from his projected 3.26 to 3.29, Bankers Life's costs increased 1 percent, wiping out 50 percent of their expected reserves. No matter how he struggled to make his projections better than precise, they were only as good as the random occurrences of the country—the essence of this notion being confirmed in April 1978, when the birth rate in Manhattan spiked 30 percent nine months after the city's total power failure and blackout. Likewise with the AIDS epidemic, Dad's polished projections for the West Coast were not even a second cousin to reality.

My many Cs with a few Bs and As in high school effortlessly became many Cs with a few Ds and Fs at the home of the Hawkeyes. Feeling no embarrassment, my bottom-feeder college grades were Dad's burden, not mine. I was *Mad Magazine*'s freckle-faced Alfred E. Neuman: "What, me worry?" My smartass, ungrateful-for-the-tuition-that-was-paid-on-my-behalf response was, "Dad, I'm pacing myself, I don't want to peak too soon."

With the purchase of a well-used '57 Chevy convertible, one fender of a color not as the others, my unrecorded college social grades improved mightily. I cruised into my junior year with the top down and a smile of impending fulfillment. The need to park with the top up was not necessarily weather dependent.

By my senior year events ten thousand miles from our tree-studded campus displaced sex as the number-one dorm banter. Vietnam, or more precisely, the draft, topped the collegiate topic pyramid. Draft avoidance became an advanced course unto itself.

Surrogate PhDs of the subject lectured on hardship and educational deferments, National Guard service (defending Iowa City against the commie hordes), and less traditional strategies: an extended holiday in Canada or the application of lipstick and eyeliner. Assuming that drag would not be my best look, I targeted Air Force OCS. While contemplating a hot Texas summer at Lackland Air Force Base, the Selective Service Powers smiled upon me and I was dealt the ace of spades of draft status, 4A; I was inoculated against forced service. Of course I could have enlisted, but why? Most thought Vietnam was of no consequence, should we be bothered . . . and most important, my mother began once again to smile. Mom's younger brother had been killed in WWII, and for most of my senior year she had been masking a dark foreboding about Vietnam.

> **ABIGAIL, 1776:** To me a small tax was a just tax, and loyal we should be to the king that granted our lands. But Charles was as the Patriots. He felt conflict was necessary, a belief shaped by a fear that to state otherwise would be a sign of his unwillingness to sacrifice. For my dear Charles the hard decision was the right decision. It did not matter that I believed otherwise, Charles was the man of the house, he and his friend John Dotson would fight the Redcoats. Even though I was told it was only for three months it pained me to know Charles would be in harm's way. In the year to come the pain twisted inside me as the husbands of other women claimed they could not serve. Claimed they were needed on their farms and in their shops.

It is a certitude, the sun rises in the east. It was with no less a certitude that after graduation my application for employment at Bankers Life rose to the top of the pile. July 11, 1966 was my first day of employment. My boss was Mr. Hurd; later I learned that he had once worked for my father. The first two months at Bankers

Life were spent reading, punctuated with more reading. Bankers Life underwriting manuals, the company's Dead Sea Scrolls, set forth all the truths, policies, and procedures that governed the actuarial department. Stacked high in a corner of my cube were bound volumes of actuarial tables. Pick any person, tell me an age, tell me their sex, tell me the county they lived in, and after fifteen minutes of computations I confidently knew that their life expectancy was another 35.5 years. These tables didn't tell me whether a person was going to be happy or sad, whether they enjoyed Italian food or jazz, or whether they had a cute sister, but I did know that on average they were going to live 35.5 more years. Not raw material for great conversation over a Friday night beer.

Things got better. Couldn't have gotten much worse unless they converted the actuarial tables to Roman numerals. I moved on to reviewing the underwriting performed in the fields. Bankers Life had a field office sales force that marketed insurance in more than half the states of the union. My job was to keep the sales force honest, make certain that they were charging an equitable rate for the services we were providing. Our premiums were based on our best estimate of the cost of providing insurance coverage; no excess profit. Later, on Wall Street, I learned another pricing theory: How much money do you have, and how little can I offer you for all of it? This business concept being introduced to America in the 1800s by Jesse James.

After my first year at Bankers Life I received my annual raise. It was 2.5 percent. I remember the number because pretty much everyone received 2.5 percent, as if they took the rainfall in inches one month and then declared that's what everybody received as a percent increase.

By the time I finished my first year at Bankers Life I understood my father's passion. Dad was an amateur radio operator. In our cellar of exposed floor joists and pipes, with its always-damp concrete floor, were his radios, his friends. Behind our house, looking for all the world like the clothesline for the Jolly Green Giant, were antennas Dad had carefully erected. Every workday evening, after conferring with Uncle Walter, Dad would descend to the lowest reaches of our home and deposit himself in a swivel chair next to our old kitchen table; the only illumination the yellow glow of radio tubes. If the ionosphere was stable and the sunspots quiet, his radio rays could bounce around the world, allowing him to converse with fellow amateur radio operators in distant lands.

Hour after hour Dad would sit at his radio, transmitting, "W3NG, CQ, W3NG, CQ." His call sign being W3NG and CQ meaning that he wanted to speak with someone. If another amateur heard his signal, he would acknowledge Dad's call sign and reference his own call sign. The two would then converse back and forth on the radio—where they lived, the weather, and God knows what of no importance. To confirm and document their radio linkup, my father and his new radio buddy would mail each other cards. These were similar to postcards each radio operator had printed up. My father had thousands, each one with a large W3NG on one side with his address and specifics of his radio equipment on the other. Dad would dutifully mail off a card to the fellow he had spoken with, hoping to receive a card back. Like a humble man's mosaic of the world, two walls of our basement were completely covered with postcards; hundreds from Illinois and Iowa, some from every state, dozens from Canada and Mexico, many from Europe, a few from South America, one prized one from Africa, and two from Japan. Later, during my stays in England, I realized that my father descended into the basement as a British gentleman might stroll down the street to the corner pub after supper. The Brit didn't go to the pub to drink, he went for camaraderie. My father wasn't an actuary when he had a microphone in his hand; he was a man of the world with hundreds of friends.

I married sweet Alice the second summer of my tenure with Bankers Life. My real achievement at the University of Iowa was not a degree, it was stealing Alice away. We met in History 42 in 1964, the year the Ford Mustang was launched, another memorable event. On a scale of 0 to 10, I wasn't more than a 6 and Alice was no less than a 9.5. We met when she was on the rebound and I was able to offset my large nose and lanky body with quick wit and a caring personality. We graduated in June 1966 and were engaged in early 1967 with a summer wedding right behind.

Just like in the movies, after the wedding we moved into our one-bedroom garden apartment. The good news is that it was air-conditioned with covered parking; the bad news was that furniture was minimal. For several years our living room lamps sat on the boxes they were shipped in—boxes Alice cleverly disguised as end tables by draping them with green "table" covers she made from discarded curtains.

> **JUNIE, 1831:** Sunshine and I were married in the fall, part-way through September. Marse Edward and Miss Louisa gave us all of Sunday off, but that wasn't the best present they gave us. Marse Edward let Sunshine use some of his lumber so's he could build a room on the back of the kitchen house, a room just for Sunshine and me. Of course it wasn't just for us a year later. Our boy was born the next summer. I had a hard time. Almost bit clean through the new mama hickory branch.

After about six months of married life Alice came down with the stomach flu. We didn't know why, but it continued. Finally Mrs. Lawson, the principal at the school where Alice taught second grade, suggested that she might be with child. On September 2nd, 1968, Andrew signed on as a member of our family, cared for by the smiling nuns at Holy Cross Hospital. One small problem. Alice had requested a daughter. No problem, reorder. On August 20, 1969, not quite twelve months after Andrew was born, our second child was hatched. Whoops! David became Andrew's younger brother. This time we waited to reorder; wanted to get it right. On March 2, 1971, I met Jennifer, wrapped in her pink blanket. Alice had her daughter and I had two pals to share my electric trains.

In time the ghost of Edward Temple took pity upon me, and Bankers Life assigned me to a special project. I was tasked to learn as much as I could about the emerging managed health-care industry. First, if I may, a short synopsis of health care. For a thousand years or so the delivery of medicine worked rather efficiently. Sick people paid doctors, or medicine men, with money, chickens, or whatever they had. If they had nothing to barter, the doctor healed for free. In the mid-1900s health insurance appeared. This insurance was straightforward and had all the levers in the right direction. If you were really sick and were admitted to a hospital, the health insurer would pay the bill, or at least a major portion. The levers were in the right direction because no one wanted to go to a hospital just to have an insurance company pay a bill; most all tried mightily to stay away.

In the early seventies a new notion paraded onto the health-care stage, clothed in a low-cut dress and seductively named health maintenance organization, quickly shortened to HMO. The HMO fan club put forth an enticing argument. An HMO would provide a full range of benefits, from well-baby care to wart removal; thus, an individual would be more inclined to obtain preventive health care, avoiding the potential for a minor health problem swelling into a catastrophic event that demanded an expensive hospitalization. "An ounce of prevention is worth a pound of cure." A congenital defect in the HMO theory, though; namely, all of a sudden people had a higher propensity to consume health-care services. Because the HMO was paying, warts were being removed that otherwise would have been tolerated for life.

To control costs HMOs attempted to manage utilization by inserting themselves between the patient and the physicians. All of a sudden an HMO employee with a heavy New Jersey accent was instructing a female beneficiary in Mobile to go to an OB/GYN whose name sounded as if he were an ambassador to the UN. Likewise with the physicians; another HMO employee, who had flunked high school biology, was on the phone admonishing a fifty-year-old physician in Fresno, who had graduated at the top of his class at Harvard, that his practice patterns weren't appropriate: "You should have provided a routine exam, not an extensive exam."

As one of their products, Bankers Life offered health insurance. Not wanting to miss any new industry trends, they assigned me to study the developing HMO industry, and report back my conclusions . . . wow, they must think I'm smart. Great assignment. I could trash the actuarial tables and engage my creativity—a major portion of such creativity being applied to demonstrating to my new boss a need for me to travel to faraway lands . . . any zip code not in Iowa. The mother of all HMOs was the Kaiser Health Plan, thrown together by Henry Kaiser to provide health care to his California shipyard workers during WWII. I spent the better part of a day crafting a memo to my boss that justified my need to journey to the land of fruits and nuts. A month later I was on connecting flights through Chicago and then out to LA.

To say I was naïve insults the term naïve. With the address for the Kaiser offices in hand, I dutifully rented my Budget rental car and pulled out of LAX heading east on Century Boulevard with the expectation that I would soon cross Sepulveda, the street on which Kaiser was located. Not realizing that LA was bigger than the third moon of Pluto, several stops for directions were required before I located my host HMO. Kaiser's management offered few insights relevant to Bankers Life, but the LA trip had eye-opening attributes. Later that day my first night in a grown-up hotel, the Marriott at LAX. Great bar, great band, great-looking women. Most of them could have been in *Charlie's Angels*.

The LA field trip was a warm-up for the Big Apple. A New York law firm specializing in health care, Epstein & Becker—later I used them when I sold to AIG—was hosting a conference on HMOs. Another sculptured memo to my boss pleading the absolute need to attend was followed by a nod of approval. Scheduled to leave on Sunday afternoon, I skipped church and spent most of Sunday morning packing and repacking in an attempt to arrange my shirts so they wouldn't wrinkle; wanted to make a good impression with my conference counterparts from Cigna, Prudential, and Travelers. A couple of years later I learned that hanging a shirt in the bathroom with the hot water running magically made it appear just pressed. Later still I merely instructed the hotel butler to iron my shirts when he unpacked my bag.

To Chicago on an American 727 and then into LaGuardia on another. Grabbed my bag from a squeaking turnstile and headed to the curb. I knew things were different when I slid into the cab. Between me and the driver was thick bulletproof glass, smeared with what appeared to be bodily fluids. English was neither the primary nor secondary language of my turban-headed driver. By pointing to the name Waldorf-Astoria on my typed itinerary, communication was established. Twenty dollars later I was in front of the Waldorf. Standing on the sidewalk I gazed down Park Avenue toward the Pan Am building. Like an early explorer at the rim of the Grand Canyon, silent awe. The lobby of the Waldorf-Astoria made me recalibrate my opinion of the LAX Marriott. Got myself checked in and called home—the first of probably ten thousand calls home made over the next fifteen years.

The conference was great, but not because of any insights gleaned into health-care policy. Rather, the words of one speaker made me rethink Bankers Life. The speaker was Phil Bredeson; he went on to become the mayor of Nashville, later the governor of Tennessee. Phil was an entrepreneur who had made a pile of money in the hospital business and then charged into the HMO arena. While his speech rambled, one line resonated. Phil declared that HMOs were not a social program, they were an industry. Everyone I had spoken to previously had referred to HMOs in the context of more benefits for the masses. Phil's contention was that, if developed just right, an HMO could spew out wondrous profits for its owners. Phil spoke a language not heard in Des Moines.

Other Des Moines differences at the conference included a couple of expensive dinners—so expensive that their cost didn't fit into the constraints of my travel per diem. Most of the folks at the conference were New York and Hartford types; their uniforms were different from those worn in the land of combines and silos. Their ties didn't appear as if cut from cardboard and while my shoes looked like they might have steel safety toes embedded under the leather, theirs had fine stitching with elaborate wing-tip designs. Most of their shirts were adorned with gold cuff links, and a few were monogrammed. I'd never seen a monogrammed shirt. At first I assumed the initials were a manufacturer's logo. And their suits were tailored and fitted for them; mine had that one-size-fits-all look. I was so impressed that I sauntered into a Manhattan men's store, thinking I just might purchase a New York suit. In Des Moines, $89 bought a suit with two pair of pants. That would have just about covered the alterations for the pinstriped I coveted.

> **JOHN, 1942:** Marched probably a quarter mile and then lined up in front of this building, then inside for our uniforms. I never seen so many clothes. Any size you needed. I couldn't believe what I got. Six pair of socks, six skivvies, pants, shirts, jackets, shoes, and boots. I stared with my mouth open like to catch flies. I'd never had new shoes or boots. I'd never had much of anything new. And for certain sure never six of anything.

When I checked out of the Waldorf-Astoria, the concierge warned me that the cab ride back to La Guardia would burn no less than an hour and a half given the traffic at the time I was scheduled to depart. One of the fellows from Travelers suggested an alternative. A helicopter shuttle service had hourly flights from the top of the Pan Am building, a few blocks from the Waldorf, right to La Guardia. It would be a quick fifteen-minute trip, skimming over midtown traffic, with a stunning view of Manhattan. I had my father's

Argus C-3 camera, so I hoped to shoot some photos to dazzle my Midwestern friends.

I was scheduled to hop on the late-afternoon flight. The helicopter was going to cost $30 more than a cab, but this was a once-in-a-lifetime type of adventure for an Iowa boy. After a quick, but non-cheap, lunch at the Waldorf, I was walking down Park Avenue with suitcase in tow when I heard a crash from above, then screams, then blood. Didn't know what happened, but somebody was dead. She was dead right there in front of me. Both pieces of her were dead, laying in an expanding pool of blood that flowed over the curb and into the gutter.

I didn't take the flight home to Des Moines that evening. I spent another night at the Waldorf, only part of it in my room. For the first time in my life I drank three martinis, trying to wash away the pool of blood on the sidewalk.

Only after I read the newspaper back in Des Moines did I find out the full story. One of the struts on the landing gear of a helicopter that had just landed on the top of the Pan Am building collapsed. The still-spinning blades dropped down and dissected several of the disembarking passengers before one of the blades hit the concrete roof, broke off, and hurtled into the street below, killing the young woman on the sidewalk.

After a few days of regaling my young Bankers Life associates with my death-defying trip to New York, I began to ponder the conference. With more than a little hesitancy, with more than a little trepidation, I drafted a memo to my boss suggesting Bankers Life could use the savings from an HMO program to generate additional profits, versus providing more benefits for the same cost. It took me several paragraphs of preamble before I raised this new flag in my memo. No one saluted. A week of silence from above, then a transfer back to the actuarial department. I had defecated on Edward Temple's grave.

I was toiling in the actuarial department for two or three years before I met Li. Bankers Life employed their own cleaning crews.

They were white folks. Pretty much everyone in Des Moines was white folk. One day a new face in the cleaning crew picked up the trash in my office. Some type of Oriental guy, maybe forty years old or so. An Asian in Des Moines was similar to a Martian in Manhattan. I'm not sure I'd ever seen one before in the Bankers Life building. He was a quiet gentlemen; walked in, kept his eyes low, dutifully emptied the trash can, and was silently off. Around the same time I started a night course on Mondays and Wednesdays. I remember the days because Monday Night Football hit the airwaves with Howard and Dandy Don. Real entertaining. The night course was advanced statistics, an evolutionary step in my career at Bankers Life. We'd have a break halfway through class; this is when I stole a quick cigarette. I only smoked when absolutely certain my parents weren't within miles.

One night during my smoke break I saw an Asian man from another class puffing away. I made note of my second Martian sighting. A couple of weeks later the gentleman emptying my trash wore a bright-green shirt that was way too large for him. Later that night during my smoke break I saw the night-school Asian wearing a green shirt that was way too big for him. There weren't two Martians after all. We nodded toward each other.

The next day when he came into my office to empty the trash we spoke briefly. Li was Vietnamese. He and his wife and three kids had stolen out of Vietnam when the Americans cranked up their helicopters for the last time and headed east. Iowa's Governor Ray was one of only a few who had responded to President Carter's plea to support Vietnamese refugees—those who got the hell out of Dodge when Ho Chi Minh's armies swept through Saigon.

During many two- or three-minute conversations I got to know Li. He had been a medical technician in Saigon, working in an American outreach program in remote villages. For the first month in the United States his family was supported by a church group; then he paid his own way. His wife worked in a dry cleaning shop and he had the job at Bankers Life, plus another one stocking at the Safeway from 3:00 to 11:00 a.m. Two nights a week he was taking a course to brush out the accent in his English.

Li's goal was to see his kids well-educated and professionally employed. He hoped that at least one of them would become a doctor. Later I learned that all three of his children were girls, a surprise. A female and a physician didn't compute in Des Moines. Until the sixties Bankers Life would only hire single females. If a woman working at Bankers Life married, she had to resign immediately. In my world back then, women weren't professionals. Of course I rethought this when I saw Margaret Thatcher pull up her pantyhose and kick the Argentines in the balls. I had the opportunity to meet Margaret and plead Hank's case in Williamsburg years later. Sorry, getting way ahead of myself.

Li made me ponder my future. My father was living a good life. I knew this because he said he was; but it was a life of postcards and actuarial tables. Likely I would mirror my father's existence. I would work hard, but not too hard. I would enjoy my vacations and holidays, I would welcome my annual raises, in thirty years I would have a subdued, nonalcoholic retirement party, during my retirement I would spend more and more time enjoying a hobby of no consequence or passion, then die and slowly rot in the ground. I looked at Li and he was, as we would say in Iowa, shoveling the manure with a short-handled shovel. He wasn't coasting; he was working two jobs, his wife was working another; they had a goal. And the goal wasn't to go from two to three weeks' vacation after ten years of employment. They were striving to achieve an unreachable goal. They were pulling themselves up the American success ladder.

It is interesting what human beings can accomplish if they have to versus how little they accomplish if they are allowed to. When a light aircraft crashes in the wilderness of Alaska, the bush pilot and his two passengers walk three days through freezing snow, eating nothing but toothpaste retrieved from a toiletry kit, and finally stagger into a remote trading camp. Meanwhile, we have another human being, manufactured by the same God as the downed bush pilot, lying on a couch watching *I Love Lucy* reruns. While this poor soul doesn't possess the initiative to interview for a job, he is able to muster the strength to waddle to the front door to see if the mailman has dropped off a welfare check. In a way, and I don't mean to be ungrateful when I say this, but Dad and I weren't trying our hardest to get ahead. We were content. I found myself believing that being content made me discontented. Or, as Peggy Lee sang, "Is That All There Is?"

It wasn't an easy decision. It wasn't a popular decision with my parents. I decided to leave Bankers Life. I wanted to work harder and smarter than everyone else so I could have more than most for my family. That previous sentence is not honest. My family would have had more than enough if I had stayed at Bankers Life. My kids would never have gone hungry in our warm and secure home. Rather, it was me wanting to get on the playing field; if I worked as hard as Li and applied myself, big rewards would be waiting. Clearly, I had a magnificent head start on Li. I was a white male, over six feet tall, who spoke perfect Midwest English and had an Anglo-Saxon name pronounceable to all. I owned dark-blue suits and I could name the starting quarterback for every NFL team. If Li could move up his success curve from where he was, I should take a risk, a risk to do better.

I decided to go into business. But what business? Without excess capital the choices were limited. Becoming a consultant seemed to be the most cost-effective. Stationery, business cards, airline tickets, and an answering service would be my manufacturing plant. A problem: My reservoir of experience was not impressive as gauged to any existing industries. What made sense was for me to consult in a new industry where there were no gray-haired sages—that new industry being the expanding HMO industry. I had already visited one HMO and had attended an HMO conference; I could place this sliver of experience under a magnifying glass when presenting to prospects.

Made another tough decision: I decided to leave Des Moines. Mom and Dad, and for certain my boss Mr. Hurd, thought Alice and I were crazy to give up a good job and a close-by family. But given that I was targeting the HMO industry as my marketplace, Washington, DC, was the source of all good. HMOs were being spawned by a giant federal grant program that incubated fledgling HMOs. The administration and money spigot for this program was in Washington. Actually, in a suburb of Washington: Rockville, Maryland.

EMILIE, 1624: Father counseled us of a magnificent new land. Acres for all with opportunity for all. His friend, Mister Raymonds of the Gloucestershire Council, told of the New World. Crops, livestock, and fishes more than one could partake. Told we that in London a play recounted the emeralds and pearls that hung from trees as leaves in the land at our journey's end. When asked how far, told a fortnight to London and two months at sea. At the end of the journey in the most lovely place, Jamestown, on the James River of the New World. Told that those before us built delightful cottages where we could live. Those before would greet us and bestow upon us gracious hospitality.

Alice and I flew in for a weekend of house hunting and returned discouraged. A $20,000 house in Des Moines cost a daunting $40,000 in the Washington area. We ended up buying a less-than-perfect house for a little over $30,000. I won't say that we lied and cheated to acquire a mortgage, but we did manage some ambiguities. The mortgage company wanted copies of my W-2 statements. This I could provide. I didn't mention that my pending resignation rendered them irrelevant. To help with our pleadings for a loan, much ado was made about Alice resuming her teaching profession. We didn't add that this would be at least ten years away, given the age of our three munchkins.

On a sweat-dripping hot August weekend Alice and I packed up our worldly possessions and squeezed them into a U-Haul trailer, which was carefully and hopefully hitched to the bumper of our Ford Maverick. The trip to DC was memorably awful; consider an un-air-conditioned car, 95-degree humid afternoons, three kids aged three, four, and five, and a goldfish in a jar.

LUKE, 1851: Sand as hard as rock, looking down, no footsteps to confirm our progress. Slowly at first, just a breeze. A furnace, but a breeze. Then harder the wind blew, all white. Our goal, the mountains, no longer in front of our path. A glance to the right, to the left, no mountains. In the wind not sand, but a vapor of alkaline. Burning eyes and burning throat, choking and gagging on air of salt. At that moment everything I had, or thought I would ever have, thankfully traded for a gulp of cool water. Walking, staggering on, praying the Captain would scream a halt, commanding everyone to take a swallow from a keg, but he marched on, his head bowed, not bowed in defeat, but bowed to study the compass he held, the compass pointing west.

I glanced back, Arch shuffling, his eyes two slits on a caked white oval. Mother's bonnet pulled from her hair to cover her face. Mary, poor Mary, her arms on Father's shoulders, walking behind his lead, with her face buried in his shirt.

Progress was slow; we stopped every hundred miles to add a quart of oil because our Ford had lost bladder control. As we passed through Peoria my confidence was elbowed out by a mob of mental doubters. I kept glancing in the rear-view mirror, perhaps hoping to see my father and mother overtaking me in their Chevy, wanting to tell us that Bankers Life demanded I return. That day, while heading east on I-80, I would have gladly taken a 20 percent pay cut to have my old job back. The only thing that kept me going was thoughts about Li.

He had come to this country with no friends, no job, no money, and little understanding of the language. He didn't turn back.

I had no clue. Not only didn't I have a clue, I didn't know there was a mystery. The avalanche of prerequisite administrative tasks that accompanied the birth of my company almost caused a corporate stillbirth. Bell Atlantic had no enthusiasm for installing business phones for a startup entity. Blue Cross, Travelers, Aetna, Cigna—no one wanted to provide health insurance for a company with two employees. Plus, none of this mattered because no building manager was prepared to lease space to a company with neither a current address nor a balance sheet.

In time the ugly pile of obstacles was tunneled under by the application of immense imagination and sleight of hand. And these were the easy problems. The hardest challenge was convincing a prospect that he or she should contract with a vagrant consultant from Des Moines. My age was another hindrance; being closer to acne than to gray hair puts one at a disadvantage when marketing experience and brain power. I persisted. I learned that 90 percent of marketing is showing up. I traveled, I traveled, and I traveled some more. It wasn't easy travel, either. It was hard travel and cheap eating. More often than not I ate dinner at a fast-food place; for 99 cents a small Coke, fries, and a grilled meaty substance on a sesame seed bun.

JACK, 1864: It was after Sharpsburg—or Antietam, as the war's victors commended it to history—with sparse rations, that I ate, gagged, my first horsemeat, repugnant to taste, repugnant to mind. Two years later, with my skin stretched taut over bone, the smallest slice of stallion or mare was most craved for.

After two months of toiling in the vineyards of health care, my first sprout. With a muted sigh of relief I signed up a developing HMO in Philadelphia. For a princely fee of $250 a day I generated financial projections for their recently spawned HMO. I struggled mightily to make their deliverable better than perfect. I quickly grasped that building a company is not unlike rock climbing. Just as one firm handhold allows a climber to lever himself into a higher position to stretch for the next handhold, one satisfied client provides the credibility to ask for a larger assignment from the next prospect.

The good news was that my company had revenues that first year; the bad news, business expenses and personal expenses were higher. And I quickly add, personal expenses weren't tabulated with nights out at the movies or steaks on the grill. Our lifestyle in Rockville was 100 percent Midwestern austerity. Alice saved the day. The cost of daycare and all the other expenses of a working mom would have swallowed most of any salary she would earn by going back to teaching. Plus, with three kids in the most malleable time of their life, a stay-at-home mom seemed prudent. So Alice became a babysitter; she took in Megan and Joey. Their mom was a nurse at Holy Cross Hospital who was happy to pay Alice $1.25 an hour to care for her two offspring. The $50 a week earned from childcare covered our grocery bill, plus $10 of walking-around money.

As a respite from her babysitting career, Alice enrolled in freebie night courses at the local community college, the first a course in accounting. Alice had assumed the role of my corporate bookkeeper, but her college schooling in elementary education didn't touch on debits and credits. If the truth of the matter be known, the real reason she enrolled in night school was that her brain was turning to pudding. With five children at home, three of ours and two revenue-generating toddlers, Alice's professional development was limited to reading *See Spot Run* and keeping the fingerpaints out of the apple juice. Night school allowed her to interact with *Homo sapiens* who were potty trained and spoke in multisyllabic words.

ABIGAIL, 1777: Today as others, up before the sun. The chamber pot emptied and cleaned, some small chores accomplished before Sarah's questions and Baby Charles's needs. Bread and jam for Sarah after her face washed and her hair stroked. Then she pretends to feed her doll as I nurse Baby Charles. To the field all three to say good morning to Mrs. Brown. I on the milking stool with Baby Charles in the sling. Sarah picks handfuls of grass and offers Mrs. Brown her breakfast. My hands once soft are no longer. Mrs. Brown looks back and down as to say, "Why so?" By the time the bucket is half full, Mrs. Brown has no more. Then down the path from the meadow to our house. The foul smell from the privy calls out to be filled with earth. Into our home, then to the field for the day's chores. For each chore done, another one standing ready. A dinner for Sarah with answers to questions always asked. The last nursing of Baby Charles, Sarah's prayers said, then they to sleep. Baby Charles's soiled napkin washed and hung by the stove. An entry in my journal and then in the quiet and darkness of the house I can speak uninterrupted with my worries.

I struggled through the second year of business, only to have my ego raise the ante by convincing me to hire a couple of folks I could resell as consultants. Within a few months I waded into major trouble. Our billings were up because I had more people in the field, but cash flow fell into a crevasse. Rent and salaries had to be paid right away. Clients tended to pay 60, 90, 120 days after the work was completed. A second mortgage filled the void between payables and receivables that year. When I started my company I wouldn't have considered risking my home equity for the enterprise. But just as a Vegas blackjack player will often double his wager in an attempt to win back a string of losses, a businessman will sometimes double the stakes, his loans, to stay in the game. At the end of my first three years as president of my own company I had slid from a modest family net worth to personal guarantees that stacked higher than my combined home and car equities . . . as they say, I was upside-down.

There were few Saturdays I didn't work a full day at the office. Sundays Alice and I tried to protect; church attended more often than not. For me, taking our three jumping-jack kids to Sunday morning services was not unlike having a hand grenade with a loose pin in my jockey shorts; always a feeling of impending disaster as our three youngsters squirmed on the wooden pews. For cheap Sunday afternoon entertainment Alice and I would wander through Potomac in our Ford Maverick, perusing open homes. Potomac, adjacent to Rockville, was considered the upper crust. Houses didn't sit on quarter-acre lots, they were artfully poised on superbly landscaped two- or five-acre parcels. Homes weren't priced at $25,000 to $75,000, they were a princely $300,000 to $500,000 and even more.

When I first strolled through one of these mega-homes, I was stunned; never stood in a house that had ceilings higher than eight feet. Most Potomac homes had ten-foot ceilings, others eleven or twelve. The higher ceilings seemed logical once I read that Clare Boothe Luce claimed that one required high ceilings for lofty thoughts. Joining the ceilings and walls were eight- to twelve-piece crown moldings in intricate designs. The mini-mansion exteriors were elegant masonry, handmade brick set in Flemish bond. Aluminum siding had long ago been excommunicated. Floors weren't plywood hidden with wall-to-wall carpeting, they were eight-inch planked and pegged hardwoods buffed to a luster. Homes in Potomac were different from anything in Des Moines. Curiosities at first; later they became much more.

—— ⌘ ——

For five years my company's revenues followed a steady crawl upward. Earnings weren't steady, earnings were scary. Things were so bad that a couple of years I risked going to jail. No, I didn't rob a bank, I just didn't make timely FICA payments for employees. I borrowed from the IRS. Of course the Feds wouldn't have used the term "borrowed" in the indictment. I got myself in a steel box. I couldn't afford to close down the business because the debts—all personally guaranteed by me—exceeded the assets, assets that were somewhat nebulous . . . how much is a used typewriter really worth?

Many nights I would have gladly bargained with the devil and forfeited a few years of my life expectancy to be back in Des Moines. At three in the morning I would find myself roaming a dark house, pausing to peer into the kids' bedrooms, their cherub heads resting on pillows that were collateral for Citizens Bank. One major advantage, though: Standing Carl Sagan-like on the edge of a financial black hole is better than fresh contact lenses. Vision becomes acutely clear and the decision process elegantly simple. "Alice, shall we have a picnic this Sunday with the kids? Or perhaps I should go into the office and push out a deliverable early with the hope that the client pays in a timely manner, thus permitting me to avoid defaulting on the line of credit that we personally guarantee. Gee, guess I'll go into the office, sweets, if that's okay with you?"

It all held together. By the eighth year cash flow was no longer exciting, it was merely an item of interest on the monthly financial statements. I was off the personal guarantees and more than five hundred employees marched in my army, the vast majority of whom were more competent than less. Wait, that's neither a fair or kind statement. Most were great. Alice and I expended immense energy into cultivating the workforce. Alice had her finger on the morale of the company. If somebody was having a personal problem, we tried to help. A lot of money was lent at zero interest. Plus we put in some programs that were hyper-employee-friendly. Because Alice and I had run out of money on our honeymoon, the company implemented a "honeymoon bonus" for the staff. For any employee who married, we provided an extra week of vacation, not charged to them, and handed over a $2,500 bonus check.

Another of my favorites—but there was a hidden agenda with this one—was the American Car program. If an employee bought a GM, Ford, or Chrysler product, we picked up half the monthly car payments, including paying the taxes on the imputed compensation. Employees collectively purchased over 250 American cars. The hidden agenda: In our inventory of prospects were numbers of union health plans. The company had a nice write-up from the UAW praising our "Buy American Program." This scored big points with union prospects.

On our Sunday afternoon tours of the mega-houses of Potomac, one builder had shone above all others: Pat Cullinane. Real estate agents spoke in hushed tones when referencing Pat's homes. I came to learn he was a Renaissance man, with interests spanning hunting to opera. He was unmarried, with a private nine-hole golf course circling his bachelor pad. Pat's propensity to consume didn't include the sinkholes that open up in the financial pastures of most married males. Pat had no need to save for college tuitions or to contribute to the happiness of an orthodontist. Because he didn't need to maximize personal revenue, Pat only built a single house every two years or so. And he only built them if he liked you . . . and if your really big check cleared.

We went back to Des Moines three or four times each year to visit Mom and Dad. My sister was in Kansas with her husband. It was a two-day drive each way. Our Ford Maverick had been gleefully traded in for a Chevrolet Capri; it had air conditioning, a more impressive invention than the wheel itself. From the Capri we later traded up to an Oldsmobile 98 with its Rocket V-8 engine, and then a silver Cadillac, shod with optional Vogue tires. I never had the nerve to drive the Cadillac to Des Moines, so we kept the Oldsmobile as the Des Moines shuttle bus. Two days out, two days back allowed for a three-day visit if I was willing to blow up an entire week. Three days with my parents was probably just about right. Mom and Dad loved the kids, but they were used to tranquility. As a parent I saw three children;

my parents saw thirty fingers. Mom's collection of Hummel figurines moved to the highest shelf in her china cabinet as our Oldsmobile crunched down on my parents' gravel driveway.

Speaking of cars, one of the Sunday-night programs I watched as a kid was *Route 66*. These two young guys, Buzz and Todd—I told you they came in pairs—were vagabonds who somehow could afford the newest model Corvette. The weekly plots were strained, but the speeding Corvettes were great. Back in the late fifties the only two-seat sportscars in the United States were the Corvette and Thunderbird. A fuel-injected Corvette was one sexy beast; as a teenager I had a poster of a maroon '61 Vette on the back of my bedroom door. I tell you about *Route 66* as backdrop to *Magnum P.I.* By the early eighties TV producers had moved up the exotic car curve. Magnum drove a red Ferrari 308 in this weekly series. My boys were old enough, and the TV censors were aggressive enough, that the males of my family could savor the program together. It was my first exposure to a Ferrari. As a teenager I knew the various International Harvester models. As an adult I learned the technical aspects of a Ferrari Daytona, Boxer, and 308 Spider. In Des Moines a Corvette was a fantasy; in Rockville a Ferrari was an objective.

"Sell too soon" is often the key to making money. If you have a stock and the price goes up, you may want to sell. You don't realize a profit until you sell. Don't worry about getting the highest price, worry about monetizing a gain. I decided to monetize my company. I engaged E. F. Hutton to send out feelers suggesting that my company might be available if the appropriate consideration was tendered. Attempting to make us seductive to a potential purchaser, I squeezed cash onto the balance sheet, bought a marble conference room table to host purchaser prospects, and was fitted for my first Italian suits.

Over a six-month period a dozen or so potential buyers knocked on our door, so to speak. A few of them sponsored TV programs; big names were prepared to acquire the company. We selected a company I had never heard of before, American International Group, known in the insurance industry as AIG. They weren't a health-care company, rather, casualty and life. AIG was listed on the New York Stock Exchange, and my initial review of them was somewhat startling. Hank Greenberg, their chairman and chief executive officer, had been written up in many prestigious financial periodicals, all of which included the observation that Hank was the toughest of the tough. Cursing and yelling were hallmarks of his management style. Never a single off-color word had been uttered at Bankers Life . . . at least that I had heard.

On the other side of the scale, the financials of AIG were staggeringly impressive. Not only was AIG's balance sheet the financial equivalent of a *Playboy* centerfold, but the company also had a magnificent growth rate. Greenberg had started with a little more than nothing at AIG and soon had the company nibbling at the heels of Cigna and Travelers. In fifteen years he had built an insurance conglomerate larger than Bankers Life, which had been hawking its products for seventy-five years.

AIG had another stellar quality: They offered the highest purchase price. I pondered the notion of selling my soul to the devil. Then I pondered my net worth after a transaction with AIG. Hank Greenberg's money machine got top billing in my mind's billboard.

A few hundred thousand dollars' worth of attorneys' fees and we had an executed sale agreement with AIG. On the closing date Alice and I flew to New York and cabbed to the offices of Wayland Mead at 70 Pine Street, AIG's corporate offices. Wayland was their corporate counsel. A platoon of attorneys from Epstein & Becker were there both to represent me and to demonstrate, by their sheer numbers, the validity of their multipage invoices for professional services. Across a large conference room table documents were dealt out and signed. Epstein & Becker attorneys, as mothers might gently lay down their babies in bassinets, secured the just-executed documents and gently placed them in their open brief-cases. We all stood and shook hands. In the lobby I thanked my attorneys for their professional assistance, and Alice and I hijacked a cab back to La Guardia, where we darted onto an Eastern shuttle. Our net worth had just gone up exponentially, but it didn't matter. I was squeezed between two business guys and Alice was relegated to a center seat several rows back: open seating with the masses.

My middle seat was a harbinger. My net worth had gone up by the third power and nothing changed. If I drank three martinis I continued to wake up with a headache. Plus, there was no doubt in my mind that my son David was still more impressed that his best friend's father had shot a six-point buck and drove home with it strapped to the hood of his pickup than with the fact that I had made a killing for far bigger bucks that would feed us a lot longer.

Several corporate gurus included Hank Greenberg in their list of "Ten Best CEOs." I could see why. What I admired most about Hank was that there was an absolute to his life. That absolute being his total commitment to building AIG and churning out profits. Like a Sherpa with a two-hundred-pound pack on his back, Hank carried AIG from $50 million in revenues to $9 billion. He drove the company with his uncompromising will to make AIG a financial behemoth. Institutions that held AIG stock spoke of Hank in reverent terms. Why shouldn't they? With a 15 percent yearly growth rate, Hank could have had horns and a tail and most any major AIG shareholder would have welcomed him to a family baptism.

It is one of those facts of life: People you like, tend to like you. I think Hank liked me. The reason being, I told him the truth. I could be frank; I had independence. AIG bought my company and I had a pile of AIG stock sitting in my safe deposit box. If he fired me, my net worth wouldn't have gone down a nickel. I could have retired. Most of his senior managers had big salaries but no serious net worth. They lived in fear of being fired. If you live in fear of being fired, you never want to make a mistake. Everyone makes mistakes. So the only way not to make a mistake is to blame your mistakes on someone else. Hank was used to listening to senior executives explain why their problems were caused by someone else's misdeeds. I just told him the truth.

A little over a year after he purchased my company, we had a morning meeting in the Big Apple to review our operations. Attending were Hank, his CFO, Ed Matthews, me, and my CFO. We had missed our numbers. I had projected that we would make X dollars in the first quarter, and we made less. Hank looked at me and said, and this is the way he talked, "Your staff that put together your quarterly projections, are they goddamn liars or are they goddamn incompetent?" A long silence as my CFO contemplated a career move to another planet. I responded, "Those two notions are not mutually exclusive. My staff could well be both incompetent and liars." There was a stunned silence, and before Hank could speak, I added, "Mr. Greenberg, these projections are mine; these are the bad assumptions I made, and this is the action I'm taking to fix my mistakes." He paused for a moment and jumped into the next subject. As we wrapped up the meeting Hank asked if I would be interested in joining him for doubles at his club. I passed, mumbling something about visiting an important client. Before leaving, his CFO, Matthews, told me that he'd figured I was a dead man after my first response to Hank.

I wish I could have accepted Hank's offer to join him for a few sets of tennis, but I hadn't ever picked up a tennis racket. There weren't a lot of tennis courts in Des Moines. If he had asked me to pitch horseshoes or maybe roll some duckpins, I could have held my own. But Hank did have me up to his club. Actually it was AIG's club. Morefar—yes, Morefar—in Brewster, New York. Only Hank's friends were welcomed. The entrance feature was a large No Trespassing sign. Morefar was your basic two hundred acres of manicured grounds with a few million dollars of bronze artwork along the fairways. It's one thing to own a great set of golf clubs, it is another to own a great golf resort.

Tennis or not, Hank wanted to see me at his club. I drove up on a Saturday, having taken the 6:30 a.m. shuttle to La Guardia. Joined Hank for lunch. Not more than fifteen seconds of pleasantries, then business. He commented on the $40 million that my company made pre-tax the previous year. Told me he expected me to generate $50 million the next year. I didn't say no, just told him it would be a real stretch, but that I would commit to the challenge. Then he did something seductive. He explained that my annual bonus would be 20 percent of the difference between last year's earnings and this year's earnings. So if I could get the number up to $50 million, my bonus would be $2 million.

On the drive back to La Guardia I considered the impossibility of his challenge. It had taken ten years to grow my company from zero to $40 million in earnings; he wanted another $10 million in a year. But by the time I was on the shuttle flight back, I was thinking about the $2 million bonus. Pulling a million off the top for Uncle Sam, I'd net out a million. A million dollars corresponded nicely to the price tag of the homes Alice and I coveted. Another correction. I was coveting the homes. Alice was smiling and agreeing. Why not? Smiling and agreeing is cheap and keeps everyone happy. She probably never considered that I might actually spend a dump truck load of money for an estate to shelter my ego.

You have heard the term "burning the lifeboats"; meaning, one takes a nonreversible action, knowing the ship is either going to reach its destination or everyone pays the big price. I burned the lifeboats: I put money at risk for an earnings destination. Alice and I had been conspiring with Pat for a couple of months and finally had our mega-house designed. Pat's price for the 10,000-square-foot abode was just a smidgen under a million dollars. I don't think he could bring himself to hand us a quote that had seven digits. To get myself motivated to hit Hank's goal I gave Pat a nonrefundable

$50,000 deposit to hold while he worked up the construction drawings. I figured that if I didn't earn my $2 million bonus with Hank, I could walk away from the deposit. Somehow the fear of losing the $50,000 deposit was more of an incentive to me than the potential of getting another $2 million. The brain works in strange ways.

To hit the $10 million incremental gain that would allow Hank to waterski behind my slave ship, I needed all my employees to row at double-time. My superstars were Rigby, Jackie, Merwin, Bob, and Bruce. There were another few hundred employees, but these were the Reggie Jacksons of the earnings playoffs. They hit revenue home runs. They got you from A to B by sheer force of will.

A quick story about one of my superstars. Bruce had a major report due on a Monday for a most demanding LA client. He worked at the office all weekend, not even stopping to go home Sunday night. From the office he dashed home on Monday morning, took a shower, hopped in his Datsun, and sped off to catch an early United flight to LA. Halfway down the Dulles access road, Bruce fell asleep at the wheel. His Datsun drifted off the road, then flipped over a couple of times. Crawling out with a bloody forehead, Bruce grabbed the client's report, then asked a cab driver who had stopped to offer assistance to take him to Dulles so he could catch the United flight. The report got delivered.

Another observation. Money is like manure. If you spread it around, things grow. While all my key staff had some significant net worth because of the sale to AIG, they all had unique and unrealized personal goals that I used as stalking horses. Rigby coveted a Porsche 928, while Jackie was looking to take a two-month sabbatical to hike Taiwan. I crafted individual bonus awards that addressed each key employee's fantasies/desires. All they had to do was make sure I didn't lose my deposit with Pat.

Even though I had the "A Team" motivated to maximize earnings, we needed to pull a rabbit out of a hat to hit Hank's target. In time a rabbit called. His name was Mike Miller, Vice President of Development for a large hospital chain in California. They were contemplating the purchase of an HMO, Health Plan of America, trading as HPA. Before they wrote a big check they wanted to sign up a company to manage HPA. Mike asked if we would be interested. After a few questions by me, designed only to suggest I was pondering my response, I replied in the affirmative. I was familiar with HPA; it was a modest-size health plan with fifty thousand members or so, but it could potentially generate a management fee of several million dollars a year, making Hank's target possible. Mike's call came on a Friday afternoon. I suggested to Mike that I could be in their offices on Monday. He called back a couple of hours later stating that his staff would meet me Sunday afternoon at the Doubletree Hotel in Orange. They were in a rush to close on HPA with a board meeting on Monday morning to approve the purchase. That weekend Alice and the kids and I had planned on going to the Shenandoah Mountains for a long-anticipated weekend of hiking and horseback riding. Sorry, Alice.

On Saturday I was in the office preparing for the HPA presentation, and that evening I was on a United flight to LA; then down 405 in my Hertz-mobile and into the Orange County Doubletree by midnight. Took a long walk the next morning to get some oxygen into my brain cells and then watched the Washington Redskins lose to the Cardinals. A bad harbinger; turned out it wasn't. Later in the afternoon I met with six senior staff of the hospital chain. All sharp folks. They came at me with a machine-gun fire of technical questions. Would you subsidize the family rate with singles? Do we need federal qualification in the marketplace? Would you capitate the primary care doctors? Would you require preauthorization for outpatient surgery? I was fortunate; I was on my game. I fired return volleys of unambiguous answers. After they caucused for a little over a half hour they smilingly announced that my firm would be selected if I could present to their board on Monday. I agreed.

That evening I called Alice and reported my victory. She packed a suitcase, took it to Dulles the next morning, and paid a skycap twenty bucks to sneak it on the United LA flight. I would have extra clothes for an extended California stay.

I probably should tell you more about Alice. She was pivotal to the success of our businesses. I was the fighter pilot; she was the crew chief on the ground. When I came home from missions she made sure that the family unit was a tranquil base for me. She sheltered me from day-to-day household frustrations and carried more than her share of family chores. Alice was much more than a great partner; as Debbie Boone sang, she was the light of my life. I knew I was blessed with Alice. I knew this because of what other guys said, or more correctly, what they didn't say. If you ask a married man what was the best thing he ever did, and his answer is along the lines of "Got accepted to Notre Dame," "Bought Microsoft stock early on," or perhaps "Accepted a job at GE," what they didn't say tells you something. For me, the answer was unequivocally, "Married Alice."

While the HPA opportunity was rife with wondrous potential, it also shared aspects of having a mountain lion as a house pet. HPA's owner was a serious hospital chain; they could have taken a big bite out of our ass if we didn't deliver. But we did. I lived out of my room at the Doubletree for just under three months. While I was able to recruit a dozen or so key folks to direct traffic at HPA, I needed to be around to make sure all the animals were in their cages and the warthogs didn't try to mate with the swans. But, New York also beckoned, also demanded.

Every quarter Hank had a "Presidents Meeting," comprised of all the heads of the AIG divisions and subsidiaries. It brought back memories of my third grade teacher, Miss Forshay; she always collected the homework and never took prisoners. There were about twenty-five AIG presidents, their individual operations ranging from $100 million to $1 billion in revenues. Many had to fly in from remote locations, including China, so I couldn't complain if

I had to take the American LA/New York red-eye back to the Big Apple.

To accommodate the various presidents attending a "Presidents Meeting" at AIG's offices on Pine Street, a dozen or so small tables would be put together to form one large square. Chairs were carefully placed around this table, each chair being identified for a specific president. I and the other presidents would stand behind our designated chairs, not unlike the Queen's Guard waiting for the monarch's review. In time Hank would stroll in with folders under his arm. He would sit; everyone else would follow his lead. Hank would randomly select an individual and start interrogating him—all were hims—about his operation. After verbally removing this president's fingernails, Hank would move to the president to the right and begin an autopsy of his operation. This continued for two or three hours while Hank, in perfect order, challenged one by one the professional confidence of the entire group. Periodically a white-jacketed Asian gentleman would enter and quietly serve Hank tea. No one else was asked whether they would enjoy a refreshment, nor were any hygiene breaks taken.

During the length of the meeting there were no subsidiary conversations. The only words spoken were between Hank and the president he was dissecting. If someone walked into the room and took a still photograph of the meeting, and then made a large print of the photo, one could readily determine which individuals Hank had drawn and quartered. Those yet to be called upon were sitting erect at the table with their hands folded in front. Others were hunched over, pummeled and broken. High-paid executives were nothing more than a row of dominoes pushing one against the other, with some still standing. I was told that two presidents had resigned within the past few years because they couldn't take the AIG pressure to hit their numbers; they walked away from big paydays. Not me, I was tough, mentally tough. I could handle any pressure sent my way.

WARREN, 1943: Roland's death occasioned no pause. Weeks more of flight ops followed. But there was a toll; a toll paid most every day. The empty bed—a bed where another of my squadron mates had slept the night before. It wasn't the death of a human that took its toll, it was the death of a person, a young man who had laughed with me at dinner messes, who spoke of his mother, his sister, his dreams. Each of these deaths chipped away part of my hope, my humanity, and worst, my sanity.

After the meeting adjourned Hank would summon a few of the just-roasted presidents to join him for lunch in the corporate dining room. I was anointed twice. The dining room was on the uppermost floor of 70 Pine, with almost a 360-degree view of the city. As Hank sat, another white-jacketed Asian silently placed a small table beside his chair for his folders. I didn't see this concept again until I was having dinner with Alice at the Hôtel de Crillon in Paris, where a waiter placed a similar table next to Alice's chair for her purse. Then three courses, three courses served by a half-dozen white-coated waiters. During lunch, while I pretended to enjoy the scrod that was always served, Hank would provide a cutting critique of various presidents who were not his lunch guests. I knew that I was similarly critiqued when not breaking bread with Hank. But I didn't care. I enjoyed corporate America. The traffic was exhilaratingly heavy, the limos big, and the destinations seductive.

It was one of those California perfect days, a warm 75 degrees and a bright sun making life and future look secure. Alice and I were drifting down Rodeo Drive in Beverly Hills. I had been in California working on HPA for most of the winter; Alice had flown out to spend a three-day weekend with me. So there we were, strolling past Gucci, Ferragamo, and Zegna. We had just finished lunch at the Rodeo Café, spinach salad and a carafe of white wine. Didn't want to chance offending the locals by ordering cheeseburgers.

All was well. Wait, what's that on the left? A boutique auto sales showroom, Selection Export/Import. We'll just go in and take a quick look. There it was, by the front window, bathed in golden California sunshine. Several middle-aged professionals in their pin-stripes soaking in the image. Parked, with Targa Top removed, a polished red, newly arrived Ferrari 308. With tan leather interior and Quattrovalvole engine, sheer sheet-metal sensual.

The salesman, who I later learned was an out-of-work actor by the name of Gregg, shuffled over. "How much?" I asked. "If you buy it today, $49,500. We just had a deal fall through for it and we need the cash flow." I knew $49,500 was $5,000 below the market. My mind cheerfully ran the calculations. *I'll buy this car and save $5,000. If I buy two hundred of them, I'll save a million dollars.* I quickly decided to save only $5,000. I called my friendly banker and wired the money. An hour after innocently entering the showroom Alice and I were back in our suite in the Century Plaza. *Can this be? Did we just purchase a Ferrari?* I quickly called my buddy Rigby. He thought it was great; but then he was on his third wife.

I had one bad night; the HPA West Coast pressure cooker got to me. After a 7:00 a.m. Monday meeting in San Francisco I scampered to the airport to grab a flight to LA for a noon meeting. Following several hours of legal Trivial Pursuit with some attorneys and investment bankers in LA, I rented a Hertz-mobile and drove the hundred miles up to Santa Barbara. There I had dinner with a fellow I was trying to recruit for HPA. For two hours I tried to speak eloquently and convincingly as to why he should join the great HPA venture. He wouldn't commit. After dinner I headed to the Santa Barbara Airport to catch a flight back up to San Francisco so I could plop in my hotel bed and steal six hours of sleep before the next day's imagined adventure. Damn! Coastal fog, all flights out of Santa Barbara were canceled.

I stood in the beige stucco terminal and stared at the cancellation notices. I had been in high gear since 6:00 a.m. In fact, I had been in high gear for the last six months, whipping between the

East and the West Coast like a jai alai ball in a final match. Here I was, stranded 2,500 miles from family, with no way to convey my tired bones to San Francisco, where my hotel mattress longed for my warm body. The cancellations popped my emotional bubble. From a pay phone I called Alice and whimpered for ten minutes or so. She, like most clever wives, had learned long ago that husbands are merely tall children. Sweet Alice verbally patted me on the head and assured me everything would be fine; I should just find a hotel room in Santa Barbara and sleep the good sleep. Having gotten the needed sympathy vote, I hung up and hopped into another Hertz-mobile and averaged seventy miles an hour to the Los Angeles Airport. There I caught the last PSA flight to San Francisco. A little after 1:00 a.m. I was safely tucked in my bed in San Francisco.

That night on the flight from LA up to San Francisco, I stared out the window at the blackness. Every few minutes a cluster of lights from the towns far below drifted slowly by. An embarrassing guilt wrapped me. A few hours before I'd been on the phone to Alice, complaining that life was not fair because I was tired with no way to crawl to my hotel. In each town that slid under the PSA flight that night there were people with real problems: lost jobs, sick children, dying parents. In each pocket of humanity that I glided over many, if not most, would have thanked God to exchange their circumstances with me. In San Luis Obispo, the guy working seventy hours a week in the 7-Eleven, hoping not to be robbed and shot, would gladly assume my role in the play of life. The migrant worker parked on a rural roadside outside of Fresno, with his wife and two kids sleeping in the back of their rusted-out Chevy, would cry with happiness to be given my "problems." I had fallen into the trap of self-pity. Before descending into San Francisco I put my forehead against the window of the plane, looked up to the stars, and promised I would never again forget my blessings. It was a promise I did not keep.

With an absolute discipline on expenditures and by forcing the revenue engine into high gear, overlaid with more than our fair

share of luck, we achieved our earnings target. Yearly profits bubbled up from $40 million to just over $50 million. Of course we
weren't allowed to grade our own papers. The AIG internal audit
guys flew down from the Big Apple and scrubbed our numbers;
they smiled and concurred. We hit our heroic target; somebody
owed me a big bonus.

I didn't know if I should call AIG and ask, "Where's my
money?" or just wait. I took the Des Moines polite, silent
approach. Plus, I wouldn't have had the nerve to ask if my $2
million bonus check was in the mail. It showed up. No questions, no hesitancy, a check arrived minus withholdings for federal and state taxes. Pride bubbled as I endorsed a seven-digit
check and slipped it to the teller with a deposit slip, less $50 in
cash.

> **PATRICK, 1860:** It was at the end of my first week with the
> Mulcahys that I got paid. I was paid a quarter dollar and a
> half dime. It was the first money I ever had for myself. That
> night I sat on my cot and stared at the coins in the light of
> the lantern. I rubbed them together. I held them together. I
> held them apart. I wiped them clean with my shirtsleeve.
> The next day I walked through Boston with one hand in my
> pants pocket holding the quarter dollar and half dime. I
> walked in big steps with a smile.

We bought the house. After setting aside a little extra from the AIG
bonus check for our contribution to Reagan's national deficit, we
gave Pat half a million as a 50% initial payment on my castle. While
I had no hesitancy in writing a check for a mega amount, I didn't
have the guts to tell my parents how much we were spending . . .
how much I was spending. Yes, it was my house, not Alice's; Alice
was enthusiastic, but her enthusiasm was for my happiness, not for
seven bedrooms, eight full baths, and three half baths. And, let me
quickly explain why seven bedrooms required eight full baths . . . a

friend advised that once past the twentieth wedding anniversary there is nothing more conducive to a tranquil marriage than his and hers bathrooms.

MILLY'S SISTER, 1903: The ship came to a big city. We walked far. We walked to a tall building. There were many rooms in the building. Our room was up many steps. There was one privy for everyone. It smelled bad.

It was right after Pat broke ground for my grand abode that the gods at 70 Pine Street embraced me. An early-morning call from one of Hank's cadre of administrative assistants at AIG set the plot, my presence was required at a meeting in LA. The meeting was not of note; rather, the mode of transportation that chiseled the event. I was to rendezvous with Hank and the AIG comptroller, Howie, at the AIG corporate hangar. For five long hours I would be in an aluminum cocoon with Hank.

My initial enthusiasm for being Greenberg's new travel companion soon morphed to fear. Even though I was a mature businessman with a couple of gray hairs, ran a company with close to a thousand employees, and negotiated hundred-million-dollar transactions, self-doubt first bubbled, then churned. What do I wear for the flight? Do I carry a briefcase? Should I be prepared to brief Hank on the performance of my company? If he drinks bourbon, should I drink bourbon? If he reclines his chair and dozes off, should I do the same, or perhaps should I stand at attention? Am I allowed to use the same restroom that he uses? Does a corporate jet even have a restroom? I felt like I was going on my first business trip years earlier at Bankers Life.

Not wishing to risk being late, I arrived at Teterboro two hours before the planned departure; I quickly located the AIG hangar and deposited myself in their lounge, where I was distressed not to see an AIG aircraft poised on the apron. After a few minutes of panic, one of the young female AIGers advised that the corporate aircraft would be arriving with Hank at our scheduled departure time. Mr. Greenberg was in Hartford for the day, either spreading wisdom or plundering.

At 5:00 it was there. Bigger than anything else on the ramp. Later I learned it was a Gulfstream IV—referred to by those in the know as a G-IV. It was larger and flew further and faster than any of the competing corporate jets. Only the top of the Fortune 500 food chain savored their very own G-IVs. With whitewalls and undercoating, the plane had a sticker price of $20 million. In time I came to think this price was seductively reasonable. After passing the mirrored walls of the galley, one entered the first cabin; here four individual and fully articulated seats awaited Hank and his blessed. In the second cabin another four seats around a conference table, this evening covered with a fine linen tablecloth and set for dinner. In the next cabin a credenza on one side and a double bed on the other. Behind this cabin a lavatory. In the front of the aircraft another lavatory for those whose name was not Hank Greenberg.

A great trip. A magnificent trip. A life-changing trip. Hank, Howie, and I in three of the four overstuffed seats in front, rotated so that we faced each other. An extremely attractive young woman served drinks: "What brand of vodka would you prefer?" After our second drink she offered a choice of three entrées. I ordered whatever Hank and Howie didn't take. I wanted to make certain they could have seconds, shouldn't have worried. Once we were comfortably ensconced around the table expansive platters of food appeared, enough to provide sustenance to an African village.

At forty thousand feet, while chasing the sunset, with a bottle of red more empty than full, I heard Hank speak for the first time about things other than AIG business. He talked about the country and how screwed up things were. Everybody else worried about Japan overtaking the United States; Hank said China was a sleeping bear, not Russia or Japan. Hank should know. Other than our ambassador to China, he had spent more time there than any other US businessman or politico.

By the last pour of wine Hank was reminiscing about his youth. As a kid he'd hated the name Maurice Greenberg and stole the name Hank from a famous ball player, "Hammerin'" Hank Greenberg. By the age of eighteen Hank was in the army killing Krauts while they were trying to kill him. Told us it was what made him what he was. Said that liberating Dachau, stepping over women and kids begging for a scrap of food, hardened him up for kicking ass in business.

When we landed Howie and I sped off to the Century Plaza in a limo; I think Hank spent the night in the plane. That night I lay in bed and replayed the flight and pondered the airplane. I used material goals as motivators. That was how I got my Ferrari and the brick monument to my ego. This night I coveted a G-IV. That's not quite right; I wanted what went with the G-IV. The absolute ability to travel in comfort and efficiency, that's what I wanted. No connecting through Atlanta or Dallas praying that the inattentive mother with two squirming kids didn't have the seat next to me.

Howie and I spent two intense days in our LA attorneys' office negotiating a merger deal. We finished up early the afternoon of the third day, and Howie had the limo driver cruise through Bel Air. Made me recalibrate my opinion of the homes in Potomac. After the tour we swung past LAX and Howie jumped on a shuttle to San Francisco and I darted back to the Century Plaza to have drinks with a potential client. Then I soloed over to the Polo Lounge, where I enjoyed a bold red and an impressive braised lamb while reflecting on my first trip to LA years before, driving around in a Budget rental car. The next morning limo'ed back to the Burbank FBO for a flight home in Hank's G-IV.

Let me tell you about an FBO. It is one of those codes for people in the know—something like S&C, the Skull & Crossbones of Yale. FBO stands for Fixed Base Operator, this being a small but well-appointed terminal at selected airports. The FBO serves only private jets. No cab lines, no crying babies, no ticket lines, no canceled flights. Only pilots, flight attendants, and aircraft poised at the ready.

On the flight back Hank spent two or three hours with a fellow I had never seen before. A lot of the talk concerning aircraft leasing. I sat dutifully in the back so not to infringe. An hour before descending into Teterboro this fellow told me that Hank wanted to speak with me. It was a good conversation. It was a scary conversation. After fifteen seconds of pleasantries Hank commented that I had hit my numbers. Didn't say "great job," didn't say "good job," just said that he saw that I hit my numbers. Told me he would expect a $20 million increase the next year. Asked if I could do it. Given that I was in the womb of corporate opulence, sipping a fine wine, negative thoughts didn't seem appropriate. Appropriateness probably had nothing to do with it, I was just a wimp. But Hank didn't stop with the earnings target. He told me that AIG had been kicking ass in Asia but was spinning its wheels in England and Spain. Wanted me to take responsibility for developing the health-care portion of AIG's business in those two countries. Wanted me to have a profitable operation of health-care business in both countries within two years. After the challenges, he served up the carrots. He offered me stock options. He'd grant me 100,000 options if I hit my annual earnings target and another 250,000 options if I got things cooking in Europe.

After we landed in Teterboro I pushed a cab driver to break his record to La Guardia; needed to hop a shuttle down to Washington. Like a cold bucket of water on my face, I sat in the US Air shuttle lounge with a few hundred people, staring at monitors as flights were delayed because of thunderstorms. Took me five hours from LA to New York, took another five hours from New York to Washington.

Sitting in the terminal I had time to dissect and evaluate both my life and my conversation with Hank. From the sale of my company I had a substantial block of AIG stock. It was the kids' college money and retirement money for Alice and me, with enough left to take care of us for the next twenty years or so if I decided to throw away my briefcase and become a professional badminton player. By hitting my bonus the previous year I got an extra million dollars after-tax. Remnants of it were resting in our savings account until we settled on the house Pat was building. But I had plenty of net worth, even after the mega-house purchase, enough not to worry. Still, I kept thinking. I'd purchased the house. I'd never actually dreamed I could own a mini-estate. Why not the plane? Why not a G-IV for Alice and me? With the stock options Hank was offering, in three or four years I could cash them in for more than the price of a G-IV. Sitting in the US Air terminal with a few hundred of the unclean distorted my logic. I needed a G-IV, a G-IV was in my crosshairs.

One of the problems with business is that while you're struggling mightily to entice new business in the front door, the competition lures your hard-won customers out the back door. If I was going to burn brain cells on developing Europe for AIG, I needed to station sentries to protect our domestic business. I spent the first month of the new year beefing up our resources on the homefront. HPA was such a critical client—close to a million dollars a month in profits—that I didn't delegate management responsibility, I kept it; requiring my span of oversight to arch from California to Europe. A lot of frequent flyer miles.

In developing England and Spain, I decided to divide and conquer. Initially I would only go after one. Since my Spanish was limited to *no comprendo*, I figured it best to target my British cousins first. With only two years to earn my stock options by generating meaningful business in Europe, scooping revenue minnows in Great Britain wouldn't do. I needed to harpoon a whale.

I spent over a month in England learning the principles of their health-care system. It was different, real different from the United States. No matter how a Brit might try to explain it, their health care was socialized medicine. If a Brit got sick, they went to a government-paid doctor. Everybody got care; that was the good news. The problem was that some of the waiting lines for care were long. By the time some poor sick Limeys got to the front of the line they were dead. It was Britain's way of rationing health care without ever using the term rationing.

In time my whale broached. It was BUPA, British United Provident Association, based in London. BUPA was the only private health insurance company operating in the UK. It served the upper crust. People with a grand salary, or a title, could purchase private health insurance and move to the front of the socialized medicine line. A contract with BUPA could be both the foundation for building a British-based health-care business and my down payment on a G-IV.

Quickly I came to like the British. They were polite, educated, and worldly. The latter the result of their owning half the world a hundred years before. Owning being a euphemism for occupying. While the average Brit was a delight, quick witted and uncomplaining with an affinity toward Yanks, at the higher levels of management working with them was frustrating for anyone who had spent a few years in the quick-draw Manhattan corporate world of "What's the deal," "Screw you," and "I'll wire the money."

My first meeting with the BUPA president and his senior staff consisted of fifteen minutes of productivity jammed into three hours. One hour was consumed with pleasantries, and the second two hours with a leisurely corporate lunch served on a white tablecloth, with sterling silver and fine china. Only a few oblique references to business, and these were in the stratosphere: "So, what do you Americans think of Mitterrand's socialist pump-priming programs?" I wanted to counter by asking whether they thought Tom Landry and the Dallas Cowboys were being left behind by the new West Coast offense. But I didn't; I politely persisted. The upside of the slow pace was that over several months I got to know England and came not only to like its people, but to admire them. After a few unproductive meetings, there was some movement. I felt I could close them.

As BUPA's management began to thaw, more and more trips to London. My standard conveyance became the Concorde. Of course the Brits never said "the Concorde," they left out the "the." So my trips were on Concorde, five scheduled flights a week out of JFK and three out of Dulles. If London beckoned me on a day that there were no flights from Dulles, I would take a helicopter up to JFK.

I have to hand it to British Airways; the entire supersonic experience was a level above superb. Caviars and fine wines in the passenger lounge were a perfect prelude to the journey. While the aircraft itself was rather confining—small seats and windows no more than seven inches wide—the service was orchestrated to perfection. Between cocktails, hors d'oeuvres, three courses, and a final curtain call of robust cognacs and an expansive cheese selection, the three-hour flight across the Atlantic quickly disappeared into my stomach.

PATRICK, 1859: Depending on the winds the Captain bragged the journey would be a quick four to six weeks. It was eight weeks before we saw America. 'Course the *Hannah* was stocked only with enough stale and rotting food for six weeks. The hunger the last two weeks didn't matter, it was an old acquaintance to all of us.

Two things told you that you were moving fast. One was a digital readout in the front of the cabin. For the better part of the flight it consisted of four digits with no decimal point. Twelve hundred miles an hour was the cruising speed. The second confirmation of almost incomprehensible speed was the airframe. If you walked forward to the front galley, stopped by the cabin entry door, and placed your hand near the metal frame, it was too hot to touch: serious air friction at the front of the plane.

Of course there was another indisputable indicator that one was flying fast. On occasion you arrived before you took off. The scheduled departure time out of London's Heathrow was 11:00 a.m. A short three and a half hours later the graceful Concorde landed in Dulles at 10:00 a.m., an hour before it had taken off. I could have a leisurely Saturday morning breakfast at the Ritz, with extra heavy cream on my blueberries, and be on my awning-covered patio in Potomac the same day, grilling burgers for the kids' lunch.

For my first few London excursions the Four Seasons was my home away from home. The hotel was right on Hyde Park. It was my choice because it was familiar—familiar in that I had been staying at a lot of Four Seasons in the United States. In fact, I considered the Four Seasons bar in Manhattan to be my personal rec room. My business associates in London recommended the Ritz. I tried it and unemotionally abandoned the Four Seasons . . . well, Jane Wyman did divorce Ronald Reagan.

Even though the Ritz was seventy-five years old—the same as Bankers Life—everything was fresh and polished to a sheen. The public rooms were magnificent. The dining room looked as if it would be appropriate for a coronation, while the hallway from the reception area down the center of the hotel reflected—okay, give me this one—the opulence of the Hall of Mirrors in Versailles. But what was really special were the people and the location. Not to take anything away from Nigel, the concierge at the Four Seasons, but observing the staff at the Ritz was like watching a ballet. Everything was efficient, precise, and beautiful. And the Ritz's location was superb. Walk out the front, turn right down Piccadilly, up through the Burlington Arcade, and a quick turn onto Bond Street. Drop into Beale & Inman for a Brioni suit; they had my measurements on file. Perhaps a couple of scarves for Alice at Hermes, then dash into Asprey for a new set of cuff links.

For a great lunch I could just walk out of the Ritz, take a quick right and then a quick left, and I was at Wilton's, the place to go for Dover sole. Took me a while to catch on; the maître d' had to explain it to me. If you walked in at one in the afternoon they greeted you with a "Good morning." If you arrived at two in the afternoon you received exactly the same greeting. I finally asked, "Why 'Good morning' in the afternoon?" The response was "Sir, it is not afternoon until you enjoy lunch at Wilton's."

After lunch at Wilton's, I could dart across the street and visit Chester, Chester being my salesperson at Turnbull and Asser. There I would consider their newest selections of fabrics—"We particularly like the Egyptian cotton blues"—and perhaps order a few custom-made shirts. Of course they had my measurements in their records . . . as well as Winston Churchill's.

The house that Pat was building for my family was in the enclave of Round Hill. A dozen or so homes, all on well-attended grounds, each owned by nouveau riche. Alice and I would be the nouveau-nouveau riche. Having committed to the house, I was like the drunk at the bar, ordering one more round for everyone before closing. "Pat, don't you agree a tennis court would be perfect over here, and is there any way we could have a pool house, with a kitchen and bath, connected by a trellis to the loggia on the back of the main house?" No going back; I had to make those numbers for Hank.

It was Ben Franklin who gave me a heads-up as to the problem with AIG. Yes, I'm referring to the Mr. Franklin who did the thing with the kite. Ben made the observation, I believe in one of his annual *Poor Richard's Almanack*s, that the eighth wonder of the world is the power of compounding—compounding being the notion that while a number that increases by a fixed percentage each year becomes a larger number each year, the incremental growth is not linear; it moves toward exponential.

An example, by your leave. If I ask you to save a penny today and two cents the next day and four cents the next day and eight cents the following day, and keep doubling this rate of growth for thirty days, do you think you could have the financial ability to accomplish this? The vast majority of people answer with a quick yes. But if you do the math you'll find that by the thirty-first day, you'll need to have saved over $10 million.

When AIG was a $5 billion revenue company, a 15 percent growth required us to pull a three-quarter-billion-dollar-sized rabbit out of a hat for the year. At $10 billion, we needed a one-and-a-half-billion-sized rabbit, with really big ears. Could we grow at a 15 percent rate for the next ten years? If you extrapolated, the answer was a resounding no. Soon some president of an AIG subsidiary might glue really big ears onto some skunks and call them rabbits to hit his numbers for Hank.

It was right after I started to worry about AIG's long-term growth that I saw "The Movie." Probably several tens of thousands of words of dialogue. One line from the script seared my brain. The movie was *Wall Street*. Great movie if you're a guy: tough, macho business talk, a couple of great-looking women, a motorcycle, limos, a beach house, and the requisite corporate jet with a sexy attendant. The plotline was pretty simple. A young Manhattan stockbroker stalks a big account—this big account being in the form of the exceedingly well-coiffed Gordon Gekko, played by Michael Douglas. He is your basic Wall Street predator who buys a company for $100 million, quickly sells off half the assets for $50 million, coldly breaks the union, robs the retirement fund, then liquidates the squeezed-to-the-bone, efficient company for a $50 million dollar gain. Greed is everything for Gordon. As the plot thickens, to curry Gordon's favor the young broker helps him make a run at purchasing a second-tier airline that employs the broker's father as a unionized mechanic. After a lot of plot development and conflict, the father chastises his son for his lifestyle. The son shoots back that his father is just jealous because he hadn't made any big Wall Street money. The father's response was the line that branded my mind: "I don't measure a man by the size of his wallet." This declaration, combined with a line from a British play I would see the following year, changed my life.

The powers to be at AIG gave me another assignment. They asked me to go to a G7 conference. When I first heard G7, I wasn't sure what part I could play—perhaps carrying a tray of hors d'oeuvres to the heads of state. It turns out that AIG had been wining and dining the British government to curry favor and a favorable nod. AIG had an absolute lock on China, but they were was thinking ahead. In 1997 the Red Chinese were going to execute their sovereign right to direct traffic in Hong Kong, this metropolis having been a British-leased property for the past hundred years or so. Hank was trying to establish AIG handholds in Hong Kong with the Brits before the flag of the Red Star was raised over the Peninsula Hotel. My assignment was to intersect with Francis Pym, who was Margaret Thatcher's Secretary for Foreign and Commonwealth Affairs, so that I could hand-deliver a letter to him. When I asked why hand-deliver versus hitting up the AIG petty cash to purchase a few stamps, I was told it was the gesture that counted, not the letter.

Hank likely asked me to play postman because Washington, DC, is only a hundred miles or so from Williamsburg, Virginia, the site of the scheduled G7 conference. Plus, I had been mingling for months with the senior BUPA staff in England, so Hank figured I probably knew my way around the niceties of the British gentry. I wouldn't slap Pym on the back and laughingly ask him what he did for fun every Fourth of July.

Williamsburg, described in the most cynical manner, is like Disneyland; it looks great, but it's not real. Original Williamsburg was the kettle in which much of the stew of American democracy simmered. The town fell into disrepair during the 1800s. The Rockefellers showed up in the early 1900s, and with immense energy and even more money rebuilt it to appear as it did in the 1700s. The town is really quite charming, if you're into colonial houses with their handmade bricks, Flemish bond, and twelve-piece crown moldings, all surrounded by gardens and more gardens.

Pym was a very pleasant chap. Our conversation journeyed awkwardly through his World War II service and his days at Cambridge. For many senior British businessmen and bureaucrats, good morning, good afternoon, good evening, I attended Oxford, I attended Cambridge, are all considered to be greetings. The British should follow the lead of the military, display rank. Mint some gold Os and some gold Cs. If one attended Oxford, one could merely attach a gold O to each shoulder of one's suit. Likewise a gold C for Cambridge. It would avoid the forced funneling of a conversation toward confirming which school one attended. Must say, I never felt obligated to mention my days at the University of Iowa . . . Go Hawkeyes!

The best part of my colonial excursion was an introduction to Margaret Thatcher. She had command presence; when she walked into a room everybody else became shorter. It was obvious why our cowboy president and she were pen pals. The other good news is that I got swept up in the official visit. The American government, plus Commonwealth of Virginia officials, were out to impress the Germans, Italians, Japanese, French, and a few also-ran countries. One of the more impressive events was a formal candlelight dinner at the mansion that once housed the first governor of the Virginia Colony. American history was put into perspective when my seatmate, a German minister, casually commented that he likely owned a pair of shoes that were older than the governor's house.

One subject grated our Virginia hosts. For all who would listen, and even if you didn't want to, Virginia State officials lectured that the first settlers in the United States weren't the heralded travelers who arrived on the *Mayflower* and established Plymouth Colony. They wanted everyone to know that Virginia was the site of the first colony, and that the history books lied and Massachusetts was guilty of false advertising. Under the guise of a historical outing, but more like busing the jury to view evidence, everyone in attendance was shuffled off to Jamestown, about ten or fifteen miles from Williamsburg. Our little caravan of limos and buses stopped at a few other sites of pre-Plymouth settlers as well. A few of these sites were being excavated, with much excitement when half a button or a part of a musket was sifted from a large mound of earth.

At the original site of Jamestown, a museum housed artifacts that had been recently unearthed. I had to burn close to an hour while some overly enthusiastic woman with a PhD in digging in the dirt excitedly told of their most recent discoveries. A couple of her finds got my attention, one being a grouping of brass buttons, each the size of half a dollar; they would have shamed the buttons on my Brioni blazers. Also a hand-carved ivory comb with the name "Emilie" along one side caused me to pause. I couldn't imagine having the time to carve twenty or more individual teeth in a piece of ivory. These settlers had time on their hands in the evenings; they weren't busy billing clients so they could hit their earnings targets.

> **EMILIE, 1627:** In the darkness of evening, a commotion. Father up, people yelling. Father from the cottage goes, Nathan and I peer through the window, much movement, much running, no direction. Then Father back. Events told quickly, Jamestown attacked by four boats of Indian warriors, muskets fire from the stockade and they retreat, no more danger. Slowly but often, news from other villages. Massacres. Women, children killed, but not quickly without pain. Homes burnt, crops burnt, supplies burnt. Our lives ashes.

My sister called Alice while I was in Williamsburg. I think she felt more comfortable talking to Alice than to me about my mother; told Alice that when she'd last visited Des Moines, Mom didn't look well at all. Sis spoke to my father, who said Mom was fine, but my sister had her doubts. She asked if I could visit with Mom and Dad, and since I owned a health-care company, could I have Mom checked out. At the time I wasn't sure what was expected of me. My health-care experience was along the lines of raising $100 million in convertible debt for an HMO, not assisting some internist in interpreting a blood workup.

We were scheduled to visit my parents for Thanksgiving. Unfortunately the Brits don't celebrate Thanksgiving. I had finally had the immovable object, the BUPA management team, rolling, and I didn't want to risk losing momentum by pausing. I needed to keep my shoulder to the wheel. I twisted myself into an ugly pretzel that Thanksgiving. While holding my breath I told Alice that I was going to miss Thanksgiving, but if she would take the kids out to Des Moines, I would join them a couple of days later. She smiled, most likely not a genuine smile, and said she understood.

My plan was to fly from London to Chicago, and then take a puddle jumper down to Des Moines and be with the family for a day or so. I had anticipated taking a Friday morning flight out, but ended up staying in London for the day. On Friday evening the BUPA senior staff wished me a cheerful weekend as they drove off in their Bentleys and Jaguars, leaving me five thousand miles away from my expectant family. I had promised Alice that I would pull in to Des Moines on Saturday evening and we could have dinner with the family, and I would be with her and the kids on the flight home on Sunday. Later that Friday evening I sat at the Ritz bar and pondered the wart-covered reality that made my promise to her no more than a wishful fantasy: I was obligated to be in California on Monday morning for an HPA Board Meeting. I couldn't go from London to Des Moines, back to Washington, then to LA, so I just got a direct flight from London into LA. On Saturday night I was cruising forty thousand feet above Des Moines and my loving family, with three hours to go before I would reach LA.

Choosing between a right and wrong option usually lends itself to the simple application of logic and ethics. It is the wrong and wrong options that tear you apart. It is wrong to miss a family gathering; it is wrong not to meet your commitments to a client. How do you choose?

I stopped in Des Moines for half a day on my way back from California for a dinner with the folks. The kids and Alice were already nested in our freshly minted home in Round Hill. I studied my parents at the dining room table. They were old; their shoulders were rounded, their hair was grayer, they moved slower. Even their eating was slower. On my flight home that night I promised myself that I would visit Mom and Dad more often.

I felt worse than bad about missing Thanksgiving. At first I rationalized: I wasn't in Vegas losing the family savings at the craps table, I was babysitting a mega-business prospect. It didn't work, though; I'd missed Thanksgiving, the High Mass and Gold Standard of family holidays. I had shortchanged my family. I was an unworthy member of the class of husbands and fathers. So I did what most guys do, I tried to buy off my guilt. I planned a family trip dripping with extravagance. Clearly, the more I spent, the fainter any remembrance of my transgression.

Ferrari introduced a new model, a Ferrari Testarossa. Think spaceship. A big twelve-cylinder engine in the back, lower than low to the ground, and multi-finned gills that flowed from the front wheel-well back through the door and into the back fender. Every car magazine had one on their cover. Even *People* magazine and *Popular Science* showcased the car. Probably the most exotic auto ever produced. A serious waiting list. My friendly Ferrari dealer informed me it would be a minimum of two, more likely three, years before I could purchase one. The waiting list was long, and the list price was high, just a few pennies under $90,000. However, one could be purchased. I bought a red Testarossa in Texas (sounds like a fragment of a limerick) by overpaying $120,000 to a speculator: instant gratification. In college my mantra had been, "What, me worry?" My new mantra was, "What, me wait?"

MORDECAI'S UNCLE, 1911: Each day you made money—maybe just pennies—but you wanted to spend it, because you could not walk down the street without seeing something you wanted, something new to eat, new to wear. In a shop window, on a wall, on a leaf of the *New York Herald* blowing jerkily downstreet, inducements uppermost; and it made it so hard to chink those few pennies back and put them under the brick (from which we both stole, I'm sorry, sorry when temptation hurt too much, for an apple, or an orange, or God help us, one stick of chocolate. But we put it back, and put the blows and outcries behind us, and went short to make up).

If someone exercises every day they will develop a robust cardiovascular system. If they then become sedentary, their heart will, in time, have less tolerance for physical stress. Money, or the lack of it, has similar effects on the human. Without excess money one goes through life experiencing the frustrations that most encounter on a day-to-day basis: waiting in a long line to pick up license plates, standing in rain while the parking attendant tries to find the keys he misplaced, being told by the dry cleaner that your suit is not ready as promised. We learn to simply accept the tedium and annoyances that punctuate life. Our frustration tolerance is well tuned. Money reduces the frustration factors. Someone else goes to pick up the car tags. Our limo is out in front of the office building; no need to wait in line in the parking lot. Our closet is resplendent with suits, one less is not noticed. When something does surface to frustrate individuals with significant net worth, their lack of frustration fitness shows. They can't cope with inefficiency or delay.

After my Santa Barbara meltdown I tried to remember my blessings and not allow my emotions to be taken hostage by some random occurrence. But one spring afternoon at National Airport I abdicated the control of my anger. I needed to be in Boston for a 3:00 p.m. meeting. As usual I darted out of my office later than intended for a scheduled noon departure on Northwest. A little extra gas and I was pulling into National; entered the line for airport short-term parking, and, one by one, drivers inched to the ticket dispensing machine, pulled a ticket, watched the gate rise, and proceeded. Then my turn. I pushed the large red button, no ticket. Twenty feet away I spotted a parking attendant in a booth; a quick honk stole her attention. At a pace slower than the plodding of a death march, she approached the ticket machine and rendered her pronouncement: "It's out of tickets."

"No problem. Can you just hand me one from the booth?" I asked.

"No, I need my supervisor's permission." With the speed of a receding tide, she sidled back to her booth. There she picked up the phone. Something was said. I waited. It was hot in the car. There was no retreat; cars were lined up twenty deep behind me, steel guard-rails on either side. Ten minutes to noon. Not much time.

I waited another minute and walked up to the booth. I smiled and asked, "How are we coming?" In a monotone she responded, "My supervisor is coming."

"Does the supervisor have the tickets?" I asked.

"No, I do, but he should be here."

Back to my car. Visions of the important Blue Cross executive sitting in a conference room wondering where I am. Perhaps the plane would be late departing. Several of the cars at the end of the line surrendered. There were only a half dozen or so behind me. Again I asked the attendant for relief. No response, no concern. She was reading a novel. Another five minutes. I started to gnaw on the steering wheel. Then, with no supervisor in sight, the attendant strolled to the dispenser. She handed me a ticket.

Incredulously I asked, "Why couldn't you have done this twenty-five minutes ago?"

She answered, "You're holding up the line."

I responded with a rich and full inventory of expletives such as not heard since the Nixon tapes were edited.

I missed the flight. I was an hour late to the meeting and aged at least two years on the flight up to Boston while contemplating the cursing and table-pounding Blue Cross executives. However, I

was the one who'd had the tantrum. I'd treated the parking attendant with less compassion than dictated by the Holy Scriptures.
While some of my Manhattan friends would criticize me for not
having pistol-whipped her on the spot, I did verbally mug her. By
the time I was on the flight home that night, after a successful
meeting in Boston, guilt settled heavily on my shoulders. Here I
was, an executive with a robust salary, an impressive home, an
exotic car, expensive suits, and a wonderful family, screaming at a
young woman who made less in a day than I probably made in an
hour. By the time my flight screeched onto the runway at National
Airport I had myself convinced she was likely working two jobs to
support her children and sick husband, only pausing to teach Bible
school after singing in the choir.

I had been a bully. In a letter he composed to a friend, Robert
E. Lee made an eloquent statement as to what distinguishes a bully
from a gentleman. I stumbled upon it while helping Jennifer with
an American history project.

*The forbearing use of power does not only form a touchstone, but the
manner in which an individual enjoys certain advantages over others is
a test of a true gentleman.*

*The power which the strong have over the weak, the employer over
the employed, the educated over the unlettered, the experienced over
the confiding, even the clever over the silly—the forbearing or inoffen-
sive use of this power or authority, or a total abstinence from it when
the case admits it, will show the gentleman in plain light.*

*The gentleman does not needlessly and unnecessarily remind an
offender of a wrong he may have committed against him. He cannot
only forgive, he can forget; and he strives for that nobleness of self and
mildness of character which impart sufficient strength to let the past be
but the past.*

The much-anticipated family trip, the trip of my repentance,
redemption, and restitution for the missed Thanksgiving, was an

Oscar winner in the category of conspicuous excess. A remarkable trip—well, terrific for 80 percent of the family. Andrew, David, Jennifer, Alice, and me in the Air France Concorde lounge. Then off to Paris. Three days of perfect weather and all the stupid tourist things that are great: "Say hello to the Mona Lisa, kids." A short flight into Heathrow, then two cabs to the Ritz: "Victor, may I introduce my children?" The Tower of London, Dover sole, Westminster Abbey, Dover sole, Big Ben, Dover sole, and the changing of the guard. From London a train to Cheltenham, then to Liverpool. In life it was larger than suggested by the brochures. The pier was overwhelmed by the QE2, shorthand for the ocean liner *Queen Elizabeth II*. Across the gangplank, a quick photo with the captain, a QE2-emblazoned life ring on the wall behind, then to our staterooms, first-class staterooms.

> **EMILIE, 1628:** Then down to our quarters, one deck below. The stink was worse than of all the barnyard animals in the hottest month of the hottest summer. No person could suffer this smell.

The first day of our crossing, crossing being the expression confirming that one was shredding a large bundle of disposable income for transportation, was full of enthusiastic discovery: libraries, casinos, spas, pools, piano bars, and fine dining. The last hour of the crossing was the most memorable: sailing past the Statue of Liberty, around the tip of Manhattan ("Kids, there's the AIG building"), then pirouetting in the Hudson River and snuggling against a West Side pier.

The four days between the first day and the last hour were boring, punctuated with naps and eating. Two days into the crossing I would have written a big check to be picked up mid-Atlantic and whisked to a traffic jam with honking horns. In my cosmos of contentment, the perfect QE2 cruise would be to board in Baltimore mid-afternoon, cruise north, enjoy an elaborate and formal dinner, sail in past the Statue of Liberty, disembark, and spend the night at the Four Seasons in Manhattan.

The business gods rewarded me for taking my family to Europe and back; the BUPA contract was signed within a week of disembarking in New York. It would be a good year for me and my company. Quickly Concorded back to London for a signing celebration dinner with a six-pack of BUPA's management team. Great sea bass at the Park Lane followed by ports, Cuban cigars, and male bonding. It was closer to dawn than dusk by the time I was horizontal at the Ritz. Was able to sleep until late morning before catching a limo to Heathrow and shuffling onto Concorde. For most of the flight home I relived the effort that I'd put forth in bringing BUPA's pen to the agreement. The fact that it was a struggle made the flight home a savoring event. Tried not to think of Spain; before long I would need to get my derriere into Madrid and start rummaging through their health-care system. Deplaned at Dulles. Alice was at the gate to meet me. She never came to the airport to meet me. My mother was dead. She died of a heart attack.

The funeral was rushed and unexpected. I should have spoken, but I didn't. Some minister spoke. He didn't know my mother. He kept using phrases like, "I'm sure if I had known her . . ." If it weren't for Alice, nothing would have been done correctly. My father was in a daze. My sister was totally distraught. I was embarrassed and just didn't know what to do. I couldn't wait to get out of Des Moines. If I wasn't in Des Moines I wouldn't have to think about Mom being dead. That's not right. I didn't want to think of all the times I didn't call or visit.

JOHN, 1941: It took about a year from when I saw the doctor's car till Ma passed. She died, but she really didn't die.

She got bedrid and slept more and more each day till one morning she just didn't wake up. Sort of like a drop of water in the sunlight. You look at it and you see it, but it just keeps getting smaller and smaller and then it's not there no more. Pa made a box for Ma out of sidings from the old chicken coop. Billy and me dug the grave, took most of a day. Got a piece of oak board and rounded one edge for a marker. Used a red-hot spike to burn in her name and dates. Tried to get the letters and numbers real straight and perfect.

As I began my second year of my Herculean effort to achieve Hank's challenge, a mob of business priorities and problems each fought to be my number one concern. Is HPA still on track? Is the just-signed BUPA contract being implemented effectively? Who are the key players in the Spanish health-care industry? By the way, do you know a competent interpreter? Why are our HMO membership numbers down? Should we use Hutton or Bear for our debt offering? Why did my corporate counsel resign with only two weeks' notice? Where did all our surplus working capital disappear to?

Time became by far my most critical resource. There just wasn't enough of it. Since the rotation of the earth wasn't going to slow, I needed to squeeze more out of twenty-four hours. I built myself a helipad on the side of our property in Round Hill; spent a little extra money and made it out of cobblestone to match our sweeping cobblestone driveway. Went a little crazy and used a darker cobblestone to form an "H" in the center, denoting a helipad from the air. With the helipad in place I could be elevated directly from my side lawn and then an unwavering straight line to the Wall Street heliport; I was in AIG offices two hours after I kissed Alice good-bye. I chopped more than two hours from the drive to National Airport, waiting for the shuttle, jetting to La Guardia, and limo'ing into the city. I gave myself an extra two hours. I put twenty-six hours in the day.

It was likely around my twentieth trip to London that my horns started to protrude. Staff were implementing the deal with BUPA and I wanted to confirm all was tranquil with my new big British client. Alice was with me and the concierge at the Ritz got us tickets to a play that he confidently reported was quite fabulous. Only in Great Britain can a grown man say "quite fabulous" without grinning.

The Ritz Rolls-Royce dropped Alice and me off at a West End restaurant for a pre-theater dinner. Probably Dover sole. By the time I finished a week or two in London I'd eaten enough Dover sole to have the fish added to the endangered species list. After dinner, a short walk to the theater. As always, Michael, the head concierge at the Ritz, had us in one of the first rows, center. The play was *Little Shop of Horrors*. A musical comedy, a life-changing comedy.

In *Little Shop*, a nerdy guy, Seymour, worked at a flower shop, nurturing an exotic plant never before seen—a bizarre plant, with both mystical powers and primeval needs. The powers being that it could speak and had the ability to grant any wish. Its primeval need being human blood for its nourishment. Each day, in a deep and foreboding voice, the plant would demand, "Feed me." With every serving of human blood the plant grew, and as it grew it required more and more blood.

At first Seymour could satisfy the plant with a pinprick on his finger. For these meager blood offerings his wish was granted. Being a guy, Seymour's wish entailed something tall and blonde with large mammary glands and taut Ligaments of Cooper.

The plant kept growing, kept demanding more blood, kept repeating, "Feed me." Not wanting to risk losing the blonde, Seymour fed the plant more and more of his blood. Finally, as the plant's size increased by several magnitudes, Seymour was forced to sacrifice whole humans to satisfy the plant's daily need for blood.

The music was great, the acting was polished . . . but the play left me scared. Clearly AIG was the plant and I was Seymour. Every year AIG's earnings had to be compounded at the same high, hero-ically high, rate. To maintain the same rate of growth we needed more and more earnings, earnings derived from human blood and human sacrifice. Business travel, missed birthdays, missed piano recitals, missed softball games, each of these only being a drop in the pond, but the ripples combining to distort the picture of the happy family. Over the next several days I thought long and hard about the play. I rethought *Wall Street*: "Don't measure a man's worth by the size of his wallet." I thought about "Feed me." Could it be? Had I sold my soul to the devil for the promise of cars, houses, and planes?

For the first few days after *Little Shop of Horrors* I tried to convince myself everything was okay. Great wife, three healthy kids. I suppose that alcoholics convince themselves that they don't have a problem. Slowly my thoughts turned from questions and doubts to answers and certitude. I was risking the family to impress Hank and to win Seymour's blonde—the stock options. Why was I compromising my family to have a higher net worth? Took me a while to understand. It was a three-letter word. It started with an "e," ended with an "o," and had a "g" in the mid-dle. But surrender was not easy. I'm a competitive guy. While I was wealthier than 95 percent of the population, why not more than 99 percent? I knew the answer. I just didn't want to accept it. I kept coming up with reasons as to why I was on the corporate jet, being whisked off to the next critical business meeting.

It was after seeing *Little Shop of Horrors* that Alice crushed me with the weight of my mammoth ego. During dinner at Old Angler's, a leisurely dinner being my cover for drinking an entire bottle of a superb red, I was replaying yet again for Alice my defense: I worked hard for the family, I struggled mightily to give them everything they wanted. Then a simple question: Alice asked where might the tennis rackets and tennis balls be? Since years ago I had spent over $75,000 to have Pat build a tennis court on our Round Hill property, why no rackets and tennis balls that would allow the family to play? Her observation leaving no escape, the tennis court was a broad brushstroke on my carefully painted mural of success, it was not for family enjoyment . . . no one in our family played tennis.

A few weeks after *Little Shop of Horrors* shook my resolve, and a few days after Alice performed her egoectomy on me, I was in LA, with a charter flight scheduled to transport me, *Star Trek*-style, back home. Before departing LA, I changed my destination, instructed the pilots to divert to Des Moines. I decided at forty-plus years of age it wasn't too late to seek fatherly advice. Gave my father a ring and told him I would be stopping by. Pulled into the Des Moines FBO around noon and stole a cab to Dad's house. We sat in the living room and talked. Dad asked about the kids. I was surprised that he knew so much about each one. While we spoke I grabbed a couple of quick glances at the outdated TV in the corner of our living room. The one Mom got so many years before so she could flirt with Dino in color.

Then the reason for my visit; I told Dad that I had a tough decision to make. Told him that I was torn between giving up my job to spend more time with the family or pressing on to hit a grand slam home run. Being an actuary, with the need to work with unambiguous data and information, he asked if a grand slam home run was my way of saying that I wanted to make more money. I said yes. Then Dad asked a question that shocked me because of its directness and its clarity: "What is your net worth?" If I had known he was going to ask, I would have considered how to respond in a manner that made the figure diminutive, hidden under a blanket of obscurities. But because the question was direct and precise, I gave a direct and precise answer. It shocked me when I said the number.

Dad sat silently; then he recalled our family vacation in '55; that summer the family loaded up our Chevrolet Bel Air and drove to California for an actuarial seminar Dad was attending. After a couple of days in LA, Dad and Mom took my sister and me to the just-opened Disneyland. We were the first kids in Des Moines to go there. Dad asked if I remembered that on the trip we would stop along the road and look at various tourist attractions, asked if I remembered stopping to see the World's Largest Ball of Twine that somebody proudly displayed in front of their store. I told him that I did. He paused for a few moments; then he told me that struggling to accumulate more money than was required for family happiness had no more merit than working mightily to wrap the biggest ball of twine. Neither effort was worth jeopardizing family tranquility.

On the way back to the FBO I called the pilot. Told him we would be going to Teterboro, not Washington. I wanted to meet with Hank. Next a call to sweet Alice, told her I wouldn't be home as planned, but I would for certain be only a day tardy. As always she was understanding, but quickly added that regardless of any happening, I had to be home the next evening; it was my birthday and she and the kids had a life-changing present for me . . . life-changing? A two-hour flight, a limo to the lower tip of Manhattan, and I was checking into the Vista Hotel at the World Trade Center. After responding to a dozen or so business faxes that greeted me at the reception desk, and after another call to Alice, I walked over to the North Tower and took the express elevator up 106 floors to Windows on the World. Slipped the maître d' a twenty-dollar bill so I could steal a table by the window. Had to perch myself at the bar for close to an hour waiting for a table to clear. With a dry Smirnoff martini and a promiscuous bowl of peanuts, I watched the shadow of the Statue of Liberty begin to stretch to the east as the sun set. I stared past Brooklyn toward Europe; the sky was turning from gray to black. Thought of my trips to England. I wondered if there would be any more.

By the end of my second martini a table opened next to my recently purchased window, a window with a view up Manhattan toward Long Island. Over a thousand feet below, a loose weave of dotted lights extended north and disappeared on the horizon. In the middle a black rectangle, Central Park, the bucolic preserve for joggers and muggers. Spent close to two hours with an overpriced Chardonnay, a pedestrian sea bass, and much contemplation. It had been fourteen years since the family had squeezed into our tired Ford Maverick and headed toward Washington, towing a U-Haul trailer full of hopes and fears. It had been a great fourteen years. We'd had a goal, and both Alice and I put our shoulders to the wheel to achieve the goal. We built a successful company and earned financial security for ourselves. And we did this while raising three clean-cut kids who always said "please" and "thank you."

But there was a problem. The problem was my dinner companion that evening. Somehow during the last few years I had silently shifted my focus from obtaining "the" objective to obtaining the "next" objective. I had unwittingly conspired with the devil to build myself an endless wheel, just like a hamster in a cage; and I had come to believe that my Gucci jogging shoes and Ferragamo sweats somehow made running on it twelve hours a day an exciting and rewarding life.

NANANAWTUNU, 1679: What made the white man different, I wondered. Not much. They worked, they slept, they loved their children. But there was a difference. Their want was not a certainty. Their want was greater than whatever they possessed. A farmer with two cornfields wanted three. A settler with one cow wanted another. Their wants were the distance of their vision, not their reach. This caused a stirring, a discontentment, a willingness to sacrifice themselves and others to move closer to their wants. Wants that always outpaced them no matter how mightily they struggled.

Before heading back to my hotel room at the Vista I strolled over to the bar. As I caressed an Irish coffee more reflection on my first years working at Bankers Life. I had been wrong. At Bankers Life I had mistaken contentment for boredom. I had given no value to balance. A balance among family, professional achievement, and financial security; a financial security that was a by-product, not the product of a company. A company that served its customers as well as possible . . . I owed Dad an apology.

At 7 a.m. my phone in the hotel room rang, picked it up to hear Alice and the kids singing "Happy Birthday." Best wakeup call ever. Some quick conversation with the kids; they were planning to take Alice and me to Old Angler's for a birthday dinner. Damn, can I blow out forty-three candles in front of a restaurant full of patrons? Next Hank's office called, he had a half hour slice of time mid-afternoon. Made some business phone calls and then took a walk through the lower part of Manhattan. I had never done this before. That's not true. I had taken a lot of walks through Manhattan. But I was always rushing someplace, looking down at my watch. This day I wasn't walking so much as wandering. I paused on my stroll and studied the bronze plaques on more than a few dark gray structures; two hundred years of history had been staring at me during the past few years. One plaque caught my eye; displayed on Trinity Church it described how George Washington had prayed within St. Paul's chapel following his inauguration as our first president. I entered by a side door, lit a candle for Mother, then sat in a back pew and silently thanked God for my blessings.

Had a leisurely lunch at a Battery Park deli. Likely the first leisurely lunch I ever had in Manhattan. Through the window I watched the young Wall Street clerks eating their bagged lunches on park benches; most probably on tight budgets, just like Alice and me when we first started out. Strolled back to the Vista and packed my bag. Down to the lobby and out to Liberty Street, three blocks east up to Pine, then the AIG building.

One of Hank's efficient assistants parked me in an anteroom; told me Hank was running late, he had Henry Kissinger in his office. I felt like I'd just received a reprieve from the governor; the delay gave me some time to consider my lines one more time. I was going to tell him I was leaving. I knew Hank. This would be a personal affront. Plus, I was one of the guys shoveling coal into their revenue boiler.

Hank already knew something was up; visits with him were scheduled at least a week in advance. When I was ushered into his office no thirty seconds of pleasantries; I was direct. Told him all the right things: I would help with the transition, owed him a debt of gratitude, learned a lot. He didn't care. Nobody left Hank of their own accord. He fired them. He told me I'd be getting a letter from their corporate counsel. But then something unexpected, after he said he was going to fire me, he asked how I was getting home. I told him the shuttle. He said he would have an assistant arrange for a helicopter to take me from Teterboro down to my home. The guy still liked me.

In the limo over to Teterboro I called Alice. Told her I'd be home as promised for my birthday. Her voice was bubbly as always as she teased me about the birthday present the kids had chosen for me. Then some quick updates on the latest happenings in the family: Jennifer made cheerleader, Andrew received two college acceptance letters, and David thought he might make the varsity basketball team. I didn't tell Alice I was retiring my briefcase. During dinner at Old Angler's I would share with her and the kids what I knew would be most welcome news.

A half hour later the helicopter was heading down the Hudson, taking a right after the Statue of Liberty. As we turned south I looked back at the tip of Manhattan, following Liberty Street past the World Trade Center. There it was, Hank's temple. After a half hour Philadelphia rose in the haze to the left. Another half hour and we were over the western suburbs of Baltimore, then Frederick to the right, down over Route 270, the Potomac River on the horizon, an arcing turn into Round Hill, a slow hover over my property, my cobblestone helipad in front of us, down a few feet, down a few feet more, a slight jolt, and on the ground. Alice halfway between the helipad and our home, standing in the light of the evening sun. Big smile on her face, the smile she always had. Right behind stood Andrew, David, and Jennifer, all three with Cheshire Cat grins. All holding something behind their backs.

I didn't wait for the pilot; I opened the door and pulled my suitcase from the seat next to me and headed straight toward my family. Then in unison Alice and the kids pivoted so that I could see what they had been hiding behind their backs. Andrew, David, and Jennifer each held a tennis racket, Alice held two.

This day the best birthday of my life . . . my new life.

Tom

Epilogue

———✦———

WHILE THE CHAPTERS THAT COMPRISE *LETTERS TO AMERICA* ARE America's story, two chapters are also the author's story.

In the John chapter, John becomes best friends with Tom Lane, another member of an Army Special Brigade stationed in England, training for the invasion of Fortress Europe. In this chapter, in 1943 Tom Lane marries Hazel, a waitress at the Queens Hotel in Cheltenham, England; he does this after borrowing $100 from his sister Dorothy in the United States. During the invasion of Normandy on June 6, 1944, John survives while his friend Tom Lane is killed. At the end of the war, before returning to America, John visits Hazel in Cheltenham. There he meets "little Tommy," who was born two weeks after his father, Tom Lane, was killed at Omaha Beach. The author is "little Tommy," his father, Tom Lane, and his mother, Hazel.

"Little Tommy" was adopted when he was two years old by his father's sister Dorothy (who lent her brother the $100) and her husband. His name was changed from Tom Lane to Tom Lane Blair, and he was raised in America . . . and became Tom, the main character in the Alice's Husband chapter.

As in the Alice's Husband chapter, the author married Alice, had three children (Andrew, David, and Jennifer), started a company in the health-care industry, built a home in Round Hill, Maryland, with a helipad and a tennis court, sold his company to AIG, and realized in time that the priorities of his life were skewed: too much focus on the next heroic financial challenge versus savoring the moments.

Also, as with the Tom in the Alice's Husband chapter, the author took his family to Europe; while there the author, his wife, his three children, and his grandchildren traveled to All Saints Church in Cheltenham, England, where his father had been married sixty-two years before. There he and his wife Alice renewed their wedding vows on their fortieth wedding anniversary. But, unlike his father Tom Lane and his mother Hazel, who stood together in the church door in 1943 with no family present, on this day of renewing vows, Tom Lane's son, three grandchildren, and twelve great-grandchildren stood in the very same church doorway.

POST DEDICATION: To Alice, the love of my life.